THE GREEK WORLD IN THE FOURTH CENTURY

The Greek world in the fourth century BC sometimes appears as the overlooked stepchild in the study of ancient Greek history, sandwiched between the brilliant achievements of classical Athens and the accomplishments of Alexander the Great. Yet this was the time of Plato and Aristotle, of Scopas and Lysippus, continuing the developments of the classical era while preparing those of the Hellenistic period to come. Athenian democracy settled into nearly one hundred years of stability, while the Greeks in Asia and the west reached a *modus vivendi* with their neighbours.

The papers collected in this volume present a systematic survey of the struggles of Athens, Sparta and Thebes to dominate Greece in the fourth century – only to be overwhelmed by the newly emerging Macedonian kingdom of Philip II. Additionally, the situation of Greeks in Sicily, Italy and Asia is portrayed, showing the geographical and political diffusion of the Greeks in a broader historical context.

Lawrence A. Tritle is Professor of History at Loyola Marymount University in Los Angeles. He has published widely in the field of ancient Greek history and is the author of *Phocion the Good* (1988).

THE GREEK WORLD IN THE FOURTH CENTURY

From the fall of the Athenian Empire
to the successors of Alexander

Edited by Lawrence A. Tritle

London and New York

First published 1997
by Routledge
11 New Fetter Lane, London EC4P 4EE

Simultaneously published in the USA and Canada
by Routledge
29 West 35th Street, New York, NY 10001

Selection and editorial matter © 1997 Lawrence A. Tritle;
Individual chapters © 1997 the contributors

Typeset in Garamond by Florencetype Ltd, Stoodleigh, Devon
Printed and bound in Great Britain by Biddles Ltd,
Guildford and King's Lynn

British Library Cataloguing in Publication Data
A catalogue record for this book is available from the British Library

Library of Congress Cataloguing in Publication Data
The Greek world in the fourth century: from the fall of the
Athenian Empire to the successors of Alexander / edited by
Lawrence A. Tritle.
      Includes bibliographical references and index.
      1. Greece–History–To 146 BC. 2. Greece–History–Spartan
and Theban Supremacies, 404–362 BC. 3. Greece–History–
Macedonian Hegemony, 323–281 BC. I. Tritle, Lawrence A.,
1946–   .
            DF231.G74   1996   96–11436
            938'.06–dc20   CIP

ISBN 0–415–10582–X (hbk)
ISBN 0–415–10583–8 (pbk)

CONTENTS

CONTENTS

MAPS AND PLATES

MAPS

PLATES

NOTES ON CONTRIBUTORS

W. Lindsay Adams is Associate Professor of History at the University of Utah and author of the forthcoming work, *The Struggle for Macedonia: Cassander and the Transition of Power, 323–301 BC.*

Charles D. Hamilton is Professor of History and Classics at San Diego State University and author most recently of *Agesilaus and the Failure of Spartan Hegemony* (1991).

Waldemar Heckel is Professor of Ancient History at the University of Calgary and author of *The Marshals of Alexander's Empire* (1992).

Julia Heskel is currently a consultant with The Winthrop Group, Inc., a Cambridge-based firm specializing in corporate and institutional history. She is author of *The North Aegean Wars, 371 to 360 BC: the Struggle over Ampipholis and Chersonese* (1996).

Steven Lattimore is Associate Professor of Classics at the University of California, Los Angeles and author of *Marble Sculpture from Isthmia, 1967–1980* (1996).

Mark Munn is Assistant Professor of History and Classics at Pennsylvania State University and author of *The Defense of Attica* (1993).

Stephen Ruzicka is Associate Professor of History at the University of North Carolina, Greensboro and author of *Politics of a Persian Dynasty: The Hecatomnids in the Fourth Century B.C.* (1992).

Cynthia Schwenk is Associate Professor of History at Georgia State University, Atlanta and author of *Athens in the Age of Alexander* (1985).

ix

Richard J. A. Talbert is Kenan Professor of History and Classics at the University of North Carolina, Chapel Hill and author of *Timoleon and the Revival of Greek Sicily* (1974).

Lawrence A. Tritle is Professor of History at Loyola Marymount University, Los Angeles and author of *Phocion the Good* (1988).

CHRONOLOGY

(All three digit dates [as below] are BC; fourth century refers to fourth century BC, etc.)

404 Athens surrenders to Sparta and her allies, ending the Peloponnesian War; regime of the Thirty Tyrants begins (to 403)
403 Dionysius I takes power in Syracuse
399 Trial and death of Socrates
396 Campaigns of Agesilaus in Asia Minor
395 Outbreak of the Corinthian War
394 Persian defeat of the Spartan fleet at Cnidus
387/6 King's Peace ending the Corinthian War
   Dionysius I captures Rhegium
   Plato's visit to court of Dionysius
379/8 Liberation of Thebes
378/7 Second Athenian League founded
377 Mausolus succeeds as satrap of Caria
375 Jason becomes *tagos* in Thessaly
371 Theban defeat of Sparta at Leuctra; rise of Epaminondas at Thebes
370 Death of Jason
367/6 Outbreak of Satraps' Revolt
367 Death of Dionysius I
362 Battle of Mantinea and death of Epaminondas
360/59 Philip rises to power in Macedon
357/6 Outbreak of the Social War between Athens and her allies
356 Outbreak of Third Sacred War in central Greece
   Dion rises to power in Syracuse
355 Social War ends

PREFACE AND
ACKNOWLEDGMENTS

The Greek world in the fourth century has long remained the over-looked step-child in the study of ancient Greek history. Sandwiched between the Classical Age of Pericles and the exploits of Alexander, the fourth century has often received either superficial treatment or postscript status as an era of decline and decay, an age of feeble accomplishment. The present volume of essays aims at redressing this perception. It has been conceived as a basic work for university students as well as an introduction for the general reader. Each author has provided an essential account of what the student should know about each region of Greece. Attempts have been made to minimize the inevitable overlap and clash of opinion in a work of multi-authorship. Yet readers should keep in mind that Athenian, Spartan, or Macedonian perceptions of events would have varied and so too will those of modern scholars.

A brief word needs to be said regarding the use of names and places. Familiar latinized forms, e.g., Demosthenes, Alexander, Corinth, Rhodes, as found and used in the *Oxford Classical Dictionary*, have been used throughout in order to ensure clarity. Unfamiliar personal names and places have been transliterated or otherwise rendered in the clearest way possible.

The support of many people stands behind the preparation of this volume. Among those whose assistance and advice requires acknowledgment are Mary Lou Zimmerman Munn, for her editorial assistance to Mark Munn's discussion of Thebes; E. Badian and H. E. Yunis, who read early drafts of Julia Heskel's chapter on Macedon and the North; F. W. Walbank, who provided suggestions on Richard Talbert's discussion of the Greeks in Sicily and South Italy; the late Professor David M. Lewis, who made available to Professor Talbert his chapter on Dionysius I in the recently published

Cambridge Ancient History; E. N. Borza and S. Ruzicka for permission to use their maps of Macedonia and Anatolia respectively; and R. J. A. Talbert for use of maps from his *Atlas of Classical History* (London, Routledge, 1985). The editor wishes to thank Margaret Edwards for all her efforts in producing the text, and finally Richard Stoneman, who was interested enough in this project to take it on and see it through to publication. To all these, and to the students who asked the questions in the first place, a great debt of gratitude is due.

ABBREVIATIONS

Titles of periodicals are generally abbreviated in accordance with those listed in *L'année philologique*. Names of ancient authors are abbreviated as listed in H. G. Liddell and R. Scott, *A Greek–English Lexicon*, 9th ed. rev. by Sir H. S. Jones and R. McKenzie (Oxford, Clarendon Press, 1940), pp. xvi–xxxviii. For standard reference works, the usual abbreviations are followed, e.g., *CAH* = *The Cambridge Ancient History*, ed. by J. B. Bury, *et al.*, 1st edn, 12 vols, Cambridge, Cambridge University Press, 1923–39 (both second and third editions are in progress); *RE* = Pauly-Wissowa, *Real-Encyclopädie der classischen Altertumswissenschaft*. So too for standard collections of inscriptions, e.g., *IG* = *Inscriptiones Graecae*; Tod = M. N. Tod, ed., *A Selection of Greek Historical Inscriptions*, vol. II. *From 403 to 323 BC* (Oxford, Clarendon Press, 1948); Harding = P. Harding, *From the End of the Peloponnesian War to the Battle of Ipsus* (Cambridge, Cambridge University Press, 1985).

The following should also be noted:

Barr-Sharrar	Barr-Sharrar, B. and Borza, E. N., eds, *Studies in the History of Art*, vol. 10. *Macedonia and Greece in Late Classical and Early Hellenistic Times.* Washington, DC, National Gallery of Art, 1982.
Beloch, *GG²*	K. J. Beloch, *Griechische Geschichte*, 2nd edn, 4 vols in 8. Strassburg, Berlin, Leipzig, Trübner and de Gruyter, 1912–27.
Borza	E. N. Borza, *In the Shadow of Olympus. The Emergence of Macedon.* Princeton, Princeton University Press, 1990.

Cargill	J. Cargill, *The Second Athenian League. Empire or Free Alliance?* Berkeley, University of California Press, 1981.
CAH² 6	D. M. Lewis, J. Boardman, S. Hornblower, and M. Ostwald, eds, *The Cambridge Ancient History*. Vol. VI. *The Fourth Century BC.* 2nd edn, Cambridge, Cambridge University Press, 1994.
FAC	J. M. Edmonds, *The Fragments of Attic Comedy*. 3 vols in 4. Leiden, Brill, 1957–61.
FGrH	F. Jacoby, *Die Fragmente der griechischen Historiker*. Vol. 1–2, Berlin, Weidmann, 1923–26. Vol. 3. Leiden, Brill, 1940–58.
FHG	C. Muller, *Fragmenta Historicorum Graecorum*. 5 vols. Paris, Didot, 1874–83.
Hammond	N. G. L. Hammond, *A History of Greece to 322 B.C.* 3rd edn, Oxford, Clarendon Press, 1986.
Hammond–Griffith	N. G. L. Hammond and G. T. Griffith, *A History of Macedonia*, Vol. II. *555–336 B.C.* Oxford, Clarendon Press, 1979.
Hammond–Walbank	N. G. L. Hammond and F. W. Walbank, *A History of Macedonia*, Vol. III. *336–167 B.C.* Oxford, Clarendon Press, 1988.

1

INTRODUCTION

Lawrence A. Tritle

THE END OF AN EMPIRE

In 404, after twenty-seven years of war, plague, and hardship, the Peloponnesian War ended. Athens' triumphant enemies watched as the 'tyrant' city's walls were dismantled to the tune of the flute. But within a short time, Sparta would replace Athens as the villain, and former allies, Thebes and Corinth, would join Athens, their former enemy, in challenging Spartan power in the Greek world in a mostly inconclusive struggle now known as the Corinthian War (395–387/6). This conflict ushered into Greek political relations the quest for *hegemonia*, hegemony, that so characterizes Greek inter-state relations for the next half-century. During this period Sparta, Athens, and Thebes sometimes challenged each other while at other times allying with one against the other in a bid to control and dominate Greece. Along the way to the famous Peace of Philocrates, accepted by most of the Greek states in 346, there would be many developments and accomplishments: politically, inter-state diplomatic arrangements would be shaped by the ancient Greek equivalent of a general peace conference, the *koine eirene* or 'common peace;' militarily, the traditional hoplite style of warfare would be revolutionized by the Thebans Epaminondas and Pelopidas and then perfected by Philip and Alexander of Macedon; again politically, the Athenians would improve upon their popular form of self-rule, democracy; in the arts, many aspects of the Hellenistic style would emerge from fourth-century innovations.

The negotiations that completed the Peace of Philocrates brought an uneasy peace to the Greeks; uneasy because now they were even more aware of the growing power – and place in Greek affairs – of the Macedonian kingdom to the north. Long subject to internal as well as external strife, Macedonian kings had frequently been forced to accommodate and accede to the demands and impositions of their southern neighbors. This, however, began to change in 360/59 with the accession of a young, vigorous and brilliantly adept king, Philip II. Between his accession and the Peace of Philocrates, which he essentially dictated, Philip would unite Macedon as never before, establish its control over the northern Aegean littoral, and advance south into old Greece, gaining control of Thessaly and intimidating central Greece and beyond.

Philip's advance, his dominating position in the Greek world, would arouse in Demosthenes and the Athenians determined opposition and a real challenge to the Macedonian hegemony. After eight years of failed negotiations, debate, and fighting in an undeclared 'Northern' war in the Aegean, the issue would be resolved on the battlefield at Chaeronea in 338/7. The satisfaction of victory, however, was brief for Philip, as he was murdered (in 336/5) while celebrating his daughter's wedding. Demosthenes and many others believed that fate had delivered them from the tyrant. Alexander, heir apparent now king, showed himself to be Philip's son – though he would later dispute this, claiming to be the son of Zeus – and quickly marched into Greece, where at the Isthmus the assembled delegates of the League of Corinth established by his father would recognize him as leader, or *hegemon*, of the Greeks.

Soon Alexander was off to the East, never to return to Greece, in his celebrated conquest of the venerable Persian Empire, as well as other kingdoms and peoples even farther east (334–23). He left behind a quiet, subdued Greece, not surprising in view of his brutal destruction of Thebes and the enslavement of more than 30,000. When Alexander died in Babylon (10 June 323), his death ignited conflicts to the ends of his Empire: in the west, the Greeks, again energized by the Athenians, launched the Lamian War in an ultimately unsuccessful attempt to end the Macedonian domination (323/2); in the east, thousands of Greek mercenaries left marooned by Alexander to guard the perimeter gave up their posts in a bid to return home. Few succeeded in that goal, as Alexander's marshals, now fighting to control his Empire, killed many and forced others to return to their frontier forts and settlements. The struggles of Alexander's successors, the *Diadochi* as they were labeled by nineteenth-century scholars, would occupy two generations in a conflict that actually passes beyond the limits of this book (i.e., to 281 and the final battle of Corupedium after which the three great

Hellenistic kingdoms of the Ptolemies [Egypt], Seleucids [Asia], and Antigonids [Macedon and Greece] appear). The conflict that ranged over Greece, Asia, and Egypt was violent and few of the original figures would survive. But at the end of the century, at the Battle of Ipsus (301), an intermediate end of sorts was reached. Here the Indian elephants of Chandragupta, a 'gift' to Seleucus exchanged for the Indus river valley that Alexander had conquered, stomped the very breath out of Antigonus the One-Eyed and so ensured the partition of Alexander's Empire. Greece would remain under Macedonian domination and the Greek–Macedonian imprint that would lead to the hellenization of the eastern Mediterranean world was well under way.

PREVIOUS APPROACHES AND CURRENT TRENDS

The modern study of ancient Greek history is actually rather recent. Its origins may be assigned to William Mitford (*The History of Greece*, written between 1778 and 1810), who was urged in the task by Edward Gibbon, his brother officer in the South Hampshire militia. Mitford's approach was notoriously Tory and this prompted a liberal Whig response, first by Connop Thirlwall whose *History of Greece* (1835–44) was soon overshadowed by that of his friend, London banker and politician George Grote (*A History of Greece*, 1846–56). However, the first modern historians of ancient Greece were little enamored with the fourth century BC. Mitford saw the strong hand of Philip of Macedon as a blessing for the Greeks, bringing an end to their interminable squabblings and that worst of political evils, mob-rule, i.e., democracy. Even in Mitford the theme of decay, the eclipsed brilliance of the fourth century, may be discerned; this theme would be further defined by Grote, who exerted tremendous influence on his contemporaries both at home and abroad.[1] This vision of the fourth century as decadent, as a mere appendage to the great 'classical' fifth century, or as an uninspired and uninspiring prelude to the greatness of Alexander, can also be seen in the literature of the twentieth century, including the first edition of the *Cambridge Ancient History*.[2]

Today, the nineteenth century's perception of decline may be recognized as a result of the underlying historiographic and philosophic concepts of the Enlightenment. With the impact of Rankean methodology and ideas about the past, later refined in a sense by a critical spirit of inquiry directed to recovering the true texture of the past (resulting from the work of W. Dilthey, B. Croce, R. G. Collingwood, and M. Oakeshott), historians today are more inclined to study a period without raising the specter of 'decline' and to attempt an understanding of that era from within.[3] As a result, the fourth century today is seen neither as decadent nor as declining, but rather as both changing and yet remaining the same in many ways.

A brief word ought to be said about matters of chronology, namely 'What is the fourth century?' It must be obvious that the Greeks, with their idiosyncratic manner of keeping time, would have been a bit mystified by our notion of periodizing the past. But in a way they too divided the past into digestible chunks, ranging from Hesiod's ages of man (e.g., Gold, Silver, Heroes), to Thucydides' and Xenophon's 'History of My Times.' Periodization is at once an asset and a liability to the historian. It suggests a unity and order that is more apparent than real. The arbitrariness of designating a 'period' as the fourth century surely is apparent, as also the reality that recognition by those contemporaries so defined is a bit presumptuous. Yet the modern world since the Renaissance has perceived time as divided into centuries, with each being somehow unique. Various recent works, for example the new edition of the *Cambridge Ancient History*, have devoted separate volumes to the 'fifth' and 'fourth' centuries. Such periodizing suggests additionally that the fourth century as an era is as distinct as any other, and that it is more than a postscript to the 'classical' period or a mere introduction to the great Alexander. The chapters that follow this introduction bear out this historiographic reality, as the individual contributors have defined their period, nuancing the term 'fourth century' with respect to the particular circumstances implicit in their subject. Readers should not be alarmed or imagine this to be disunity; rather it is yet another characteristic of the historian's craft.

THE SOURCES

In terms of sources the great deficiency of the fourth century is the absence of an extant historical work the caliber of Thucydides or Herodotus. The Athenian Xenophon is possibly an exception to this, as his many works, e.g., the *Hellenica*, *Anabasis*, *Agesilaus*, and *Hipparchius*, provide a rich source of material for the period down to *c.* 362. His moral tone, however, as well as his prejudices complicate his use but, for the first third of the fourth century, Xenophon is a source that must be confronted.[4] More difficult yet are the various contemporary historians of note, e.g., Ephorus, Theopompus of Chios, the various 'Alexander' historians (e.g., Ptolemy [later first king of Ptolemaic Egypt], Aristobulus of Cassandreia) who survive in scattered fragments or in the works of later authors. Of these latter, Diodorus of Sicily and his *Bibliotheke*, or 'Library,' is possibly most important for the historians of 'old' Greece in the fourth century. Though there are various problems with Diodorus and his adaptation of his material (particularly competing chronological systems), it seems clear that he was not quite the dunce that some modern scholars suggest.[5] For the 'Alexander' historians, the most important author is clearly Arrian of Nicomedia. A contemporary of the Roman Emperor Trajan, Arrian was an able writer who made good sense of the material that he found recording the campaigns of Alexander.[6]

A major source for nearly all Greek history and literature for the modern historian and reader is Plutarch of Chaeronea. Like Diodorus and Arrian, Plutarch dates from the Roman period. His many lives of famous Greeks, including fourth-century personalities such as the Athenians Demosthenes and Phocion, the Spartans Agesilaus and Lysander, the Theban Pelopidas, and finally Alexander the Great, provide all sorts of useful information that Plutarch garnered from extensive reading of contemporary accounts. This applies additionally to the many works – political, philosophical, religious – that are to be found in his *Moralia*, including here too useful works that he did not write but which became attached to his corpus, most notably the *Lives of the Ten Orators*. Moreover, his firsthand knowledge of many places he wrote about, Thebes and central Greece, and Athens especially, provide an additional dimension to the life dramas he tells.[7]

Oratory became increasingly important in Greek society, especially Athens, from the end of the fifth century and emerged as an equally important source of information for politics (both domestic and foreign) and society. The 'canon' of ten orators, Antiphon, Andocides, Lysias, Isocrates, Isaeus, Aeschines, Lycurgus, Demosthenes, Hypereides, and Dinarchus, contains many speeches written both by these orators and less well known figures (e.g., the Athenian Apollodorus) whose speeches were assimilated to those of their better known contemporaries. These speeches, too many for detailed review here, provide useful information regarding the struggle between

Athens and Macedon, e.g., Demosthenes' *Olynthiacs* and *Philippics*; the nature of political rivalry in Athens, e.g., Aeschines' *Against Ctesiphon*; and the battle for hegemony in Greece during the fourth century, e.g., Isocrates' *Panegyricus*. These sources pose numerous problems: chief among these is the question of veracity and the problems of exaggerating what these speakers proclaim about their own importance and the extent to which their opinions reflect those of their contemporaries.[8]

While the fourth century may lack an historian the quality of Thucydides, it is also true that there is a much greater body of epigraphical evidence that grows continually. This is especially true regarding Athens, where popular decrees, treaties, and proclamations were engraved on stone and placed on public display. Much valuable information regarding the functioning of the Athenian democracy, both at home and abroad, is thus preserved.[9]

Information of a similar nature is provided in the work of Aristotle, especially his *Politics*, which bears closely on fourth-century developments, and the *Constitution of the Athenians*, which either belongs to him or to a follower in his school.[10] Less valuable are the works of Plato, laden with imagery and myth and directed toward philosophical speculation. A similar body of literary composition is to be found in comedy. The last two surviving plays in Aristophanes' corpus, the *Ecclesiazusae* and *Plutus*, relate attitudes and conditions in Athens and the rest of Greece *c.* 390s. Unfortunately, Middle Comedy, i.e., that following on Aristophanes and the other poets of the fifth century, has survived only in fragments, but enough of these exist to provide some interesting social and economic commentary for the period.[11]

Finally, there are a number of later authors, travelers and geographers such as Pausanias (*A Description of Greece*) and Strabo (*Geography*).[12] Strabo, for example, preserves much useful earlier material, such as that from Ephorus dealing with the Peloponnesus and the early Hellenistic writer Megasthenes on India. Antiquarians such as Athenaeus (*Deipnosophistai*, or, 'The Learned Banquet') and others, also preserve various details and events mentioned by earlier and now lost authors. This information is both a blessing and a curse, as it is sometimes distorted in the retelling while the context is obscured or garbled in the transmission. Such information must be evaluated carefully, keeping in mind its manner of preservation as well as the purpose that it was adapted to serve by the transmitter.

NOTES

1 See A. Momigliano, 'George Grote and the Study of Greek History,' in *Studies in Historiography*, New York, Harper and Row, 1966, pp. 56–74, for a useful introduction.

2 See e.g., E. Barber, 'Greek Political Thought and Theory in the Fourth Century,' *CAH*, 1927, 6: 510. A later example is C. Mosse, *Athens in Decline, 404–86 BC*, London, Routledge & Kegan Paul, 1973.

3 See e.g., R. G. Collingwood, *The Idea of History*, Oxford, Oxford University Press, 1946, pp. 76–85, 164–5, and A. Marwick, *The Nature of History*, New York, Knopf, 1971, pp. 98–105.

4 See below Hamilton, pp. 43–4, who provides a useful bibliography, and S. Hornblower, 'Sources and Their Uses,' *CAH*,[2] 6: 7.

5 See below Talbert, pp. 137–9, who discusses Diodorus and the western Greek historians, Timaeus and Philistus. For an example of Diodorus' chronological problems, see below p. 200.

6 A recent survey is P. A. Stadter, *Arrian of Nicomedia*, Chapel Hill, University of North Carolina Press, 1989.

7 The bibliography on Plutarch is immense. For a good introduction to his career, work, and methods, see D. A. Russell, *Plutarch*, New York, Scribner's, 1973.

8 See the comments of Hornblower, ibid., pp. 17–18.

9 The major collection of inscriptions for fourth-century Athens is *Inscriptiones Graecae*, vol. II; a second edition began in 1913 by J. Kirchner and a third in 1981 by D. M. Lewis *et al.* For a list of the volumes and descriptive comments see A. G. Woodhead, *The Study of Greek Inscriptions*, Cambridge, Cambridge University Press, 1959. Two collections of sources in translation relevant to the study of the fourth century are M. Crawford and D. Whitehead, *Archaic and Classical Greece*, Cambridge, Cambridge University Press, 1983, and J. Wickersham and G. Verbrugghe, *Greek Historical Documents: The Fourth Century BC*, Toronto, Hakkert, 1973; see also Harding and Tod, listed in the Abbreviations.

10 See P. J. Rhodes, *A Commentary on the Aristotelian Athenaion Politeia*, Oxford, Clarendon Press, 1981. There is at present no up-to-date commentary on the *Politics*.

11 See the collection of fragments in *FAC*, listed in the Abbreviations.

12 Pausanias, see C. Habicht, *Pausanias' Guide to Greece*, Berkeley, 1985; Strabo, see R. Syme, *Anatolica: Studies in Strabo*, ed. by A. R. Birley, Oxford, Clarendon Press, 1995, and Hornblower, 'Sources,' p. 21.

2

ATHENS

Cynthia Schwenk

Defeat and surrender to Sparta were an inauspicious beginning to the history of Athens in the fourth century. Yet the Athenians remained a major force in the inter-state affairs of Greece in the fourth century. Their significant role in Greece persisted despite the fact that Athens was often on the losing side and that the Athenians had lost their empire and the tribute that went with it in 404. The Athenians suffered under the immediate post-Peloponnesian War Spartan hegemony which supported the reign of the Thirty Tyrants, 404–403. In the King's Peace of 387/6, marking the end of their participation in the Corinthian War (395–387), the Athenians regained enough stature to have their control of Lemnos, Scyros, and Imbros acknowledged as an exception to the general rule of freedom to all Greek states in the mainland and islands. The creation of the Second Athenian League (378/7) marked Athens' full recovery as a power; the League lasted, despite setbacks, until 338/7. Although the Athenians did not fight at Leuctra in 371, their Theban allies immediately informed them of the victory and what turned out to be the end of Spartan hegemony. In a reversal so typical of Greek affairs in the fourth century, the Athenians later fought their former Theban allies at Mantinea (362) and contributed to the end of the Theban hegemony. Athenian support of the Phocians during their attempt at hegemony ended when Athens agreed to terms with Philip in the celebrated Peace of Philocrates (346). Finally, Athens, aroused by Demosthenes, encouraged opposition in Greece to Macedonian power at Chaeronea in 338, and again in the Lamian War (323/2).

Alexander's death and the Lamian War in central Greece, events which traditionally separate the Hellenic and Hellenistic Eras of ancient Greek Civilization, seem an appropriate end point as well for a history of fourth-century Athens. The Lamian War resulted in defeat for Athens and, despite various intrigues between Alexander's generals and various leaders in Athens, the outcome remained the same in 300 as it had been in 322: Athens no longer had the power of a sovereign state. The appropriate chronological definition, therefore, of 'fourth-century Athens' is 404/3–323/2, but the *caveat* expressed in the Introduction should be kept in mind: fourth-century Greece is a modern perception.

There are other constructs, both modern and not so modern, which continue to influence and perhaps even distort the narrative of fourth-century Athens. Recent scholarship has challenged a number of these assumptions. They include the notion that Athens reverted to fifth-century imperialist ways;[1] that the roles of general and politician diverged sharply;[2] that there was a failure of the city-state.[3] The nature of the source material available for Athenian history has itself encouraged conflicting interpretations. Beyond the basic sources for fourth-century Greece as a whole are two additional categories of sources which in their abundance are the result of a democratic polity and thus uniquely Athenian. The extant speeches of the orators provide a fascinating, if not entirely reliable, glimpse into the lives of prominent Athenians.[4] They are also a rich resource for learning about social, economic, and legal aspects of Athenian life. Additionally, inscriptions, though found throughout the Mediterranean world, are relatively abundant for Athens not only because Athens was a democracy and thus prone to publish popular proceedings, but also because excavations at Athens have been conducted for a longer time and more extensively than most other sites in Greece. As for the philosophers, the Aristotelian *Athenaion Politeia* provides much useful information concerning the Athenian democracy in the later fourth century, though many details have been vigorously debated. The rest of the Aristotelian corpus, excepting the *Politics* perhaps, as well as the Platonic works, are less helpful.[5] The source material is, therefore, relatively abundant yet not entirely satisfactory.

DEFEAT AND THE THIRTY TYRANTS

The terms of Athens' surrender in 404 were negotiated by the Athenian Theramenes and executed by the Spartan Lysander. Athens agreed to a series of stringent terms: the destruction of fortifications including the Long Walls that ran from Athens to the Piraeus; the relinquishment of all its foreign possessions; the reduction of its fleet to twelve ships; the return of all exiles; and an alliance with Sparta. Though the Athenians faced the fourth century without their previous resources, they still possessed their city and their freedom. By 404, total destruction of a polis and enslavement of its inhabitants were not innovations, and the Athenians might easily have expected such treatment. In fact, Sparta's allies in the recently completed war, Thebes and Corinth, led the other members of the Peloponnesian League to propose such an action but failed in the face of Spartan opposition. The motives for Sparta's decision range from sentimental – the memory of Athens' role in the Persian Wars, to realpolitik – the destruction of Athens would benefit Sparta's 'allies,' in particular Thebes and Corinth, much more than Sparta. Whatever Sparta's reasons, Athens was fortunate. Had Sparta chosen to carry out the League's proposal, the history of Athens would have been very different.

As the terms of surrender were carried out and Lysander supervised the destruction of the Long Walls, the exiles returned and took measures to produce a more oligarchical form of government. The final outcome of their actions was the appointment of a committee of Thirty to frame a new constitution for the Athenians. Critias, a student of Socrates and member of the 'Four Hundred' in 411, emerged as leader of this group which earned for itself the title 'Thirty Tyrants,' since it quickly became clear that the ostensible purpose for the creation of the Thirty was the excuse to provide these men with the power to run the state as a narrow oligarchy. The appointment of the Ten to guard the Piraeus and the Eleven to carry out police duties such as seizure and executions as well as the appointment of a Council of Five Hundred, to which all judicial functions of the state had been transferred, were the prelude to a series of numerous trials and condemnations. Democrats in opposition were an obvious choice for attack, but the Thirty also struck down fellow oligarchs who protested their policies and even wealthy citizens and metics in order to confiscate their property. According to tradition, protests by Theramenes, a member of the Thirty, led the Thirty to enroll the Three Thousand citizens. Nonetheless, this larger body could not change the power structure nor end the policy of condemnations; it did, however, make clear who had *lost* the privileges of citizenship. It is no coincidence, therefore, that many Athenians chose exile.

As two opposing factions now emerged, the Athenian state experienced political stasis. The situation prompted the involvement of other poleis such as Megara, Corinth, Elis, Argos, and, especially, Thebes. Although staunch enemies of Athens during the recently completed war, these poleis had quickly become dissatisfied with Sparta, their leaders, and were willing to help exiled Athenians overthrow a tyrannical regime, one propped up by Lysander, who was now making enemies both at home and abroad. The occupation of Phyle, a border fort between Boeotia and Attica, by Thrasybulus and some seventy Athenian exiles, was the first military challenge to the Thirty. The Thirty responded by requesting aid from Sparta. The Spartans dispatched a garrison of 700 men which the Thirty placed on the Acropolis and subsequently financed. When they were unable to take Phyle, the Thirty seized Eleusis after putting some 300 Eleusinians to death. Then Thrasybulus and his 'men of Phyle' successfully seized the Piraeus. Critias, still leader of the Thirty, led all his forces, including the Spartans, to the Piraeus, but lost his life in the resulting battle on the height of Munychia, overlooking the port.

In response to the 'Battle of Munychia,' the Three Thousand elected a body of Ten to replace the, by now, very unpopular Thirty. Those who were left from the original Thirty retired to Eleusis and established a third faction in opposition to those led by the newly appointed Ten in the city and those led by Thrasybulus in the Piraeus. When Thrasybulus prepared to besiege the city walls with the aid of reinforcements, both the Ten in the city and those in Eleusis appealed to Sparta. Lysander arrived at Eleusis and acted to cut off supplies to the Piraeus, but he was replaced by King Pausanias before he could do much damage. Pausanias secured Thrasybulus' cooperation and enabled the establishment of a general amnesty which included all but the Thirty, the Ten who had succeeded them, the Ten who guarded the Piraeus, and the Eleven who had served as police. By September of 403, *nomothetes* ('law-givers') began the task of revising the constitution. Those in Eleusis were initially allowed to remain separate from the state, but by the end of 401, Eleusis returned to Athenian jurisdiction.

The Athenians now owed Sparta two debts of gratitude for its actions since the siege of Piraeus had ended the Peloponnesian War. The first, already discussed, was the decision not to destroy Athens; the second was Pausanias' intervention, which assured for the Athenians a return to their democratic constitution. The Athenians were fortunate in Pausanias' moderation and apparent goodwill toward their state. Whatever his motives, this policy reversed the earlier decision to support oligarchy. This change of heart proved to be a great benefit for the Athenians.

Pausanias had cut short the process of stasis that had ruined other poleis. Yet that the Athenians did not forget the trials, condemnations, and executions by the Thirty was revealed by the political trials (Socrates' was one of many) and machinations which occurred after the democracy was restored.[6] The experiment with the Thirty, as well as Lysander's part in supporting them, however, had sent a message to *all* Athenians to confine their quarrels within the state. Thus an additional debt of gratitude was owed to Sparta – that Sparta remained powerful enough long enough for the strongest passions and hatreds created during the rule of the Thirty to subside.

INTRIGUE WITH SATRAPS AND THE CORINTHIAN WAR

Within less than a decade the Athenians moved beyond their gratitude and defied Sparta by challenging the terms of their surrender. During the period between the restoration of the democracy in 403 and the outbreak of the Corinthian War in 395, two factors created a situation that enabled the Athenians to regain their status as a sovereign state. Both factors concerned Sparta and were legacies of the Peloponnesian War. Even before the war had ended, Sparta had to deal with suspicious satraps and therefore the Persian king; Spartan actions aggravated this situation after 404. Moreover, the end of the war only served to exacerbate discontent within the Peloponnesian League, particularly between Sparta and her most prominent allies, Corinth and Thebes. Both factors worked to Athens' advantage.

Sparta enjoyed an ambiguous relationship with Persia. In exchange for financial subsidies to build and maintain the fleet which had won the war for Sparta, Sparta was to surrender to the Persian king all claims to the Asiatic Greek cities. This agreement belied Sparta's published war aim of protecting the freedom of the Greek states against Athenian aggression. Although Persia received the designated states at the end of the war, subsequent Spartan policies alienated Persia. First, Sparta supported Cyrus' attempt to usurp the Persian throne by placing the 'Ten Thousand' under his command. Second, Sparta chose to wage war against Persia in response to an appeal from the Ionian city-states. The arrival of Agesilaus in Asia Minor in 396, after desultory campaigns by Thibron and Dercyllidas, changed the complexion of the hostilities and provoked a stronger

Persian response. In 397, the Persians created a fleet and made the Athenian Conon its commander. Conon had been in Persian service since Aegospotami in 405 and more recently had worked for Evagoras of Cyprian Salamis. His great victory at Cnidus in 394, therefore, was a double boost to Athenian morale: the Spartans had been defeated and the commander, although in Persian employ, was an Athenian.

Athens participated indirectly in the Persian War against Sparta through her citizen Conon and other Athenians who fought for and were paid by Persia. Athens, the state, participated more directly against Sparta closer to home by playing upon the discontent of Sparta's allies, the second factor which was to work to Athens' advantage. The discontent was apparent even before the end of the Peloponnesian War, and at its end Sparta's actions further exacerbated the situation. These actions belied the Spartans' professed motive for now fighting Persia – the freedom of the Asiatic Greek states – and gave the allies, as well as the defeated Athenians, justification for instigating war against Sparta. The Greek malcontents were further encouraged when Timocrates of Rhodes arrived in Greece with Persian gold and an offer of a Persian alliance against Sparta. This meant that intrigues with satraps and possible Persian financial support were no longer options exclusive to Sparta.

Theban actions in 395 provided the Athenians the opportunity to declare war against Sparta. A dispute between Phocis and Locris, perhaps provoked by the Thebans, prompted Phocis to appeal to Sparta, which declared war on Thebes. Thebes, in turn, appealed to Athens for an alliance and Athens accepted, signing a separate alliance with Locris as well. When Pausanias arrived in Boeotia, too late to help Lysander who had died in battle at Haliartus, he chose to negotiate a truce. Sparta also lost its foothold in Thessaly at this point and early in 394 Agesilaus was recalled from his Asian campaign. The success of this challenge to Spartan authority led Athens to join with Thebes, Corinth, and Argos in an alliance which gathered at the Isthmus of Corinth, attracted additional members, and declared war. Thus the Corinthian War began in July 394 with the battle at the Nemea river near Corinth and, despite attempts on both sides to end hostilities during the next seven years, ended only with the King's Peace in 387/6 (see Plate 1, the funeral monument of Dexileos, an Athenian cavalryman killed in one of these battles).

During the Corinthian War the Athenians operated as an equal once again. Even before the outbreak of war, Athens had begun to

Plate 1 Funerary stele of Dexileos, 394 BC. Kerameikos Museum, Athens.
Photo: Art Resource.

rebuild its Long Walls and had fought at Haliartus. After the war began, Athenians fought at Coronea later in the same summer of 394 and sent Iphicrates to the Isthmus to help contain Sparta in the Peloponnesus. Iphicrates had made improvements in the weapons and shields of the peltasts, the lighter-armed foot soldiers who were especially effective in skirmishes, raids and ambushes, exactly the type of land warfare waged for the remainder of the Corinthian War. Just how effective the peltasts could be was shown in 390 when Iphicrates and his force were able to defeat a Spartan regiment of 600 hoplites and then recover Piraeon, Sidon, and Crommyon, all recently captured by Agesilaus.

Even before the ambush and disgrace of 390, the Spartans had attempted in 392 to negotiate a peace. The Spartan Antalcidas went to Susa with a proposal that the Greek cities of Asia Minor be subject to the Persian King and that all other Greek states remain autonomous, except for Lemnos, Imbros, and Scyros, which were to remain in Athenian control. The Athenians refused the terms. After Cnidus, Conon, with the help of Persian gold and the victorious fleet, proceeded to finish the rebuilding of the Long Walls to the Piraeus (see Plate 2); he may have also been responsible for the recovery of Lemnos, Imbros, and Scyros, all under Athenian control by 392 when Antalcidas made the proposal. Apparently, the Athenians felt strong enough and safe enough – Sparta was confined to the Peloponnesus and Athens had restored her walls – to continue hostilities.

After Antalcidas' failed attempt at peace, Athenian participation in the hostilities took place mainly at sea. Operations against Sparta around Aegina continued but were frustrating. Farther from home, however, Athens was more successful. By 390, Athens had sent some ships to its honorary citizen and ally, Evagoras of Salamis on Cyprus, who had revolted from Persia. In 389, Thrasybulus was sent to support Rhodes against possible Spartan incursions. He sailed by way of the Hellespont, the area most vital to Athenian interests, and was successful in bringing Thasos and Samothrace, the Chersonese, Byzantium, Chalcedon, and most of Lesbos into alliance with Athens; he even helped reconcile two kings in Thrace. Thrasybulus' alliances as well as his levy of a commercial tax on those allies were successful because Athens was outwardly still cordial with Persia. Exactions of a more violent type led to Thrasybulus' murder at Aspendus in Pamphylia. Iphicrates very quickly succeeded Argyrrhius, the first replacement, and successfully ambushed the Spartan Anaxibius to gain the upper hand in the Hellespont. By

Plate 2 The walls of Conon in the Piraeus of Athens, *c.* 394 BC. Photo: L. Tritle.

387, therefore, Sparta held only Abydus and Sestos, but even these states were blockaded by Iphicrates; the skirmishes from Aegina were a draw; and Agesilaus' 388 invasion of Acarnania was at an impasse. It was time for Sparta to visit the King in Susa.

THE KING'S PEACE

It was once again the Spartan, Antalcidas, who proposed peace to the Persian King with conditions similar to those he had proposed in 392. All Asian Greek cities plus Clazomenae and Cyprus were to be under the Persian King; all others were to be autonomous, excluding Lemnos, Imbros, and Scyros, which were to remain under Athenian jurisdiction. Just *which* state – Athens or Sparta – would be favored by the king was not as apparent as might be thought. Athens was still officially allied with Persia through Pharnabazus. On the other hand, Tiribazus (last heard of imprisoning Conon) favored the Spartans, and it was a Spartan who made the peace offer and effectively gave up any claims to the Asian Greek cities. Peace among the Greek states as well as peace *with* the Spartans would free the King for affairs closer to home, especially the revolt by Evagoras of Cyprus. In fact, Athens' relationship with Evagoras as well as Persia's recently acquired control over Clazomenae had to be strong reasons for the King's selection of Sparta as guarantor of the peace. Once Sparta was designated, Antalcidas returned to the Hellespont and took over the Spartan fleet at Abydos. With more ships provided now by the King as well as Dionysius of Syracuse, Antalcidas was able to blockade the Athenians and stop the grain ships. That blockade, along with raids still coming from the Spartan base at Aegina, persuaded the Athenians to end hostilities and send representatives to Sardis. In 386, representatives of the states reported to Sparta and made their formal acceptance. The only difference between these terms and those proposed in 392 concerned Thebes and the Boeotian League. Rather than accepting a Boeotian League (without Orchomenus), Sparta, when challenged by Thebes to sign for the League, insisted that each Boeotian city sign separately. The Thebans yielded when Agesilaus began mobilizing the Spartan army for a march north. Sparta's treatment of Thebes, both at this time and subsequently, exemplifies Sparta's abuse of power over the next fifteen years.

While the King's Peace marked a setback to Theban ambitions and left Sparta in a position more powerful in some ways than after the Peloponnesian War, it very quickly became apparent that this peace provided long-lasting benefits to Athens. Athens' role as a leading power was confirmed and the Peace freed her from old ties. Athens was neither forced back into a role of subservience to Sparta nor bound by the alliances made in the Corinthian War. The Spartans once again became preoccupied with domination in Greece since help to the Asiatic Greeks was no longer their concern. Persia concentrated on trouble-spots closer to home, such as Cyprus and Egypt. These circumstances left Athens free to pursue a policy in the Aegean that resulted in the alliances which became the basis for the Second Athenian League.

Before turning to perhaps the most interesting of Athens' creations in the fourth century, the Second Athenian League, it is appropriate to stop and consider conditions within Athens. The men who led Athens in the immediate post-war period had also been active at the end of the Peloponnesian War. With the exception of Iphicrates, who only began his career in the post-war period, they were gone by the time of the King's Peace.[7] The coincidence of the loss of the old generation of wartime leaders and their dreams of recovering the Empire, with the imposition of the King's Peace, marked the end (or beginning?) of an era. No matter how unrealistic the notion of a 'unified Greek state' was on the part of the orators, Gorgias or Lysias or Isocrates, their suggestions reflect that at least some people were realizing that new solutions were in order.[8] A question to consider, therefore, is whether the changes in policy affected by the Athenians after the King's Peace were just adaptations of the old imperialist motives to the changed conditions or whether there was a discernable change in policy.

Economic conditions certainly affected Athens' actions. In 404, Athens lost the tribute from the Empire, as well as the fleet. Hopes of a renewal of an imperial financial base to complement the newly obtained fleet ended with the King's Peace. Acknowledgement of that fact came in 377 when, presumably in the context of the foundation of the Second Athenian League, the Athenians initiated an assessment of private property and rationalized the machinery so that they could more easily obtain the *eisphora* or property tax. This direct taxation, first imposed as an exceptional measure during the Peloponnesian War, had become more usual by this time. The creation of the symmories (groups), by which the wealthier citizens were responsible to the state to provide the assessment and then to collect from their fellow citizens, indicates as well that Athens was willing to support her new league despite the financial obligations involved.

The make-up of the citizen body and the machinery of democracy have been the topic of recent studies which, in one way or another, stress that *all* levels and factions of Athenian citizens voted, for example, to pursue war and empire in the 410s and the 390s, or to accept the King's Peace, or to continue with the *eisphora* just mentioned above.[9] There were, however, some changes that did affect the functioning of the state. While the economic losses mentioned above affected the entire citizen body, the wealthy for the most part were able to maintain their lifestyle; those of the lower classes often could not. The result, therefore, was a 'significant increase of tension between the have and the have-not.'[10] Strauss argues that the potentially strong tension was mitigated, however, by the large number of casualties suffered by the thetic class at the end of the Peloponnesian War.[11] Thus the potential for serious stasis after the Thirty Tyrants was not as strong as it might have been. For whatever reasons, and despite continued trials throughout the fourth century, the Athenian democracy functioned well.

The status and condition of the other elements of Athenian society appears to have experienced even less change. In contrast to Sparta, there is no evidence to suggest that the status of Athenian women either improved or worsened. In fact, most of the evidence to document women's lives in all of classical Greek society comes from Athens of the fourth century and even later. It is the fourth century which produced a decree of the state that commended a citizen for 'contributing to the health and safety of the Boule and the Demos, and the Children and the Women and the other Possessions.'[12] The role of women as separate from the citizen body was characteristic throughout the classical period. The position of slaves, as well, remained the same. The call to emancipate slaves in order for them to fight at Arginusae in 406 did not indicate a change in attitude, but rather the desperation of the moment.[13] The decline in the number of slaves due to the desertions late in the Peloponnesian War adversely affected their individual owners as well as the mining industry and the workshops - one more economic setback to Athens' prospects at the end of the Peloponnesian War.[14]

THE SECOND ATHENIAN LEAGUE

The years between the King's Peace and the formation of the Second Athenian League proved to be productive for Athens. As mentioned above, the King was tending to affairs closer to Persia; Sparta's actions affected Athens much more. Sparta's continued assertion of power ranged from the break-up of Mantinea in 385 and the reduction of Phlius by 379 in the Peloponnesus, to the suppression of the newly formed Chalcidian League in the northern Aegean, also in 379. Sparta's garrisoning of the Cadmea, the citadel at Thebes in 382, which was strongly condemned by all Greek states, including Athens, was in fact advantageous to the Athenians because it meant that the Thebans were contained within their own borders. Spartan concerns, therefore, for maintaining military hegemony in effect gave the Athenians a free hand to pursue their own interests. By 384, Athens had made a defensive alliance with Chios. Soon after, alliances were made with Byzantium, Methymna, and Mitylene in Lesbos, and the Odrysian king, Hebryzelmis, all within the parameters set by the King's Peace.

The events which led to the formal establishment of the Second Athenian League were provoked by the outcome of events in Thebes (see also below pp. 77–8). In 379 the Thebans succeeded in expelling the Spartan garrison from the Cadmea through a bold and well-organized coup. Although Xenophon and Diodorus differ in details, both confirm that Athenians played a part in the liberation.[15] The presence of Spartan troops in central Greece, however, was strong inducement for Athens to abide by the letter of the truce and to bring to trial and convict two Athenian generals for their complicity in the affair.[16] Subsequent events are recorded most fully in Diodorus and are not contradicted by Xenophon, who, incidently, does not mention the creation of the Second Athenian League *per se*.[17] After the 'liberation,' the Thebans began uniting Boeotia and preparing for war, while the Athenians took advantage of the unsettled conditions by invoking the King's Peace and successfully making alliances with disgruntled Spartan allies. Athenian successes led to the formation of a new league which made an alliance with Thebes. While the Spartans began preparing for war, Sphodrias, who had been left in charge at Thespiae, at the instigation of either Cleombrotus (Diodorus) or the Thebans (Xenophon) or his own misguided ambition (Hammond and Bury), decided to invade Attica.[18] Athens' anger at this outrageous breach of conduct was assuaged by three Spartan ambassadors who happened to be in Athens, perhaps in response to Athens' new league, and who assured the Athenians that Sphodrias would be brought to justice. When Sphodrias was acquitted, Athens declared that the truce with Sparta had been broken and proceeded to prepare for hostilities. It is at that point that Diodorus notes the enrolment of Thebes into the *synedrion* of the allies, Athens' relinquishment of cleruchies, both past and in the future, and subsequent to those two actions, Athens' success in eventually enrolling seventy members.[19]

Many authors have ignored Diodorus' sequence of events and have synchronized Athens' alliance with Thebes, Thebes' membership in the league, and the creation of the Second Athenian League, and put all three events after and in reaction to the Sphodrias affair. The narrative as it stands, however, is reasonable. It is consistent with the idea that the creation of the League was a process rather than one isolated event. It also helps to explain why Athens took the drastic step of abolishing cleruchies and promising other stringent guarantees: those steps were the price that Athens paid to persuade her present and potential maritime allies to remain members despite Thebes' admittance which could only involve those allies in a land war in which they had no interest.[20] Athens had to consider an alliance with Thebes even before the Sphodrias affair. Despite the expulsion of the garrison, there was a strong Spartan presence in central Greece and that meant the possibility of a Spartan–Theban alliance. The price Thebes paid for the guarantee of Athenian support against Sparta was membership in the new league, which meant adherence to all the stipulations, most particularly the acknowledgement of the 'autonomy' clause from the King's Peace with Athens as the acknowledged *hegemon*.[21] Whatever the exact sequence of events, the raid and subsequent acquittal of Sphodrias were the determining factors for Athens. At that point the Athenians chose to renounce the truce with Sparta and became more committed to Thebes. The hostilities lasted, despite attempts at peace and even the attainment of a short-lived peace in 375, until Sparta's defeat by Thebes at Leuctra in 371.

Athens carried out hostilities against Sparta as *hegemon* of her newly constituted Second Athenian League (see Map 1). The document, the so-called 'Aristoteles' Decree,' (*IG* II[2] 43), records the provisions and the membership of the league (see Plate 3).[22] It began with the usual dating formula which places the decree in the spring of 377. The motive, recorded next, would have been the one goal that the Thebans and the rest of the allies would have in common: that the Spartans leave the Greeks free and autonomous. The next few lines, which were purposefully erased, were probably a reference to the King's Peace.[23] The offer to enroll was accompanied by the

21

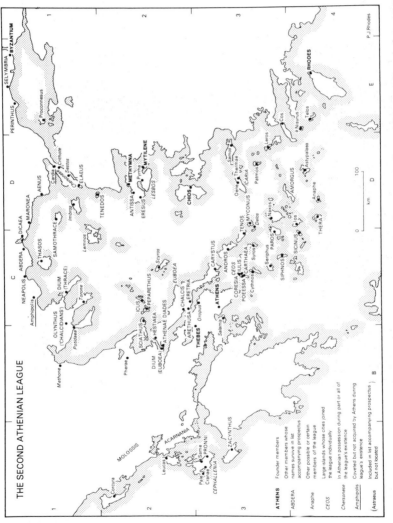

THE SECOND ATHENIAN LEAGUE

Map 1 The Second Athenian League, from R. J. A. Talbert, *Atlas of Classical History*, Routledge, 1985.

Plate 3 The Decree of Aristoteles stele, 378/7 BC. Epigraphical Museum, Athens. Photo: Epigraphical Museum.

guarantees that the members would remain free and autonomous with their own constitution and the assurance that they would be forced to receive neither garrisons nor governors, nor to pay tribute. The Athenians pledged to give up any private or public possessions in any ally's territory and not to acquire any such possessions in the future. There followed the notice that any ally who was attacked by land or sea would be aided by the League and, finally, written safeguards against any changes or deletions to the decree. The names of the members were inscribed below the decree and on the left side of the stele in various hands, a sure indication that the names were indeed inscribed as the states were enrolled.[24]

Assessments of Athens' role in the Second Athenian League have often been influenced by scholar's opinions as to whether Athens reverted to its former fifth-century imperialistic ambitions during the fourth century. The provisions of the League were innovative and had obviously been created to assure allies that Athens would not return to the most hated practices. How conscientious the Athenians were in maintaining their promises must be judged solely within the context of Athens' treatment of the members of the *synedrion* of the Second Athenian League only, *not* its treatment of other Greek states – whether enemy, neutral or ally of Athens and/ or the League. And within that context, it would appear that what made the sixty-some members the 'privileged inner circle' was that Athens did continue to honor its agreements with those members for a considerable length of time.[25] How the Athenian *demos* dealt with other states should be judged within the context of Greek inter-state relations in the fourth century and, more particularly, the context of the Spartan and Theban hegemonies. Even in the worst instances of arrogant treatment by Athens – with other states or within the Second Athenian League during the Social War in the 350s – Athens did not come close to some of the excesses committed by Sparta or Thebes or even fifth-century imperial Athens.

The first six years of the Second Athenian League were productive and successful. Chabrias won a decisive victory over Sparta at Naxos in 376 which led to the addition of more members and confirmed Athenian supremacy in the Aegean until the 320s. The generals Timotheus and Iphicrates were popular and active in the Ionian as well as the Aegean and had enrolled the full membership by 371.[26] The renewal of the King's Peace in 375 between Athens and Sparta recognized the Peloponnesian League *and* the Second Athenian League but did not last very long. Hostilities resumed until another peace was negotiated by Callias in June of 371, when both Sparta and Athens were more willing to share hegemony.[27] The Athenians had reached another stage in regaining power and prestige. Athens had managed to bring some seventy members into its league, and Sparta was forced to acknowledge the partnership.

THE THEBAN HEGEMONY

As Athens regained its position of equality among the Greek states and leadership in the Second Athenian League, its primary concern was Thebes, a reluctant member of the League from the beginning. If the Thebans, indeed, were responsible for the ill-fated raid by Sphodrias, then their effort was well rewarded. Since 378, Athens not only helped Thebes maintain a military presence against Sparta in central Greece, but Athenian naval activities also kept Sparta involved in a second front. Thus Thebes was able to expand in Boeotia and very quickly flaunt the provisions of the King's Peace as well as the Second Athenian League. A possible confrontation with Thebes in 375 was avoided when peace between Athens and Sparta quickly broke down. As mentioned above, Athens and Sparta had resolved their differences in 371 and called a peace conference at Sparta. When the Thebans insisted on representing all of the Boeotian states, the Spartan army under Cleombrotus quickly marched into central Greece, confronted the Boeotian army at Leuctra, and suffered an astounding defeat. Theban potential had become reality (see below, pp. 81–6).

The Spartan defeat was unexpected and required a major readjustment in Greek inter-state relations. The Athenians received the Theban herald and his news coldly and then decided to take advantage of the situation by calling a conference of all states that wanted to maintain the King's Peace of 371 with the Second Athenian League the guarantor. All of the Peloponnesian states except Sparta and Elis made a defensive alliance with Athens. The assurance of Athenian support contributed to innovative changes in the Peloponnesus. Tegea instigated the formation of an Arcadian Alliance and plans for the creation of Megalopolis. The Mantineans reinstated their city from the pieces scattered by Sparta in 385. Other cities took advantage of the situation by ousting pro-Spartan oligarchies. It was, however, the Thebans who went to the Peloponnesus to support these changes. In addition, they worked for the quite significant liberation of the helots in Messenia and the creation of Messene and the new Messenian state. This Theban activity both in the Peloponnesus as well as closer to home in central Greece and Thessaly led the Athenians to negotiate a new alliance in 369.

Although 371 has become a pivotal date for the history of the Greek states in the fourth century, the year 369 is the significant one for the Athenians because that is when they chose to ally with Sparta, the only other state, despite its defeat at Leuctra, capable of confronting the Thebans. And the Thebans were soon to show how formidable they had become. Even the combined forces of Athens, Sparta, and Corinth were unable to keep the Thebans' second expedition from getting past the Isthmus and helping to make the new Messenian state a reality. Despite Athens' alliance with Alexander of Pherae, the majority of Thessalians showed their reluctance to have any native leader and chose Thebes as their protector. An even bigger jolt occurred in 367 when it became obvious during negotiations for a renewal of the King's Peace that the King favored Thebes as the guarantor. It is no surprise that the Peace was not renewed – Sparta would not recognize Messenia, Athens wanted Amphipolis,[28] and neither was willing to accept Pelopidas and the Thebans as the guarantor. In 366, along with a third Boeotian expedition to the Peloponnesus, the Thebans also seized Oropos, a border town between Athens and Boeotia which Athens claimed. The Athenians' disappointment over lack of support from their Peloponnesian allies contributed to their decision to make a defensive alliance with the Arcadians. Yet the Arcadians were engaged in hostilities against Sparta, also an ally of Athens. This ambiguity was to continue until 362.

Athens fared better in the north Aegean. By 367 Athens had renewed claims to Amphipolis and dispatched Timotheus, son of Conon, to enforce the Athenian claim. Although Athens was never to regain Amphipolis, Timotheus was successful in freeing Samos from Persian control and adding Potidaea to Athens' list of allies. The Theban naval expedition to the Hellespont in 364 under Epaminondas' leadership resulted only in alliance with Byzantium. That alliance, however, and the rival fleet's potential for causing mischief among members of the Second Athenian League or other Athenian allies, resulted in Timotheus' continued activity in the Aegean.

The various hostilities set in motion after 371 culminated in the battle at Mantinea in 362. By the time an armed Athenian force returned to the Peloponnesus in 362, Athens' contradictory alliances had been resolved. Hostilities between Elis and some cities of the Arcadian League had caused a break-up of the Arcadian League into two factions. Athens allied with the Mantinean faction, which allied with Sparta as well as Achaea and Elis. The other faction was led by Tegea and was allied with Thebes, Argos, and Messenia. Although there was no clear-cut victor, the death of Epaminondas, combined with that earlier of Pelopidas in 364, meant the decline of Theban participation in matters anywhere but central Greece. In central Greece, however, Thebes remained powerful enough to keep the Athenians occupied on land, as well as provoke the Phocians into a Sacred War, the Third, in 355.

THE SOCIAL WAR

After Mantinea, it might be expected that the Athenians would now take their place as *hegemon* in the affairs of the Greek states. Hegemony, however, remained just out of reach on account of circumstances beyond Athens' control. First, Athens' loss of empire after 404 and Sparta's loss of Messenia after 371 meant that by 362 the city states in Greece were more evenly matched. Thebes, of course, is the best example of this phenomenon. Second, and more significant, there were more participants – both Greek and foreign. Thessaly had already become a state with which to contend since Jason of Pherae had swiftly marched into Boeotia and negotiated an armistice in 371, after Leuctra. In the 360s, the Athenians had to deal with his successor, the unscrupulous Alexander of Pherae, who intrigued with Thebes and Macedonia as well as members of the Second Athenian League. Persian satraps had been involved in Greek affairs since at least the Peloponnesian War, but a satrap like Mausolus of Caria, who became active in the early 350s, was a different proposition. Although a loyal satrap to the king, he also acted independently of both king and any Greek states and he was intent on building power in the southeastern Aegean. Finally, the Persian monarchy was resurgent. In 358, Artaxerxes III ascended the throne and quickly brought all of western Asia under strong Persian control.

Despite these new factors, the Athenians had managed to hold their own against these states until 357. The generals Chabrias, Iphicrates, and Timotheus were still in action. By 362, Athens had recovered from threats posed by the creation of a Theban navy as well as the maneuvering of Alexander of Pherae. Although his attempts to take Amphipolis were unsuccessful, Timotheus did manage to bring Samos, Sestos, and some Chalcidian cities, including Potidaea, into the Athenian sphere and to recover Byzantium. And in 357, Athens recovered the Chersonese after many unsuccessful attempts. A number of cities on Euboea allied with Athens at that time as well. Complacency, however, did not settle in. In the same year Philip captured Amphipolis. A more serious threat to the integrity of the Second Athenian League was Mausolus of Caria who supported the revolts of Rhodes, Chios, and Cos against Athens. The general Chabrias died heroically in defeat at Chios. Due to the maneuvering of Chares, Timotheus, and Iphicrates, the two generals who had been so instrumental in the creation and maintenance of the Second Athenian League, were first recalled to Athens and then prosecuted. The net result was Athens' loss of both men and Chares' sole naval command. In order to obtain funds to continue hostilities against the members of the League in revolt, Chares was soon forced to support the satrap, Artabazus, in his revolt against Persia. Chares' actions, however, provoked Artaxerxes to demand that the Athenians recall Chares and make peace with the rebellious allies. The independence of Rhodes, Cos, and Chios was recognized, and each received Carian garrisons as the Social War ended.

The Social War, 357/6–355, can be seen as the culmination of a policy on the part of a number of states to aggrandize themselves at the expense of the Second Athenian League as well as other Athenian alliances.[29] What distinguishes this war is that the general Chares commanded most of the operations and acted treacherously not only against rebellious states but also against allies of Athens and his own colleagues. There is other evidence to support the conclusion that Athens did not behave well during this war. It is therefore no wonder that scholars have used Isocrates' speech 'On the Peace', which was given at the cessation of hostilities and included a scathing criticism of imperialist tactics, to support their contention that the Athenians continued their fifth-century imperialist posture throughout the fourth century.[30] Cargill would argue, however, not only that Isocrates' condemnation is much more confined to practices during the actual Social War but also that, in the same speech, Isocrates acknowledged Athens' good behavior between the foundation of the Second Athenian League and 357.[31]

INTRIGUES WITH PHILIP AND THE SACRED WARS

After 355, the Sacred War against Phocis and further actions by Philip of Macedon were to prevent the Athenians from ever getting the chance to recover their Aegean hegemony. The Phocians had seized Delphi soon after the Social War began. When the Third Sacred War was declared, Athens allied with Phocis against the Thebans, still a formidable enemy to Athens. What began as a war setting the Greek states of the Phocians, Athenians, and Spartans against the Thebans, Locrians, and Thessalians quickly became the means by which Philip would become directly involved in Greek affairs. He began by attacking Pherae on the invitation of Thessalians led by the Aleuads of Larisa. In response, the tyrants of Pherae asked for help from the Phocians. Although the Phocians successfully defeated Philip in 353, by 352, Philip and the Thessalians defeated and killed many Phocians, including their leader, Onomarchus, at the battle of the Crocus Field. An Athenian fleet, commanded by Chares and stationed in the Gulf of Pagasae, was only able to rescue some survivors after the battle.[32] The subsequent arrival of an Athenian contingent, both cavalry and infantry, did keep Philip from getting past Thermopylae in 352.

Philip continued, however, to separate both members of the Second Athenian League and other Athenian allies from Athenian control. Already during the Social War, Philip captured Amphipolis, Pydna, Potidaea, and Krenides.[33] Philip added Methone, the last Athenian ally on the Thermaic Gulf, shortly after the end of the war. By 348, he had captured Olynthus, which meant that he had full control of the Chalcidice as well. Closer to home, Philip took advantage of discontent against Athens in Euboea. The end result of the Euboean campaign, notwithstanding Phocion's victory at Tamynae, was Athenian recognition of Euboean independence.[34] Therefore, despite Demosthenes' delivery of his first *Philippic* and *Olynthiac* orations that had inspired the Athenian alliance with Olynthus, the Athenians began negotiations that led to the Peace of Philocrates of 346.

The events surrounding the Peace of Philocrates became both the cause of and the opportunity for a number of political trials which began in 346 and did not end until 330. The conditions of the Peace were straightforward: the Athenians and the Second Athenian League (no other allies, including the Phocians) and Philip and his allies were to keep what they had. There is no doubt that all members of the embassies sent to Philip were responsible for the negotiations and agreed to those terms, including the two youngest members, Demosthenes and Aeschines (see Plates 4 and 5). To be a part of such a group meant a rise in Demosthenes' political fortunes.[35] In less than a year, however, Demosthenes had separated himself from what was already looking like a disgraceful agreement when he entered an accusation of misconduct against Aeschines.[36] Aeschines' trial did not take place until 343, at which time he was acquitted.[37] Philocrates, tried at the same time, was condemned. The antagonism between Aeschines and Demosthenes continued into the Lycurgan era when, in 337, Aeschines indicted Ctesiphon for proposing to reward Demosthenes with a crown. Speeches by both Aeschines and Demosthenes are preserved from the trial, which did not occur until 330 but did offer further opportunity to rehash the events of 346. Events surrounding the Peace of Philocrates, therefore, prompted a political rivalry which would both color subsequent events in Athens' history and obscure modern scholars' attempts to present a coherent narrative.[38] The example of the speeches developing out of the Peace of Philocrates serves as a cautionary reminder to anyone hoping to use as primary sources the extant orations which both 'instruct and perplex posterity.'[39]

Philip's actions were the chief reason for the change of heart concerning the Peace of Philocrates. No sooner had the Peace been signed than Philip captured Thermopylae, received the Phocian surrender, and ended the Third Sacred War. The Athenians took emergency actions to defend the state, although those measures turned out to be unnecessary. Despite Philip's offer in 343/2 to reconsider the Peace, which Athens refused, and the chance that Philip might not return from his Thracian campaigns of 342–339, events moved inexorably toward confrontation. By 338, Philip had besieged Byzantium and Perinthus, encroached upon Athens' control of the Chersonesus, established friendly tyrants at Oreus and Eretria, and had seized the grain shipment at Hieron. By 338 the Athenians, under the leadership of Demosthenes, had reinforced Byzantium so that Philip abandoned his siege, won back Euboea, obtained backing from the Persian king, and negotiated a number of alliances, including ex-allies, ex-members of the Second Athenian League, and – the real coup – Thebes. The occasion for Philip's expedition into central Greece was the declaration of a Fourth Sacred War against the Amphissans and the subsequent invitation to Philip to handle the matter. The confrontation happened at Chaeronea where Philip met a coalition of Greek states and defeated them.

Once more the Athenians could have easily expected harsh treatment from the victor; once more the terms were more generous than what might have been expected. If *agathe tyche* (good fortune) had

Plate 4 Demosthenes. Roman copy of Greek original by Polycuctus (*c.* 280 BC). Vatican Museum, Rome. Photo: Vatican Museum.

Plate 5 Aeschines. Herm from a Roman copy of a Greek statue of the fourth century BC. Vatican Museum, Rome. Photo: Vatican Museum.

eluded Demosthenes at Chaeronea, at least it played a part after-wards. The Athenians did still have their navy, which is most likely why they were allowed to keep their freedom and territory as well as Salamis, Samos, Scyros, Imbros, Lemnos, and the administration of Delos. The Second Athenian League, however, was dissolved, and Athens became a part of the 'Greek League' established by Philip, which met in Corinth. Although unhappy with these circum-stances, Athens was about to experience the benefit of fifteen years of peace.

LYCURGAN ATHENS

Athenian recovery was accomplished under the guidance of Lycurgus. Mitchel makes a strong case for a Lycurgan policy which encom-passed all aspects of society and not only made Athens strong again militarily but also energized the society patriotically and spiritually.[40] But Lycurgus did not work alone. All of the political leaders were patriotic Athenians and thus worked with Lycurgus.[41] Their coop-eration was in spite of personal likes and dislikes and their differing points of view as to how best serve Athens.

This development, which appears so prominently in the literary sources, prompted scholars in the nineteenth century to imagine that after Chaeronea, Athenian leaders – much like British parliamen-tarians – created a 'coalition government' of four distinct parties.[42] Such a view is clearly self-deceiving, but the complexities of our sources, even an intact epigraphical document, often leave room for differing interpretations regarding the political atmosphere. The Law Against Tyranny of 337/6 illustrates this (see Plate 6). The Law (first published in English in 1952) condemns anyone who would become tyrant or contribute to tyranny or the overthrow of the Athenian people or their democracy, including the Council of the Areopagus, either individually or as a group.[43] In 1958, Sealey expanded on the general consensus that this decree was directed against the Areopagus by suggesting that Demosthenes, who had been responsible for its renewed activities, was the real target.[44] Alternatively, the Law Against Tyranny can be seen as a means to protect the recently revived Council from being compelled to legitimize a would-be tyrant.[45] No one has ever suggested that any of the leaders in Athens would contemplate tyranny. In fact, the possibility that tyranny might be imposed from outside Athens was one more incentive for political leaders to cooperate for the good of Athens.

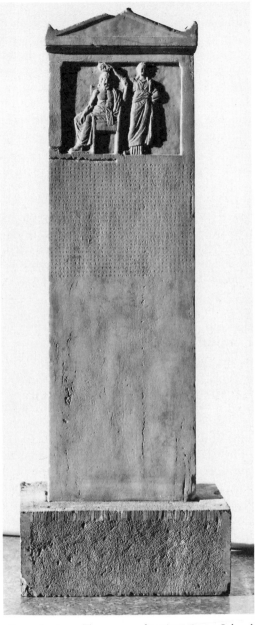

Plate 6 The Law Against Tyranny stele. American School of Classical Studies at Athens: Agora Excavations. Photo: American School of Classical Studies Museum.

The political narrative for the Lycurgan era is short. Philip's assassination in 336 did not end Macedonian hegemony, which only became stronger under Alexander. When Alexander returned to central Greece in 335 and destroyed Thebes, Athens was once again in a very precarious position – Demosthenes had urged the Thebans to overthrow the Macedonian garrison – but once again the Athenians and their leaders were spared, thanks to the negotiations of Phocion and Demades (see below, pp. 104, 192–3). The choice to withhold support from Agis' revolt in 330 is more evidence that the leaders were behaving prudently, at least in foreign matters.

As support of the rebellion would have violated the terms of the Greek League, so also would have the pursuit of any independent foreign diplomacy. Yet the epigraphical record shows that the Athenians did maintain, throughout the period, an unofficial diplomacy. That Macedonians or friends of Macedon were granted honors and sometimes even citizenship should come as no surprise.[46] The bestowal of honors to men who had been allies of Athens at Chaeronea,[47] or honors to a relative of the Memnon of Rhodes who fought for Persia against Alexander,[48] points to the fact that Athens was maintaining diplomatic relations despite the League of Corinth.[49] These informal ties began immediately after Chaeronea and continued throughout the Lycurgan period. By 323, even before Alexander's death, Athens was actively engaged in seeking allies against Macedonian rule.[50] When news of Alexander's death did reach the Greek city-states, Athens was prepared once again to head opposition to Macedonian rule.[51] The defeat of the Greek states by the Macedonians in the Lamian War, 322, confirmed the fact that the city-state was no longer able to withstand the more powerful forces without.[52]

Athens had the wherewithal to lead a coalition because Lycurgus had worked to enhance his city financially and materially. He rationalized the finances, raising the state revenues from 60 to 1200 talents.[53] The epigraphical evidence shows in detail his reorganization of the religious festivals and offerings.[54] And Lycurgus was able to finance a building program second only to that of Pericles in the fifth century.[55] The building project on the Pnyx, which included two large stoas and an enlargement of the auditorium, is perhaps most symbolic of this era (see Plate 7). It was a grand design which was not completed.[56]

Along with the physical changes brought about during this era was the creation of the more ephemeral classic 'Greek ideal.' Lycurgus

Plate 7 The *Bema* or speaker's platform in the Pnyx, a meeting place of the Athenians, in the Lycurgan period. Photo: L. Tritle.

had also established authorized texts of Aeschylus, Sophocles, and Euripides, as well as bronze statues. His well-rounded program, played out within a context of peace, established Athens as a city-state to be admired and emulated in what was to become the Hellenistic era. To speak, therefore, of a 'failure of the city-state,' is to denigrate the substantial accomplishments of the Athenian polis.[57] The city-state of Athens not only produced great art and literature in the fifth century; it also survived the changing fortunes of the fourth century in order to bequeath to western civilization its first classical tradition.

NOTES

1 For example, Hammond, p. 516, notes after his discussion of the Social War, 'Athens' second attempt to win an extensive empire and dominate the Greek world ended in failure and exhaustion.' The so-called Athenian imperialist aims are considered throughout this chapter; see especially notes 25 and 31.

2 L. A. Tritle, 'Virtue and Progress in Classical Athens: The Myth of the Professional General,' *AncW*, 23 (1992), 86, discusses modern scholars who still maintain this construct. In 'Continuity and Change in the Athenian *Strategia*,' *AHB*, 7 (1992), 125–9, Tritle argues that rather than a divergence between the two roles, the fourth century offered oratory as an alternative means to political power.

3 Hammond, p. 525: 'The turmoil in and between the Greek states was ultimately due to the failure of the city-state as a political form to meet the spiritual, social, and economic needs of the citizens.' For a more optimistic assessment, see note 57.

4 I. Worthington, 'Greek Oratory, Revision of Speeches and the Problem of Historical Reliability,' *Classica et Mediaevalia* 42 (1991), pp. 55–74, addresses one aspect of the problem. His *A Historical Commentary on Dinarchus*, Ann Arbor, University of Michigan Press, 1992, provides general bibliography on the historical aspects of the orators.

5 See J. Ober, *Mass and Elite in Democratic Athens*, Princeton, Princeton University Press, 1989, pp. 338–9: 'It was arguably the failure of the elite to control political ideology that led them to devise and write formal political theory which would explain what was wrong with the system they failed to dominate.'

6 B. Strauss, *Athens after the Peloponnesian War*, Ithaca, Cornell University Press, 1986, p. 104, notes 'a substantial amount of disunity in Athens.'

7 Strauss, *Athens*, p. 163: 'War and politics – but mostly politics – took a heavy toll of the Athenian political elite from 395–386.'

8 J. B. Bury and R. Meiggs, *A History of Greece*, 4th edn, New York, St. Martin's Press, 1975, p. 346, mentions all three men.

9 M. H. Hansen, *The Athenian Democracy in the Age of Demosthenes*, Oxford, Blackwell, 1991, provides an exhaustive bibliography which

includes a full list of his many previous works on the subject of the working of all aspects of the democracy. Strauss, *Athens*, p. 59, stresses that the restoration of empire would benefit *all* classes. Ober, *Athens*, p. 305, gives an innovative view of the working of the Athenian state in terms of the relationship between mass and elite and demonstrates the tension between the 'social reality of inequality and the political ideal of equality.'

10 Strauss, *Athens*, p. 57.

11 Strauss, *Athens*, p. 81, 'By 405, a good part of the political power of the thetic class was at the bottom of the Aegean.' The Appendix, pp. 179–82, details the evidence for hoplite and thetic casualties in the Peloponnesian War.

12 *IG* II² 410 ll.14–16.

13 Xen. *Hell.* 1.6.24.

14 Strauss, *Athens*, pp. 46–7 discusses the make-up of the 20,000 deserters.

15 Xen. *Hell.* 5.4.9; Diod. 15.25.4–26.2.

16 Xen. *Hell.* 5.4.19.

17 Diod. 15.28–30. Cargill, pp. 56–61, considers the ancient sources as well as the more recent interpretations.

18 Diod. 15.29.5; Xen. *Hell.* 5.4.20; Hammond, p. 483; Bury, *Greece*, p. 350.

19 Diod. 15.29.7–30.2.

20 A. P. Burnett, 'Thebes and the Expansion of the Second Athenian Confederacy: *IG* II² 40 and *IG* II² 43,' *Historia* 11 (1962), 11. See also Cargill, pp. 60–1.

21 Cargill, p. 59.

22 Cargill, Chapter 2, provides a full text, both in Greek and translation, with commentary.

23 Cargill, pp. 16, 31; Cargill's choice of 367 (p. 32), when the Thebans came in favor with the King, seems the most reasonable time for the clause to have been erased.

24 Cargill, pp. 45–7.

25 Cargill, p. 67.

26 Cargill, p. 65 n. 46 for date; on p. 66, Cargill argues for completion of membership drive by 375.

27 R. Sealey, *A History of the Greek City-States ca. 700–338 B.C.*, Berkeley, University of California Press, 1976, pp. 415–19, discusses the sources and various possibilities.

28 Sealey, *History*, p. 430, suggests that Athens' renewed claim to Amphipolis occurred in conjunction with the alliance with Sparta in 369. In *Demosthenes and His Time*, New York, Oxford University Press, 1993, pp. 77–83, Sealey argues that, rather than misguided posturing or reference to old glories, Athenian claims on Amphipolis and the Chersonese were 'a response to changes occurring independently in the north and threatening Athenian interests' in reference to Thessaly, Macedonia, and the northwest frontiers of the Persian Empire (p. 77).

29 Cargill, pp. 165–79, discusses in detail how those various states were involved.

30 See note 1 for Hammond's view.

31 Cargill, p. 177. See also Sealey, *History*, pp. 432–3.
32 Hammond, p. 543, goes so far as to assume the fleet was part of a joint Athenian–Phocian attack.
33 Sealey, *Demosthenes*, p. 111, notes that while at the time these states were not much of a loss, in retrospect they provided the firm economic and maritime basis for Philip's further expansion.
34 L. A. Tritle, *Phocion the Good*, London, Croom Helm, 1988, pp. 76–89 discusses the campaign in detail.
35 Sealey, *Demosthenes*, p. 145. Sealey also notes (p. 146) Demosthenes' flurry of activity in Athens subsequent to the first embassy.
36 Ibid., pp. 156–7, suggests political survival as the motive for Demosthenes' action.
37 Philocrates' condemnation in the same year underlines the unpopularity of the Peace.
38 See Sealey, *Demosthenes*, pp. 150–7, for the latest in a long line of reconstructions of the events and motives. E. M. Harris, *Aeschines and Athenian Politics*, New York, Oxford University Press, 1995, pp. 8–16, establishes a methodology for the critical use of the orations; he devotes pp. 57–101 to a full discussion of the three embassies connected to the Peace.
39 Bury, *Greece*, p. 433.
40 F. W. Mitchel, 'Lykourgan Athens 338–322,' *Semple Lectures* II, Cincinnati, University of Cincinnati, 1970, p. 190, stresses this 'comprehensive program of reconstruction, reform and revitalization,' throughout.
41 Mitchel, ibid., p. 189.
42 Mitchel, ibid., p. 173; n. 62, p. 180, provides bibliography for the four-party structure. More recently, Sealey's discussions of Demosthenes in both *Demosthenes* and *History*, and Tritle's discussion of Phocion in *Phocion* take for granted the flexibility of alignment. Harris, *Aeschines*, p. 149, reaches the same conclusion in regard to Aeschines.
43 B. Merritt, 'Greek Inscriptions, 5. Law Against Tyranny,' *Hesperia* 21(1952), 355–9. For bibliography and discussion, see C. Schwenk, *Athens in the Age of Alexander*, Chicago, Ares, 1985, pp. 33–41, no. 6.
44 R. Sealey, 'On Penalizing Areopagites,' *AJP* 79 (1958), 71–3. He continues to hold this opinion, *Demosthenes*, p. 201.
45 Schwenk, *Athens*, p. 41.
46 *IG* II² 240 (Schwenk, *Athens*, no. 7, esp. p. 46); *IG* II² 253 (Schwenk, *Athens*, no. 51, esp. p. 250). Both decrees were proposed by Demades, who cultivated good relations with Macedon.
47 *IG* II² 237 (Schwenk, *Athens*, no. 1); *IG* II² 238 (Schwenk, *Athens*, no. 2).
48 *IG* II² 356 (Schwenk, *Athens*, no. 58).
49 See also *IG* II² 336 (Schwenk, *Athens*, no. 31, esp. p. 169).
50 *IG* II² 370, although fragmentary, is the epigraphical evidence for the treaty between Athens and Aetolia mentioned by Diod. 17.111.3. Both *IG* II² 367 and *IG* II² 365 are dated to 323 and record honors to men who contributed to the war effort, according to Schwenk, *Athens*, pp. 392, 400.

51 Tritle's comment, (*Phocion*, p. 96) that 'Philip's genius and Macedonian power explains Chaeronea, not Athenian decline or the incompetence of Athenian generals' pertains as well to the Lamian War.

52 Sealey, *Demosthenes*, p. 3: 'The intrusion of Macedon into Greek affairs was the triumph not of an idea but of armed might.'

53 Plut. *X orat.* 841B–844 attests Lycurgus' building program and policies; the archaeological record corroborates the former.

54 *IG* II² 333 (Schwenk, *Athens*, no. 21); *IG* II² 334 + *Hesperia* 28 (1950) 239–47 (Schwenk, *Athens*, no. 17).

55 Mitchel, *Lykourgan Athens*, pp. 192–3, 196–7, 200, 203–5, 207, 210–11, discusses the building program.

56 H. A. Thompson and R. L. Scranton, 'Stoas and City Walls on the Pnyx,' *Hesperia* 12 (1943), 299, date the plan to the closing years of the Lycurgan era. On p. 301, they comment: 'In the breadth of its conception, as also in the sheer mass of its fabric, this program might well be counted the greatest of Lykourgos' public works, a fitting climax to his career and a splendid, if pathetic expression of his faith in Athens.'

57 See M. I. Finley, *The Ancient Greeks*, Harmondsworth, Penguin, 1975, p. 82: 'There were not many important figures in Greek cultural life between the years 500 and 300 who were not associated with Athens for at least part of their career, including some of the bitterest critics of her system.' Much the same sentiment is voiced by P. J. Rhodes, 'The Polis and its Alternatives,' *CAH*² 6: 591: 'cities and leagues persisted, and asserted as much independence as circumstances allowed. Greek political institutions did not fail, but showed remarkable vitality.'

3

SPARTA

Charles D. Hamilton

The surrender of Athens in spring 404 marked the end of the Athenian Empire and of the fifth century; the victory of Sparta can be said to begin the fourth. For over thirty years, from 404 to 371, Sparta dominated the political affairs of Greece, although not without opposition. For nine years Spartan hegemony in Greece was not contested, but then the conflict known as the Corinthian War broke out. From 395 until 386 a coalition composed of Athens, Corinth, Thebes, Argos, and other Greek states, and funded by Persia, struggled to curtail or overthrow Sparta's position as premier power in the Aegean. At the Battle of Cnidus in 394 Sparta suffered an irreversible naval defeat at the hands of the exiled Athenian admiral Conon, commanding a Persian fleet. Thereafter Sparta pursued a more moderate objective of retaining its hegemony within Greece itself. In the King's Peace (also known as the Peace of Antalcidas for the Spartan diplomat who negotiated it, or the Common Peace), Sparta agreed to surrender the Greeks of Asia Minor to Persian control in return for an end to Persian subsidies to its Greek enemies, Persian recognition of *de facto* Spartan domination of Greece, and the principle of autonomy for all Greek states, large or small.[1]

Over the next five years Sparta worked to establish its control by interpreting the autonomy clause of the peace to its advantage, isolating and threatening its former enemies. This process culminated in wrongful intervention in Theban politics and the seizure of the Theban acropolis (the Cadmea) in 382. A puppet government and a garrison were installed, and Thebes remained under Spartan control until Theban patriotic exiles returned to liberate the city late in 379. The struggle which followed, in which Sparta attempted to regain control of Thebes and Boeotia, is known as the Boeotian War. It resulted in growing discontent with Spartan aggression, the establishment in 377 of the Second Athenian League, and ultimately in the fateful Battle of Leuctra. In 371 a Spartan-led Peloponnesian force met the army of the reformed Boeotian League under Theban leadership on the plains of Boeotia; the outcome was a decisive defeat for the Spartans, who lost 700 of their citizen-soldiers and the commander, King Cleombrotus. In the aftermath of this battle Spartan allies defected in great numbers, and the way opened for an invasion of the Peloponnesus.

The great Theban general Epaminondas led an invasion in 370, and another in 369, with the result that the city of Mantinea was refounded, Megalopolis was formed in Arcadia, and the territory of Messenia in south-western Peloponnesus – for well over three centuries considered a province integral to the Spartan state – was liberated. At a stroke Sparta lost control of the richest agricultural land in the Peloponnesus, and the helots to work it; the very foundations of the socio-economic system of Sparta were threatened. Moreover, Sparta in its bastion of Laconia was now ringed round from north-east to south-west by a hostile coalition consisting of its inveterate foe Argos, Mantinea, Megalopolis, and finally the rebuilt city of Messene. For the remainder of the 360s Sparta struggled to recover control of Messenia and to undo the work of Epaminondas. The second Battle of Mantinea in 362, although indecisive in other respects, sealed Sparta's fate and left Messenia independent.[2]

The story of Sparta's history in the period from 362 until the Macedonian conquest of Greece is largely a sad epilogue to the glory days of hegemony: Spartan kings, Agesilaus and his son Archidamus, ventured abroad in mercenary service to foreign kings and states in the vain hope of acquiring enough money to hire mercenary armies to reconquer Messenia. Agesilaus died at the end of his campaigns in Egypt, and Archidamus fell fighting in southern Italy in service to Tarentum. Sparta abdicated its role as a great power in the affairs of Greece when Philip of Macedon began to menace his neighbors by focusing on the reconquest of Messenia to the exclusion of all else. The single episode of Spartan political and military initiative in this period was Agis' organization of a revolt against the Macedonians which culminated in the Greek defeat at Megalopolis, after Alexander had launched his invasion of the Persian Empire. For the remainder of the fourth century Sparta played no appreciable role in Greek history.

The central question which scholars have posed about Spartan history in the fourth century is how and why Sparta fell from its position of undisputed domination of Greece at the beginning of the period, to that of a second- or even third-rate power, consumed with concern over merely local affairs in the decade after Leuctra. Was Sparta's failure primarily political, or did it result from deep-rooted social and economic causes with implications in the military realm? To put the matter another way, was the failure of Spartan hegemony the result of policies deliberately chosen, of political and diplomatic aims pursued from among several possible options, or were more fundamental changes – linked to the very fabric of society and imperfectly understood – responsible for its collapse as a great power?[3] Any attempt to answer this question rests, in large measure, on the less than satisfactory sources which we possess for the subject.

The first and most important account of Spartan, and Greek, history in the early fourth century is that of the Athenian Xenophon, who was a contemporary witness of events.[4] Born in 427, Xenophon was a young man at the time of Athens' capitulation, and he had connections to Socrates' circle. He left Athens to join the mercenary army, supporting the Persian prince Cyrus in his abortive attempt to overthrow his elder brother, the Persian King Artaxerxes. After Cyrus' death at Cunaxa, Xenophon remained with the Greek forces, eventually becoming their commander on their retreat from Mesopotamia across Armenia to the Black Sea. Xenophon appears to have remained in Asia Minor until his force was incorporated into the army of which the Spartan king Agesilaus took command in 396. Banished from his native Athens, Xenophon became a close friend of Agesilaus and was rewarded with an estate in the Peloponnesus, where he retired to raise a family and to write a number of works including two historical accounts, the *Anabasis* (the story of the Ten Thousand Greek mercenaries in Cyrus' army) and the *Hellenica* (a general account of Greek history from 410 until the Battle of Mantinea in 362); an account of the Spartan government and way of life (*Constitution of the Lacedaemonians*); a flattering and highly partial account of Agesilaus as king and commander; and several treatises on such matters of concern to a Greek aristocrat as hunting and horsemanship. There is also a long, romanticized work, the *Cyropaedia*, which purports to be an account of the education of Cyrus the Great, the founder of the Persian Empire. Xenophon's writings are obviously of the highest importance as the products of a contemporary witness, but his historical works in particular suffer from many defects, including bias and partiality toward Sparta, omissions of many important events, and inferiority to his two fifth-century predecessors, Herodotus (in narrative power) and Thucydides (in intellectual rigor and political insight). We are indebted nonetheless to Xenophon for the main lines of development of events in fourth-century history down to 362, and his account must form the basis on which any chronological study is built. His *Hellenica*, supplemented by the *Agesilaus* and his *Constitution of the Lacedaemonians*, provides an invaluable source of information about Sparta in this period.

We possess relatively few other contemporary sources for Spartan history. The Athenian orators make a number of incidental references to the subject, but Isocrates' *Archidamus* is the only lengthy and detailed speech ostensibly devoted to issues in Spartan history. Inscriptions, given the attitude toward writing and written documents in Sparta, provide little helpful information.[5] The sections of the anonymous writer known as the Oxyrhynchus historian, recovered in a treasure trove of papyri from the Egyptian village of Oxyrhynchus, have been recognized as supremely valuable, but unfortunately they are limited to only a few years of our period, from 397 to 395.[6] Of the other two major fourth-century historians, Ephorus and Theopompus, only fragments remain, although Ephorus seems to have been the main source for Diodorus of Sicily for this period, and both writers were known to and used to some degree by Plutarch, especially in his lives of Lysander, Agesilaus, Pelopidas, and the lost Epaminondas.[7] In several other works, such as his collections of *Sayings of Spartans* and of *Kings and Commanders*, and in his *Constitution of the Lacedaemonians*, Plutarch preserves valuable evidence.[8] Also from the Roman period, the Latin writers Cornelius Nepos and Justin and the Greek travel writer Pausanias occasionally provide useful scraps of information.

One further source of information must not be neglected, although it must be treated with great care: the works of the fourth-century philosophers. The corpus of Plato includes numerous references to Spartan customs and institutions, as does Aristotle's *Politics*. The difficulty with Plato in particular is that he tended to admire certain aspects of the Spartan way of life, as indeed did Xenophon, and he may well have exaggerated or glamorized Spartan institutions and uncritically accepted elements of what one scholar has referred to as 'the Spartan mirage.'[9] Aristotle's incidental remarks about certain Spartan political institutions, such as the ephorate and the powers of the kings, derive in all likelihood from his lost *Constitution of the Lacedaemonians*. His remarks about Spartan demographics, and in particular his famous comment about *oliganthropia*, bear the stamp of authenticity of a contemporary witness, and a critical one at that. In sum, this completes the sorry catalog of historical data for Sparta in the fourth century. It is from this information that modern scholars have wrestled with the difficulties of writing the story of the Spartan hegemony and its failure.

SPARTAN HEGEMONY, 404–395

In antiquity, credit for the military defeat of Athens was given to the brilliant Spartan admiral, Lysander, and the judgment of modern scholars is little different.[10] But the victory at Aegospotami was not accomplished by Spartans alone; they were aided by their Greek allies in the Peloponnesian League and by some Greeks who had rebelled from Athens' control, and by massive subsidies from the coffers of Persia. Indeed, the price for Persian financial aid, agreed to by the Spartans in 411, was the recognition of Persian rule over the Greek communities along the Aegean coast of Asia Minor. This concession, of course, made mockery of the Spartan claim at the outbreak of the Peloponnesian War that they were fighting 'to free the Hellenes' from Athenian tyranny.[11] Whether or not cries of protest went up against such perfidy immediately after Sparta signed its agreement with Persia, it is certain that the Spartans were vilified for their act in later decades.[12] To return those Greek cities 'liberated from Athens' to Persian control, of course, was to undo the work of Athens over three quarters of a century *vis-à-vis* Persia. Not surprisingly, this issue became problematic at the end of the war.[13]

The reduction of Athens was the first priority of the Spartans after their victory at Aegospotami. Lysander closed the Hellespont to Athenian shipping and began the siege of the city. While a portion of his fleet interdicted further supplies of food to Athens and Kings Agis and Pausanias surrounded the city and the Piraeus, Lysander himself sailed through the Aegean accepting the surrender of cities formerly subject to Athenian control. Thus was spent the autumn and winter of 405–4, and after a six-month siege Athens had been starved into submission. In the spring of 404, almost twenty-seven years to the day that the Thebans had initiated hostilities by entering Plataea, Athenian envoys sought peace terms from the Spartans. At a conference of its Peloponnesian League allies, Sparta determined to offer peace to Athens on the following terms: evacuation of all foreign territory of the empire (already a *fait accompli*); destruction of the walls of the city, of the Piraeus, and the Long Walls linking the two; reduction of the fleet to a token squadron of twelve; and the adoption of the *patrios politeia*, the 'ancestral constitution.' To its credit, Sparta decided to reject the proposal of the Thebans and the Corinthians to execute all adult males, enslave the women and children, and destroy the city itself.[14] No doubt this came as a welcome relief to the Athenians, since they had meted out precisely such treatment to several enemies during the war, perhaps most notably the Melians in 416. Not long after the formal capitulation of Athens, internal political squabbling over the nature of the ancestral constitution led to the establishment of a panel of thirty, backed by a Spartan garrison and harmost (military governor). For eight months this government, which came to be known as the Thirty Tyrants, ruled ever more harshly and oppressively.[15] In the end, a group of Athenian exiles led by Thrasybulus seized first Phyle and then the Piraeus. When full-scale civil war developed between the factions, the Spartans intervened. The king Pausanias superseded Lysander in command of Spartan troops in Attica and negotiated a reconciliation. The Thirty Tyrants fell from power and the democracy was restored in 403. For almost a decade, however, Athens remained subservient to Sparta in foreign policy and may have been, as some scholars believe, a member of the Peloponnesian League.

The overthrow of the Thirty Tyrants was the first step in the unraveling of Sparta's settlement of the war. But we have anticipated events and, in order to understand the significance of this development, we must examine in detail Sparta's post-war settlement. Lysander more than any other shaped it, and the treatment of Athens provides a model of how other states' affairs were settled. First, Lysander installed in power in each state a decarchy or group of ten from among his own partisans; the decarchies are analogous to the Thirty in Athens. This was done throughout the former Athenian Empire, both in states in Asia which were to be returned to Persian control and in those of the Aegean that were to be 'independent.' In most instances Spartan harmosts and garrisons were also installed, to maintain order, prop up the new regimes, and assure that the states newly freed from Athenian control would have the proper political orientation. Finally, Sparta assessed and collected tribute from these states, probably along the lines of what the Athenians, and before them the Persians, had done previously.[16] Thus, in effect, the Spartan hegemony rested on the three props of political subordination, military control, and financial exaction. Although such a policy for the reshaping of the Greek world seemed to violate the aims with which Sparta had entered the war against Athens in 431, few outside Sparta were in any position to offer effective opposition. The same was not the case within the Spartan polity.

There is evidence, although less clear than we might wish, to suggest that a vigorous debate was engendered within Sparta over the issue of Sparta's role in foreign policy after 404, and in particular over the implications of one policy or another for the Spartan way of life. Doubtless the central issues were discussed among the *homoioi* or peers, those of citizen status, but opinion tended to crystallize around three individuals, the two kings and Lysander, each of whom may have represented the head of a faction.[17] Lysander stood for the most radical and innovative policy, that of a strong imperialist presence abroad in the Aegean and in Greece. In this he was supported at home by a number of individuals who may have hoped to profit from the opportunities afforded by command as harmosts, and abroad by his partisans among the decarchs. King Pausanias seems to have represented conservative opinion, most closely aligned with those who, before the war, merely wished to restrain Athens from interfering in the affairs of Sparta's allies, and who would have restricted Spartan influence to the Peloponnesian League. There were many in Sparta who took this traditionalist view, and probably many of Sparta's traditional allies in the Peloponnesian League favored such a foreign policy. King Agis was opposed to Lysander personally, and perhaps to his policies of expansion abroad as well, although there is evidence to suggest that Agis and his supporters would have welcomed a strong Spartan presence in central and northern Greece, not merely in the Peloponnesus, together with Spartan influence if not direct interference in the internal affairs of other states. Several states such as Thebes and Corinth took alarm at this policy, and in time they would work vigorously to counteract it.

The debate over such issues came to a head shortly after the conclusion of the war and it focused on the question of whether or not Sparta should utilize gold and silver in the form of coined money, in violation of the Lycurgan prohibition against this practice. Sparta of course had no currency of its own; it was foreign silver and gold, the booty of the war and the tribute now flowing in to the state annually, that was in question. The incident that brought the matter to public attention was the peculation by Gylippus, the hero of Syracuse and lieutenant of Lysander, who had been instructed to convey a large amount of money home to Sparta. He could not resist the temptation to dip into the bags of money, but he failed either to take note of the receipt tallies, or to alter them. Thus the authorities quickly discovered the discrepancy between the monies enumerated and those delivered, and a search of Gylippus' house revealed the stolen funds hidden beneath his roof beams.[18] Gylippus was indicted for fraud and possession of money in violation of the Lycurgan law, but the case raised public interest and precipitated discussion of the impropriety of employing money. It was recognized that Sparta could not continue on the course of maritime imperialism on which Lysander had set it without modifying its economy of barter into an international money economy, and the *gerousia* voted to allow the use of money for public purposes but to continue to forbid its possession by private individuals. This attempted compromise, needless to say, was unworkable, and in the next few decades more and more Spartans found ways to amass and retain wealth in contravention of the law.[19] For the moment, however, the issue appeared to be settled, but it illustrates one of the many implications of Sparta's new foreign policy of imperialism. Unfortunately it is very difficult to gauge how significant this particular development was in the changing picture of Sparta's socio-economic conditions in the early fourth century.

The next area of controversy in Sparta's post-war settlement concerns the fate of the former states of the Athenian Empire located in Asia Minor. According to the agreements of 411, Sparta was to turn these territories over to Persian control in return for receiving Persian subsidies in the war against Athens.[20] But Sparta was also not to make peace with Athens without the agreement of Persia. The situation was complicated by the fact that King Darius, under whose authority the treaty had been made, died early in 404, before the surrender of Athens. Both his elder son, Artaxerxes, and his younger son, Cyrus, who had cooperated with Lysander in prosecuting the war against Athens with vigor, were away from the coast at the Persian capital when Athens sued for peace. The Greek sources give no indication that any Persian representative took part in the negotiations at Sparta which led to peace. To further complicate matters, we learn that Cyrus was suspected (rightly, it would seem) of a plot to assassinate Artaxerxes, who was named to succeed their dead father. Cyrus was imprisoned for a time, but released at the instigation of his mother Parysatis, and then returned to his position as *karanos* or overlord of the western Persian satrapies. Just when this occurred is a matter of some debate, and it is impossible to tell with certainty. In all likelihood, however, Cyrus did not return to the coast much before the fall of 404, i.e., a good six months after the surrender of Athens; and he may not have returned until an even later date. However that may be, it is clear that the Spartans, and particularly Lysander, had to settle the affairs of the Greeks of Asia Minor before the return of Cyrus. The process of establishing pro-Spartan decarchies in place of the previous pro-Athenian governments was begun in the aftermath of Aegospotami (autumn 405) if not before, and it continued through the winter and probably until the summer of 404; Lysander did not sail back to Sparta until after the surrender of Samos in September.[21] At some point in the spring or summer of 404, Tissaphernes, the Persian satrap with whom the Spartans had actually negotiated the treaty of 411, demanded the return of those cities freed from Athenian control to Persian suzerainty. Lysander must have handed them over to him, decarchies, garrisons and all. The fate of the garrisons is unclear; they may or may not have been retained in support of the decarchies, but if retained they would have come under the overall control of the Persians. But friction soon developed with Tissaphernes, and when Cyrus returned a majority of the cities revolted from Tissaphernes to him. This situation led to Spartan involvement once again in Persian affairs.

Cyrus continued to plot to overthrow Artaxerxes and he used his position to recruit Greek mercenaries for his planned march into the interior of the Persian Empire. There was no dearth of soldiers available for service after 404, and Cyrus had several captains recruiting armies throughout Greece for him. Hostilities with Tissaphernes soon broke out, and he used them as an excuse for the gathering of his forces. Eventually he summoned the various contingents to join him in Asia and in the spring of 401 he set out to confront his brother. The objective of the march was kept a secret from the rank and file of the Greeks, although suspicions grew the farther they marched from the coast. Eventually Cyrus' army met Artaxerxes' near Cunaxa north of Babylon, and in the ensuing battle Cyrus was killed, although his Greek troops cleared the field before them. The subsequent fate of the Greeks, fascinating as it is, does not concern us here; Xenophon's *Anabasis* provides the details. What does concern us is the fact that Tissaphernes returned from Assyria to Ionia and demanded the submission of all of the Greek cities there. Most of them had cast their lot with Cyrus, and they now sent a plea to

Sparta for assistance. The Spartans, in fact, had sent aid to Cyrus at his request, presumably because they recognized a debt of gratitude to him for his help in defeating Athens. In any case, the Spartan government sent a warning to Tissaphernes to cease and desist from doing any harm to the Greek cities and, when he ignored the ultimatum, they dispatched Thibron with an army to aid the Greek cities. Thus, in 400, began the war which would in time bring a Spartan king (Agesilaus) to Asia and would pit Sparta against the might of the Persian Empire.

The decision to protect the Greek cities of Asia Minor from Tissaphernes represented a reversal of the treaty of 411 with Persia, and it marked a turning point in Spartan foreign policy. The imperialist faction of Lysander must have supported this decision, but others in Sparta may well also have welcomed the opportunity to improve the tarnished image which surrender of these cities to Persia had brought upon Sparta. The army sent abroad affords us another insight into a development of considerable importance. In addition to a contingent of allied soldiers, the Spartans sent several thousand *neodamodeis*. These troops are mentioned for the first time in this context and, while the sources nowhere tell us exactly who they were, there is general agreement among scholars that they represent freed helots who were pressed into service.[22] During the Peloponnesian War the earliest indications of that manpower shortage to which Aristotle alludes appear. The number of Spartan citizen-soldiers is beginning to diminish, and Sparta starts to turn to alternative sources of manpower, including the use of helot contingents. In the fourth century *neodamodeis* are mentioned again and again, and it is clear that they have begun to supplant the traditional citizen hoplites in Sparta's ever more numerous wars abroad.

Sparta's decision to intervene militarily on behalf of the Greek cities met with a rather mixed reaction from other Greek states. Both Thebes and Corinth declined to supply troops for the expedition, but Athens sent a cavalry contingent. Sparta's other Peloponnesian allies were more cooperative.[23] At just about the same time as the war in Asia was beginning, the Spartans made a set of demands upon the state of Elis in the Peloponnesus. Elis had control over the sacred site of Olympia and the operation of the Olympic Games, and it had excluded the Spartans from participation since 420. Preoccupation with the war against Athens had prevented Sparta from dealing with Elis. Now in 400 they sent an ultimatum, demanding not only that Elis allow Sparta to participate again in the Panhellenic Games and allow King Agis to sacrifice to Zeus, but also that Elis grant independence to several border towns. Elis refused and called upon other states to assist, particularly Thebes and Corinth. These two did not assist Elis, but they failed to march out with the Spartans either when called upon to do so. In any case, King Agis invaded Elean territory and left garrisons in towns which came over to him. When he prepared to launch another invasion, Elis sent envoys to negotiate terms, eventually surrendering control over its dependent towns, tearing down the walls of its ports, and allowing Sparta access to the games. Sparta's war upon Elis sent a clear message to states such as Thebes and Corinth which were becoming ever more fearful of Spartan intentions: Sparta would intervene in the internal affairs of other states, even those technically allied, when it seemed useful to do so.[24]

THE CORINTHIAN WAR, 395–386

Sparta's hegemony weighed heavily on the states of Greece. Those which had been members of the Athenian Empire had received pro-Spartan oligarchies, been garrisoned, and had tribute imposed upon them. Several states such as Elis, Messenian Naupactus on the Corinthian Gulf, and Trachinian Heraclea on the borders of Malis and Locris experienced the harsh hand of Spartan military intervention. Even the activities of Spartan commanders operating in Asia Minor ostensibly on behalf of the Greek cities there seemed to some to threaten the establishment of a wider Spartan empire. Against this background of fear, concern, and perceptions of Spartan aggression and expansion, war came about.

In antiquity, the common explanation of the origin of the Corinthian War was that afforded by Xenophon: Persia corrupted faction leaders in several Greek cities and bribed them into war against Sparta.[25] In this view, Timocrates of Rhodes visited Thebes, Athens, Corinth, and Argos to test the waters. He proposed Persian subsidies to help finance military activities in Greece to create a two-front war for Sparta and thus reduce some of the pressure Persian forces were feeling in Asia Minor. Sparta's principal allies in the Peloponnesian War, Thebes and Corinth, not only felt deprived of any meaningful influence at the conference table which ended the conflict and were denied a share of the booty of the war, but were also required to pay their share of costs associated with the waging of the war. Therefore they proved susceptible to Persian machinations. Defeated Athens, subservient to Sparta for a number of years after 404, had begun to consider ways to reassert its predominant role in Aegean affairs. Thus, when the Athenian admiral Conon, who had fled to Cyprus after Aegospotami, took employment in Persian service against Sparta, some Athenians sailed to join him. And finally Argos, long a rival and opponent, was eager to challenge Sparta's position in the Peloponnesus. The chief allies, Thebes, Athens, Corinth, and Argos sent representatives to Corinth in 395 to form a council to conduct operations and to recruit other states. Many others from central Greece and even from the Peloponnesus joined, and a coalition force was formed at Corinth. In this fashion a coalition of states began the conflict known as the Corinthian War.

An alternative explanation is afforded by the Oxyrhynchus historian.[26] He asserts that an anti-Spartan faction in Thebes wanted a preventive war but realized that they could not secure allies unless Sparta appeared to be the aggressor. Thus they engineered a border conflict between the central Greek states of Phocis and Locris. When the Phocians turned for assistance to Sparta and the Spartans dictated terms of settlement for the dispute, the Thebans had their opportunity to portray the Spartans as meddling aggressors. When Sparta sent forces into Boeotia under Lysander, with a second army to follow under King Pausanias, Thebes appealed successfully to Athens for an alliance. Modern scholarship tends to emphasize the underlying causes of the war, especially the widespread perception of the threat of Spartan aggression, while acknowledging the role of Theban intrigue and of Persian subsidies in bringing the conflict to a head.[27]

It is not possible to discuss the military aspects of the war in detail here.[28] Suffice it to say that after Lysander was killed in battle at Haliartus in 395 and King Pausanias was tried *in absentia* for failure to recover his body by fighting, Sparta recalled King Agesilaus from his successful operations in Asia Minor. Two battles in Greece of the classic hoplite type proved indecisive, at the River Nemea near Corinth in July and near Coronea in Boeotia in August 394 (see below, pp. 71–3). The same was not the case with the naval defeat suffered by the Spartans at Cnidus in summer 394; there the Persian fleet under Conon and Pharnabazus swept the Spartans from the sea and ended Sparta's short-lived naval hegemony. For the remainder of the war the fighting was largely confined to operations from fixed positions in and around Corinth, and to naval activities in which the Athenians went some distance to re-establish their fifth-century domination of the Aegean, initially with the support of Conon and the Persian fleet. Eventually the Spartans were forced to recognize that they could not win the war in both theaters and, predictably perhaps, they chose once again to abandon the Greeks of Asia in order to reimpose their hegemony in Greece proper. Abortive negotiations to this effect occurred in 392, but it was not until the Spartan admiral Antalcidas defeated an Athenian squadron and closed the Hellespont in 387 that a definitive peace agreement was finally reached. According to its terms, the Spartans surrendered the Greek cities to the Persian king, and all the other poleis were to have their autonomy guaranteed, regardless of their size. The principle of autonomy seemed a firm cornerstone upon which to base the peace, since the war had occurred in large measure over real or perceived violations of the autonomy of the Greek states by the Spartans. The question was, would autonomy actually govern the relations of the states?[28]

SPARTAN DOMINATION, 386–371

At the conclusion of the Corinthian War the generation of leaders who had shaped Spartan politics after 404 was gone: King Agis had died after the Elean War and been succeeded by his half-brother, Agesilaus; Lysander had been killed at Haliartus; King Pausanias had fled into exile in 395. Agesilaus became the chief political figure in the aftermath of the so-called King's Peace of 387/6, and it was he and his policies which dominated the Greek world for almost two decades, although not without opposition from within Sparta. Pausanias' two sons, Agesipolis (until his death on campaign in 381), and then Cleombrotus, focused the opposition to Agesilaus.[30]

Acting as the guarantor of the King's Peace in Greece, Sparta took measures to assure itself of control there. Agesilaus used the principle of autonomy to dissolve the Boeotian League, which Thebes dominated, the novel political association of Argos and Corinth, and the nascent Athenian maritime alliance system. Next, Sparta moved against Peloponnesian states, intervening in the affairs of Mantinea and Phlius. Mantinea was forced to tear down its walls and disperse its population among five villages which originally formed the city; and Phlius had to accept pro-Spartan exiles in place of its governing class after a long siege. Sparta's objective in these actions, as in Elis fifteen years earlier, was to punish those who had challenged Spartan leadership in foreign policy or whose government was not sufficiently docile. For many, however, such intervention seemed to violate the principle of autonomy.

The culmination of such interventionism occurred when Sparta meddled in the internal affairs of Thebes.[31] In the 380s the government of Thebes was divided between pro- and anti-Spartan factions. In 382, a Spartan commander *en route* to operations against Olynthus in the Chalcidice encamped before Thebes and accepted an invitation from the pro-Spartan faction to seize the Cadmea and to assist in a *coup d'état*. Phoebidas carried out this plan and helped to install the pro-Spartans in power, arresting or driving out their opponents. When this act was denounced at Sparta as an unjustified act of aggression in peacetime against an ally, which clearly violated the autonomy of Thebes, Phoebidas was brought to trial. Agesilaus argued in his defense that the outcome was the important thing, and that if it was judged in Sparta's interest to secure control of Thebes, then the initiative of the commander who had achieved this result should be applauded. Although a mild fine was imposed on Phoebidas, Sparta kept its garrison on the Cadmea and supported its partisan, Leontiades. By contrast Ismenias, the anti-Spartan leader, was arrested, brought to trial himself, and convicted on charges of accepting bribes from and conspiring with Persia. His execution on these charges, given Sparta's own record of having collaborated with Persia and having accepted 'subsidies' in the war against Athens, struck many contemporaries as stark hypocrisy. Even Xenophon, otherwise a biased champion of Sparta, could not refrain from condemnation of this 'impious act.'[32]

Sparta appeared to be at the peak of its powers in 379, after the successful completion of its campaign to reduce the aggression of Olynthus against its Greek neighbors.[33] But the Spartan hegemony was less securely based than it might have seemed to contemporaries, and it would be shaken before the end of the decade. The first shock came when a group of Theban exiles slipped back into their city and carried out a counter-coup against the pro-Spartan clique. Not only did they engineer the overthrow of Leontiades' government, but they also intimidated the Spartan garrison commander into evacuating the Cadmea. Angry and alarmed at this turn of events, Agesilaus demanded that the Thebans readmit the Spartan garrison, and when they refused to do so he sent his colleague, King Cleombrotus, with an army to operate in Boeotia. Thus began the Boeotian War, which saw Agesilaus himself lead two invasions into enemy territory, and which culminated in the Battle of Leuctra in 371.[34]

Agesilaus' object was to reassert control of Thebes and Boeotia, and to punish those who had overthrown his partisans. He hoped initially to achieve these goals through the agency of Cleombrotus, but the latter returned to Sparta without accomplishing much. But there was one fateful result of his mission. Cleombrotus left a Spartan, Sphodrias, in command of a garrison in Boeotia, and that worthy conceived the idea of marching into Attica in an abortive attempt to seize the Piraeus. When his attempt became known, the Athenians sent envoys to demand justice at Sparta. The Spartans promised to bring Sphodrias to trial, but in the end, again through Agesilaus' influence, they acquitted him of wrongdoing. The Athenian response was to break off relations with Sparta, declare that they were responsible for breaking the peace, and to seek an alliance with Thebes. Shortly thereafter the Athenians formed their Second League and went to war against Sparta.[35]

The ensuing conflict was fought on land in Boeotia and at sea, in both the Aegean and the Ionian theaters. A surprising number of Greek states accepted Athens' invitation to join the Second Athenian League, and Sparta found itself facing stiff opposition. Negotiations in 375 attempted to break a military stalemate, but the resultant renewal of the Common Peace was short-lived and war resumed. Once again, in 371, the belligerents sought a diplomatic solution to their difficulties. But the refusal of the Theban Epaminondas to allow the various cities of the reformed Boeotian League to sign for themselves unless the Spartans allowed the towns which they controlled in Laconia and Messenia to do the same sent Agesilaus into a rage. He struck the name of the Thebans out of the treaty and Sparta sent King Cleombrotus into Boeotia with an army. On the plain of Leuctra the Peloponnesian army, which outnumbered the Boeotian force opposed to it, met defeat at the hands of Epaminondas and his tactical innovations: the massed depth of fifty shields on one wing, and the use of cavalry to exploit a gap in the enemy phalanx (see below, pp. 81–6). The effect of this Spartan defeat was far greater in the diplomatic than in the military realm. It was the beginning of the end for Sparta's position in Greece.[36]

DECADE OF CRISIS, 371–362

Many of Sparta's allies, even within the core of the Peloponnesian League, defected after the news of the defeat at Leuctra became known. This development was the result, at least in part, of dissatisfaction and concern that had been growing over Sparta's high-handed treatment of other states ever since the King's Peace. The Theban generals Epaminondas and Pelopidas seized the initiative in exploiting Sparta's growing diplomatic and political isolation, and they undermined an Athenian attempt to negotiate another peace shortly after Leuctra. Instead, Epaminondas led a large army of Boeotian and other Greek forces in an invasion of the Peloponnesus in 370.[37] His objective was to continue exerting pressure upon Sparta and to reduce even further its military capability. The invasion force pushed down into Laconia itself, but a defense led by Agesilaus at the Eurotas River convinced the Theban not to attempt to attack Sparta city. After ravaging much of the territory, Epaminondas led his army north into Arcadia and then south-west into Messenia, where he liberated the helots and proclaimed the rebirth of the Messenian polis. Exiles were recalled from Sicily and elsewhere to repopulate the new city, and stout walls were constructed below Mount Ithome (see Plate 8, the walls of Messene, and below p. 259). In addition, the ancient city of Mantinea, which the Spartans had caused to be destroyed in 385, was rebuilt, and a new city, called Megalopolis, was created in Arcadia as a focus for the many scattered small communities of that region (see Plate 9, a view of the Thersilion and theater, and below p. 259). Now Sparta was ringed round by a series of fortified cities, each of which was hostile to it and committed to the containment of Spartan military activities as the price of its own existence. In the following year the Thebans came again, but since there was little to ravage in the southern Peloponnesus, their operations were largely confined to the northeastern portions of the area, where additional allies of Sparta defected to their cause. The Spartans had appealed to Athens for assistance at this time, and the Athenians, judging the Thebans a greater threat to their interests than the militarily constrained Spartans, agreed to aid them and sent a force to the Isthmus. Thus a shift occurred in the power politics of Greece, in which Sparta and Athens were now allied against the reality of what scholars call the Theban hegemony. For almost a decade, from 371 to 362, Thebes was the dominant power in Greece, and Theban influence stretched far south into the Peloponnesus and north into Central Greece, Thessaly, and even Macedonia.

Throughout this period the Spartans focused their attention on the recovery of Messenia. The loss of their richest agricultural territory, together with the helots to work it for them, had reversed 350 years of history, and they were unable to adjust to this situation.

Plate 8 The walls of Messene. Photo: R. Stoneman.

Plate 9 Thersilion, viewed from theater at Megalopolis, *c.* 370–50 BC.
Photo: S. Lattimore.

Unfortunately, their military capabilities were not equal to the task
of the recovery of Messenia. For one thing, the pool of manpower
available to them from their alliance, the old Peloponnesian League
which had been the lynchpin of their military leadership for about
a century and a half, was much depleted. By the mid-360s only
Laconia itself and a handful of states in and around the Isthmus of
Corinth in the northeastern Peloponnesus remained loyal to Sparta
and could be counted on to supply contingents to any Spartan-led
army. For another, Spartan military effectiveness had been declining
for decades, the result of a process which is almost completely undoc-
umented in our sources and is therefore not well understood by
modern scholars.[38]

What we do know is that at the time of Leuctra there were only
some 1,500 full citizen-soldiers of Sparta left, in contrast to the
5,000 Herodotus reckoned at the time of the Persian War in 480.[39]
Aristotle, writing about fifty years later than Leuctra, stressed the
oliganthropia ('shortage of men') from which Sparta suffered in his
day.[40] It is not clear whether this decline was the result of an absolute

reduction in the numbers of the Spartan population, i.e., a true demographic trend which was the product of a diminished birthrate among the citizen class, exacerbated perhaps by losses in battle, or of an artificial shift that resulted more from socio-economic trends, such as the accumulation of more and more wealth in the hands of women so that fewer and fewer males could qualify for admission to the *syssitia* or common messes, and therefore for the privileges of citizenship; if the issue of land availability was a crucial part of this development, then obviously the loss of Messenia would have played a central role in the further reduction of the citizen numbers. We also know that the Spartans were forced to several expedients to cope with this situation. The most notable of these was the growing practice, already noted, of employing so-called 'enfranchised' helots or *neodamodeis* as troops. Finally, there is evidence of social unrest within the body politic, reflected in the so-called conspiracy of Cinadon and in two plots which Agesilaus encountered during the first invasion of Laconia by Epaminondas.

The conspiracy of Cinadon (397) involved a plot to stir up and arm many elements within Sparta against the *homoioi*, the citizen class.[41] Most notable is that the dissidents included not only helots, as one might have expected, but also *perioikoi* and a group not previously mentioned, the *hypomeiones*. These latter, to judge by their name, were the 'inferiors' and it is assumed that they represented former *homoioi* who for some reason had lost their civic status. The plot was discovered in the first year of Agesilaus' reign and brutally suppressed by the Spartan authorities, but it suggests that at the beginning of the fourth century there was serious social unrest within Sparta, linked perhaps to social and economic changes that resulted from Sparta's victory over Athens and, more particularly, from the decision to transform foreign policy into imperialism. The other plots occurred in 370 and involved discontented elements among the citizen population; these also were suppressed by Agesilaus. It is possible, although by no means certain, that the principal instigators in 370 belonged to the *hypomeiones*. In any case, these various incidents suggest that beneath the surface of the Spartan social order there lurked a much more complicated set of structures than the commonly recognized triad of *homoioi*, *perioikoi*, and helots.[42]

Sparta's military failure in the 360s was sudden and shocking. It produced a reversal in the power structure of Greece, both political and diplomatic. As Theban power grew, alarm in Athens and Sparta prompted attempts at a negotiated settlement to restore something like the *status quo* before Leuctra. Several such overtures to the Persian King to sponsor another common peace met with only limited success, and Sparta especially failed to achieve its goals through diplomacy, despite the efforts of the able diplomat Antalcidas. It must be recognized, however, that Sparta's own recalcitrance to admit Messenia to the family of poleis as a sovereign and autonomous state undermined its efforts to isolate Thebes and to recapture its former hegemonic position in Greek affairs. Consequently, much of Sparta's effort was spent in trying, by diplomatic or military means, to undo the results of Epaminondas' first invasion. Complicated political and diplomatic shifts among the Greek states led ultimately to the Battle of Mantinea in 362. That battle, which witnessed most of the Greek states arrayed against one another, with the coalitions led respectively by Thebes and by Sparta and Athens, was indecisive. The Theban commander Epaminondas fell mortally wounded, and Thebes' brief period of hegemony soon faded. But Sparta fared no better. The peace conference which was held after the battle reasserted the principle of autonomy and, since Messenia was included among the signatories, Sparta remained outside the treaty, isolated diplomatically once again.[43]

SPARTA ECLIPSED, 362–332

Not long after the peace conference which followed the Battle of Mantinea, King Agesilaus of Sparta, now over eighty years of age, took service as a mercenary commander to a native Egyptian dynast who was leading a rebellion against the Persian Empire. For some three years he pursued this course, directing the Greek forces employed against Persia (*c.* 363–360). Agesilaus' friend Xenophon attempted to portray this final chapter in his hero's life as another episode in a lifelong Panhellenic crusade against the inveterate foe, Persia. A more realistic as well as impartial reading of these events indicates that Agesilaus' motivation was indeed mercenary. He went to Egypt to earn enough money to recruit a mercenary army for the ongoing crusade, not to free Greeks from Persian control, but to reconquer Messenia for Spartan exploitation.[44] Agesilaus did in fact receive a substantial amount of money for his services, but he died on his return voyage to the Peloponnesus, where his body was conveyed for burial. His end was a sad commentary on a long and otherwise distinguished career, although it can be argued that it was his policies that were largely responsible for the Spartan debacle at Leuctra and afterwards.[45]

His son Archidamus succeeded him and followed in his father's attempts to reconquer Messenia. This policy meant mercenary service himself to pay for the army which Sparta could no longer raise on its own resources or from its erstwhile allies. Thus, in the 350s and 340s, while Philip of Macedon was engaged in the process of extending his power over the Greek states, Sparta stood largely to one side and did not play a significant role in events. The state did support Phocis in the Sacred War against Thebes, but Sparta withdrew into its own concerns after that conflict ended in 346 and Philip's power grew in Greek affairs. Demosthenes' attempt to forge a coalition to oppose Macedonian expansion after 340 excited no interest in Sparta; King Archidamus was abroad in southern Italy at the time, fighting in the employ of Tarentum against Lucanian enemies. He met his death there in 338, the same year that Philip was victorious over Athens and Thebes at Chaeronea. When Philip organized the League of Corinth, he could allow the Spartans to remain aloof from his new creation; their refusal to join in fact gave some credence to Philip's claim that the League was a voluntary alliance. No matter that a Macedonian army had marched into Laconia and rectified the borders with Arcadia and Argos to the advantage of those states. Sparta retained about half of its former civic territory, limited to the Eurotas valley, the Mani peninsula to the west, and the Malean to the east; its day as a great power in the affairs of Greece was long past, and there would be only one final effort to regain its former status under King Agis III.[46]

Sparta remained quiescent during Philip's preparations for his war against the Persian Empire, and even after his assassination and Alexander's accession to the throne, it took no steps to reassert its position. When Thebes revolted upon the false news of Alexander's death in battle in Thrace, the king marched south and annihilated the city. Surely Sparta rejoiced at the destruction of its nemesis for the past half-century, but no movement either for or against Macedon occurred. It was only after Alexander had invaded Asia and defeated the Persians at the Granicus and at Issus that the Great King, Darius III, sent envoys to Greece to elicit help against Macedon. King Agis III received them and entered into negotiations with Memnon of Rhodes and his successor, the commanders of the Greek contingents in service to Persia. The plan was to engineer a revolt with Persian aid, or more properly a war, since Sparta was technically independent and so could not revolt against Macedon. Agis worked to stir up dissent in Greece until, in early 331, he had organized a coalition of rebel Greeks. This group included no states north of the isthmus, however, and its object seems to have been the reduction of Megalopolis, where the main battle occurred.[47]

Agis commanded some 30,000 troops, including 10,000 mercenaries, some of whom had returned from Persian service for the occasion. Others had been recruited from the recently established mercenary base at Taenarum on the tip of the Mani. The Macedonian commander Antipater collected a force of some 40,000 Macedonians and Greeks from the League of Corinth, and battle was joined in late autumn 331. The Spartan-led coalition suffered a significant defeat, including the deaths of King Agis and thousands of Laconians, largely *perioikoi* but numbering Spartan citizens as well. Not only in this respect did Megalopolis resemble Leuctra; the political significance of the battle also overshadowed the military losses in 331 as in 371. Sparta fell from the status of a second-rate power, which it may reasonably be argued to have held since Leuctra, to that of a third-rate entity. Antipater took hostage fifty of the 'most distinguished' Spartans. The proposal of Acrotatus, the older son of King Cleomenes II, to punish those who had not fought well, even though it was not enacted, produced a permanent resentment among many. Here again, as after Leuctra, the disgrace of Spartans who had fled in the face of disaster was subordinated to the need to keep citizen numbers from diminishing even more. The net result of Megalopolis, at least for Sparta, was to reinforce its status as a power that could easily be ignored in future, and to corroborate the situation in the Peloponnesus which had been forged by the Thebans in 370 and sanctioned by Persia in 367 and by Philip in 338/7. Sparta was stigmatized once again for having collaborated with Persia, and it did not take any part in the final great revolt of the Greek states against Macedon in the fourth century, the Lamian War. Its days as a great power were indeed over and, for Sparta, the fourth century had concluded ingloriously at Megalopolis. The socioeconomic results of Theban and Macedonian intervention in the Peloponnesus would lead ultimately to the attempted reforms of Agis and Cleomenes a century later, but that story falls beyond our purview.

Although there is no agreement among scholars on the single cause for Sparta's failure in the interstate realm during the fourth century, several explanations should be noted here. First, Sparta's narrowness of vision must be recognized. Even when its diplomat Antalcidas worked to originate the idea of Common Peace, Sparta subordinated it to its own interests, manifesting provincialism, greed, and selfishness. Next, there was the undeniable socio-economic decline of the period. The impact of increasing wealth on a social system that was inflexible, at least in terms of the governing class, produced an alarming reduction in the number of citizen-soldiers, which reduced Sparta's ability to pursue its political goals outside of the polis. Finally, there was factionalism within the state, not just along the lines of foreign policy, but also over social issues and in internal politics. These divisions of opinion found expression no doubt among the various political leaders, and in no one more clearly than in Agesilaus. At first, vacillation among different policies and then the pursuit of a policy of Spartan dominance in Greece led to increasing alienation among Sparta's erstwhile allies and supporters. Future research in fourth-century Spartan history may well proceed along one or more of these lines of inquiry.

NOTES

1 See C. D. Hamilton, *Sparta's Bitter Victories: Politics and Diplomacy in the Corinthian War*, Ithaca, Cornell University Press, 1979 for detailed discussion of the events leading up to and including the Corinthian War.
2 See P. Cartledge, *Agesilaos and the Crisis of Sparta*, Baltimore, Johns Hopkins University Press, 1987 and C. D. Hamilton, *Agesilaus and the Failure of Spartan Hegemony*, Ithaca, Cornell University Press, 1991 for recent, full discussion of these events.
3 Hamilton, *Agesilaus*, presents the case for the former interpretation, attributing Sparta's failure primarily to its foreign policy, which was shaped above all by Agesilaus and was centered around his obsessive hatred of Thebes. Cartledge, in *Agesilaos*, views the Spartan failure as the result of deep-rooted socio-economic processes rather than of politics and diplomacy. E. David, *Sparta between Empire and Revolution*, New York, Arno, 1981, provides a good discussion of the impact of economic factors on Spartan policy.
4 See J. K. Anderson, *Xenophon*, New York, Scribner, 1974; W. E. Higgins, *Xenophon the Athenian*, Albany, State University of New York Press, 1977; V. Gray, *The Character of Xenophon's Hellenica*, Baltimore, Johns Hopkins University Press, 1989; and J. Dillery, *Xenophon and the History of His Times*, London, Routledge, 1995, for discussions of Xenophon's life and writings.
5 See T. A. Boring, *Literacy in Ancient Sparta*, Leiden, Brill, 1979 on this topic.
6 I. A. F. Bruce, *An Historical Commentary on the 'Hellenica Oxyrhynchia'*, Cambridge, Cambridge University Press, 1967, provides an excellent introduction to this work and its influence on later historians.

7 See C. D. Hamilton, 'Plutarch's *Life of Agesilaus*' in *Aufstieg und Niedergang der römischen Welt*, ed. W. Haase and H. Temporini, Berlin, de Gruyter, 1992. Part II, vol. 33.6: pp. 4201–21.

8 See R. J. A. Talbert, *Plutarch on Sparta*, Harmondsworth, Penguin, 1988 for translation of the *Sayings of Spartans* and *Sayings of Spartan Women*, and useful introduction.

9 F. Ollier, *Le mirage spartiate*, Paris, Boccard, 1933–43, 2 vols.

10 See D. Lotze, *Lysander und der Peloponnesische Krieg*, Berlin, Akademia, 1964, pp. 31–7; J.-F. Bommelaer, *Lysandre de Sparte: histoire et traditions*, Paris, Boccard, 1981, pp. 103–15; and Hamilton, *Bitter Victories*, pp. 40–55.

11 See Thuc. 8.18, 37 and 58 for the treaties with Sparta; cf. 1.69.12, 1.124.3 and 4.85 for the promises to liberate the Hellenes.

12 Isoc. 4. 122.

13 C. D. Hamilton, 'Lysander, Agesilaus, Spartan Imperialism and the Greeks of Asia Minor,' *AncW* 23 (1992), 35–50, discusses this topic in detail.

14 The sources are Xen. *Hell.* 2.2.20; Plut. *Lys.* 14.4; Diod. 14.3.2; and Arist. *Ath. Pol.* 34. For discussion, see Hamilton, *Bitter Victories*, pp. 45–55.

15 See P. Krentz, *The Thirty at Athens*, Ithaca, Cornell University Press, 1982.

16 For sources and discussion, see Hamilton, *Bitter Victories*, pp. 58–62.

17 I argued this in 'Spartan Politics and Policy, 405–401 BC,' *AJP* 91 (1970), 294–314, and again in *Bitter Victories*. Several scholars have rejected or modified my suggestions; see particularly W. E. Thompson, 'Observations on Spartan Politics' in *RSA* 3 (1973), 47–58, and Cartledge, *Agesilaos*, who proposes a 'model' for the working of the Spartan constitution.

18 For discussion and the sources on Gylippus, see Hamilton, *Bitter Victories*, pp. 55–8.

19 See E. David, 'The Influx of Money into Sparta at the End of the Fifth Century B.C.' in *Scripta Classica Israelitica* 5 (1979/80), 30–45, for discussion of this process.

20 See E. Levy, 'Les trois traités entre Sparte et le roi,' *BCH* 107 (1983), 221–41 and D. Kagan, *The Fall of the Athenian Empire*, Ithaca, Cornell University Press, 1987, pp. 28–50.

21 Xen. *Hell.* 2.3.7. For detailed discussion of these events and references to modern literature, see Hamilton, 'Lysander,' pp. 37–43.

22 See C. D. Hamilton, *Agesilaus*, pp. 76–8 for discussion of this class.

23 Xen. *Hell.* 3.1.4. While Thebes and Corinth are not explicitly mentioned, Xenophon's reference to 4,000 other Peloponnesians implies the absence of troops from these states.

24 The sources on the Elean War are Xen. *Hell.* 3.2.21–31; Diod. 14.17.4–12; and Paus. 3.8.3–7.

25 Xen. *Hell.* 3.5.1–2. See the discussion in Hamilton, *Bitter Victories*, Chapter 6, on this topic.

26 *Hell. Oxy.* 18.3.

27 The modern literature is cited in Hamilton, *Bitter Victories*, Chapter 6.

28 They are treated in Hamilton, *Bitter Victories* and in Cartledge, *Agesilaos*.
29 T. T. B. Ryder, *Koine Eirene: General Peace and Local Independence in Ancient Greece*, Oxford, Oxford University Press, 1965, is the essential study of the topic of Common Peace.
30 See Hamilton, *Agesilaus*, pp. 121–4 for discussion of factions in Sparta, with modern literature.
31 See Hamilton, *Agesilaus*, pp. 141–9 for discussion of this episode.
32 Xen. *Hell.* 5.4.1.
33 Xen. *Hell.* 5.3.27; Diod. 15.23.3–5.
34 There was much controversy in ancient times, as there is among modern scholars, over the responsibility of Agesilaus for Spartan relations with Thebes. See Hamilton, *Agesilaus*, ch. 6, for detailed discussion and citation of literature.
35 For the Sphodrias affair, see Hamilton, *Agesilaus*, pp. 167–74; for Athens' new league, see above pp. 19–25.
36 For the battle of Leuctra see J. Buckler, *The Theban Hegemony, 371–362 BC* Cambridge, Harvard University Press, 1980, pp. 46–69 and Hamilton, *Agesilaus*, pp. 202–11, with citations of recent literature.
37 Buckler, *Theban Hegemony*, is fundamental for the sequel to Leuctra.
38 Cartledge, *Agesilaos*, is excellent on the question of Spartan demographics. See also Hamilton, *Agesilaus*, p. 78, n. 51, for additional modern literature.
39 J. F. Lazenby, *The Spartan Army*, Warminster, Aris and Phillips, 1985, contains a good but technical discussion of manpower questions and the Spartan military organization.
40 Arist. *Pol.* 1270a 29–32. See the solid discussion of this topic in P. Cartledge, *Sparta and Lakonia: a Regional History 1300–362 B.C.*, London, Routledge and Kegan Paul, 1979, pp. 307–18.
41 E. David, 'The Conspiracy of Cinadon,' *Athenaeum* n.s. 57 (1979), 94–116 and Hamilton, *Bitter Victories*, pp. 125–8, discuss this event.
42 E. David, 'Revolutionary Agitation in Sparta after Leuctra,' *Athenaeum* n.s. 58 (1980), 299–308 and C. D. Hamilton, 'Social Tensions in Classical Sparta,' *Ktema* 12 (1987), 31–41, provide discussions of these issues.
43 Xen. *Hell.* 7.5.26–27; Diod. 5.89.1–2.
44 See Hamilton, *Agesilaus*, pp. 252–4.
45 See Hamilton, *Agesilaus*, pp. 256–7.
46 See C. D. Hamilton, 'Philip II and Archidamus,' in *Philip II, Alexander the Great and the Macedonian Heritage*, ed. W. L. Adams and E. N. Borza, (Washington DC, University Press of America, 1982, pp. 61–83, and P. Cartledge and A. Spawforth, *Hellenistic and Roman Sparta: A Tale of Two Cities*, (London, Routledge, 1989), Chapter 1.
47 E. Badian, 'Agis III,' *Hermes* 95 (1967), 170–92, discusses the attempt of Agis in great detail; more recently, see Cartledge and Spawforth, ibid., Chapter 2.

4

THEBES AND CENTRAL GREECE

Mark Munn

Thebes in Boeotia was, for a brief period, the most powerful state in fourth-century Greece. Its rise and decline is best understood in a regional context, as part of the history of central Greece. North of Athens and Attica, central Greece is sometimes considered to end at the coastal narrows of Thermopylae. Beyond mountains north of Thermopylae are the plains of Thessaly where, along with the plains of Boeotia, the most populous towns north of Athens lay. The overlapping and sometimes competing interests of Boeotians and Thessalians dominated the politics of this portion of Greece. This chapter will therefore embrace the affairs of Boeotia and Thessaly.

CENTRAL GREECE AT THE END OF THE FIFTH CENTURY

The scale of personal wealth based on agriculture was the greatest, of all parts of the Greek world, in Thessaly. Political privileges were traditionally restricted to landowners, and the wealthiest of these were termed 'dynasties.' As in Laconia and Messenia under Spartan domination, this long-established privileged elite depended on the agricultural labor of serfs with no political rights, the *penestai* ('poor'). Thessalian aristocrats were perennially on guard for signs of discontent among the *penestai*, but they were unable to unite for any common political purpose. By the later fifth century pressure on the aristocrats was coming from another quarter.

A growing number of town-dwellers, free men whose livelihoods depended on commerce and industry rather than agriculture, rallied behind leaders who challenged the exclusive authority of the dynasts. In the late fifth century, political movements along these lines resulted in turmoil and bloodshed in some Thessalian towns, primarily Larissa, home of the powerful Aleuad family.

Factional fighting within Thessaly created favorable conditions for outside intervention, and by the end of the fifth century Sparta had become the greatest external force in Thessalian affairs. The foundation of a Spartan colony at Heraclea north of Thermopylae (426) was instrumental to Spartan expansion. Many Thessalians feared or resented this encroachment and they responded with raids and open warfare (Thuc. 3.92–3, 5.51, 8.3.1). In the final years of the Peloponnesian War the Spartans lost Heraclea (Xen. *Hell.* 1.2.18), but the surrender of Athens in 404 enabled them to devote more attention to central Greece. The Spartans offered an alliance to the Thessalians, ostensibly to protect them against the Macedonian King Archelaus. By doing so, they appealed for the support of the widening factions of the political reform movements in Thessaly. Yet lingering mistrust of Sparta, and the influence of dynastic families more sympathetic to Macedon, led to the rejection of this overture.

The strongest challenge to the old aristocracies of Thessaly came from Lycophron, the ruler of Pherae. Alone of Thessalian towns, Pherae controlled an important seaport, Pagasae, where much of the trade of Thessaly was handled. Lycophron and his townsmen represented a powerbase fundamentally different than that of the dynasts of the Thessalian interior. Lycophron aspired to dominate Thessaly and be elected *tagos*, 'leader' of the ancient confederacy of all Thessalian communities. By tradition the *tagos* held supreme command of a united army numbering 6,000 cavalry and over 10,000 hoplites, with still more light infantry provided by subject allies (Xen. *Hell.* 6.1.8–9). But in the face of local rivalries, the Thessalians had been without a *tagos*, and their confederacy without true coherence, since before the Persian Wars. In 404 Lycophron, 'hoping to rule all of Thessaly,' won a bloody battle against the Larissaians and other Thessalians (Xen. *Hell.* 2.3.4). Despite this victory, both Larissa and supremacy in Thessaly remained beyond Lycophron's grasp. With Spartan help, Lycophron later succeeded in seizing Pharsalus. But the ensuing struggle of Lycophron and his successors at Pherae achieved, with one brief exception, little more than continued bloodshed through the first half of the fourth century. This condition of great wealth squandered on fruitless in-fighting became almost a proverbial description of the state of affairs in Thessaly (Isoc. 8.117–18; Dem. 1.22).

Between Thessaly and Boeotia lay the smaller, oligarchically constituted states of Phocis, East and West Locris, tiny Doris and Malis, and, to the west, the tribal confederacy of Aetolia. Among these states, so long as Peloponnesian arms were ascendant, political alignments were mostly pro-Spartan. That these states should act more or less in concert was, however, an exceptional condition. After Athens had submitted to Sparta, the Aetolians sided with the Eleans in a brief war against Sparta (Diod. 14.17.9–10), and Malians felt the anger of Sparta when the Spartans reasserted control of Heraclea (Diod. 14.38.4–5). The mutual animosity of the Phocians and Locrians had erupted into open warfare during the Peace of Nicias (Thuc. 5.32.2; Diod. 12.80.1) and it would ignite more than one great war in the fourth century.

Boeotia was under the sway of Sparta in the second half of the fifth century, largely because the propertied families dominating politics found the Spartans more sympathetic to their interests than the Athenians. For a brief period in the mid-fifth century, the Athenians had forced the establishment of democratic governments in the towns of Boeotia. An oligarchic rebellion in 447 ended this episode, and led to the establishment (or re-establishment) of a Boeotian confederacy aristocratic in outlook and deeply suspicious of outside intervention. Though decades later some Boeotians still favored a more liberal constitution on the Athenian model (Thuc. 4.76.2), this conservative confederacy controlled Boeotian politics for some sixty years.

The constitution forming the Boeotian confederacy gave political authority only to those possessing a certain level of wealth (*Hell. Oxy.* 11.2, 3–4, see Harding 15), probably measured in holdings of land. The propertied class governed through local councils, and participated in federal government in proportion to their representation in the eleven federal districts into which Boeotia was divided. Thebes, Orchomenus, Thespiae, and Plataea (before its conquest by Thebes in 427) each comprised two districts, Tanagra made up a district of its own, and six other Boeotian towns formed the remaining two districts. Each district elected one Boeotarch, who was an executive officer and military commander, and sixty councillors to a federal assembly that met at Thebes. Each district also fielded up to 1,000 hoplites and 100 cavalry. This army of 11,000 hoplites and 1,100 cavalry probably represented an estimate of the number of able-bodied landowners, from rich to moderate means, who were the enfranchised citizens of the towns of Boeotia.

A larger population of free but unenfranchised Boeotians formed a subservient class, available as light-armed troops in time of war.

A united Boeotian army was a match for the Athenians (Thuc. 4.94.1; Xen. *Mem.* 3.5.2–4, *Hipp.* 7.1). Such an army concentrated in central Greece was an essential ally to the Spartans in their war against Athens. The Spartans assured themselves of Boeotian support primarily by favoring Thebes, the leader of the Boeotian confederacy. Thebes acquired, for instance, the territory, the votes on the confederate council, and the right to elect two additional Boeotarchs that had belonged to Plataea, after that town fell in 427 (Thuc. 3.68.3; *Hell. Oxy.* 11.3, see Harding 15). On a smaller scale, the systematic pillaging of Attica from the Spartan fort at Decelea in northern Attica funneled profits chiefly to pro-Spartan Thebans (*Hell. Oxy.* 12.3–5).

These sources of gain were disrupted by Athens' surrender in 404, and as a result Boeotian support for the Spartan cause, and the balance of power within the Theban leadership, underwent a dramatic shift. Sparta's refusal to expel or enslave the defeated Athenians and divide up their territory meant that there was no windfall of spoils for the victors. The tithe to Apollo from the booty of the defeated enemy was dedicated at Delphi by the Spartan commanders, Agis and Lysander, who thereby appropriated symbolic credit for the victory and the right to divide the final portions of booty. Resentment against Sparta among her allies was an inevitable result.

By late 404, the revolution at Athens produced a stream of political refugees, many of them men of wealth and influence. Rather than scorned as defeated enemies, these Athenians were welcomed in Thebes as fellow-victims of Spartan arrogance by the growing anti-Spartan circle. In defiance of a Spartan order not to harbor these exiles, the Thebans voted publicly to give them sanctuary, and privately assisted them in preparing for their return to Athens (Diod. 14.6.1–3; Plut. *Lys.* 27.2–4). Within a year these exiles had overthrown their enemies. The vital support given to these exiles created bonds of friendship between them and influential Thebans which endured for a generation.

THEBES AND THE OUTBREAK OF THE CORINTHIAN WAR, 401–395

For nearly a decade after the Peloponnesian War Thebes remained formally bound by treaty to Sparta, but had no intention of cooperating as the Spartans punished enemies and humbled reluctant allies. When, in 401, the Spartans summoned allies to join them in punishing Elis, the Thebans and the Corinthians refused (Xen. *Hell.* 3.2.25). The same two states probably refused again to follow the Spartans to Asia Minor to make war against the Persians in 399, as they certainly did in 396 (Paus. 3.9.3; cf. Diod. 14.36.1–2). Just as with the Peace of Nicias (421), peace between Sparta and Athens dissolved the basis for cooperation between Thebes and Sparta.

The Spartans, meanwhile, were intervening in central Greece in a manner certain to make the Boeotians uneasy. In 400 the Spartans seized the former Athenian naval post at Naupactus (on the Corinthian Gulf) and turned it over to the Locrians (Xen. *Hell.* 3.2.30–3.1; Diod. 14.34.2–3). The following year the Spartans moved north and re-established a Spartan governor at Heraclea, expelling or executing their enemies (Diod. 14.38.4–5; Polyaenus *Strat.* 2.21). The same year probably saw the entrance of a Spartan army into Thessaly. Archelaus of Macedon, a supporter of the Aleuads of Larissa, had just been assassinated, and Lycophron of Pherae seized this opportunity to expand his influence. The Spartans provided Lycophron with troops to take Pharsalus from the forces of Medius, dynast of Larissa.

If any single state were capable of offering serious opposition to Sparta, it was the Boeotian confederacy. It is not surprising, then, to find the Spartans attempting to isolate their Boeotian enemies. The war against the Persians for the sake of the independence of the Greeks in Asia Minor gave the Spartans the banner of a 'just cause' under which to rally support among the Greeks. Theban refusal to support this war could be turned to the advantage of Spartan propaganda, especially when evidence began to appear of communications between the Persians and the enemies of Sparta in Greece (*Hell. Oxy.* 2 = Harding 11A, 7).

When, in 396, the Spartans sent an army to Asia Minor under the command of Agesilaus, a summons of allies was answered by all but the Boeotians, Corinthians, and Athenians. A public incident dramatized the rift between the Spartans and Boeotians, allegedly corrupted by Persian gold. Agesilaus' departure ceremony at Aulis on the Boeotian coast was halted by Theban horsemen at the command of the Boeotarchs (Xen. *Hell.* 3.4.3–4, 5.5; Plut. *Ages.* 6.4–6, *Lys.* 27.1–2). This action forced the Boeotians into a public stance opposing Agesilaus, leader of all Greeks against the barbarians. The Spartans could now describe the Boeotians as favoring Persians against the rest of the Greeks, just as they had done in the time of Xerxes (cf. Xen. *Hell.* 6.3.20, 5.35).

The Spartans soon found more cause to level public blame at their enemies in Thebes. Timocrates of Rhodes, a Persian agent, had been dispatched with money to stir up war against Sparta. Recipients of his gifts included the most influential politicians at Thebes, Ismenias and Androcleidas (Xen. *Hell.* 3.5.1–3; *Hell. Oxy.* 2.2, 13.1; Plut. *Lys.* 27.1). In any actions against these, the Spartans could now claim justification in punishing the betrayers of Greece (cf. Plut. *Ages.* 15.6; Xen. *Hell.* 5.2.35).

War erupted in summer 395, triggered by a border dispute between the Locrians and Phocians that gave pretexts to both Sparta and the Boeotians, the latter incited by Ismenias and Androcleidas. When the Boeotians blocked arbitration of the dispute, the Spartans prepared two armies to invade Boeotia (*Hell. Oxy.* 13.2–5; Xen. *Hell.* 3.5.3–5; Diod. 14.81.1). Lysander assembled the Phocians and other central Greek allies at Delphi. King Pausanias led a Peloponnesian force north from Corinth. Both armies were to descend simultaneously on the strategic Boeotian town of Haliartus. Initially the Thebans enjoyed only the support of the Locrians and fellow Boeotians, and their allegiance was none too certain. Moreover, Lysander successfully split the Boeotian confederacy by persuading the Orchomenians, chief rivals of Thebes in the west, to join him. His way to Haliartus thus opened immediately.

Lysander's march on Haliartus was ill-fated. In a hasty attack Lysander and nearly 1,000 men were killed, after which his allies withdrew. All that remained when Pausanias arrived were the bodies of the dead. Encouraged by this victory and anticipating the arrival of their new allies, the Athenians, the Thebans dictated terms to Pausanias, allowing him to recover the bodies on condition that his army immediately evacuate Boeotia. The Thebans had prevailed, and Spartan plans for a swift seizure of power in central Greece were ruined, for the moment (Xen. *Hell.* 3.5.5–25; Diod. 14.81.1–3; Plut. *Lys.* 28–9).

The Spartan invasion had given Thebes the alliance of Athens and, after victory at Haliartus, Argos and Corinth stood ready to join them. Still, the Spartans could muster considerable strength in the Peloponnesus and recall the army under Agesilaus in Asia Minor. Perhaps more ominous for Thebes was Lysander's legacy. Before he died, Lysander had brought Orchomenus over to the Spartans, and it remained so for the rest of the war. Boeotia was thus divided, and to the Thebans the most immediate enemy in the ensuing war were the people of Orchomenus (Andoc. 3.20; Xen. *Hell.* 5.1.29, cf. 6.4.10).

THE BATTLES OF THE NEMEA RIVER AND CORONEA, 394

Later in summer 395 the Thebans and their allies met at Corinth to determine a plan of action. Central Greece was recognized as the most vulnerable area of Spartan influence. Accordingly, an allied army, chiefly Boeotian and Argive, was sent to Thessaly. United with Medius of Larissa, still locked in conflict with Lycophron of Pherae, these allies captured Pharsalus from its Spartan garrison. The allies then returned south and seized Heraclea with the help of friends inside the town. The Spartans taken at Heraclea were executed and other Peloponnesians were invited to leave. Heraclea and its territory were returned to the previous inhabitants. South of Heraclea, Phocis remained the center of Spartan support in central Greece and the chief threat to Boeotia. Following the success at Heraclea, Ismenias marched on Phocis at the head of an army numbering almost 6,000 Boeotians, local allies, and Locrians. The Phocians advanced to meet them and got the worst of a hard-fought battle (Diod. 14.82.5–10).

By spring 394 the Corinthians and Argives were anxious to move the war against Sparta forward into the Peloponnesus. The coalition, however, hesitated to act, probably because it seemed perilous to attack Sparta without additional allies. But by midsummer, with Agesilaus returning from Asia Minor, the allies had to break Spartan power in the Peloponnesus first, or be caught between two armies. Thus they assembled at Corinth and set out toward Laconia. They soon learned that the Spartans had reached Sicyon behind them, where they threatened Corinth. The allies doubled back and took up a position facing the enemy across the Nemea River in the plain to the west of Corinth.

Both sides were roughly equal in number, but in the ensuing battle Spartan expertise and unified command proved decisive. Command in the allied force was held in rotation and the battle plans varied accordingly. The Thebans were responsible for opening the battle. On their day of command, they arrayed their own hoplites on the right flank in an exceptionally deep formation and put the Peloponnesians facing them to flight. The Athenians, however, at the far end of the allied line were outflanked by the Spartans and routed, resulting in the eventual collapse of the entire allied line (Xen. *Hell.* 4.2.16–23).

The battle at the Nemea River was the largest land battle yet fought between Greek armies, but it solved nothing. Both sides suffered heavily and the allies lost any hope of carrying the war against Sparta into the Peloponnesus. Corinth itself was in danger of falling to the Spartans.

Within a few weeks of the defeat at the Nemea River the allies had to reassemble to meet Agesilaus, now descending through Thessaly. The Thessalians might have posed an obstacle to Agesilaus, but they were too deeply divided to resist his passage. Agesilaus tried diplomacy to sway Thessaly toward Sparta, but his ambassadors were arrested in Larissa; he negotiated their release and then withdrew (Plut. *Ages.* 16.3). Moving south past Thermopylae, Agesilaus gathered reinforcements before entering Boeotia and found the Thebans and their allies encamped south of Orchomenus, near Coronea at the foot of Mount Helicon (Plut. *Ages.* 17.1; Xen. *Ages.* 2.6–9).

On the day of battle at Coronea, the Thebans and the Spartans again led from the right and again each was victorious. This time, unlike the rout at the Nemea River, the Thebans were prepared to meet the Spartans. Turning from their pursuit of the Orchomenians, broken in the first onslaught, the Thebans reformed and attacked the Spartans. The Thebans inflicted many casualties on the Spartans before forcing them to open their line and let them pass through (Xen. *Hell.* 4.3.16–19, *Ages.* 2.9–12; Plut. *Ages.* 18). The Thebans won the battle of the formations, but having moved off the battlefield while the Spartans attacked their flanks, they left the Spartans in possession of the tokens of victory – the bodies of the dead.

WAR'S END – THE KING'S PEACE, 387/6

The carnage of the two great battles of summer 394 discouraged both sides from seeking another head-on confrontation. The battles established the fronts of the war in Greece, which now focused on the plains around Corinth and Orchomenus. The largest contingents on both sides were engaged in the Corinthia. But for the Boeotians, the Corinthia was a sidelight to the real conflict – the contest between the Orchomenians, supported by Spartans and Phocians, and the rest of the Boeotians led by Thebes. After 394 our sources tell us nothing of this Orchomenian war, except that it proved costly in men and property, with no significant change in the balance of power in Boeotia (Andoc. 3.20).

Under these discouraging conditions, it became apparent that Ismenias' and Androcleidas' leadership at Thebes depended upon Athenian success against Sparta in the wider arena of the Aegean. Though the Thebans played no part in Conon's victory at Cnidus – the one bright spot for the allies in summer 394 – they strengthened their bond with Athens by sending skilled workmen and stonemasons to Athens to help the Athenians in rebuilding the walls of the Piraeus (Xen. *Hell.* 4.4.9, 8.10; Diod. 14.85.3).

The fighting in the Corinthia continued with both sides gaining then losing again. The Spartans attempted to prevail with diplomacy and, in winter 392, proposed a peace recognizing the status quo. Such terms were agreeable to the Thebans, now ready to acknowledge the independence of Orchomenus in return for peace (Andoc. 3.13, 20, 28). But the Athenians rejected the treaty and rallied the allies to recapture Lechaeum and rebuild the Corinthian long walls in spring 391 (Xen. *Hell.* 4.4.18; cf. Diod. 14.86.4). The Spartans quickly recaptured Lechaeum (Xen. *Hell.* 4.4.19; cf. Diod. 14.86.4), but were soon stunned by Iphicrates' defeat of a Spartan regiment at Lechaeum (Xen. *Hell.* 4.5.11–17). The stalemate at Corinth thus dragged on as the close balance of forces wore down both sides with little prospects of change. The complex web of Greek and Persian diplomacy, however, eventually brought a solution.

Between autumn 388 and spring 387, the Persian king Artaxerxes II decided that it was time to end his war with the Spartans. He announced in an edict the terms that all combatants must swear to uphold in order to obtain peace, or face war against him and those Greeks who agreed to the settlement (i.e., the Spartans). This edict became known as the King's Peace (Xen. *Hell.* 5.1.31; Diod. 14.110.3).

Ever since they had opened negotiations with Persia in 393/2, the Spartans had argued that peace between Persia and Sparta should bind the parties to enforce the independence of all Greek towns outside of Persian dominion. This seemingly benevolent clause was a mask for the long-standing Spartan practice of dissolving the political unions of their enemies in the name of freedom and autonomy. Such had been the Spartan rallying cry against Athens during the Peloponnesian War (Thuc. 1.139.3) and more recently in the war against Elis (Xen. *Hell.* 3.2.23). Now, if peace were made with Persia, the Spartans could pursue this policy of 'liberation' in Greece without distraction, and potentially with Persian might on their side.

Persian might and Spartan successes in the Hellespont compelled the Athenians, by spring 386, to accept the king's edict, leaving their allies no choice but to do the same (Xen. *Hell.* 5.1.25–31; Diod. 14.110.2–4). When the Theban ambassadors announced their intention to take the oath on behalf of the Boeotians, the Spartans refused. According to Xenophon, Agesilaus demanded that the ambassadors swear 'as the edict of the king said, that every town, great or small, will be autonomous' (*Hell.* 5.1.32). In other words, Theban authority would be recognized for Thebes alone, and the Thebans must acknowledge the autonomy of *every* Boeotian town. To accept would mean that the deliberative, administrative, judicial, and military institutions that united most of Boeotia under Theban leadership would cease to exist. The Theban ambassadors, unwilling to accept the responsibility for thus disbanding the Boeotian confederacy, departed, bringing this issue back for debate at the confederate assembly at Thebes. Meanwhile, Agesilaus commanded Spartan allies to prepare for a campaign against Thebes, now without allies outside of the Boeotian confederacy.

The Thebans complied with Spartan demands before Agesilaus had completed the first stage of his muster (Xen. *Hell.* 5.1.33). The fact that the Thebans had previously attempted to reach a settlement with Sparta reveals that Boeotian resolve to oppose Sparta was thin and easily shattered. The independence of Orchomenus must have been a source of constant annoyance to the Thebans, since it symbolized a viable alternative to fighting and dying in order to maintain Theban dominance in Boeotia. Within Thebes an influential group opposed war with Sparta. Leontiades, of a prominent family with a long history of cooperation with Sparta (Hdt. 7.233; Thuc. 2.2.3), had seen his political influence yield to that of Ismenias (*Hell. Oxy.* 12.1–2, cf. 2.1–2). He and his supporters were still active, and ready to lead Thebes as political fortunes now shifted in their favor.

CENTRAL GREECE UNDER SPARTAN SUPREMACY, 386–379

The dissolution of the Boeotian confederacy was chief among Spartan achievements in the settlement of the Corinthian War. The Thebans, again allied to Sparta, dutifully served in 385 when the Spartans suppressed Mantinea (Isoc. 14.27–8; Plut. *Pel.* 4.4–5; Xen. *Hell.* 5.2.1–7). Outside of Boeotia, the most conspicuous change resulting from the settlement in Boeotia was the warming of relations between Thessaly and Sparta. A united Boeotia had been able to bring the Thessalians, except for Pherae, into the alliance against Sparta. Now, though Thessalian factionalism prevented a formal alliance with the Spartans, leading Thessalians made possible closer ties with Sparta (Xen. *Hell.* 5.3.9, 6.1.4).

Yet the Spartan settlement of Boeotian affairs was inherently unstable and Spartan influence north of the Peloponnesus fragile. Spartan hegemony depended upon the local leadership of friends of Sparta. But if compliance with Sparta stood in the way of local interests, such as re-establishing Theban leadership in Boeotia, then the local popularity of pro-Spartan leaders would be undermined. At Thebes, Ismenias and Androcleidas worked to achieve just this. By 383 leading Thebans and Athenians were quietly exploring the possibility of cooperation between Athens and a renewed Boeotian confederacy (Lys. 26.23; Xen. *Hell.* 5.2.34). At the same time, ambassadors from both states discussed an alliance with the Olynthians, then solidifying their control of a league of towns in the Chalcidice and in Macedonia (Xen. *Hell.* 5.2.15, 34). In spring 382, Chalcidian enemies of Olynthus appealed to the Spartans for support. The Spartans could not neglect this appeal, for it was time to check the activities of their enemies in central Greece.

After Sparta had resolved to go to war against Olynthus, the Spartan commander Phoebidas gathered forces for the campaign. At Thebes, Ismenias had proposed a resolution forbidding any Theban from serving in the Spartan-led expedition. Leontiades, opposing this resolution, was thwarted in the face of growing support for Ismenias and Androcleidas. But the arrival of Phoebidas at Thebes, early in summer 382, made possible a decisive shift in Theban policy. After consulting with Leontiades, Phoebidas seized the Cadmea. With this Spartan support, Leontiades then arrested Ismenias who was soon condemned to death in a miscarriage of justice that even bothered the pro-Spartan Xenophon. His following was smashed and many, including Androcleidas, fled for their lives to Athens (Xen. *Hell.* 5.2.25–31, 35; Plut. *Pel.* 5.2–3; Diod. 15.20.1–2).

Phoebidas' occupation of the Cadmea was the most outrageous act yet committed by the Spartans. The self-proclaimed champion of Greek independence, Sparta had openly trampled on the independence and autonomy of Thebes and used specious charges to eliminate her opponents there. In immediate effect, these events merely demonstrated what every observer knew, namely, that the Spartans were prepared to use any pretext to gain their ends.

With his opponents swept aside, Leontiades provided military assistance to the Spartans (Xen. *Hell.* 5.2.34, 36, 41). More than this, through Leontiades and their garrison on the Cadmea, the Spartans now had 'the Thebans and the rest of the Boeotians completely in their control' (Xen. *Hell.* 5.3.27). Far to the north, the Spartans ended successfully their two-year war against Olynthus without serious distraction in central Greece. The only power not under their influence was Jason of Pherae, the vigorous successor to Lycophron, who exercised leadership over a growing circle of allies. The Spartans were now prepared to check Jason. Shortly after the Olynthian War in 380, a Spartan force expelled Neogenes, a supporter of Jason and tyrant of Histiaea in northern Euboea, in the name of liberty (Diod. 15.30.3–4). A direct confrontation between Jason and the Spartans would surely have followed had Spartan supremacy in central Greece not suffered a stunning blow at its vital link, Thebes.

THE THEBAN UPRISING OF 379/8

Before the coup at Thebes in 382, Thebans and Athenians had been working towards a wider anti-Spartan alliance. This process was violently disrupted by the occupation of the Cadmea and the execution of Ismenias. But the anti-Spartan Theban exiles in Athens engendered a new phase of close collaboration among Sparta's enemies. Not even the assassination of Androcleidas by Leontiades' agents at Athens (Plut. *Pel.* 6.2) could distract the efforts of the exiles and their Athenian friends. Their plans for the restoration of an independent Thebes were put into action at the beginning of winter, 379/8.

A group of conspirators led by Melon and Pelopidas covertly entered Thebes and assassinated Leontiades and his chief colleagues in the pro-Spartan oligarchy. Immediately, the conspirators rallied widespread support among the Thebans, even though the Spartan garrison still held the Cadmea. Athenian forces waiting on the frontiers of Attica were essential to the success of this uprising, for only with this reinforcement could the Spartan garrison be securely blockaded. As soon as the coup at Thebes was announced, the Athenians made an alliance with the newly liberated Thebans, and sent a substantial force to Thebes to suppress Boeotian support for the Spartan garrison on the Cadmea, and, more importantly, block arrival of reinforcements from the Peloponnesus.[1]

A Spartan army was sent to relieve the garrison at Thebes, but it was stopped in the Megarid by Athenian and Theban forces holding the passes into Boeotia. When the garrison finally surrendered, the Thebans and Athenians relaxed their guard, allowing King Cleombrotus to bring a Spartan army into Boeotia. Cleombrotus marched to Thespiae, west of Thebes, where the most substantial forces still loyal to Sparta were located. He made a show of strength, but did not march directly against Thebes. With Athenian troops still at Thebes, Cleombrotus hesitated to provoke a war with Thebes *and* Athens. But he made known Sparta's demand that the murderers of Leontiades be brought to justice. So that there be no doubt about Sparta's resolve, upon returning to the Peloponnesus Cleombrotus left a strong force at Thespiae under the command of Sphodrias (Xen. *Hell.* 5.4.13–15; Diod. 15.27.1–3, 29.5–6; Plut. *Ages.* 24.1, *Pel.* 13–14.1).

The remainder of the winter saw intense diplomatic activity, as the new Theban leaders attempted to persuade the Spartans not to intervene at Thebes. The Spartans refused to see the murders of their friends as a purely internal matter, and remained firm in their demand that the Thebans surrender the conspirators. Meanwhile, the Spartans lobbied to convince the Athenians that this affair was no business of theirs. Cleombrotus' show of strength underlined Spartan arguments and the Athenians soon repudiated their alliance with Thebes, punishing the generals who had advocated it (Xen. *Hell.* 5.4.19, 22; Isoc. 14.29).

Thebes now stood isolated and might well have been forced to yield had Spartan aggression not again provoked the Athenians. Near the end of winter, Sphodrias attempted to capture the Piraeus in a surprise night march from Thespiae, some forty-five miles away. The attack failed when Sphodrias' army was discovered at dawn deep in Athenian territory but still far from its objective. As with Phoebidas' Theban coup, we are left wondering who ordered this bold move (Diod. 15.29.5–6). Several sources claim that the attack was secretly encouraged by Pelopidas in order to embroil Athens in war with Sparta (Xen. *Hell.* 5.4.20–1; Plut. *Ages.* 24.3–5, and *Pel.* 14). This account makes sense only in light of the attack's failure: if it had succeeded, Pelopidas' scheme would have sealed his own doom.

THE BOEOTIAN WAR AND THE NEW BOEOTIAN CONFEDERACY, 378–371

Sphodrias' aborted attack propelled the Athenians back into alliance with the Thebans, and both readied their defenses against the Spartan onslaught. In early summer 378, Agesilaus invaded Boeotia. Joining his army with the garrison at Thespiae, he advanced against Thebes with nearly 30,000 men to confront a combined Theban and Athenian army half as large. In the face of such odds, the allied commanders, Gorgidas of Thebes and Chabrias of Athens, employed a disciplined defensive strategy over the next two summers and denied Agesilaus an opportunity to use his overwhelming manpower (Xen. *Hell.* 5.4.38–55; Diod. 15.32–4.2; Plut. *Ages.* 26, *Pel.* 15).

By spring 376 the Thebans and Athenians regained control of the passes leading into Boeotia. By crossing the Corinthian Gulf, the Spartans could still maintain their garrisons in Boeotia, but these were now beleaguered. As in the Corinthian War, the Athenians bore the brunt of the sea war against the Spartans. Their victories at Naxos (376) and at Alyzea (spring 375), however, forced the Spartans and their allies onto the defensive on all fronts (Xen. *Hell.* 5.4.59–66).

In spring 375 the unexpected victory of a small Theban unit over a much larger Spartan force revealed how vulnerable Spartan military supremacy was. The garrison from Orchomenus, numbering about 2,000 men under Spartan command, was returning from a raid into Locrian territory. At Tegyra it unexpectedly met a small Theban force of hoplites and cavalry commanded by Pelopidas. Pelopidas led his troops forward in a tight formation and succeeded in forcing through his opponents' line. Rather than withdrawing after this breakthrough, Pelopidas turned his men against the divided enemy, forcing them to flee. Already prominent in Theban leadership from his role in the overthrow of Leontiades, Pelopidas achieved at Tegyra the first of a series of distinguished military victories, and made famous the name of the elite troops he led. These were the Sacred Band, the elite corps of the Theban forces that Gorgidas had led against Agesilaus in 378, destined to make a name for themselves more than once in the course of the Theban ascendancy of the fourth century (Plut. *Pel.* 16–19; Diod. 15.37.1–2).

Soon afterwards the Thebans carried the war into Phocis. The Spartans took strong measures, sending Cleombrotus to reinforce the Phocians. By summer 375, however, the true front in the war had shifted to the negotiating table. The Spartans were ready to prevent further losses by reaching a settlement. The Athenians were anxious to confirm their gains. The Thebans, however, were just beginning to rebuild their confederacy by force of arms. Peace now would prevent them from consolidating their power in Boeotia, and they spoke out against the settlement that their Athenian allies had reached with Sparta. But to refuse the treaty would force the Thebans to stand alone, and this they were not ready to do. In the end, all parties swore to uphold the peace that the Athenians and Spartans had negotiated (Xen. *Hell.* 6.2.1; Diod. 15.38.3–4; Nep. *Tim.* 2.2).

The Boeotian War signaled the rebirth of the Boeotian confederacy. Immediately after the overthrow of Leontiades the Thebans had elected four leaders of the uprising to the high office of Boeotarch, thus formalizing their intention of restoring the confederacy and their leadership in it (Plut. *Pel.* 13.1, 14.1). Thebes traditionally elected two Boeotarchs; the two additional Boeotarchs represented Plataean territory taken in 427, but lost after the dissolution of the confederacy in 386. In 378 the Thebans again laid claim to Plataea, then controlled by a Spartan garrison. This was but one example of the Theban claim to represent the legitimate interests of all of Boeotia against the narrow oligarchies supported by Sparta. The towns of Boeotia encouraged this rising tide of Theban influence, either by agitating against their pro-Spartan regimes, as happened at Thespiae, or by providing a stream of men ready to fight under Theban leadership (Xen. *Hell.* 5.4.46, 55; Diod. 15.26.3).

The Boeotian confederacy reborn in the years after 378 was not a simple re-creation of the confederacy dissolved by Sparta in 386. Part of the appeal of the new leadership at Thebes was their recognition of the political rights of a larger class of Boeotians than before, probably by lowering the property qualifications necessary for voting rights. The new Boeotia was thus more democratic. At the same time, the new confederacy was more tightly controlled by Thebes. Sovereign authority was exercised by an assembly of all enfranchised Boeotians meeting at Thebes. Under this system, the predominance of Theban interests was assured by the Theban majority in the assembly and the Theban majority of four out of seven Boeotarchs.

Theban domination was the inevitable product of a confederacy born while Boeotia was at war. Boeotian towns joining the Theban cause were given a place in the new confederacy, but powerful rivals forced into submission (Thespiae and later Orchomenus) were denied representation, at least on the executive board of Boeotarchs. The peace of 375 gave but a momentary pause in the process of Theban aggrandizement. Plataea, granted independence by the peace of 375, fell victim to a Theban surprise attack in 373, when the Plataeans were seeking a protective alliance with Athens. Overwhelmed, they surrendered without a fight and abandoned their town and territory. This incident polarized Athenian opinion, already wary of the growing strength of Thebes. But the Athenians accepted the explanations of their Theban allies and refused to support the Plataeans, most likely because cooperation with Thebes was once again essential as war with Sparta had broken out again (Diod. 15.46.4–6; Isoc. 14).

From 373 until 371, the conflict suspended in 375 was renewed. Resistance to Thebes at Thespiae was crushed by the expulsion of many citizens and by razing the town walls. The Thebans made war on Phocis and Orchomenus, and Cleombrotus was again posted in Phocis with a Peloponnesian army some 10,000 strong, reinforced by troops as far north as Heraclea. The war did not last long, and as before it was brought to a close at the initiative of the Athenians and Spartans.

Both sides had exhausted their resources in costly naval campaigns in the Ionian Sea, and both wished to end their dispute on terms offering no advantages to the Thebans. The treaty of 371, like those of 386 and 375, stipulated that all Greek towns should preserve their independence. When the Theban ambassadors wished to sign the treaty in the name of Boeotia, Agesilaus prevented them, demanding that each Boeotian town sign independently. This time the Thebans refused and were ready to remain in a state of war. Enemies of Thebes, even some Athenians, were said to be pleased at the thought that Thebes would now be humbled by the armed might of Sparta (Xen. *Hell.* 6.3.1–4.3; Diod. 15.50.4–51.3).

Meanwhile, commitments to Orchomenus and Phocis had prevented the Spartans from helping Polydamas of Pharsalus, their most important ally in Thessaly, against the growing strength of Jason of Pherae. By 375 Thessaly was united under Jason, now *tagos* of the Thessalian confederacy (Xen. *Hell.* 6.1.18). Sparta's inability to oppose Jason in Thessaly meant that their influence farther north, at Olynthus, had also withered. Now, with Thebes unwilling to accept the terms of a general peace negotiated at Sparta, the Spartans saw an opportunity to crush the chief obstacle to their supremacy in central Greece.

THE BATTLE OF LEUCTRA, 371

Immediately after the peace conference, Spartan ambassadors demanded that the Thebans comply with the general treaty, restore Thespian and Plataean exiles and grant independence to all Boeotian

Plate 10 The Boeotian Plain: the view toward Leuctra. Photo: M. Munn.

communities. The Thebans replied that they had never interfered in Spartan internal affairs, and the Spartans had no right now to interfere in Boeotian. Such arguments had not concerned the Spartans in the past, nor did they now. Spartan authorities immediately ordered Cleombrotus to lead his army in Phocis against the Thebans. In a brilliant march from Phocis along the southern side of Mount Helicon to the shore of the Corinthian Gulf, Cleombrotus annihilated several Boeotian garrisons then turned north to threaten Thebes. The Thebans, anticipating a direct invasion from Phocis, had assembled at Coronea on the north side of Helicon. Now they withdrew in haste to head off Cleombrotus, encamped between Thespiae and Thebes at a place known as Leuctra (see Plate 10).

Epaminondas had played a major role in provoking this conflict. Recognized for his political leadership, Epaminondas had represented the Thebans in the council of Athenian allies in 375, and in the negotiations at Sparta in 371. Now that diplomacy was past, his leadership was to be tested on the battlefield. Cleombrotus' bold move had left the Boeotarchs, among whom was Epaminondas, undecided about the wisest course of action. Furthermore, not all Boeotians were committed to the prospect of dying for Thebes. Their army numbered some 6,000 hoplites and they could see that the Spartan army facing them was twice as large. Epaminondas had to inspire his troops and this he did by a combination of propaganda – spreading word of favorable omens and suppressing pessimistic opinions – and discrimination, dismissing those Boeotians least willing to fight.

Epaminondas' strategy was simple, ingenious, and terribly risky. Its essence was to place his Theban troops on the left end of the Boeotian battle line directly facing the Spartans. In previous engagements, the Thebans and the Spartans had opposed each other on the right end of their own lines. When the armies had fought, as in 394, both right wings had won, but each time the Spartans came out on top in the second phase of battle, when the victorious wings engaged. Now Theban and Spartan forces would engage immediately. Moreover, Epaminondas anticipated that Cleombrotus would employ the traditional Spartan maneuver of wheeling his overlapping units so as to engage the Theban left flank. But Epaminondas planned to strike the Spartans before they completed this flanking maneuver, giving his deeply massed Thebans the advantage of an unimpeded attack, spearheaded by the Sacred Band under Pelopidas.

Epaminondas realized that the battle depended on the outcome of a contest between Thebans and Spartans. The allies on both sides did not really matter, making the odds for Epaminondas much more favorable, since Theban hoplites actually outnumbered the 2,000 Laconian hoplites, of which only some 700 were Spartiates. In this regard Epaminondas' acumen as a statesman was as critical as his tactical genius, because he correctly judged that the allies of *neither* side were enthusiastic for the fight and would shrink from the full fury of combat.

Initiative for opening the battle lay, according to Epaminondas' plan, with the Spartans. Just as Epaminondas anticipated, Cleombrotus moved to attack, extending his line and wheeling his right flank. A Spartan cavalry attack failed and the retreating cavalry brought disorder to Spartan ranks as Theban infantry quickly advanced. Epaminondas' attack hit the Spartan line hard. Men went down in fierce fighting, and the Spartans were immediately on the defensive. The attack fell on Cleombrotus' position and the king fell, mortally wounded. Surrounded by his bodyguard, Cleombrotus was carried back from the battle line, while elite Spartiate soldiers were cut down as the Spartan line buckled. With the command group in retreat, the remainder of the Spartan line drew back, as did the allies. Unable to reorganize, the Spartans fell back to their encampment and at this point both sides broke off the engagement.

The Thebans had carried the day and now possessed the battle-field and the corpses strewn across it. Some Spartans were minded to regroup for a second attack, but the surviving commanders determined that the allies were unwilling to fight again. The following day the Spartans petitioned the Thebans for permission to collect their dead. After erecting a trophy from the arms of the defeated, Epaminondas granted permission, first to Sparta's allies, who had trivial losses, and then to the Spartans, forced to acknowledge that most of the over 1,000 corpses on the field were theirs, of whom some 400 were Spartiates. Theban losses numbered about 300.

The battle of Leuctra was over, although it was several days before both sides recognized that there would be no further fighting. Messengers from both sides summoned reinforcements. A Theban request for Athenian aid was met with silence. Their ally Jason of Pherae, however, responded instantly, marching south with a force of 1,500 mercenaries and 500 cavalry. When Jason arrived at Leuctra, the Thebans proposed a joint attack to destroy the Spartans and their remaining allies. Jason persuaded Epaminondas and his colleagues that victory was already theirs, and it would be wiser to avoid further risks and allow the Spartans to withdraw from Boeotia.

Plate 11 Theban Victory Monument at Leuctra. Photo: M. Munn.

The Spartans departed under cover of night, meeting their relieving force a day's march away, in the Megarid. With the gloom of defeat hanging over them, they all returned to the Peloponnesus and disbanded.[2]

The trophy made up of the arms of the fallen Spartans was remembered not long afterward in an epigram inscribed on the base of a monument dedicated to Zeus at Thebes. It reads in part, 'The Thebans are superior in battle, proclaims the trophy at Leuctra that announces the victory won by the spear' (Harding 46 = Tod 130). The Thebans replaced the trophy with a bronze monument on a tall stone base, erected perhaps on the spot where Cleombrotus fell and the victory was won (see Plate 11). Permanent trophies had previously been erected to mark Greek victories over Persians, as at Marathon (Paus. 1.32.5), but this was the first such battlefield memorial to a Greek victory over Greeks (Cicero *Inv. Rhet.* 2.23).

THEBES AND THESSALY AT THE CROSSROADS, 371–369

Thebes remained nominally an ally of Athens, but the bonds of mutual defense against Sparta were broken. Theban power was ascendant and could no longer be contained by either Sparta or Athens. In the months following Leuctra, the Thebans secured Boeotia, first capturing a stronghold of Thespian exiles, later reducing Orchomenus. The Phocians were compelled to join the widening alliance of Thebes. In less than a year the Thebans could count almost all of central Greece as allies, including the Thessalians under Jason of Pherae (Diod. 15.57.1–2; Paus. 9.14.2–4; Xen. *Hell.* 6.5.23).

Jason, meanwhile, was demonstrating his own strength. On his way north from Leuctra he removed the northernmost bastion of Spartan influence by destroying Heraclea in Trachis. Opposition to his dominion in north central Greece was evaporating. From Malis north to Perrhaebia and Macedon, and from Epirus to Magnesia, regions surrounding Thessaly had been brought into alliance with Jason as *tagos* of the Thessalian confederacy. Not since the sixth century had the power of Thessaly been united behind a single leader, and Jason was preparing a demonstration that might secure for him the recognized supremacy now slipping away from Sparta.

The summer of 370 would see the first gathering at Delphi for the Pythian games since a devastating earthquake a few years earlier. The question of how to fund the rebuilding of Apollo's temple had for some time been the talk of the pious and the powerful (Diod. 15.48.1–4; Xen. *Hell.* 6.4.2; Tod 133, lines 9–10; Tod 205 = *Parian Marble*, A71). In spring 370 Jason commanded his allies to assemble thousands of animals as sacrificial victims to be escorted to Delphi by the armed forces of Thessaly. Through his control of Delphi's Amphictyonic council, and by sponsoring the greatest gifts to Apollo's shrine, Jason expected to preside over the festival and games. But shortly before Jason was to leave for Delphi he was struck down by assassins. Several of the assassins who fled to towns outside of Thessaly were honored, reflecting a widespread apprehension at Jason's rapidly rising power. Just as Jason had made himself *tagos* of

Thessaly and commander of the largest citizen army in Greece, he might well, it was feared, have become a tyrant over all Greeks (Xen. *Hell.* 6.4.27–32; Diod. 15.57.1–2, 60.1–2, 5).

Jason's leadership was not easily transferred. His brothers jointly assumed the powers of *tagos*, but these soon fell by the wayside and his nephew Alexander claimed supreme authority in Pherae. Alexander sought to reclaim the leadership over Thessaly, but Jason's remarkable legacy was crumbling. Following Jason's death, the Aleuads of Larissa appealed for Macedonian support against the power of Pherae, and in 369 the new king of Macedon, Alexander II, came to the aid of his family's ancient friends in Thessaly, sending a garrison to Larissa. At the same time, members of the Thessalian confederacy were reforming their union so as to separate it from the tyrannical power of Pherae and the influence of the Aleuads. Thessaly was again divided from within (Diod. 15.61.3–5, 67.4).

As the power of Thessaly collapsed with Jason's death, the power of Thebes emerged. Theban supremacy within Boeotia had been established by practices that were no less authoritarian and, at times, no less brutal than those of the Pheraean tyrants. But Thebes was not ruled by a tyrannical dynasty, and the greater durability of the emergent Theban supremacy can be explained by the resilience of the constitutional government of Thebes. Power, in practical terms, lay with the seven annually elected Boeotarchs. The most influential Boeotarchs came from the leaders of the uprising of 379/8, men who had proven their leadership in battle, foremost among them Pelopidas and Epaminondas.

Theban supremacy outside of Boeotia was another matter. Most alliances with Boeotia were attracted by the power of Thebes rather than compelled by it. Theban leadership relied upon voluntary adherence in the face of a common enemy. It also depended on the charisma and abilities of the generals who led allied ventures, making the reputations of Pelopidas and Epaminondas valuable assets for the Thebans. As with Jason's leadership in Thessaly, the wider influence of Thebes was closely tied to the careers of these commanders.

THEBANS AND PELOPONNESIANS, 370–365

Late in 370, Pelopidas and Epaminondas entered the Peloponnesus on a campaign demonstrating the full consequences of Leuctra. The Arcadians, once part of the Spartan alliance, were now feuding among themselves, attempting to form their own confederacy. Those still friendly to Sparta appealed for support against their enemies, who in turn appealed unsuccessfully to Athens for aid. Denied, these then turned to Thebes and gained an alliance. Within weeks an army representing all of central Greece invaded the Peloponnesus in the cause of ending Spartan aggression (Diod. 15.62; Xen. *Hell.* 6.5.19, *Ages.* 2.24).

As the Spartans withdrew from Arcadia, some 40,000 hoplites and as many light troops and unarmed followers assembled at Mantinea, where the Thebans laid their plans carefully for the invasion of Laconia. Outlying towns quickly fell or voluntarily surrendered. The Spartans devoted their sparse manpower to the defense of Sparta itself, barely holding back the tide of Theban and allied assaults on the unwalled town. The Spartans witnessed their countryside, untouched by war for centuries, subjected to weeks of devastation and plundering. At length, Epaminondas led his army west for the most important stage of this campaign – the liberation of Messenia (Xen. *Hell.* 6.5.23–32; Diod. 15.63.4–64; Plut. *Pel.* 24.1–2, *Ages.* 31–2).

Long held in servitude or scattered abroad in exiled communities, the Messenians yearned for their homeland. Exiles were invited to return and join the Theban force at Mount Ithome, where tradition and a strong defensive position favored the foundation of an independent Messenian capital. Argives, kinsmen of the Dorian Messenians, presided over the ceremonies of refoundation, while the Theban-led army swiftly constructed walls, houses, temples, and streets. Within weeks the bulk of the allied army returned home leaving a substantial garrison to protect Messene, as the newly rising city was named. The foundation of Messene assured that Spartan power would never recover from the blow struck at Leuctra (Paus. 4.26.5–27; Diod. 15.66–7.1; Plut. *Pel.* 24.5).

In summer 369 the Arcadians, Argives, and Eleans, eager to continue the war of revenge and plunder against Sparta, recalled the Thebans to their support. Epaminondas, now at the height of his prestige, again commanded an allied invasion force. This time, the Spartans, now supported by the Athenians, prepared to block his advance by closing the way into the Peloponnesus at the Isthmus of Corinth. Epaminondas was not intimidated. In a dawn attack he forced his way through the Spartan position and joined his Peloponnesian allies. Epaminondas directed his attention first against Sicyon and Pellene, to the west of Corinth, and then against Epidaurus and the towns of the Argolic peninsula. Allies of Sparta now saw their land plundered, and several (notably Sicyon and

Pellene) renounced their allegiance to Sparta (Xen. *Hell.* 7.1.15–22; Diod. 15.68.1–70.1).

The Spartans, experienced in a wider field than Peloponnesian politics, played a card that had restored their fortunes before. They appealed to the king of Persia to offer an alliance to all willing to uphold a common peace in Greece. The satrap Ariobarzanes, a Spartan friend, represented the interests of King Artaxerxes, and in spring 368 his emissary summoned the warring parties to a conference at Delphi. Agreement was impossible. The Spartans demanded that Messene be restored to them, and that the Thebans give the Boeotian towns their independence. Agreement, however, was probably not what the Spartans expected. When the conference broke up, the Spartans acquired the services of 2,000 mercenaries with the financial backing of Ariobarzanes. War in the Peloponnesus continued (Xen. *Hell.* 7.1.27; Diod. 15.70.2).

The Thebans now recognized that power in Greece depended upon successful engagement in the high-stakes politics of money and manpower governing relations between the Persian king and the Greeks. Artaxerxes had long experienced difficulty in maintaining control of distant satrapies, especially Egypt, and was always interested in negotiating support with a strong Greek power. In 367 the Thebans sent Pelopidas on an embassy to make the king a friend of the Thebans. Joined by ambassadors from the chief states of the Peloponnesus and challenged by Athenian and Spartan ambassadors, Pelopidas had no difficulty making the case for Thebes in persuasive terms. Since the time of Xerxes, the Thebans had been Persian friends and enemies of Persia's Greek enemies. Moreover, now triumphant over Sparta, they were manifestly the most powerful state in Greece. The Theban proposal was simple: let Messene be free, and let the Athenians keep their navy off the seas. All agreeing would become allies of the Thebans and the Persians, and would make war on those not agreeing. In view of the ascendancy of the Thebans, and the simplicity of their proposal, Artaxerxes issued a proclamation inviting the Greeks to abide by these terms. Pelopidas brought this edict home, and early in 366 the Thebans invited all independent Greek communities to join them in upholding it. The king's edict, however, was not backed by immediate military compulsion and none of the Greeks at war with Thebes agreed to its terms (Xen. *Hell.* 7.1.33–40; Plut. *Pel.* 30).

The Thebans, prepared to reduce their opponents one by one, sent Epaminondas on his third expedition into the Peloponnesus in summer 366. Breaching defenses held by Athenians in the Corinthia, he marched westward against Spartan allies in Achaea. He forced the Achaeans into alliance with Thebes and liberated the towns of Dyme, Calydon, and Naupactus. He thus brought the states on the Corinthian Gulf, excepting Corinth, under Theban control. The following spring, suffering the consequences of isolation and fearing yet another Theban campaign through their territory, the Corinthians entered negotiations for peace. Sparta's remaining allies in the Peloponnesus followed suit, and in 365 the terms Pelopidas had brought from Artaxerxes the previous year were renegotiated into a peace treaty. The treaty stopped short of binding the Peloponnesian states in alliance to Thebes but it left the Spartans, still vainly claiming possession of Messene, stripped of all allies except the Athenians (Xen. *Hell.* 7.1.41–2, 4.6–11; Diod. 15.75.2, 76.3; Isoc. 6.11, 91).

The Thebans resolved momentarily their direct involvement in Peloponnesian conflicts. But neither the internal politics nor the external relations of the Peloponnesian communities had been stabilized. The Thebans would soon be compelled to return to the Peloponnesus, to establish a dominant order by force of arms.

THEBANS AND THESSALIANS, 369–364

The struggle by Alexander of Pherae to dominate Thessaly began with the murder of his predecessor in 369 and did not end until he was murdered by his brothers-in-law eleven years later. His failure to unite Thessaly as Jason did has been ascribed to his temper as a more ruthless but less efficient tyrant. A more compelling explanation of the troubled course of Alexander's career can be found in its timing. Jason consolidated his power in the vacuum left by the receding influence of Sparta, while Alexander's career coincided with the high point of Theban strength.

As Alexander built his power in Thessaly, his opponents sought outside support. At first, Macedonian influence prevailed in the north, as the forces of Alexander of Macedon supported the exiled aristocracy of Larissa. The core of the Thessalian confederacy, the more broadly based oligarchs of the Thessalian towns, turned instead to Thebes. In response, in summer 369 Pelopidas marched north and compelled the Macedonians to withdraw from Larissa and Alexander of Pherae to renounce his claim to command the Thessalian confederacy. Pelopidas entered Macedon and brought Alexander of Macedon into alliance with Thebes. To assure this alliance he took hostages from the Macedonian nobility to Thebes; among these was King Alexander's younger brother, the future king, Philip, about thirteen years old (Diod. 15.61.3–5, 67.3–4; Plut. *Pel.* 26.1–4).

The assassination of Alexander of Macedon and complaints against Alexander of Pherae prompted Pelopidas and a colleague, Ismenias (son of the Ismenias put to death by the Spartans in 382), to return to Thessaly and Macedon in summer 368, this time as ambassadors, relying on Theban prestige rather than arms, to negotiate a resolution of these disturbances. In Macedon, Pelopidas received oaths of friendship and a fresh round of hostages from Ptolemy, the regent. In Thessaly, however, Pelopidas and Ismenias were arrested by Alexander of Pherae and imprisoned at Pharsalus. In response, the Boeotians sent an army and two Boeotarchs to free them. Alexander, meanwhile, made an alliance with Athens and received reinforcements. The Thebans, unable to make any headway against the forces of Alexander and Athens, withdrew under difficult circumstances, to the disgrace of their commanders. The following spring a second Boeotian expedition, commanded by Epaminondas, entered Thessaly. Through a campaign of attrition, Epaminondas pressured Alexander to accept a truce and to release his captives. Pelopidas and Ismenias returned home (summer 367) and soon departed on another embassy, this time to the Persian king at Susa (Diod. 15.71.2–7, 75.1–2; Plut. *Pel.* 27–9).

For the next two years the struggle between Alexander and the Thessalian towns continued: Alexander consolidated his hold on the outlying regions of Magnesia and Phthiotis and inflicted defeats upon the armies of the confederacy. In summer 364 Pelopidas was sent to support the Thessalian confederacy against Alexander with an army of 7,000 hoplites and 700 cavalry. After uniting with the allied Thessalians at Pharsalus, Pelopidas found Alexander waiting in the hills of Cynoscephalae with more than 20,000 men. Relying on a rapid attack to compensate for inferior numbers, Pelopidas assaulted the extended positions of Alexander's army. Pelopidas' initiative, and his skillful use of cavalry, gave him the advantage which he pressed home in a charge against Alexander's own position. Pelopidas was killed in the action, but Alexander's forces broke. Despite the loss of Pelopidas, this victory was turned to the advantage of the allies when Boeotian reinforcements arrived and forced Alexander to surrender and to become an ally of Thebes. Strategically, the Theban position was greatly strengthened by this campaign, which robbed the Athenians of the alliance of Alexander and secured Thessaly for their friends. Honors paid to the memory of the fallen Pelopidas in Thessaly and at Delphi added to a sense of solidarity between Thessalians and Thebans. But the loss of a renowned commander would prove to be a severe blow (Diod. 15.80–1; Plut. *Pel.* 31–5.2; Harding 49).

Another benefit secured for Thebes by the Thessalian campaigns of 364 was the loyalty of a majority of representatives on the Amphictyonic council. Six of the twelve states participating in this council of the ancestral patrons of Apollo's shrine at Delphi were among the traditional allies of a unified Thessalian confederacy. This was the first time such an alignment had been achieved since it was momentarily realized by Jason of Pherae, and there is good reason to believe that the Thebans used their influence during the following year. In 363, eleven prominent Delphians, friends of Athens and of Phocis, were banished by decree of the Amphictyons (*IG* II² 109). Probably in the same year, the Amphictyons fined the Spartans 500 talents for their seizure of the Cadmea nearly twenty years earlier, on the grounds that the act was a violation of Delphi's Pythian truce (Diod. 16.23.2, 29.2; Just. 8.1.4–5; Aristid. *Eleusinios* 258). The validity of this grievance was never acknowledged by the Spartans, but a religious sanction against Sparta was useful propaganda for the Thebans when, also in 363, they announced plans for another major campaign into the Peloponnesus (Xen. *Hell.* 7.4.40–5.3).

THE HEIGHT OF THEBAN SUPREMACY AND THE BATTLE OF MANTINEA, 364–362

In 364 the Thebans turned to a new sphere of activity, the sea. Their alliance with Artaxerxes challenged Athenian sea power, and plans began as early as 366 for the construction of a Boeotian fleet. Naval activity was hardly alien to the Boeotians. By the latter years of the Peloponnesian War the Spartans had relied upon the Boeotians for more ships than the Corinthians (Thuc. 8.3.3), and since then the Boeotians had maintained a naval presence along both coasts (Xen. *Hell.* 5.4.56–7, 6.4.3). Now, with 100 triremes to be constructed according to Epaminondas' plan, the Thebans designed a program for naval supremacy.

In 364 Epaminondas sailed for the northeastern Aegean, toward the Hellespont where years before Persian-backed Spartan fleets had twice defeated the Athenians. This time, however, there was no decisive engagement, and no substantial result. Epaminondas attempted to persuade key Athenian allies, Byzantines, Chians, and Rhodians, to rebel and ally with Thebes. He received expressions of goodwill, but no commitments. The fleet returned unscathed, and could have put to sea to more effect in another year had not other priorities intervened. The Boeotian fleet never sailed again.[3]

Another side of Theban supremacy was displayed in summer 364. The Thebans learned of a conspiracy of Boeotian exiles and Orchomenians to overthrow the democratic government at Thebes. Striking first, Theban authorities had the 300 members of the Orchomenian cavalry arrested and sentenced to death. Still more dire penalties against the ancient enemies of the Thebans were decreed by the Boeotian assembly at Thebes: Orchomenus was to be razed, its men put to death, and its women and children sold into slavery. An expedition carried out this decree, swelling the ranks of anti-Theban exiles awaiting the day when the cycle of vengeance would turn the other way (Diod. 15.79.3–6; Paus. 9.15.3).

As the Thebans focused their activities on the sea and on Orchomenus, the power struggle in the Peloponnesus reached a symbolic crisis in the summer of 364. The Arcadians engaged the Eleans in battle in the precinct of Zeus at Olympia during the Olympic Games (Xen. *Hell.* 7.4.28–32; Diod. 15.78.1–3). The Arcadians controlling the sanctuary then feuded over use of the treasures deposited there. An aristocratic faction based in Mantinea opposed liquidating the sacred funds, as proposed by a democratic faction in Tegea, supported by a Theban garrison (Xen. *Hell.* 7.4.33–5.3; Diod. 15.82.1–4).

By winter 363/2 it was evident that the Thebans would support their friends in Arcadia, and that the ensuing conflict would decide the leadership of Greece (so the contemporary Xenophon [*Hell.* 7.4.18 and 26] saw the event). By the beginning of summer, Epaminondas had entered the Peloponnesus with allies from central Greece, including forces from the Thessalian confederacy and from Alexander of Pherae. Epaminondas attempted to take Sparta by surprise, but Agesilaus spoiled his plans (Xen. *Hell.* 7.5.8–19; Diod. 15.82.5–84.3; Plut. *Ages.* 34.3–8). At last, Epaminondas arrived at the southern end of the plain of Mantinea where his enemies awaited him. Epaminondas had the larger army, over 30,000 infantry and cavalry, made up of Arcadians, Messenians, and other Peloponnesians, as well as his Boeotians. His opponents, including Mantineans, Spartans, and Athenians, numbered something over

22,000 infantry and cavalry. Epaminondas arrayed his battle line like a massive version of his formation at Leuctra and led the left wing himself against the right wing of his opponents where the Mantineans and Spartans stood. Epaminondas made a conspicuous example of himself attacking at the head of his formation. He was struck in the chest and fell just as the battle turned in favor of the Boeotians. The Spartans and Mantineans retreated, but there was no pursuit by the victors. Epaminondas remained alive long enough to realize his men had carried the day, but the victory was hollow. The Athenians had dominated their end of the line, while the Thebans held the field at the other. Both sides erected trophies and claimed victory. The greatest battle yet fought between Greeks had decided nothing (Xen. *Hell.* 7.5.20–7; Diod. 15.84–7; Polyb. 9.8.2–12; Plut. *Ages.* 35.1–2, *Mor.* 194C).

The death of Epaminondas, however, proved in retrospect to be the decisive event of the battle of Mantinea. With his passing, and Pelopidas already gone, the spark of genius and charismatic leadership was lost to the Thebans. Contemporary historians recognized this. So Xenophon and Anaximenes closed their histories with the battle of Mantinea, and two others, the Boeotians Dionysodorus and Anaxis, ended their narratives in the following year (as noted by Diod. 15.89.2 and 95.4). Another fourth-century historian, Theopompus (most likely reflected in the later work of Just. 6.8.1–9.1), signaled the event as a major turning point, notable for the decline of Thebes thereafter rather than the ascendancy of any other power. Dinarchus, a contemporary Athenian orator, likewise referred to the lifetimes of Pelopidas and Epaminondas as the period of Thebes' greatness (1.72–3), and the judgment was a commonplace among later historians (so Polyb. 6.43.2–7; Diod. 15.88.4; Nep. *Epam.* 9–10).

THEBES IN DECLINE, AND THE THIRD SACRED WAR

The standoff following the battle of Mantinea led, later in 362, to a general peace treaty between the warring sides. This agreement did not alter the conditions leading to the battle of Mantinea, however. The Spartans refused to take part because the agreement recognized the independence of Messene. Support for Sparta's enemies remained a guiding concern in the policies of Thebes. Thus in 361 a Theban army supported the Arcadians of Megalopolis against Spartan intervention, and a similar force was sent into the Peloponnesus again in 352. These expeditions sustained the principle that Thebes influenced the balance of power in the Peloponnesus, but by mid-century it was clear that this influence was diminishing.[4]

The Theban alliance was not what it had been before the battle of Mantinea. In 361 Alexander of Pherae again threatened the Thessalians, who appealed not to Thebes but to Athens. Instead of withdrawing, Alexander launched attacks against Athenian interests in the Aegean.[5] The assassination of the tyrant of Pherae in 358 ended these actions and again opened the door to outside intervention in Thessaly. The Aleuads of Larissa acquired the aid of King Philip of Macedon. Philip's military presence in Thessaly was shortlived, but his influence among the highest circles of Thessalian dynastic politics was established by marriages to the Aleuads of Larissa and the tyrants of Pherae. These connections would support Philip's more substantial entry into the contest for influence and power in central Greece (Diod. 16.14.1–2, cf. 15.61.3–5; Just. 7.6.8–9; Ath. 13.557B–D).

Neither the Thebans nor the Athenians made their presence felt in Thessaly during this period. Instead, their attentions were fixed on Euboea, once loyal to Thebes, but now mired in a power struggle between local tyrants and their opponents. In the summer of 357, the Thebans and the Athenians engaged in a brief war for dominance in the island that was won by the Athenians (Diod. 16.7.2; Aeschin. 3.85; Harding 65, 66 = Tod 153, 154).

In autumn 357 a more fateful dispute commenced. The eclipse of Pherae benefitted the Thebans by re-establishing a friendly majority on the Amphictyonic council. This bloc now voted to reimpose the penalty for sacrilege on Sparta. It also imposed a heavy penalty for sacrilege against the Phocians for their unauthorized cultivation of sacred land. The Phocians, traditional enemies of Thebes and long-time friends of Sparta, had been cowed into alliance with the Thebans after Leuctra, but had demonstrated their disaffection for Theban leadership even before Epaminondas' Mantinean campaign (Xen. *Hell.* 7.5.4). Now the Thebans used the Amphictyonic council as a platform on which to rebuild their prestige, first by humbling the Phocians (Diod. 16.23.2–3; Paus. 10.2.1).

The pronouncement against the Phocians was provocative, the Phocian reaction even more so. Urged on by their leading statesman, Philomelus, the Phocians resolved to take control of Apollo's sanctuary, thereby denying the Amphictyons' authority to issue decrees on Apollo's behalf. They gained the covert support of the Spartans, who stood to benefit by this move, and of the Athenians. In spring 356 the Phocians seized Delphi, eliminating their opponents and restoring their friends, exiled in 363, to positions of leadership. The Phocians then sent ambassadors to the chief states of Greece to justify their actions and to seek allies. Meanwhile, the outbreak of fighting between the Phocians and the Locrians marked the opening of a conflict soon to spread more widely.[6]

The Locrians appealed to the Boeotians, who called upon the Thessalians and all other Amphictyons to declare war in the name of Apollo against the Phocians. Between autumn 356 and spring 355 practically all central Greece united against the Phocians. The Phocians, meanwhile, gained defensive alliances with the Athenians, the Spartans, and other Peloponnesians. But most of the fighting on the Phocian side was left to mercenaries, who were attracted in large numbers by the high rate of pay offered by the Phocians, with the treasures of Apollo at their disposal (Diod. 16.27.5, 28.4–30.2).

The Third Sacred War saw ten years of fighting concentrated in Phocis, Locris, and western Boeotia. A series of battles in summer 355 between the Phocians and their opponents led to a rout of the Phocian army and the death of Philomelus (Diod. 16.30.3–31.5; Paus. 10.2.4). The Amphictyonic forces, however, did not press their victory home and Onomarchus, Philomelus' successor, rallied the Phocians, suppressed dissent, and used the resources from Apollo's sanctuary to double the Phocian forces. Onomarchus moreover weakened his opposition by encouraging Lycophron of Pherae, Alexander's successor, to take the offensive against the Thessalian confederacy.

Onomarchus' strategy brought the Phocians numerous victories in 354: he forced the Amphissans in West Locris into alliance and captured Orchomenus. After the Thessalians summoned Philip of Macedon to join them against Pherae, Onomarchus entered Thessaly to confront Philip. With a larger army and using catapults for support in an open field engagement, Onomarchus twice defeated Philip and his Thessalian allies (Diod. 16.32–3, 35.1–2; Polyaenus *Strat.* 2.38.2).

This triumph was followed, in 353, by Onomarchus' return to Boeotia, where he dealt the Thebans a further blow by the capture of Coronea. Philip, meanwhile, rejoined his Thessalian allies in attacking Pherae, and Onomarchus went to the support of Lycophron. When the two armies met on the plain bordering the Gulf of Pagasae they were nearly equal in size, but Philip and the

Thessalian cavalry determined the outcome. Six thousand Phocians and mercenaries, and Onomarchus himself, were slain in the rout that followed, and 3,000 were taken prisoner. These Philip put to death by drowning, as punishment for plundering Delphi (Diod. 16.35.3–6, cf. 61.2; Paus. 10.2.5).

This episode in the Third Sacred War was a turning point for central Greece. Philip followed the defeat of the Phocians with the capture of Pagasae and a march on Pherae. Lycophron surrendered Pherae to Philip on terms allowing his departure to Phocis. Philip had triumphed in Thessaly and was acclaimed head of the Thessalian confederacy. The mantle of Jason, contended by Alexander and Pelopidas, now passed to the king of Macedon.[7]

Philip might well have pressed home the defeat of the Phocians in this year, but the Athenians manned the pass at Thermopylae and prevented his march south. From 352 until 346, the Third Sacred War ground on with the mutual devastation of Phocian, Locrian, and Boeotian territory. In 351, the Phocians, led by Phayllus, Onomarchus' brother, captured key strongholds in East Locris and the pass of Thermopylae. Phocian influence may have been responsible for a momentary resurgence of the Pheraean tyranny, prompting Philip, in 349, to divert his attention to Thessaly. Otherwise, until 346, there was no significant change in the positions of the combatants.[8]

Exhaustion of the Boeotians finally brought the Sacred War to an end. The riches of Delphi had repeatedly repaired losses that would have ruined states many times as populous as the Phocians. Boeotian manpower losses were perhaps not as severe as those suffered by the Phocians, but they were harder to replace. The Boeotians also employed mercenaries on their side (Paus. 10.2.4), but their resources were severely limited. Revenue was generated by hiring Boeotian manpower to Persian satraps and to Artaxerxes III (Diod. 16.34.1–2, 40.1–2, cf. 44.2; Polyaenus, *Strat.* 7.33.2). The apparent paradox of sending troops away from Boeotia during war becomes comprehensible if these troops are recognized as mercenaries under Theban commanders. While they were maintained in paid service, able to return later to Boeotia, Theban authorities received a sizable bounty enabling them to hire other soldiers.

Such measures were insufficient to maintain the Boeotian war-effort indefinitely, and by 347 the Thebans appealed to Philip to rescue the Delphic Amphictyony. Philip provided a small force, and, forming an alliance with the Boeotians over winter 347/6, planned to march south from Thessaly with a major army in the summer of 346. By these moves, the Thebans implicitly acknowledged that their bid to become the champions of the most prestigious Amphictyony of Greek states had failed. Philip filled the role the Thebans had intended for themselves (Diod. 16.58.2–3, 59.2; Dem. 5.20–2; 19.139–41, 318; Just. 8.4.4).

By thus raising the ante against them, the Thebans forced the Phocians to face the coming crisis. The Phocians summoned aid from Athens and Sparta, who prepared reinforcements for the defense of Thermopylae. But the Phocians were divided in their purpose. With the day of reckoning approaching, they sought scapegoats among themselves for misappropriating Apollo's money. Phalaecus, commanding the Phocian forces at Thermopylae, was deposed, but he refused to give up his command or to cooperate with the Spartan and Athenian allies; he then secured his personal salvation by negotiating a surrender to Philip, when at length he approached Thermopylae. As a result, Philip marched unopposed into Phocis, and received the surrender of the Phocian towns (Diod. 16.56.3–57.1, 59.1–3; Aeschin. 2.133–5).

THEBES, PHILIP, AND THE BATTLE OF CHAERONEA, 338

In summer 346 Philip, King of Macedon and Archon of the Thessalian confederacy, had achieved a position of preeminence. He had ended on favorable terms a long war with Athens with the Peace of Philocrates. As champion of the Amphictyony he had ended the Third Sacred War, and had joined that body in its deliberations over terms to be imposed upon the vanquished Phocians. Stripped of the Boeotian towns they had conquered, the Phocians were disarmed, deprived of their own fortified towns, and compelled to live in scattered villages. They were made to pay an indemnity to restore Apollo's treasury. Those personally responsible for taking Apollo's money were outlawed and cursed. Finally, the Phocians lost any official role at Delphi, and their place on the Amphictyonic council was given to Philip, who presided over the Pythian games held that summer (Diod. 16.59.4–60.1–4; Dem. 19.325, 327; Paus. 10.3.1–3; Harding 88 = Tod 172A).

The Thebans gained peace and received control of Orchomenus, Coronea, and Corsiae (Diod. 16.58.1, 60.1). But greater glory came from giving than from receiving, as Demosthenes noted (5.21).

Philip now commanded the influence over central and southern Greece that had belonged to the Thebans before the battle of Mantinea. The Thebans had good reason to be jealous of Philip. Their hopes of one day restoring their own pre-eminence perhaps influenced their decision, in 344, to send a general and troops to Artaxerxes III, then requesting Greek assistance against Egypt (Diod. 16.44.1–2). But if the Thebans longed to reverse positions with Philip, Philip would not give them the opportunity.

The most important vehicle of Philip's authority in Greek affairs was his control of the Amphictyonic council, which depended upon control of the Thessalian confederacy. Divided among themselves as always, the Thessalians would concede their united allegiance only grudgingly. Between 344 and 342 Philip strengthened his grip over Thessaly by reviving the ancient tetrarchies, four administrative districts through which the dynastic families of Thessaly had formerly exercised their control. This reform removed the balance of influence from Thessalian towns and returned it to the aristocratic families, with whom Philip's personal ties were strong (Diod. 16.69.8; Dem. 6.22; 9.26, 33; 19.260; Isoc. *Ep.* 2.1.20; cf. Harding 87).

This aristocratic Thessalian confederacy, through the Amphictyonic council, prompted Philip's next and most decisive intervention in central Greece. In 339 the Amphictyons determined that the people of Amphissa had misused land sacred to Apollo. The resolution punishing the Amphissans was passed by a special meeting of the Amphictyons attended by neither the Athenians, again at war with Philip, nor the Boeotians. Alienation between the Thebans and the Thessalians had been building since Philip's most recent settlement of Thessalian affairs. Sometime before 341 the Thessalians took Echinus, a northern stronghold, away from the Thebans, who returned the favor now, expelling a Thessalian garrison from Nicaea, another strategic stronghold in the pass at Thermopylae. The pro-Thessalian Amphictyons felt they had just cause to summon Philip to enforce their decrees, and Philip felt the time was ripe for decisive intervention in the south.[9]

Late in autumn 339, Philip brought his Macedonian and Thessalian army into central Greece. Sending ambassadors ahead to Thebes, nominally his ally, Philip requested the surrender of Nicaea and cooperation in his war against Athens. But before the Thebans could respond, Philip advanced to Elatea in Phocis, close to the borders of Boeotia. Philip had arrived to force Theban compliance much as Phoebidas had a generation earlier. Conscious of the precedent, and how Phoebidas' intervention had ignited righteous indignation against Sparta, Philip patiently waited. The Thebans showed their hostility by allying with Athens and moved to protect Amphissa and to confront Philip's army. The allies skirmished with Philip's forces over winter and spring 339/8 in anticipation of the confrontation to come in the summer (Dem. 18.169–88, 211–22; Aeschin. 3.140–51; Diod. 16.84–5.4).

Theban prestige had so diminished that their former allies in the Peloponnesus abandoned them. Efforts to enlarge the alliance against Philip succeeded only in Euboea and Megara, where pro-Macedonian factions had recently been suppressed, and among states along the Corinthian Gulf that feared Philip's recent movements to take control of Naupactus and Ambracia (Dem. 7.32; 9.27, 34; 18.234–7; Aeschin. 3.94–8). Ironically, the Thebans now championed the Phocians as victims of Philip and the Amphictyons (Paus. 10.3.3–4, 33.8, 36.3).

In spring or early summer 338 Philip captured Amphissa, having tricked the Theban and Athenian defenders with a false dispatch, reporting his retreat northwards (Polyaenus *Strat.* 4.2.8). This coup compelled the main allied army to withdraw to a new position at Chaeronea in western Boeotia, where the plain of the Cephisus River narrows, offering a defensive position not easily outflanked (see Plate 12). Philip advanced to this new position, and, a little past midsummer, was ready for battle (see Map 2). Each side commanded about 30,000 infantry, but Philip had over 2,000 cavalry, whose role would make the difference. On the day of the battle, Philip led his right wing against the Athenians, while the left wing, facing the Thebans, was commanded by his senior general Parmenion and his son Alexander at the head of the cavalry. Patience was again key to Philip's success. He withdrew his wing, pretending to retreat and so encouraged the Athenians to press forward. After they had rashly loosened their formation, thinking they had carried the day, Philip counter-attacked and prevailed. Meanwhile, his left wing was heavily engaged, but Alexander threw the Thebans into disarray with a cavalry charge that broke their line. Both allied flanks were thus routed. The Athenians lost 1,000 dead and another 2,000 prisoners. Theban casualties were also high, although no numbers are reported, beyond the 300 members of the Sacred Band, said to have fought to the death on this day (Diod. 16.85.5–87; Polyaenus, *Strat.* 4.2.2, 7; Plut. *Alex.* 9.3).

A monumental stone lion was later erected at Chaeronea as a memorial of this battle (see Plate 13). Traditions sympathetic to Thebes and

Plate 12 The Boeotian Plain: from the Acropolis of Chaeronea toward the battlefield. Photo: M. Munn.

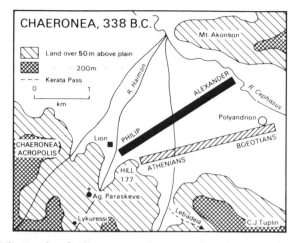

Map 2 The Battle of Chaeronea, 338/7 BC, from R. J. A. Talbert, *Atlas of Classical History*, Routledge, 1985.

the heroism of the Sacred Band have held that the Lion of Chaeronea was placed over the bodies of the last members of that elite Theban corps (Paus. 9.40.10; Plut. *Pel.* 18.5). Battlefield monuments usually honor the victors, so if the tradition is correct it would be a most remarkable deviation from practice. It would not, however, be the first exceptional battlefield monument erected by the Thebans.[10]

THE FATE OF THEBES

As victor at Chaeronea, Philip imposed terms that would assure cooperation of the vanquished, and not a few Boeotians considered this turn of events a bright new beginning. Plataeans, Thespians, and Orchomenians exiled by the Thebans years before now returned home. The Boeotian confederacy, far from being disbanded, was augmented by representation of the restored communities among the Boeotarchs. Thebes, meanwhile, was made more amenable to Philip's interests by the restoration of numerous Theban exiles. Some opponents of Philip were summarily executed, others driven into exile, and the returning partisans of Macedon were allowed to hold inquisitions of fellow-Thebans to determine who else deserved to be exiled. Finally, Philip's friends at Thebes were protected by a Macedonian garrison on the Cadmea (Diod. 16.87.3; Paus. 4.27.10, 9.1.8, 37.8; Just. 9.4.6–10).

Plate 13 The Monument at Chaeronea. Photo: M. Munn.

Philip's murder less than two years later placed all this in jeopardy. Anti-Macedonian exiles prepared to act, and the long absence beyond the Danube of the young king, Alexander, early in 335, encouraged an uprising that proceeded most rapidly at Thebes. No doubt driven by a sense that Thebes could again, as in 378, gain liberation from a tyrannical occupying power, leaders of the new crop of exiles returned to Thebes by night, murdered leaders of the opposition, and announced that liberty was at hand. Soon the Macedonian garrison was blockaded on the Cadmea, and allies were petitioned at Athens and in the Peloponnesus, all encouraged by the rumor that Alexander was dead. In less than two weeks, however, Alexander stood before Thebes, where, first of all, the movement against him had to be put down. Attempts at negotiation led only to defiance, and an assault on the walls was soon underway. Once inside, the assault became a general massacre, enthusiastically led by the Phocians and anti-Theban Boeotians among Alexander's allies. When it was over, Alexander granted the request of his allies that the Theban captives be sold, the city razed, its land divided among themselves, and the Cadmean citadel held by a Macedonian garrison. Thebes was made an example, and ceased to exist as a political entity (see also below pp. 192–3).[11]

Alexander's destruction of Thebes served its purpose for, when Alexander died twelve years later, Boeotia remained loyal to Macedon (Diod. 18.11.3–5). During the Lamian War (322), even the Thessalians joined the general cause of opposition to Macedon (Diod. 18.11.1, 12.3, 15.2–4, 38). The absence of a strong Macedonian dynast encouraged some to resist outside domination. Only the desire of those Boeotians wanting to keep what they had gained at the expense of Thebes kept Boeotia loyal to Macedon.

Yet hope, in other quarters, for the resurrection of Thebes survived. Alexander had found two prominent Theban ambassadors, one a grandson of the Ismenias executed for collaboration with Persia in 382, among the followers of Darius captured at Damascus in 333 (Arr. *Anab.* 2.15). Seven years after Alexander's death, Theban exiles recalled home by the Macedonian general, Cassander, rebuilt Thebes with the enthusiastic assistance of the Athenians (Diod. 17.118.2, 19.53–4.1, 63.4; Paus. 9.7.1–4; Harding 131). Thebes could not remain long abandoned because it was too useful a stronghold in the land fated to be, in the phrase of Epaminondas, 'the dancing-floor of Ares' (Plut. *Marc.* 21.2; cf. *Demetr.* 39–40). But by the close of the fourth century Ares' tune was played on foreign pipes. Thebes was now and forever after a creature of greater powers.

NOTES

1 The events of the Theban uprising are narrated in dramatic (and slightly varying) detail in several sources (Xen. *Hell.* 5.4.1–12; Plut. *Pel.* 8–12 *De gen.*; Nep. *Pel.* 2–4; Diod. 15.25.1–3). The vital Athenian role is described differently. Xenophon reports Athenian involvement in the initial uprising (*Hell.* 5.4.9–10), but leaves the impression that this participation was unofficial (*Hell.* 5.4.19). Diodorus describes Athenian forces sent by public decree (15.25.4–26.3), and his account is supported by the references to a formal alliance by Dinarchus and Isocrates (Din. 1.38–9; Isoc. 14.29). The Athenians must have acted openly after the uprising was under way, as Diodorus reports.

2 The chief description of the battle of Leuctra is that of Xenophon (*Hell.* 6.4.1–26), but important details are added by other sources (Diod. 15.51–6; Plut. *Pel.* 20.1–23.4, *Ages.* 28.3–6; Paus. 9.13.3–14.1; Polyaenus *Strat.* 2.3.2, 4, 8, 11, 12, 15).

3 A full-scale naval offensive was a costly undertaking and could not be managed by Theban resources alone. Epaminondas' naval program was most likely financed chiefly by Artaxerxes, who in 366 had reasons to support a rival to Athens at sea. After 364, the expense of a Boeotian fleet probably exceeded its usefulness in Artaxerxes' eyes. Brief accounts of this episode are given by Diod. 15.78.4–79.2, Isoc. 5.53, and Plut. *Phil.* 14.1–2.

4 The Peace of 361 is attested by Diod. 15.89.1–2; Plut. *Ages.* 35.2–4; Polyb. 4.33.8–9. The Theban expeditions to Arcadia are reported by Diod. 15.94.1–3, 16.39.1–7; cf. Paus. 4.28.1–2, 8.27.9–10, and Dem. 16.

5 The alliance of the Thessalian League and the Athenians is recorded in Harding 59 = Tod 147. Alexander's naval campaign may have been inspired by Epaminondas' maritime ambitions. Xenophon reports that Jason of Pherae had envisioned naval supremacy as a goal of Thessalian power (*Hell.* 6.1.11–12). Alexander went after more specific objectives, e.g., raiding the Cyclades and even, daringly, the Piraeus (Diod. 15.95.1–3; [Dem.] 50.4–5; Polyaenus *Strat.* 6.1–2; cf. Xen. *Hell.* 6.4.35).

6 The seizure of Delphi is described by Diod. 16.23.4–25.3, 27.1–28.3 (cf. Paus. 10.2.2–4). The chronology of the first years of the Third Sacred War is variously reconstructed (see bibliographical note). In this account I have followed the interpretations proposed by John Buckler, *Philip II and the Sacred War, Supplement to Mnemosyne*, vol. 109, Leiden, Brill, 1989.

7 Philip's rise to power in Thessaly is noted by Diod. 16.37.3, 38.1, cf. 31.6; Isoc. 5.20–1; Dem. 1.12–13, 8.65; Just. 8.2.1–8; Polyaenus, *Strat.* 4.2.19.

8 The Athenians at Thermopylae are reported by Diod. 16.35.5, 38.2–3; Dem. 19.83, 319–20; Just. 8.2.8. The continuing war in central Greece is described by Diod. 16.38.4–7, 39.8, 40.1–2, 56.1–2, 58.1. Philip's intervention in Thessaly is noted by Diod. 16.52.9 and Dem. 1.22.

9 The condemnation of the Amphissans is described (but not necessarily

well explained) in detail by Aeschin. 3.113–31; cf. Dem. 18.143–52. The capture of Nicaea by the Thebans is attested by Did. *Dem.* col. 11.37–51 = Philoch. *FGrhist* 328 F56b = Harding 96B; its previous possession by the allies of Philip is noted by Dem. 9.32, and [Dem.] 11.4; its recapture by Philip is noted by Aeschin. 3.140.

10 The monument, re-erected after 1902, bears no inscription identifying the dead. It stands over an enclosure excavated in 1879 and was found to contain 254 skeletons, interred with few burial goods and no weapons: see J. G. Frazer, *Pausanias's Description of Greece*, vol. 5, London, Macmillan, 1898, pp. 209–10. A tumulus at the opposite end of the battlefield, near the Cephisus river, was found to cover a pyre containing bones and a few weapons, possibly of Macedonian type: see G. Soteriades, *AthMitt* 28 (1903), 301 ff.

11 The best account of the destruction of Thebes is Arr. *Anab.* 1.7–9; see also Diod. 17.3.1–5, 4.4–5, 8.2–14; Just. 11.2–3; Aeschin. 3.156–7; Din. 1.18–21; Plut. *Alex.* 11.3–12.

5

THE EASTERN GREEK WORLD

Stephen Ruzicka

Two notable battlefield deaths conveniently frame the fourth-century history of the Eastern Greeks:[1] that of Cyrus, the Persian prince who perished at Cunaxa in 401 while trying to take the Persian throne from his brother Artaxerxes II, and that of Antigonus Monophthalmus, the Macedonian general and king who fell at Ipsus in 301 while facing a coalition of rival Macedonians. The death of Cyrus provoked reconsideration of the status of Eastern Greeks, especially Asian Greeks, and opened the door to a century-long series of liberators, defenders, protectors, and mere occupiers which culminated in Antigonus Monophthalmus and his effective combination of autonomy and autocracy.

The question of the status of Eastern Greek cities had long been central to Eastern Greek affairs. Located along the northwestern, western, and southwestern coastal fringe of Anatolia from Chalcedon to Cnidus, and outside Anatolia along the Propontic and Hellespontine coasts from Byzantium to Elaeus, and then on the islands facing the Anatolian coastline from Imbros and Tenedos in the north to Rhodes in the south, Eastern Greeks had predatory or imperialistic neighbors (see Map 3). Consequently, Eastern Greeks learned early that the cherished Greek ideal of the sovereign, self-governing city was difficult to maintain in practice. Already in the early sixth century most of the Ionian Greek cities had fallen under Lydian control; then in the mid-sixth century, they and almost all the rest of the Asian Greek cities became tributary subjects of the Persians. Freed from Persian control by Athens and other Eastern Greeks in the 470s, Asian Greeks and their Eastern Greek allies ended up as virtual Athenian subjects after the mid-fifth century, constrained in many cases by Athenian garrisons, governors, or settlers (cleruchs) and compelled to make annual tribute payments.

WESTERN ANATOLIA

Map 3 Western Anatolia. Artwork by Stephen Ruzicka and Lawrence Tritle, based on Stephen Ruzicka, *Politics of a Persian Dynasty: The Hecatomnids in the Fourth Century BC,* © 1992 University of Oklahoma Press.

During the Peloponnesian War (431–404), the Spartans and their allies fought Athens in the name of freedom and autonomy for the Greeks. But by the end of the war, thanks to Sparta's recognition of Persian claims (Thuc. 8.58.2: 'the land of Asia, as much as belongs to Asia, is the King's, and with regard to his own land let him determine to do whatever he wishes'), Asian Greek cities had again become possessions of the Persian king. For Aeolic cities along the coast opposite Lesbos up through the Troad, this meant subordination (marked by payment of annual tribute and liability to military service) to Pharnabazus, the Persian satrap (governor) of Hellespontine Phrygia who resided at Dascylium. South of this, the mainly Ionian Greek cities down to Miletus and the few Dorian Greek cities south of these belonged to Cyrus, the young son of Darius II and for the last several years satrap of Lydia and supreme military commander in western Anatolia.

Outside Anatolia most other Eastern Greek cities became members of the new Spartan empire which stretched from Byzantium to Rhodes. The Spartans commonly installed governors (harmosts), garrisons, and pro-Spartan oligarchies in these Eastern Greek cities and also collected payments or 'contributions' from them.

The entanglement of Ionian Greek cities in Persian politics made the settlement obtaining at the end of the Peloponnesian War short-lived. In 404, not long after he succeeded his father Darius as king, Artaxerxes II transferred the Ionian Greek cities from Cyrus to Tissaphernes (Cyrus' predecessor as satrap of Lydia who resided in Caria and may now have assumed control of Caria – previously always part of Lydia – as a separate satrapy), as punishment for Cyrus' alleged plot to murder the newly enthroned Artaxerxes.[2] However, supported by Cyrus' garrison troops, all the Ionian cities except Miletus successfully resisted takeover by Tissaphernes. But once Cyrus perished at Cunaxa in 401, Ionian Greek cities no longer had a defender. Tissaphernes, returning from Cunaxa where he had fought in support of Artaxerxes II, was now satrap of Lydia (including Caria again) and he demanded that all the Ionian cities be subject to him. Rather than face what had previously befallen Tissaphernes' Milesian opponents – execution or exile – oligarchs in the Ionian cities threatened by Tissaphernes sought Spartan help. This Ionian appeal – coming in summer 400 – marks the beginning of fourth-century Eastern Greek history.

SPARTANS, PERSIANS AND
EASTERN GREEKS, 400–387

In their appeal to the Spartans in summer 400, Ionian envoys requested that the Spartans 'on the grounds that they were the over-seers (*prostatai*) of all of Greece, take care also of them, the Greeks in Asia, so that their land would not be ravaged and they might be free' (Xen. *Hell.* 3.1.3). What the Ionian envoys sought most imme-diately was protection from Tissaphernes. What the envoys sought in a larger sense, though, was inclusion in the Spartan protectorate which embraced most of the Eastern Greek and other cities outside Anatolia formerly under Athenian domination.

The Spartans complied. They had themselves supported Cyrus and thereby incurred Tissaphernes' and Artaxerxes' animosity already. Initially, Spartan protection took the form of a harmost and a defense force, composed of liberated helots, Peloponnesian allied troops, and local levies, based at Ephesus. But after enlisting about 5,000 of Cyrus' former mercenaries who had made their way back to the Aegean world after Cyrus' death, Spartan commanders – first Thibron and then Dercylidas – ventured farther afield and quickly liberated Greek cities up to the Hellespont. By 398 the Spartan protectorate included not just Ionian Greek but almost all Asian Greek cities north of the Maeander River. Newly installed harmosts and garrisons in Asian Greek cities and tours by Spartan ephors, the chief elected officials at Sparta, gave apparent institutional permanence to the Spartan presence in western Anatolia. Greek cities in the Chersonesus also sought Spartan protection (marauding Thracians were the problem here), and Dercylidas effectively incor-porated these within the Spartan protectorate in 398/7, crossing to the Chersonesus and rebuilding the fortification wall built earlier across the peninsula by the Athenians Miltiades and Pericles.

While the Spartans thus extended their protectorate rather easily after the Ionian Greek appeal, various problems made long-term prospects for this expanded protectorate uncertain. So far Spartan commanders had faced Persian satraps (Tissaphernes of Lydia and Pharnabazus of Hellespontine Phrygia) who, lacking substantial military resources and relying mainly on locally levied Persian cavalry, had been swift to make truces rather than fight. Should this situation change, the Spartans would have to deploy larger forces and find a way to support them adequately. The protectorate lacked a depend-able means of paying troops: the greatest concern of Spartan officials and Asian Greeks was recurrence of pillaging and confiscations by Sparta's own forces. In practice, Asian Greek cities themselves contributed relatively few, mostly unreliable troops. In 397 Ionian Greeks persuaded the Spartans to target Tissaphernes' own land-holdings in Caria to pressure him into formally recognizing Ionian Greek autonomy, but when after much maneuvering the Spartan-led Greek force and Tissaphernes' army (which included Pharnabazus and cavalry troops from his satrapy) faced each other near Ephesus, troops from the Ionian cities and from the islands either ran away or were ready to do so. Fortunately, Tissaphernes, a veteran of Cyrus' Greek mercenaries' charge at Cunaxa in 401 and thus respectful of Greek hoplites, remained unaware of Eastern Greek defections and declined to engage.

In the aftermath of this disgraceful non-battle, the Spartans may have been ready to abandon military operations on behalf of Asian Greeks and reach some new diplomatic understanding with Tissaphernes. The Spartan ephors issued a decree, most plausibly dated to 397, which urged restoration of 'the ancestral constitutions' in Asian Greek cities and thus announced in effect that the Spartans would no longer stand behind local oligarchies established at the end of the Peloponnesian War (Xen. *Hell.* 3.4.2).[3] If, as a result, oligarchs fell from power in Ionian Greek cities – the men who had opposed Tissaphernes in favor of Cyrus in and after 404 – Tissaphernes might be more inclined to recognized the autonomy of Asian Greeks.

The Ephors' Decree threw most Asian Greek cities into political crisis, but the Spartans quickly abandoned their conciliatory stance when late in 397 they received reports of big naval preparations by the Persian king in Phoenicia. Confronted now by the prospect of large-scale Persian opposition, the Spartans redoubled their military efforts, sending Agesilaus and 8,000 additional troops to Anatolia in early 396.

Quickly settling political affairs in cities disrupted by the Ephors' Decree, Agesilaus ranged from Ephesus to the Hellespont, attacking and ravaging estates of Persian landholders to signal a vigorous offensive strategy. Most important, Agesilaus demanded full involvement by all Asian Greeks, summoning contingents from all their cities. He ordered that the rich supply horses, arms, and good riders (or serve in person) to compensate for the earlier deficiency in cavalry. Over the winter of 396/5 Agesilaus drilled intensively all the locally raised troops. Success came soon: in the summer of 395, Agesilaus advanced to Sardis itself, center of the Lydian satrapy, soundly defeating Persian cavalry in the process. Artaxerxes ordered Tissaphernes executed soon afterwards.

At this point the Persian king sought to avoid further fighting and loss to Persian holdings in western Anatolia by offering (through his *chiliarch* Tithraustes, Tissaphernes' executioner) autonomy to Asian Greeks so long as they paid 'the old tribute.' However, Agesilaus, the Spartan home authorities, and the Asian Greeks as well saw the promise of greater victory. Indeed, Eastern Greeks began to display a long-hidden enthusiasm for active campaigning. When Agesilaus, now (late 395) accorded authority over the entire Eastern Greek protectorate, sent instructions to Eastern Greek island and coastal cities to construct warships but left the numbers up to individual cities, they quickly produced and manned 120 new ships.

Taking advantage of a new truce in the Lydia–Ionia region occasioned by Tithraustes' peace proposal, Agesilaus led his army with its now extensive Asian Greek contingents north into Hellespontine Phrygia, ravaging at will and, repeating the strategy used earlier in Lydia, advancing to the satrapal center (here Dascylium) and laying waste to the whole region – cutting down trees in the beloved Persian parklands and setting fire to every structure they found. All this, like Agesilaus' earlier parading of Persian captives naked at Ephesus and his raid on Sardis, served to demonstrate to his Asian Greek troops and to Asian Greeks generally their capabilities and great prospects for success. Widespread enlistments (Xenophon reports Agesilaus receiving troops from 'everywhere') attest to the impact of his symbolic demonstrations.

There were indeed great plans for 394: to march inland and make all peoples behind the now swollen, advancing Greek army revolt from imperial control. Persian authority would perhaps soon extend no further west than the Halys River, perhaps not even that far. Eastern Greek initiative and Spartan leadership, it must have seemed, would create a realm secure from Persian intervention and far larger than that ever won by Athens.

However, Persian diplomacy and Persian funds had done their job inciting war against Sparta in Greece itself in 395 (the Corinthian War), and Spartan officials recalled Agesilaus in spring 394 to lead Spartan operations at home. Asian Greeks were not prepared to abandon entirely their expedition and expectations at this point, and all those in Agesilaus' army voted to go with him to mainland Greece and then, after victory there, take him back to Anatolia – a good testimony of the transformation Agesilaus had effected in the Asian Greek cowards and slackers of three years earlier. There was to be no end to the Spartan protectorate. Agesilaus left behind harmosts, 4,000 garrison troops, and the fleet.

Within a few months, though, the Spartan fleet no longer existed, and Spartan harmosts and garrisons were gone from almost all Eastern Greek cities. Not long after Agesilaus' departure Pharnabazus joined the expatriate Athenian Conon in command of the mostly Cypriot–Persian fleet. This had been stationed first (since 397) on the southern Carian coast and then, after Conon detached Rhodes from Spartan allegiance in 395, at Rhodes; in summer 394 Pharnabazus and Conon met and destroyed the Spartan fleet near Cnidus. Eastern Greek sailors, lacking experience and the confidence Agesilaus had instilled in the Eastern Greek land troops, fled at the beginning of the battle. In an effort to exclude the Spartans from the Eastern Greek world (and thereby keep them away from Persian holdings as well), Pharnabazus now assumed the role of protector of Eastern Greek cities – a development of immense consequence for the rest of fourth-century Eastern Greek history. After the battle of Cnidus, with Eastern Greek waters free of Spartan ships, Pharnabazus and Conon moved northward unopposed, driving out Spartan harmosts and garrisons and announcing that Eastern Greek cities were to be autonomous and without garrisons. This new Persian policy inspired nearly universal Eastern Greek defection from Sparta – undoubtedly helped by the absence of those many Asian Greek troops who had accompanied Agesilaus to mainland Greece earlier in the year. Once Pharnabazus and Conon completed their tours only Sestos and Abydos on opposite sides of the Hellespont, where refugee Spartan harmosts and garrison troops had collected, remained in Spartan hands. References to some states attaching themselves to Conon and the record of statues and other honors awarded him in the aftermath of Cnidus by Ephesus, Erythrae, and Samos probably point to local democratic victories over pro–Spartan oligarchies as another of the consequences of the battle of Cnidus.[4]

Pharnabazus' promulgation of a comprehensive policy of autonomy without garrisons announced that the Persians were appropriating the role of arbiters of Eastern Greek affairs in general. Pharnabazus' policy would in fact itself become the basis of Persia's whole Aegean policy. By 392 the Spartans were ready to surrender formally the role of protector in the Eastern Greek world, offering to recognize Persia's traditional claim to the Asian Greek cities and expressing their agreement that the islands and cities be autonomous if Artaxerxes would end Persian subsidies to Athens. Artaxerxes refused. The Persians were after all already effectively masters of the Eastern Greek world – the Spartan presence in Abydos and Sestos was evidently tolerable – and Artaxerxes preferred to maintain the status quo by ensuring continued Spartan preoccupation on the Greek mainland. Artaxerxes, however, soon found this a short-sighted and dangerous policy. The Spartans, undoubtedly hoping to gain some bargaining power, resumed operations in the Eastern Greek world after Artaxerxes' rebuff. Thanks to Pharnabazus' well-received grant of autonomy and freedom from garrisons, Eastern Greek cities were undefended, and during 391 and 390 the Spartans quickly took control of major Eastern Greek islands – Rhodes, Samos, and most of Lesbos – as well as Cnidus and the whole mainland territory from Priene north to the Gulf of Smyrna. From coastal bases they then attacked Persian estates further inland in western Anatolia.

All this ended up bringing the Corinthian War into the Eastern Greek world. For Athens, currently at war with Sparta on the mainland, the prospect of renewed Spartan domination of the Eastern Greek world was intolerable. Operating unopposed, the Spartan fleet might again block grain shipments out of the Black Sea and pressure Athens into settling the mainland conflict on Spartan terms. Consequently, in 389 Athens dispatched a fleet under Thrasybulus, who took control of Byzantium, intervened in the Chersonesus, and fought over control of Lesbos before sailing southward to plunder or extort funds from a series of coastal towns. Challenged now in the north, the Spartans resumed operations there, sending in a new commander and 1,000 mercenaries to join forces already in the Troad since 394. The Athenians countered by sending out to the Troad a 1,200-man land force of their own.

Full-blown war thus filled the Eastern Greek world again in the early 380s. Artaxerxes II was at this time increasingly concerned with deteriorating conditions in the eastern Mediterranean. Egypt remained independent after its revolt in 404 and was ready to intervene in disturbances elsewhere to delay Persian attack.[5] Evagoras, king of Cypriot Salamis, had with Egyptian and Athenian support over-run all of Cyprus and now threatened coastal regions – Cilicia and Phoenicia – opposite Cyprus. Unwilling to condone further confusion in the Eastern Greek world, Artaxerxes in late 388 finally signalled his willingness to end the Spartan-Persian conflict by appointing as satrap of Lydia the philo-Laconian Tiribazus (who had supported the unsuccessful Spartan peace initiative in 392), and then, when the Spartans sent envoys to him, Artaxerxes and the Spartans quickly agreed to the terms proposed by the Spartans in 392. The Spartans evidently immediately handed over to Tiribazus the Asian Greek cities they had taken in recent years. During 387, acting now as Persian allies, the Spartans campaigned against Athenian forces in the Hellespont and ultimately managed to capture Athens' full Hellespontine fleet. Additional ships from various Asian Greek cities and from Syracuse gave the Spartans mastery of the sea and permitted them to prevent grain ships from the Black Sea from reaching Athens. As a result, late in 387 the Athenians themselves were ready to consider peace with Sparta.

There were no negotiations. Artaxerxes handed down peace terms in the form of an ultimatum read out by Tiribazus to Athenian, Spartan, and other (mainland) Greek envoys – the participants in the Corinthian War – who assembled at Sardis toward the end of 387. Xenophon, a contemporary observer, furnishes the core of the pronouncement (*Hell.* 5.1.31):

> Artaxerxes the King thinks it just that the cities in Asia be his and of the islands Clazomenae and Cyprus, and further that the other Greek cities both small and large be left autonomous except Lemnos, Imbros, and Scyros; just as of old, these are to be Athens'. Whichever of the two [sides] does not accept this peace, I will make war on them together with those wishing these [terms], both by land and by sea and with ships and money.

By ratifying the terms of this dictated peace, important Greek states assented to the power of the Persian king to establish unilaterally the status of various Greek cities. The role coopted by Pharnabazus in 394 in the Eastern Greek world – that of arbiter – Artaxerxes now adopted on an expanded basis. Unlike Pharnabazus, Artaxerxes explicitly asserted ownership of Asian Greek cities, but this may not have been as unattractive as it had seemed in 400. Pharnabazus' autonomy had hardly kept many Asian Greek cities (and Eastern Greek cities outside Anatolia) from being attacked, blockaded, besieged, plundered, and taxed in recent years.

THE ERA OF THE KING'S PEACE, 386–336

The terms of the King's Peace determined the status of Eastern Greeks for the next fifty years. As possessions of the Persian king once again, Asian Greek cities rendered annual tribute payments and performed military service on demand. For Asian Greeks during the era of the King's Peace military service meant campaigning in the eastern Mediterranean against Egypt or against local insurrections fostered by Egypt. Right after conclusion of the King's Peace, Asian Greeks began construction of ships – reportedly ultimately 300 of them – for the war Artaxerxes mounted against Evagoras, the rebellious king of Cypriot Salamis, and once protracted preparations centered in the Gulf of Smyrna were completed (384 or 383?), Asian Greeks manned the newly constructed ships and fought through 380 under the Persian commanders Tiribazus and Orontes. They probably also saw service regularly as foot-soldiers in the successive Persian invasions of Egypt in the late 370s, late 350s, and late 340s. Six thousand Asian Greeks appear in Artaxerxes' expeditionary force in 343, and this may represent a typical levy.

On the whole, Asian Greeks appear as dutiful subjects, reconciled to subject status. Persian satraps seem to have intervened little in local political affairs, allowing tyrannies and democracies as well as oligarchies. Mausolus, the philhellenic native satrap of Caria, was an exception, moving numerous native hill-folk from the Halicarnassus peninsula hinterland into Halicarnassus and incorporating them into the political life of the city after he himself built a big palace in Halicarnassus and took up residence there (see Plate 14).[6] Occasionally, however, Asian Greek cities found themselves swept up in revolts by local Persian governors. For example, Ariobarzanes, the satrap of Hellespontine Phrygia, broke with Artaxerxes II in the early 360s to avoid replacement and garrisoned coastal cities such as Assos, Atarneus, and Adramyttium (evidently in anticipation of aid from mainland Greeks he had cultivated in recent years) which were then the targets of sieges by loyal Persian satraps (Autophradates and Mausolus) ordered to dislodge Ariobarzanes.

In succession other, initially loyal satraps followed Ariobarzanes into revolt after 365. These satrapal revolts in western Anatolia evidently grew out of the court rivalries and shifting alignments connected with expectation of the aging Artaxerxes II's death and the ensuing succession crisis.[7] One official, Orontes, called by Diodorus the satrap of Mysia, seems to have used Cyme as headquarters for his revolt, and its territory became a battlefield when Autophradates, satrap of Lydia and still loyal, attacked Orontes. After Autophradates himself and Mausolus finally broke with Artaxerxes II – or with the faction temporarily dominant at court – by 362/1,

Plate 14 Statue of 'Mausolus' from Mausoleum at Halicarnassos, *c.* 350 BC.
British Museum, London. Photo: British Museum.

the satraps and leading officials of western Anatolia formed a rebel coalition under Orontes' leadership, amassed a sizable treasury and began to assemble a large mercenary army. Asian Greek cities now furnished funds and undoubtedly quartered satrapal troops. The satraps' revolt collapsed quite suddenly with Orontes' return to loyalty late in 362/1 and his transfer of mercenary troops and cities he controlled – mostly the Ionian Greek cities – to commanders sent by Artaxerxes. There is no evidence that these Greek cities suffered for their involuntary complicity in the satraps' revolt, but individual Asian Greeks may have been among those 'bringing money' whom Orontes arrested and sent in chains to Artaxerxes to signal his good faith.

Despite the collapse of the satraps' revolt, conditions remained unsettled for Greek towns of Hellespontine Phrygia. Here no commanders sent by the king arrived to take control as in Ionia. In fact, Ariobarzanes held out for a while after 362/1 before succumbing to the treachery of his own son who then yielded the satrapy to Artaxerxes II's grandson Artabazus. During this confused time, freebooting mercenary captains seized control of various towns in the Troad and instituted ephemeral tyrannies. Artabazus himself revolted after the death of Artaxerxes II and the succession of Artaxerxes III (about 358), and for the next half-dozen years as Artabazus fought to avoid defeat and capture he used large mercenary armies which at times turned to pillaging local Greek cities: Sigeum and Lampsacus met such fates in 355. By 352 Artabazus gave up further resistance and fled to Macedonia, but now Artaxerxes III's initiation of a new attack on Egypt meant affairs in northwestern Anatolia were not the king's greatest concern, and it appears that the satrapal seat remained unfilled after Artabazus' flight. One local dynast, Hermias of Atarneus, established a virtually independent realm stretching along the coast from Assos down to the vicinity of Erythrae.

Only in the late 340s, after Artaxerxes III finally conquered Egypt (in 343/2) and then sent an army to western Anatolia under the Rhodian mercenary commander Mentor, was direct imperial authority restored everywhere in the region. Campaigning in 342 and 341, Mentor took control of places held by 'rebels' – quasi-independent dynasts like Hermias of Atarneus – and installed local governors answering directly to Artaxerxes.

By the terms of the King's Peace, Eastern Greek cities outside Anatolia were outside the King's realm and autonomous. However, Sparta's and Athens' easy conquests in the Eastern Greek world in the aftermath of Pharnabazus' autonomy proclamation of 394 had shown that 'autonomy' could be just another word for vulnerability and defenselessness. Awareness of this prompted most major Eastern Greek states outside Anatolia to buttress autonomy with defensive alliances during the era of the King's Peace.

Immediately after ratification of the King's Peace, Persian naval preparations in western Anatolia for war against Evagoras, including construction and mustering of a large, mostly Asian Greek fleet, must have provided Eastern Greeks with a sense of security – Artaxerxes certainly would not tolerate any renewed Spartan or Athenian intervention. But once naval preparations neared completion and then after the fleet departed and Persian attention focused on the eastern Mediterranean, first on the war against Evagoras and then on new preparations – in Phoenician cities – for renewed war against Egypt, various Eastern Greek states made alliances with Athens. Chios was first (in 384), followed by Byzantium (378), Methymna and perhaps then Rhodes and Mytilene (377). The individual alliance agreements, emphasizing continued maintenance of the King's Peace and the continued freedom and autonomy of those allying with Athens and promising mutual assistance in the event of attack, served a double function for these Eastern Greek states. By binding Athens to respect its allies' freedom and autonomy the alliances provided some safeguards against Athenian attack, and by securing promises of assistance from Athens the alliances provided for support in the event of renewed Spartan aggression.

This alliance, the Second Athenian League, replaced the various individual Athenian-Eastern Greek alliances in 377 when Athens and Athens' allies invited all other Greek states outside the King's realm to join them 'in order that the Lacedaemonians shall leave the Greeks free and autonomous.' Altogether, fifteen Eastern Greek states became members of the league, comprising a quarter of the total membership. Athenian guarantees regarding allied freedom and autonomy – that each ally would live under whatever constitution it wanted, receive neither garrison nor governor, and not pay tribute – and the self-imposed Athenian prohibition against Athenian ownership of any land or property in an allied state (no allotments to cleruchs, in other words) provided important additional safeguards (see also above, pp. 21–4).

For Eastern Greeks, the Spartans ceased to be a potential danger soon after formation of the Second Athenian League when in 376 Athenian ships destroyed the Spartan fleet off Naxos. Nevertheless, league membership continued to provide Eastern Greeks with safeguards against Athens itself as well as against non-members, and almost all Eastern Greek members remained part of it throughout its forty-year life.

Some important members, including three of the 'founding' members, Byzantium, Chios, and Rhodes, chose not to remain in the league, defecting in the 360s and then fighting a war with Athens in the 350s. There is no good evidence that the Athenians violated or even threatened league members' freedom and autonomy before these defections. More likely, deteriorating Athenian relations with Artaxerxes II rather than with league members lay behind the defections in the 360s.

The Athenians broke with Artaxerxes in 367 over his support for pro-Theban peace proposals for the Greek mainland and, perhaps to demonstrate their potential for trouble-making (at a time when Ariobarzanes, satrap of Hellespontine Phrygia, was in revolt) in order to prompt Artaxerxes' return to a pro-Athenian stance, the Athenians sent a fleet under Timotheus (son of Conon) into Eastern Greek waters in mid-366. Timotheus besieged then captured Samos and in summer 365 took Sestos and Crithote in the Chersonesus. The Athenians quickly sent cleruchs to Samos, signalling plans for permanent control. There was evident expectation of further Athenian action. Mausolus, for example, garrisoned coastal sites in his satrapy which faced Samos. Retaliation by Artaxerxes might be anticipated, especially since Athenian actions seem to have hampered efforts to suppress the rebel satrap Ariobarzanes. Timotheus' attack on Samos had evidently prompted Mausolus to bring his fleet back to Caria in 366, halting the attack he had been mounting together with Autophradates on Ariobarzanes.

In the eyes of Eastern Greeks, the likelihood of Persian retaliation against Athens grew in 364 when Thebes, at the moment the Persian king's most favored Greek state, launched a newly constructed 100-ship fleet, built largely with Persian funds. With these Theban ships and those of Mausolus, there was a sufficiently large naval force to challenge Athens without any additional, time-consuming preparations; Persian retaliation would undoubtedly aim at blocking grain shipments out of the Black Sea. This in turn would likely mean conflict in the Propontis/Hellespontine region and possibly also attacks on important cities allied to Athens. Neither prospect would have been tolerable for such prosperous commercial states as Rhodes, Chios, and Byzantium, and the report that the Thebans made these places their own points to Rhodian, Chian, and Byzantine alliances with Thebes during 364, made most probably to avoid damaging entanglement in any Athenian–Persian conflict (Diod. 15.79.1).

Nothing came of these alliances. The satraps' revolt precluded any Persian operations against Athens, and the Theban fleet never sailed again into Eastern Greek waters. There is no evidence that defecting allies resumed active membership in the league after 364. Regular Byzantine harassment of Athenian shipping in the Propontis in the late 360s certainly suggests a continued break between at least Byzantium and Athens. Additionally, Isocrates' references (8.125; cf. 8.36) to Athenian orators urging the Athenians not to allow on the seas those unwilling to pay their 'contributions' (the term for the levies made in connection with league operations) to the Athenians indicates allied disaffection on the part of more than one state, possibly dating to the 360s.

Statements such as these undoubtedly lay behind the Chian, Byzantine, and Rhodian belief (reported by Dem. 15.3) that the Athenians were plotting against them in the early 350s. Mausolus – no friend of the Athenians after their seizure of Samos – now stepped forward (most probably in 358/7) as protector of Eastern Greeks against any Athenian intervention, entering into a defensive alliance with Byzantium, Chios and Rhodes as well as Cos (not a member of the Athenian league but a state whose new great harbor might make it an attractive target for Athens in the event of any naval war in the Eastern Greek world) and providing a garrison for Rhodes. This set the stage for real conflict since the Athenians, still facing Theban hostility and confronting also now Macedonian threats to Athenian holdings in the north Aegean, had a special incentive to appear strong and quick to act against any 'raids' on their alliances. In 356 when the Athenians finally acted and initiated the Social War (357/6–355/4) with an attack on Chios, Mausolus and his Eastern Greek allies were ready. They repelled Athens' initial assault on Chios, then ravaged Athenian holdings on Samos, Imbros, and Lemnos, and later in the year met and defeated a reinforced Athenian fleet off Chios. Athenian mercenaries under the Athenian commander Chares now took service with the rebel satrap Artabazus, but Artaxerxes III's demand that Chares be recalled and rumors that the Persian king had promised ships to aid Athens' opponents scared the Athenians off and in 354 they made peace with their former allies, evidently affirming their freedom and autonomy.

Social War defectors included not only the original rebels, Byzantium, Chios and Rhodes, but also Perinthus and Sclymbria in the Propontis.[8] The loss of so many allies located along the Black Sea–Hellespont grain route made the Athenians more determined than ever to secure their vital interests in the Eastern Greek world. In 353 they retook Sestos (which had slipped from their control in 360 and into the hands of the Thracian king Cotys), massacring all males, selling women and children into slavery, and repopulating the city with Athenian cleruchs. In 352, soon after the death of Mausolus, the Athenians settled additional Athenian cleruchs on Samos and removed all remaining Samians. By virtual annexation, Athens thus secured the most important coastal site – Sestos – in the Chersonesus and tightened its grip on the eastern terminus of the all-weather Aegean crossing – Samos. Additional settlers sent to the Chersonesus bolstered Athens' hold on Sestos. Ironically, Athenian failure in the Social War led to a much greater Athenian presence in the Eastern Greek world.

Though formally freed from alliance with Athens by the peace concluding the Social War, defecting cities did not rely on themselves to secure their continued autonomy. In the Propontis, Byzantium and Perinthus allied with the Macedonian king Philip in 352. To the south, Rhodes remained attached to Mausolus even after the Social War and then to his successors. The garrison Mausolus originally installed in Rhodes may have served after the Social War to back local oligarchs in their overthrow of governing democrats. Chios too had a Hecatomnid garrison, at least by the early 340s (possibly installed in response to Athens' reinforced presence on Samos). Since Mausolus and his successors (his wife Artemisia and then his brother Idrieus) – the Hecatomnids – controlled various other islands, including Cos, close by the Carian coast, there was a sort of Hecatomnid protectorate stretching from Chios down to Rhodes.

None of these developments constituted a renunciation of the fundamental terms of the King's Peace. Greek cities in Asia remained the King's. Eastern Greek cities outside Anatolia remained autonomous. Sestos and Samos were of course exceptions. But since the principle of autonomy represented essentially a safeguard against revived imperialism and since Athens, while having virtually absorbed Sestos and Samos, was not seen as embarking on any new imperial ventures in the Eastern Greek world but only acting to secure its vital Black Sea grain supply, these transgressions of the principle of autonomy were tolerable violations.

Ultimately, however, Philip of Macedon brought the era of the King's Peace to an end. Having moved relentlessly eastward in Thrace since the early 350s, Philip confronted the possibility in the late 340s that Athens and the Persian king might combine efforts to push him out of the region. Artaxerxes III's restoration of direct imperial control in northwestern Anatolia (which involved the capture and interrogation under torture of Hermias of Atarneus) seemed to provide good evidence of Artaxerxes' belief in the great significance of this region and this could only indicate concern about Philip's plans. Artaxerxes, having at last reconquered Egypt, could finally turn his attention to other problems. He might now conceivably join with Athens, whose cleruchs in the Chersonesus had been persistently harassing Philip through attacks on Macedonian-held Cardia, and move against Philip in eastern Thrace. Philip evidently decided to strike first and secure his Thracian holdings by taking direct control of strong sites on the Thracian coast. Evidently claiming treaty violations, Philip attacked his erstwhile ally Perinthus in 340. Following Artaxerxes III's orders, Persian officials in Anatolia kept Perinthus supplied – undoubtedly confirming Philip's suspicions about Artaxerxes' anti-Macedonian plans in the process. Failing at Perinthus, Philip then turned in late 340 against Byzantium (which had also supplied Perinthus). Here he found ships from Byzantium's Social War allies, Rhodes, Chios, and Cos, as well as Athens, ready to assist Byzantium, and in early 339 he abandoned the campaign and withdrew.

Philip was not to be thwarted long. Turning now to the Greek mainland, he took control of mainland Greek cities after his battlefield victory at Chaeronea in 338/7 to ensure against any further Greek–Persian collusion. In the post-Chaeronea settlement, Philip left Athens the 'Athenian' Eastern Greek possessions of Imbros, Lemnos, and Samos, but dissolved the Second Athenian League. Philip himself sponsored formation of a more comprehensive alliance system, the League of Corinth. Members subscribed to the principle of autonomy in Greek interstate relations, swearing not to overthrow existing constitutions and agreeing to make war on transgressors in accordance with league council resolutions under the leadership of the *hegemon* – Philip. The league gave Philip the means to organize the Greek world for military purposes under his leadership. When he announced in 337 that he planned to campaign against Persia on behalf of the Greeks, he announced in effect the end of the era of the King's Peace.[9]

MACEDONIAN CONQUEST, 336–323

With the declaration of war against Persia by Philip and the League of Corinth, the Eastern Greek world again became a middle zone between two hostile powers, and for the next five years repeated land and naval campaigns by both Macedonian and Persian forces spread hostilities over the entire Eastern Greek world.

Initially it seemed that the war, at least insofar as it touched the Eastern Greeks, would be short-lived. With Artaxerxes III gone now (a victim of assassination in 338), the youthful Arses on the throne, the Persian court distracted by intrigue, and local satraps reluctant to raise personal armies for fear of being suspected of treasonous plans, there was little prospect of effective Persian opposition to Macedonian movements in Anatolia. Philip made liberation of the Asian Greek cities – all Persian possessions for the last half-century – his first objective, but viewed this only as a preliminary undertaking, sending his general Parmenion with 10,000 troops in early 336 while he himself remained in Macedonia.

Asian Greeks had not invited liberation, but, undoubtedly aware of Persian paralysis, they put up no resistance, and Parmenion seems to have accomplished or nearly accomplished his task in short order during 336. Crossing into Anatolia, probably at Abydos, he left a contingent under Calas in the Troad and then proceeded southward himself. Given the absence of reports of fighting, it is most likely that Parmenion received spontaneous submissions, like that reported at Ephesus (which occurred here, as perhaps elsewhere, with overturning of the local oligarchy in favor of democracy). Under Parmenion, the Macedonian program of liberating Asian Greek cities extended down the Anatolian coast at least to Ephesus. Beyond this lay Caria and the Greek cities of that satrapy, but given the pro-Macedonian stance of the Carian satrap Pixodarus these may not have been included in liberation plans.

Just what Philip planned regarding the status of Asian Greek cities is unknown. He made no pronouncements, and he died in 336 while Parmenion's campaign was still underway. Not long after this, in late 336 and early 335, the situation in Anatolia changed. Darius III, newly elevated as Persian king and firmly in control at court, made preparations for confronting the Macedonian threat. Dispatching 5,000 troops to Memnon (brother of the Rhodian mercenary commander Mentor who had overseen restoration of Persian authority in northwestern Anatolia in the late 340s and who had since died), Darius ordered him into action. Memnon displayed great initiative, pushing as far south as Magnesia by Sipylus where he battled Parmenion, then moving up to the Troad to ravage the territory of pro-Macedonian Cyzicus. Asian Greeks now had second thoughts about Macedonian prospects. Grynium and Pitane refused liberation, and while Grynium fell to Parmenion, Pitane eluded capture when Memnon's arrival forced Parmenion to abandon his siege of the city. Deployment of an additional Persian force in the Troad pushed Macedonian troops in this region back to Rhoetium on the Hellespontine coast. Parmenion, who had kept up operations after Philip's death, chose now not to fight further and withdrew to Macedonia. Despite the continued Macedonian bridgehead at Rhoetium, many Eastern Greeks evidently viewed Persian enterprise along with Philip's death as heralding the end of Macedonian expansion. In numerous cities – Chios, Mytilene, Eresus, and Ephesus – oligarchic counter-revolutions toppled recently installed pro-Macedonian democracies, turning many citizens into exiles.

When Philip's son and successor Alexander III, following up on Philip's Persian war plans, crossed into Anatolia in early 334, he found a much different situation than Parmenion had encountered in 336. Persian forces, including many Greek mercenaries, were arrayed in substantial numbers in Hellespontine Phrygia; various important Asian Greek cities such as Ephesus now had garrisons. There were, consequently, no significant spontaneous submissions except in the immediate vicinity of the Macedonian army's landing. Alexander paid little attention to Asian Greeks initially, advancing first to meet Persian defenders at the Granicus River and then after victory there moving southward to Sardis. Until Alexander reached Ephesus, he bypassed Greek cities entirely. Exiled Ephesian democrats may have appealed for Alexander's intervention (Asian Greeks had reportedly urged Alexander at Corinth in 336 to continue Philip's Persian campaign[10] – they may have been pro-Macedonian democrats fearful of oligarchic restorations which did in fact occur), but Alexander's own strategic concerns would have brought him here in any case. Ephesus had repeatedly served as a base for Spartan operations in Anatolia in the 390s and 380s, and Alexander could not afford, now that the arrival of the Persian fleet was anticipated, to leave the city in Persian hands.

At Ephesus, Alexander restored the local democrats exiled after the oligarchic takeover in 335, but intervened to stop their vendetta against oligarchic opponents. Alexander's message seems to have been that he would displace pro-Persian oligarchs and support Asian Greek democrats but would not permit ruthless anti-oligarchic strife and bloodshed. His treatment of Ephesus reportedly won Alexander great popularity among Asian Greeks and probably inspired the first spontaneous submissions by Asian Greek cities – Tralles and Magnesia on the Maeander – whose envoys surrendered their cities to Alexander at Ephesus (see also below pp. 194–7).

Seeing the response to his actions at Ephesus, Alexander evidently recognized the elements of a policy which could secure his control of Asian Greek cities and permit him, in accord with his and Philip's panhellenic propaganda, to appear as a liberator. Soon after receiving Tralles' and Magnesia's spontaneous submissions, Alexander sent a Macedonian commander, Alcimachus, with 5,000 infantry and 200 cavalry to the Aeolic and Ionian towns still subject to Persia with orders to disband existing oligarchies, establish democracies, restore their laws (in other words, proclaim their autonomy), and cancel the tribute normally paid to the Persians.

Henceforth, this was Alexander's fundamental policy toward Asian Greeks. As Alcimachus moved northward to 'liberate' Ionian and Aeolic Greek cities north of Ephesus, Alexander advanced southward with the main army. He had to lay siege to Miletus – the first time he attacked a Greek city in Anatolia – where a Persian-installed garrison, anticipating the arrival of the Persian fleet, was determined not to surrender. Alexander's fleet held off the Persian ships, and Alexander took the city. Then, despite Milesian participation in the stand against Alexander, Alexander gave surviving Milesians freedom (meaning autonomy). As he moved south, now into Caria toward Halicarnassus where Persian forces – survivors of the Granicus River battle and other troops – were preparing to meet him again, Alexander declared Greek cities between Miletus and Halicarnassus autonomous and exempt from tribute. Following a lengthy siege of Halicarnassus in which Alexander took the outer city but declined to contest for the inner citadel, he turned eastward, advancing through southern Caria and into Lycia, leaving the Eastern Greek world behind forever.

By late 334, most but not all Eastern Greek cities were free and autonomous. Outside Anatolia, such Eastern Greek states as Mytilene, Tenedos, and Chios are known to have been members of the League of Corinth. They and perhaps many other Eastern Greek states outside Anatolia may have joined as early as the time of the league's formation in 337 or perhaps at the time of Parmenion's campaign or possibly only in 334 when Alexander launched his campaign.[11] Membership meant continued recognition of the autonomous status accorded them by the King's Peace, but it also meant continued involvement in an alliance system – the League of Corinth now rather than the Second Athenian League – with a *synedrion* and an official *hegemon* (Alexander). For Asian Greeks, autonomy derived from Alexander's proclamation, and no alliance system or common peace provided a mutual bond. To judge by his provisions for Priene, Alexander himself made detailed determinations about boundaries, citizenship matters, and tax liabilities. He also evidently levied or reserved the right to levy 'contributions' and presumably set the level himself.[12] A few Eastern Greek island states were in Persian hands at the end of 334, most notably Cos and Rhodes, but Alexander's policy regarding the status of Eastern Greeks – freedom and autonomy on the basis of league membership or royal decree – served to establish him as the patron and defender of Greek interests.

Alexander's policy proved successful as a means of joining at least Asian Greeks to him. Many Eastern Greek cities outside Anatolia, however, soon had little choice but to shift to Persian allegiance. Memnon had overseen the defense of Halicarnassus, withdrawing with the bulk of surviving defenders and the Persian fleet when the Macedonians finally broke through the outer city wall. After wintering in Cos and receiving from Darius full military authority in the Aegean, Memnon initiated a Persian counter-offensive in the Eastern Greek world which continued even after Memnon's sudden death in summer 333 and resulted in Persian seizure of Chios, the cities of Lesbos, Tenedos, and cities on the Hellespontine coast. Persian proposals made at Mytilene and Tenedos – that the terms of the King's Peace should prevail (that is, Asian Greek cities belong to the King and all others be autonomous) – and the destruction there of the inscriptions recording League of Corinth membership, represent an attempt to turn the clock back and re-establish the Persian king as the protector of autonomy outside Anatolia. With the Persian fleet operating without opposition (Alexander had dismissed the Macedonian – largely Greek – fleet after taking Miletus in 334) during spring and summer of 333, resistance on the part of Eastern Greek cities outside Anatolia was futile. Not surprisingly, however, Asian Greeks made no move to break with Alexander during 333.

In the long run there proved to be too few troops available to Persian commanders in the Aegean to garrison adequately the various Eastern Greek cities they recaptured. A reconstituted Macedonian fleet began operations in September 333 and secured the vital Black

Sea grain route, chasing Persian ships out of the Hellespont and retaking Tenedos. The Persians managed to hold on to such vital bases as Lesbos, Chios, Cos, and Halicarnassus over winter 333/2, but, as Alexander had anticipated, once the Macedonian army seized Phoenicia and controlled the eastern Mediterranean in early 332, so many Phoenician, Cypriot, and Cilician ships defected from the Persian fleet that remaining Persian forces in the Eastern Greek world were helpless to resist the wide-ranging Macedonian offensive. One after another, Lesbos, Chios, and Cos all came under Macedonian control. At the same time, Macedonian officials in Anatolia pushed all remaining Persian troops out of Anatolia, liberating Miletus and Halicarnassus once and for all.

For Eastern Greeks outside Anatolia, the final Macedonian victory meant restoration of guarantees of autonomy. (Rhodes, which had furnished ships for the Persian fleet right through 332 and thus appeared particularly anti-Macedonian, received a garrison now.) For Asian Greeks, the final Macedonian victory meant the end of any threat of Persian domination. But it also meant the end of any strategic significance in Alexander's generous policy of autonomy, democracy, and freedom from tribute for Asian Greek cities, and Asian Greeks must have been apprehensive of possible change in their status.

Early in 331, while Alexander was in Egypt, Miletus and Erythrae sent envoys to him (at Memphis) to report wonderful oracular statements concerning Alexander's descent (from Zeus) and his coming achievements. These missions may be seen as attempts to assert a basis for a special relationship with Alexander, perhaps as a hedge against any change in the policy announced in 334. Erythrae itself, and the Ionian Greek cities acting together as the Ionian League, evidently accorded Alexander divine honors later in his reign, most likely in an effort to sustain a relationship with an ever more distant benefactor.

Alexander was in fact not especially concerned with Eastern Greeks after 332, though, recognizing the propaganda value of their liberation, following the battle of Gaugamela in 331 he announced generally to the Greek world the end of the Persian Empire in terms of autonomy: 'all the tyrannies have been put down and the Greeks are living as autonomous citizens' (Plut. *Alex.* 34.2). Given the long-standing fourth-century distinction between Greeks who belonged to the Persian king – Asian Greeks – and other Greeks in terms of autonomous status (accorded explicitly to Greeks outside Asia), this was a natural way to announce that Greeks everywhere were free of Persian control, but it suggests that for Alexander the fundamental meaning of 'autonomy' may have been only 'non-Persian.' Alexander's establishment of Macedonian mints in numerous Asian Greek cities between about 330 and 324 – Magnesia on the Maeander, Lampsacus, Colophon, Miletus, Abydos, and Teos – indicates that, grants of autonomy notwithstanding, Alexander viewed Asian Greek cities as part of his realm. Alexander's issuance of the Exiles' Decree in 324, commanding restoration everywhere of political exiles, offers further evidence of the autocratic interpretation of autonomy emerging from Alexander's practices.

In fourth-century terms, Alexander's policies regarding Asian Greek cities seem to be pointing to something new. Heretofore, autonomy had been a status denoting separation from empire. Witness, for example, the King's Peace: Asian Greeks belong to the King, all others are autonomous. Or the League of Corinth: Greeks, autonomous by virtue of their membership in this league, are linked to Philip (and then to Alexander) officially only by formal alliance. What seems to have been emerging from Alexander's dealings with Asian Greeks is the idea that Asian Greeks belong to the King (Alexander) but are at the same time autonomous. They are, in other words, autonomous subjects.

While Asian Greek cities no longer paid tribute, they were, unless specifically exempted, obligated to make 'contributions' (*syntaxeis*), and Philoxenus, the Macedonian official who, residing at Sardis, oversaw the collection of tribute in Anatolia after his appointment by Alexander in 331, may have been responsible for gathering Asian Greek 'contributions' as well as tribute payments from non-Greeks in Anatolia.[13] Alexander undoubtedly ceased requesting such 'contributions' soon after his final victory over Darius III and his confiscation of virtually the entire Persian treasury. Philoxenus, however, evidently retained a supervisory role in connection with Asian Greek affairs, demanding, for example, that Ephesus hand over three citizens responsible for murdering a certain Hegesias (whom Polyaenus *Strat.* 6.49 calls 'tyrant of Ephesus') and then attacking the city and carrying the men off to prison at Sardis after the Ephesians refused to surrender them. An episode such as this served to underscore the meaning of autonomy as it applied to Asian Greeks: they were autonomous, but remained subjects who exercised freedom and autonomy at the pleasure of a sovereign who could intervene in local political affairs whenever and however he chose.

THE AGE OF ANTIGONUS, 323–301

Eastern Greeks saw no real change in their status or circumstances in the immediate aftermath of Alexander's sudden death in 323. Alexander's vast empire remained intact under the joint kingship of his older brother Arrhidaeus and his (posthumously born) son Alexander IV, and Macedonian satraps continued as governors of large administrative subdivisions of the empire; Asian Greeks remained autonomous and effectively outside the realms of nearby satraps. Although the League of Corinth which various Eastern Greek states had joined came to an end after the Lamian War, Eastern Greeks outside Anatolia remained aloof from the war and thus escaped the constitutional changes and imposition of garrisons which occurred on the mainland. In other words, they, like Asian Greeks, remained effectively autonomous.

But after 322, as the protracted struggle for precedence and territory among leading Macedonian commanders began, Eastern Greeks found themselves once again in the middle of conflict. Within a decade they all (except for the Thracian Greeks) came under the control of Antigonus Monophthalmus. This long-time satrap of Greater Phrygia, *strategos* of Asia after Perdiccas' death in 321, and commander of the largest field army of the day, aspired to be the undisputed arbiter of affairs after Antipater's death in 319. In pursuit of this goal, Antigonus planned (evidently none too secretly) to replace officials throughout Asia with his own chosen friends and supporters. Favoring Antigonus' major opponent Polyperchon and fearing replacement, satraps in western Anatolia – Cleitus in Hellespontine Phrygia and Arrhidaeus in Lydia – now installed garrisons in the most important Asian Greek cities. Antigonus, head-quartered with his huge army at Celenae in Phrygia, was able to dispatch forces into Hellespontine Phrygia and Lydia at the same time. As one army chased Arrhidaeus out of Hellespontine Phrygia, thereby liberating the Greek cities of this region, Antigonus himself campaigned in Lydia to secure the cities recently garrisoned by Cleitus, taking Ephesus, besieging Cyme, and winning over the rest by force or persuasion. In the next year (318), Antigonus secured control of the Hellespont and got maritime supremacy after defeating Polyperchon's fleet. Campaigns farther eastward interrupted additional activities in the Eastern Greek world until 313, when Antigonus dispatched a fleet into the Aegean and secured the allegiance of Eastern Greek and various other island states. Finally, in

313–312, a systematic, multi-pronged campaign in Caria placed this whole region with its Greek coastal cities under him.

The Eastern Greek world had ceased to be of great strategic interest to Alexander after 332 – Eastern Greeks were simply no longer on the fringe between Greek and Persian-controlled worlds – and the propaganda value of Alexander's liberation of Asian Greek cities from 'tyranny' and the bestowal of autonomous status on them ceased to be an important consideration with the end of the Panhellenic phase of Alexander's campaign. For Antigonus, however, the Eastern Greek world remained vitally important throughout his career. Antigonus' great power and ambition prompted other leading figures – Polyperchon and then Cassander (in Macedon), Lysimachus (in Thrace), Ptolemy (in Egypt), and Seleucus (in Babylon) – to combine against him. Facing the realms of Cassander and Lysimachus, the Eastern Greek world under Antigonus was thus again a fringe world and control of it thus strategically critical.

Antigonus adopted from the first a policy of supporting Greek freedom and autonomy as a means of garnering Greek support. In 319 he excoriated Arrhidaeus, satrap of Hellespontine Phrygia, who had attempted to force a garrison on Cyzicus for having besieged a Greek city which was an 'ally' and had done nothing wrong – denying, in other words, that a satrap had the right arbitrarily to intervene in the affairs of an autonomous Greek city. In 314, just as he was facing the combined opposition of all the major Macedonian commanders (Ptolemy, Lysimachus, Cassander, and Seleucus), Antigonus announced support for Greek autonomy as his official policy, proclaiming from Tyre that all Greeks were to be free, without garrisons, and autonomous. Since Eastern Greeks were under Antigonus in greatest numbers, they were the primary beneficiaries of his ostensibly panhellenic proclamation. In 311, when Antigonus concluded a brief peace with Ptolemy, Cassander, and Lysimachus, he insisted that the terms include common agreement 'that the Greeks be autonomous.'

In the aftermath of this peace, Antigonus went beyond the mere proclamation of the autonomous status of Greek cities and instituted a more elaborate procedure that made the grant of autonomous status a means of incorporating 'autonomous' cities into a kingdom or empire so that the possession of autonomy became in fact a sign of belonging to a sovereign. Once Antigonus had come to terms with his various Macedonian opponents, he circulated a letter to Greek cities in which he recounted the genesis of the peace (of 311), emphasizing his role as advocate of Greek freedom. Antigonus dispatched at the same time representatives with copies of the treaty and an oath which, according to the treaty, Greek cities were to sign 'swearing to aid each other in preserving their freedom and autonomy,' a provision for which Antigonus claimed responsibility. Antigonus portrayed himself as the sole protector of Greek interests, bound and determined to protect Greek freedom and autonomy as long as he lived. His assertion that the oaths would serve to protect Greek interests after his death underscored his depiction of himself as the sole true defender of Greek autonomy. He averred finally that he would of course continue to do whatever he could for the benefit of Greek cities (Harding 132).

Although according to Antigonus' description of this agreement, all Greeks were to join in the oath and aid each other in preserving their freedom, it is likely that Antigonus' envoys visited only those cities within his sphere of influence – that is, those Eastern Greek cities which Antigonus had already 'liberated.' Evidence of Eastern Greek response survives only in the form of an inscription from Scepsis, a small city in the Troad, but it may well be typical. At Scepsis the citizens formally recognized Antigonus' responsibility for great benefits to the city – the peace and autonomy it will henceforth enjoy. As a mark of their gratitude, they voted to accord Antigonus divine honors – creation of a sacred precinct for him, furnished with an altar and a cult statue – and to award him a gold crown weighing 100 staters (his two sons were to get crowns of lesser value). Finally, the citizens of Scepsis all swore to the oath which Antigonus sent as (they said) they were instructed, and they voted to erect a stele recording the 311 agreement, the letter from Antigonus, and the oath which he sent.[14]

Antigonus, as a contemporary of Alexander's father Philip and as a satrap (of Phrygia) resident in Anatolia from 334 onward, was a long-time observer of mainland and Eastern Greek politics, and it was certainly no coincidence that his dealings with Eastern Greek cities contained elements of many of the different fourth-century arrangements regarding the status and security of Greek cities. In a manner reminiscent of the King's Peace, a peace agreement served as the occasion for asserting the principle of the autonomy of Greek cities. To safeguard the status thus enjoyed by Greek cities, Antigonus created an alliance system (theoretically, by the terms of the peace, to include 'all Greeks,' but in practice limited to those within Antigonus' territory) reminiscent of the Second Athenian League or the League of Corinth, but lacking any real institutional structure

– there was no *synedrion* and no provision for decision-making by league members.

Antigonus' selective borrowings provided him with a protocol for incorporating 'free and autonomous' (Eastern) Greek cities in his realm, justifying making demands on them, and making their association with him appear voluntary and self-serving. The great *strategos* (use of the royal title began only in 306) recognizes and compels general recognition of the autonomy of Greek cities; he then sends envoys to each city announcing this determination and Antigonus' responsibility for it; individual cities in turn recognize him as the indispensable benefactor from whom their possession of autonomy derives, and they swear oaths to participate in protecting mutual freedom and autonomy. Since autonomy depends in the first instance on Antigonus as benefactor, such oaths imply agreement to act to protect the benefactor – Antigonus – and not to harm him by, for example, supporting his opponents.

Because, henceforth, Antigonus could construe any of his actions as a reflection of his concern for Greek freedom and autonomy, by sponsoring the freedom and autonomy of Greek cities he actually acquired full freedom to do as he pleased with them. Eastern Greeks, in accepting their freedom and autonomy under these circumstances, effectively surrendered them at the same time. It was nevertheless a mutually beneficial arrangement. There was for Eastern Greek cities little question of standing up against Antigonus: better then to accept incorporation in his realm on terms which seemed to belie subordinate status and enshrined instead the ancient ideals of the Greek city. For Antigonus, the arrangement provided him with a useful philhellenic identity and prepared the way for the campaign for the conquest of Greece he would initiate in 307, sending his son Demetrius to the Greek mainland 'to free all the cities in Greece' (Diod. 20.45.1–2).

Eastern Greek dealings with Antigonus over the next decade (311–301) reveal that Antigonus in fact intervened at will in cities' affairs. He altered boundaries, moved whole populations, even eradicated communities, joining together eight communities in the Troad (including Scepsis) to form a new city, Antigoneia Troas, refounding the city of Smyrna, combining the territories of Colophon and Notium, and initiating the synoecism of Teos and Lebedos.[15] Recognizing his effectively sovereign role, various Eastern Greek cities sent envoys, made appeals, and communicated by letter with Antigonus. Where matters were of no great strategic interest to him, he might abandon a policy in the face of opposition, giving apparent evidence of respect for autonomy. Eresus, on the island of Lesbos, for example, got Antigonus to rescind his support for the reinstatement of the sons of certain exiles and allow the Eresians to judge the matter entirely on their own. At the other extreme, Eastern Greek states could see the risks of obstructing Antigonus' wishes in matters of great importance to him: when Rhodes refused to supply Antigonus with ships for a campaign against Ptolemy, it found itself besieged for over a year by Demetrius (305/304). Antigonus, however, never commanded or decreed. Communication used the language of diplomacy, not empire, and Antigonus unfailingly couched his intervention in the language of solicitude. Eastern Greek cities responded with divine honors, cults of Antigonus (and Demetrius), and, of course, compliance with his wishes.

For Eastern Greeks, the Antigonid age lasted until 301. Antigonid successes on the Greek mainland in 304–302, including reformation of the League of Corinth, prompted fears of an Antigonid invasion of Macedonia and roused the anti-Antigonid coalition to renewed action. Lysimachus, previously preoccupied with the pacification of Thrace, including Thracian Greek towns, crossed the Hellespont into Anatolia in 302, and over-ran cities from Lampsacus all the way down to Ephesus, installing garrisons in those that resisted and ravaging the lands of those where reinforcements prevented capture. Sailing back hastily from Greece, Antigonus' son Demetrius recovered various cities as he advanced from Ephesus north to the Black Sea. This heralded for Eastern Greeks the onset of a new era of shifting hegemonies. Once Antigonus had died in the battle of Ipsus in 301, no new individual potentate established comprehensive authority over the Eastern Greek world or even over the world of Asian Greeks. Thus no further comprehensive pronouncements comparable to those of Artaxerxes II, Alexander, or Antigonus determined the status of Eastern Greek cities.

By the end of the fourth century BC, however, Eastern Greek cities could anticipate enduring recognition of their 'freedom and autonomy,' at least so long as they remained submissive to whatever power of the moment – Lysimachus, one or another of the Ptolemies or Seleucids or later Antigonids – succeeded in asserting himself in this or that portion of the Eastern Greek world. Ironically, by grounding the relationship between city and monarch (between beneficiary and benefactor), 'autonomy' provided the means by which kingdom or empire could absorb city-state.

NOTES

1 'Eastern Greeks' is used here in the broadest sense to designate Greeks of cities of eastern Aegean islands, the Anatolian mainland, the Chersonesus, and the Propontis. 'Asian Greeks' refers generally to Greeks of Anatolia (= Asia), comprising from north to south along the western Anatolian coast, Aeolic, Ionian, and Dorian Greeks.

2 See D. M. Lewis, *Sparta and Persia*, Leiden, Brill, 1977, pp. 121–2.

3 Xen. *Hell.* 3.4.2 with C. D. Hamilton, *Sparta's Bitter Victories*, Ithaca, Cornell University Press, 1979, pp. 126–9.

4 Diod. 14.84.4; Paus. 6.3.16; Tod 106.

5 On the Persian king's concern with Egyptian problems as the background to the decision to end hostilities with Sparta, see S. Ruzicka, 'Clazomenae and Persian Foreign Policy, 387/6 B.C.,' *Phoenix* 37 (1983), 104–8. Isoc. 4140–1 attests a Persian attack on Egypt in the 380s, but does not provide a clear chronology. Whether the attack occurred in the early 380s or the late 380s remains disputed.

6 The permanent establishment of a satrapy of Caria separate from Lydia probably occurred *c*. 392: S. Hornblower, *Mausolus*, Oxford, Clarendon Press, 1982, pp. 37–8. At that time a native Carian dynast, Hecatomnus, became satrap and he and his offspring, known collectively as the Hecatomnids, governed Caria through the 330s. On the activities of Mausolus, the son and immediate successor of Hecatomnus, see Hornblower, *Mausolus*, pp. 81–90.

7 Diod. 15.90.1–92.1 recounts events of what is often called 'the Great Satraps' Revolt.' He gives the impression that this revolt, coinciding with the Egyptian king's plans for an offensive campaign, nearly crippled the Persian Empire. Recent scholarship, however, depicts it as a matter of satrapal conflicts and rivalries and not as a momentous insurgence against the king: M. Weiskopf, *The So-called 'Great Satraps' Revolt,' 366–360 BC*, Historia Einzelschriften, 64. Stuttgart, Franz Steiner Verlag, 1989; S. Ruzicka, *Politics of a Persian Dynasty*, Norman, University of Oklahoma Press, pp. 56–68, 76–82.

8 Cargill, p. 180.

9 Philip's and his allies' declaration of war on Persia, 'with the avowed intention of avenging the sacrilege of Xerxes and liberating the Greek cities of Asia Minor,' may have been 'an explicit renewal of the aims of the Delian League' (thus A. B. Bosworth, *Conquest and Empire. The Reign of Alexander the Great*, Cambridge, Cambridge University Press, 1988, p. 18), but it should be noted that Greeks themselves had long since lost interest in any such liberation enterprise. There is no evidence that Asian Greeks chafed under King's Peace arrangements and appealed for liberation as they had at the time of the formation of the Delian League.

10 Delius, a former student of Plato, represented the Asian Greeks: Plut. *Mor.* 1126D.

11 A. J. Heisserer, *Alexander and the Greeks. The Epigraphic Evidence*, Norman, University of Oklahoma Press, 1980, pp. 58–9, 77–8, 83–96, 131–9, discusses possible circumstances surrounding incorporation of various island states into the League of Corinth.

12 Cf. Bosworth, *Conquest and Empire*, pp. 253–4.
13 On the possible functions of this figure, see E. Badian, 'Alexander the Great and the Greeks of Asia,' in *Ancient Society and Institutions: Studies Presented to Victor Ehrenberg*, Oxford, Blackwell, 1966, pp. 56–60; A. B. Bosworth, *A Historical Commentary on Arrian's History of Alexander*, Oxford, Clarendon Press, 1980, pp. 280–2.
14 M. M. Austin, *The Hellenistic World From Alexander to the Roman Conquest*, Cambridge, Cambridge, Cambridge University Press, 1981, no. 32.
15 Strab. 13. 593, 597, 604; 14, 646; C. B. Welles, *Royal Correspondence in the Hellenistic Period*, New Haven, Yale University Press, 1934, 3, 4; R. A. Billows, *Antigonos the One-Eyed and the Creation of the Hellenistic State*, Berkeley, University of California Press, 1990, p. 295.

6

THE GREEKS IN SICILY AND SOUTH ITALY

Richard J. A. Talbert

The mixed fortunes of these Western Greeks[1] during the fourth century receive little more than a glance in many history courses today. That is a pity, for however baffling the personalities and events may seem to us, there is no doubting the strong impression which they left upon contemporaries in mainland Greece. To make best sense, our 'century' must be stretched at either end, to run from the Syracusans' defeat of their Athenian besiegers in 413 to the death of King Agathocles in 289.

INTRODUCTION AND SOURCES

The sense of bafflement stems, predictably, from the nature and limitations of the surviving source material. We are forced to rely heavily on a single historian, Diodorus. This in itself need not be cause for disappointment, since he was in fact a Sicilian Greek, from Agyrium west of Mount Etna, who displayed a special interest in the affairs of the island in general and of his own city in particular. He lived, however, three centuries after the one which concerns us, and the sheer comprehensiveness of his purpose – to produce a universal history in forty books – inevitably meant that for the most part he confined himself to excerpting from earlier accounts.

Yet this in turn is not all bad either. In recent years there has been considerable modification of the nineteenth century views that Diodorus' impact upon the character and purpose of his history was minimal, or that he was incapable of exploiting more than just a single source at a time. Moreover, the fact is that, however far such revisionist assessments be pressed, Diodorus does preserve for us substantial, important slices of Western (especially Sicilian) Greek history that would otherwise be altogether lost. The actual identity

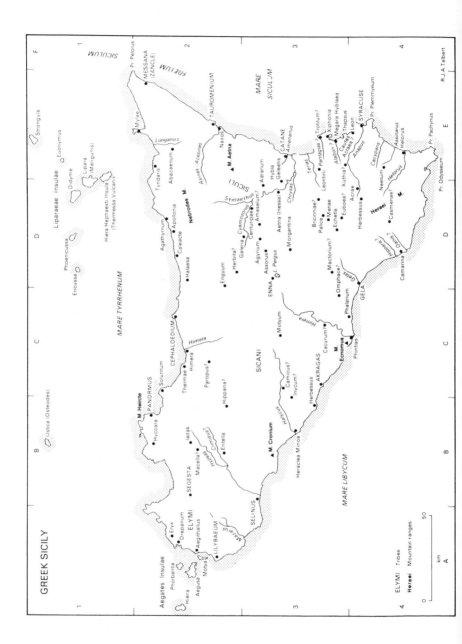

Map 4 Greek Sicily, from R. J. A. Talbert, *Atlas of Classical History*, Routledge, 1985.

of the writers preserved by him in this way still remains an enigma, though perhaps not a particularly significant one for present purposes. Much of the material relates to the two remarkable rulers of Syracuse early and late in the century, Dionysius I and Agathocles respectively. Treatment of the former must ultimately go back to the account composed by his one-time supporter and associate, Philistus. Given that apparently there never was any other extensive firsthand account of Dionysius' rule, it remains only to speculate whether Diodorus drew upon this direct (not so likely), or from one or more intermediaries (if so, who), and how much of the hostile tone is theirs rather than Philistus' own. Agathocles attracted more historians, but Diodorus' treatment in all likelihood depends most upon Timaeus of Tauromenium, who was exiled by the tyrant and thus took revenge by writing a notoriously hostile account.

Even more striking, and more damaging for our study, is the unevenness of Diodorus' coverage as it survives. His previously detailed treatment of Dionysius' campaigns and other activities all at once shrinks to just a few short remarks for the final twenty years or so of the reign, so that we remain hopelessly ill informed on the major campaigns of the late 380s and 370s. The treatment of Dionysius II, Dion and Timoleon, who are successively the dominant figures at Syracuse thereafter, is less sketchy, but still not full. He does then devote more attention to Agathocles, but once again we learn little about the last part of the reign or the handling of internal affairs because the surviving text breaks off in 302.

For Dion and Timoleon we are fortunate in being able to turn to *Lives* by Plutarch. These in their turn preserve much material from earlier accounts that would otherwise be lost. Their limitations for our purpose are that they were written more than four centuries after the events, and that each Life forms half of a pair designed to illuminate and contrast the characters of a leading Greek and a leading Roman (Dion and Timoleon are matched with Brutus and Aemilius Paulus respectively). Plutarch admires these men and sheds light on their achievements, but it is not his intention to attempt a critical assessment of them or their underlying motives such as to satisfy historians today.

In Diodorus too, the handling of causation likewise leaves much to be desired. The result is that both our main sources time and again leave us with a frustratingly weak grasp of why leading figures and communities acted as they did. In the case of Greek communities at least, archaeology, coins and a handful of inscriptions can do something to compensate for the resulting bafflement and the general lack of contemporary testimony. However, a marked determining factor of their history in the fourth century is their interaction with non-Greeks, most persistently in Italy and North Africa. The fact that nothing written from the perspective of these peoples survives (if it was ever written), and that our Greek sources typically display no more than the most cursory interest in their thinking, can make for insurmountable difficulties. It is equally awkward to convey some meaningful sense of what everyday life, rural or urban, was like for ordinary Greeks in such a turbulent period.

SICILY AT THE END OF THE FIFTH CENTURY

Greek settlement in southern Italy and Sicily dated back to the eighth century, and had gradually spread – for the most part, although not exclusively, to fertile coastal areas. By the late fifth century flourishing agriculture in general, and grain-growing in particular, had long bestowed enviable prosperity upon Greek Sicily. Here the two cities of Acragas (enriched by its exports to North Africa) and Syracuse stood out as a match for any in mainland Greece. Syracuse understandably draws most attention as the target of an immense effort to expand Athenian power and shift the focus of the Peloponnesian War. Against all odds, within two years (415–413) the Syracusans not only repulsed this assault, but also inflicted crippling losses upon the manpower and resources of their Athenian besiegers.

It is hard to evaluate the jibes made by the Athenian Alcibiades immediately prior to this Sicilian expedition about the mixed, shifting and unpatriotic populations of the cities in the island (Thuc. 6.17). What remains beyond doubt, however, and quite uncharacteristic of most sieges in classical Greece (soon ended by treachery), is the amazing unbroken unity of the Syracusan democracy throughout its lengthy ordeal. Less surprising is the ancient tradition that long bottled-up tensions erupted in political turmoil soon after 413, even if the nature of the reforms passed then at the instigation of the 'demagogue' Diocles remains obscure. An important target of the reformers was the aristocratic general Hermocrates who, after outstanding service, in 412 had been given the command of a naval squadron to assist the Peloponnesians' efforts against Athens in the Aegean. Meeting with only mixed success there, he found himself exiled in his absence in 410.

It was not for two more years that he attempted a return to Syracuse. How early he had planned it is unclear, and hardly of much significance, because all of Greek Sicily had meantime been shaken by a quite unexpected turn of events. This was invasion from Carthage at the invitation of Segesta, a hellenized community of indigenous Elymians, feuding with its neighbor Selinus in the far west of the island. There had long been Punic settlement in this region, principally at offshore Motya, Panormus and Solus, but since the Greeks' defeat of the previous Punic invasion in 480 it had evidently been modest, and no friction is recorded. So far during the Peloponnesian War various appeals to enlist the military and naval potential of Carthage had been made by Greek cities or at least talked of, even by Athens and Syracuse, but none had produced any positive response.

It remains mysterious, therefore, just why Carthage should now choose to assist Segesta against Selinus, with only modest forces in 410, but in much greater strength the following year. In part the explanation must be desire for revenge by the Punic commander Hannibal, whose grandfather Hamilcar had died fighting the Greeks at Himera in 480. Certainly in 409, after capturing and looting Selinus in a mere nine days, Hannibal moved northwards towards Himera, attracting widespread support among the indigenous Sicans and Sicels. The Greek cities of Acragas, Gela and Syracuse rushed forces to assist the defence, but Diocles as supreme commander lost his nerve. Himera too fell, with a great slaughter of its inhabitants.

Yet with this revenge exacted Hannibal merely returned home; there was seemingly no further Sicilian engagement in prospect. It is an open question, then, how far the next Punic intervention, when it came, was provoked by Hermocrates. In hopes of winning recall to Syracuse, he set himself up in the ruins of Selinus in 408/7, recruited a private army, and attacked Punic settlements and property throughout the west of the island. The Syracusans were evidently impressed. They even exiled Diocles, but still did not recall Hermocrates, and he eventually met his death trying to re-enter the city by force.

At any rate, in 406 the Carthaginians returned to the island in greater strength than ever. Their full intentions are as usual unclear, but understandably enough they made first for wealthy Acragas. Although reinforcements for its defense came from Greek communities in both Sicily and South Italy, eventually the decision was taken to evacuate the population to Gela, and the city then fell after a siege of seven or eight months.

THE RISE OF DIONYSIUS

The general panic which this catastrophe set off brings to the forefront the man who turns out to dominate the affairs of Greek Sicily, and the historical record, for almost the next forty years. Dionysius, now about twenty-five years old, was a Syracusan of uncertain background (although the extreme poverty predictably alleged against him seems hard to credit). He had joined in Hermocrates' failed attempt to re-enter the city by force, and had been wounded. Now, in an atmosphere heavy with recrimination, when no one dared speak at a meeting of the assembly, Dionysius alone was prepared to do so, and to attack the generals for the fall of Acragas. When the magistrates attempted to silence him by imposing fines, Philistus (the future historian) offered to pay enough to let him continue speaking all day.

Dionysius' taunts led to the recall of exiles (no doubt mostly fellow associates of Hermocrates), and to the election of a fresh board of generals, himself among them. However, he refused to associate with his colleagues out of distrust, and so was sent off alone with a force to reinforce the Syracusan garrison at Gela. There is no knowing, of course, what exactly he expected to gain by taking such extreme positions at a time of mounting tension, nor to what extent considerations of personal advancement already over-rode all others in his thinking.

Rather than remain at Gela Dionysius soon preferred to return to Syracuse, bringing further denunciations of his fellow generals. As a result, the assembly was prompted to dismiss the entire board and to make him general-with-full-powers (*strategos autokrator*), a traditional Syracusan recourse in crises. With that authority he at once doubled military pay, and then mobilized all men under forty for training at Leontini. While here, he staged the well-worn ploy of a failed attack on himself, which in turn justified the request for a bodyguard of 600, duly voted by the assembly. On his return to Syracuse he then made the dockyard his headquarters, behaved unashamedly as 'tyrant' (or so says Diod. 13.96.2), and married Hermocrates' daughter.

Such rapid concentration of authority need not have been all to the city's disadvantage at this stage, with the threat of a Carthaginian advance still looming. Sure enough, the Punic army proceeded from Acragas to Gela in 405. Dionysius' strategy for relieving the siege proved insufficiently decisive, so that he then ordered the evacuation of not just Gela, but also Camarina. The army's sense of outrage and betrayal at this double withdrawal led a group of cavalry to dash back to Syracuse ahead of him, wreck his house, and drive his wife to suicide. Sufficient troops remained loyal, however, for him to follow at once and re-establish his authority. An outbreak of 'plague'[2] meanwhile evidently prevented the Carthaginians from continuing their expected advance towards Syracuse, although unfortunately the passage in which Diodorus must have explained this miraculous deliverance for the city has dropped out of his surviving text and become lost. When his narrative resumes, we find the Carthaginians exacting harsh terms. Their authority in the west of the island was to be recognized; the captured cities of Selinus, Acragas, Himera, Gela, and Camarina could be resettled, but without walls, and with tribute payable to Carthage. Formal recognition was given to Dionysius' authority at Syracuse; other communities, Greek and Sicel, were to be independent.

Such Punic recognition would not necessarily secure Dionysius' position. In fact, only a short time after the Carthaginians' withdrawal there was such a strong rising against him that he seriously contemplated suicide. But with the help of Campanian mercenaries rushed in from the west of the island,[3] he re-established himself, and thereafter increasingly strengthened a personal rule that was to endure until his death in 367 and pass to his eldest son. Its nature calls for discussion, but first his extensive preoccupations outside Syracuse should be noted. Spread over thirty years and more, and by no means always informatively reported in surviving source material, these can appear bewildering in their frequency and bloodiness. Equally opaque, often, is the underlying motivation, especially when time and again stunning success seems to be canceled out by catastrophic failure.

DIONYSIUS THE COMMANDER

The beginnings at least are clear enough. Regardless of the terms imposed by Carthage in 405, Dionysius immediately wanted to bring as much of eastern Sicily as possible – both Greek communities and Sicel – under Syracusan control. Force, diplomacy and treachery all proved effective instruments. Aetna and Enna were stormed, Naxos and Catane were betrayed to him. The populations of the latter two cities were sold off into slavery; Naxos was then razed, while Catane was made into a settlement for more Campanian mercenaries.

Leontini was now left isolated, so that when Dionysius demanded that its inhabitants hand over their city and remove to Syracuse, they complied.

All this had probably occurred by 402/1. The effect was to leave Messana in the far northeast as the only Sicilian Greek city of consequence which was not yet ruined or under Dionysius' control. Naturally, alarm was felt here, as also at Rhegium across the straits. So in 400/399 a joint offensive against Syracuse was planned, but disputes forestalled its launch, and instead both cities preferred to come to terms with Dionysius. Surprisingly, he agreed, in all likelihood because he now wished to secure his rear while turning instead to a much greater objective – revenge for the Punic victories of the previous decade.

Carthage seems not to have anticipated such a bold initiative. Certainly, when Dionysius set out in full force in 397, he was able to proceed the entire length of the island: the Punic stronghold of Eryx surrendered without a blow. It was more important for him, however, to gain the offshore island fortress of Motya to the south, which he eventually did later the same year with the help of a formidable array of siege weaponry, including newly invented catapults.[4] But having thus seized so much advantage, he then proceeded to lose it all disastrously when campaigning resumed in 396. He allowed a fresh force from Carthage under Himilco to retake Motya, and to march along the north coast of the island all the way to Messana, which was captured and destroyed. Next, at a craggy site high above the coast south of there (and close to where Naxos had been), Himilco provocatively founded the new city of Tauromenium for the many Sicel supporters that he had attracted. His army and navy could not then be stopped from laying siege to Syracuse. Despite frantic appeals for help sent to mainland Greece and South Italy, both Dionysius' rule and Syracuse's very survival seemed doomed. Unlike the Athenian besiegers twenty years or so before, the Carthaginians could hardly fail – except that 'plague' fortuitously struck again, so that Dionysius was able to defeat them and dictate terms. Most of Himilco's army was enslaved, but (with whatever dark motive) Dionysius allowed all the Carthaginian citizens to make their escape home, where the disaster triggered a serious revolt in Libya.

After this second miraculous deliverance from Carthage, Dionysius resumed his efforts to strengthen Syracusan control over eastern Sicily. Mostly he was successful, although a winter assault on

Tauromenium failed (and indeed almost cost him his life). He resettled Messana, and founded a new city further along the north coast
at Tyndaris. In 393/2 Carthage took the offensive again, but the
expedition first failed to take Messana and then, despite much Sicel
support, proved no match for Dionysius. He was now able to
demand, therefore, that the Sicels (and Tauromenium) be acknowledged as coming under his authority.

With the Carthaginians thus forced to realize that the capture of
Syracuse was beyond them, and with his control of eastern Sicily
secured, Dionysius next turned to the elimination of any threat from
South Italy, in particular from the hostile city of Rhegium across
the straits, to which he laid siege in 391. He had a loyal ally in
Locri, a Dorian foundation whose support of Dorian Syracuse had
long been matched by the hostility of Ionian Rhegium. He was
driven off, however, by forces of the Italiote League, drawn from
several cities of South Italy. He therefore retaliated by allying with
the Lucanians (one of the indigenous Oscan peoples who, as we
shall see, posed an increasing threat to the Greek cities of the region);
he persuaded them to attack the Italiote League city of Thurii by
land in 390, while his brother Leptines blockaded it by sea. The
plan worked too well: the Lucanians so crushed the Thurians that
Leptines out of pity arranged peace terms.

Dismissing Leptines, the following year Dionysius himself sought
a direct confrontation with the Italiote League's forces by attacking
Caulonia, north of Locri. However, having successfully ambushed
them at the River (H)elleporus, on their way to relieve the city, he
chose to let the thousands of men captured go free. This then enabled
him to come to favorable terms with many Italiote cities and thereby
break up the League. Only Caulonia and (in 388) Hipponium were
treated harshly – their buildings razed, and the populations transferred to Syracuse. At last Rhegium was isolated, until in 387 it too
fell after a bitter siege of eleven months.

From then on, for the next twenty years until his death in 367,
it is hard to follow Dionysius' foreign involvements, mainly because
the record in Diodorus becomes so scrappy. To defeat Carthage
evidently re-emerged as his principal ambition. Just as her leaders
earlier had been reluctant to leave Syracuse undefeated, so by the
late 380s Dionysius returned to the attack on the Carthaginian
presence in Sicily. The fighting perhaps lasted as much as eight years
altogether and spread to South Italy, where Croton fell to Dionysius
and most of the other Greek cities were forced to submit. Connected

with these offensives (though not linked thus by Diodorus in his account) may have been a hugely profitable raid on Etruscan Pyrgi in 384/3, a port where we know there to have been strong Punic contacts. The climax came in two battles at otherwise unknown sites in Sicily, Cabala, and Cronium: at the first the Greeks inflicted massive casualties on the Carthaginians, and at the second it was the reverse case. So it was demonstrated that Dionysius could no more break the Carthaginians than they could him. However, this did not stop him from renewing the attempt in 368, yet again with very mixed success; but the effort was not sustained after his death the following year.

Meantime, whether for empire-building or with some hazy intention of making his position yet more secure than ever, Dionysius evidently founded settlements on the Adriatic, and made alliances with peoples on the far side of the straits dividing Italy and Greece. In similar fashion, whether out of gratitude for past help given to Syracuse, or with an eye to future need in a crisis, or just sheer love of getting involved, he was prepared to contribute resources to the frequent wars in mainland Greece – on the Spartan side, although his relationship with Athens was also cordial enough from time to time.

Throughout, the compulsive aim of all these external involvements was surely to strengthen Syracuse, and for the most part he proved successful in this. But there was a heavy price to be paid. Despite repeated efforts, he could not drive the Carthaginians from Sicily. Nor could he ever feel comfortable to see any Greek community flourish within range of Syracuse yet be outside its control (Tarentum is a possible exception, and a puzzle to which we shall return). As to hostile or uncontrollable non-Greeks, it was characteristic of him to think of having a trench dug all the way across the toe of the Italian peninsula to keep them out (Strab. 6.1.10). The major consequence of his compulsiveness was that widespread suffering, slaughter, and destruction had to persist. Not that any of this misery deflected him from his purpose. Having lived through the Athenian siege of his city in his teens, and the near inevitable prospect of its fall to the Carthaginians twice within the following decade, he knew that half-measures or indecisive leadership would never suffice to secure its future.

DIONYSIUS THE TYRANT

The same concern to strengthen Syracuse can be seen in his handling of its internal affairs too. He did not hesitate in requiring whole populations to transfer there. In addition, he maintained a large body of mercenaries, and transformed Ortygia, the original settlement of the city, into an island fortress to accommodate them apart, along with his own family and close friends. Existing state institutions evidently continued to function: magistrates held office and the assembly met, but the exercise of all authority was for Dionysius alone. Although his reaction to any sign of opposition was brutal, he does not seem to have made a great show of his power. We do not know what official title, if any, was used for his position internally: he was never so innovative as to place either it or his head on the city's coins, for example. Abroad, the only reliable testimony comes from three Athenian documents[5] where he is termed very neutrally as *archon* ('governor' or 'ruler') of Sicily. In one, a treaty made in 368/7 with him and some of his family rather than with the Syracusan state (whose representatives are nonetheless involved), the Athenians promise to send help 'if anyone attacks in war by land or by sea Dionysius or his descendants or anyone whom Dionysius rules.' Altogether it seems typical that while he thus specifically lays claim to more than Syracuse, the extent of his rule is given no further definition ('Sicily' is just a geographical term, after all), and the prospect of growth or contraction is allowed for.

The mention of Dionysius' descendants reflects once again his determination to secure the future both of his family and of his city. His first wife bore him no children before her suicide. When he sought to remarry in 398, he went to the trouble of taking two brides – Aristomache, a Syracusan, and Doris, from Locri (after his attempt to find a bride from Rhegium had been pointedly rebuffed). Aristomache bore him two sons and two daughters, Doris two sons and one daughter. All these children he used quite unashamedly for dynastic purposes, even for marriages with closer relatives than was typical Greek practice. But then his own bigamy had already shown that, like earlier Greek tyrants, he did not hold himself and his family to conventional norms. He evidently very much wanted his successor to come from the Locrian side (it alone was party to the treaty of 368/7), so to this extent it was fortunate that the oldest of all his children was a son by Doris, also named Dionysius, who did indeed succeed, with Aristomache's brother Dion serving as chief adviser.

Quite apart from exploiting the services of his children once they were old enough, at every stage Dionysius also badly needed the help of friends and relatives of his own generation. Only within this small circle, it seems, would he raise issues or listen to advice. Even so, his service was fraught with perils. Two sets of relatives by marriage doubled the chances of family rivalries. He may not have minded such heightened tension, and he was indisputably the most demanding and unforgiving of taskmasters. Few of those close to him survived unscathed. It is true that some were restored after a period of exile, but many were killed, and others (like Philistus, who turned historian of the reign) never returned so long as he lived.

It was easier perhaps to serve as one of the thousands of mercenaries upon whom his continuation in power so heavily depended. Such service could well turn out less stressful than being a member of the Syracusan citizen body, which Dionysius disarmed and treated as a completely submissive tool for the achievement of his purposes. Thus, for example, at his whim citizens could be directed to work on building the extensive fortifications that were the one form of construction in which he was prepared to invest heavily.[6] Likewise, in the constant search for revenue (another matter of marked personal interest to him), citizens could be made liable to all manner of taxes, their valuables confiscated, and their slaves freed. In the same way, land and houses were redistributed, and there were countless banishments and executions.

It would be a bad mistake to conclude that Dionysius was universally loathed as a result, however. Far from it. While tens of thousands suffered or died, many others benefitted: Dionysius welcomed refugees from elsewhere, and along with ex-mercenaries was willing to offer them citizenship and land either at Syracuse itself or in one of his new communities.[7] His constant campaigns moreover meant that there was always demand for workers at Syracuse, and quite early on too he evidently learned the political value of being seen to lend a hand personally alongside ordinary folk in whatever needed to be done.

Dionysius the popular 'man of the people' was a potent image, therefore, and needs to be set against that of the remote, cruel, paranoid monster embroidered by his enemies. For all the elements of fantasy, both images still contain a measure of truth, and do more or less accurately reflect a man who is bound to appear full of contradictions. The ruthless butcher was indeed also the intellectual who wrote poetry and (many believe) attracted the philosopher Plato to his court.[8]

Any final assessment of him surely has to be likewise mixed. His successes speak for themselves. When one Greek community after another in Sicily was falling to the Carthaginians, and Syracuse lacked leadership, he provided it and transformed the city's fortunes. Long before his death in 367, its unrivalled strength and size were a marvel to all. He himself was seen by some as the inspiring leader that mainland Greece needed to restore unity and purpose there. Up to a point he must have taken his forerunner Gelon and other tyrants as models, but he also furnished Greeks with new and influential norms for the character and conduct of the sole ruler. The result was not all admirable. His repeated attempts to remove the Carthaginians from Sicily were ultimately a failure. Meantime, the great majority of the wrecked Greek communities were not rebuilt, and there seemed no end in sight to his aggressive involvement in conflicts near and far: to him, these perhaps even gave continued justification to his rule, and certainly they put to use the mercenaries on whom he so heavily relied. To many others, however, the future as determined by Dionysius was a somber one which held out scant hope of peace or freedom or resettlement.

SUCCESSORS OF DIONYSIUS I

On this view, the rule of his son and successor did mark some improvement in the short term, because there was now at least an uneasy peace. But the main reason for it was that Dionysius II had neither talent nor inclination to maintain his father's fight against the Carthaginians or any other enemy. By nature he was lazy, not energetic, and in addition (for whatever sinister or myopic reason) his father had failed completely to equip him with suitable training or experience to take over. In fact, Dionysius II even preferred to spend more time at Locri, his mother's birthplace, than at Syracuse. Two further visits by Plato proved fruitless, for all that they may have served to influence the philosopher's own political thinking.

Inevitably, the stability of the regime was undermined. It might not have been, however, had Dionysius II chosen to take the easy option of transferring a large measure of his authority to his adviser Dion, the brother of his father's Syracusan wife Aristomache, and now the senior member of the Syracusan side of the family. Dion, ten years or so older than Dionysius II, was a complete contrast to him – high-minded, well educated, capable, ambitious, aloof. It seems predictable that they soon found it impossible to work together. It was in deciding how to resolve the tension that Dionysius II fell short of his father. The negotiations with Carthage in 366 (after Dionysius I's campaign during the last year of his life was not resumed) offered an opportunity. When indiscreet, even treasonable, correspondence sent privately by Dion to the enemy was brought to him, Dionysius II's reaction was not to execute Dion at once, but merely to exile him to mainland Greece, even leaving his property untouched.

Only around 360 did Dionysius II at last decide to seize all Dion's assets, and it was this confiscation along with other grievances that now impelled him to try and overthrow Dionysius II by force. In Greece there was no widespread enthusiasm for the venture, even among other Syracusan exiles. But Dion did succeed in attracting a miscellaneous assortment of supporters, in particular certain members of Plato's Academy who were convinced that Greek states would truly benefit if philosopher-kings were to become their rulers. He eventually set sail from Zacynthus in 357, with a total of five ships and one thousand men. Dionysius, at Locri, had a substantial fleet waiting to intercept them, but in risking a more southerly route across the open sea they were blown off-course in a storm, landed first on the Libyan coast, and then made for Minoa, a small Punic town in south-west Sicily. Here the Carthaginians turned a blind eye, content enough not to obstruct incipient civil strife among the Greeks.

Dion attracted much support, and not least because Dionysius II's forces were still expecting him to approach from a quite different direction, he was able to take over Syracuse; only the fortified island of Ortygia continued to hold out. Reinforcements, too, soon reached him from mainland Greece, led by another Syracusan exile there, Heraclides, who decisively smashed Dionysius II's fleet. Dion may have claimed to come to Syracuse in order to restore its liberty, but once in control he proved so cold and autocratic that he rapidly lost the citizens' support. In fact, in 356 he was forced to withdraw to Leontini. But a Campanian mercenary commander, Nypsius, then came so close to recapturing the city for Dionysius II that in desperation Dion and his followers were recalled. With their help Nypsius was then driven back, and eventually after much fighting even Ortygia was liberated in 354.

With Dion's declared objective of freeing Syracuse now fully attained, it was natural for there to be keen interest in what his next steps would be. Unfortunately, despite all his recent vicissitudes, he did little to show that he had learned the value of maintaining popular support. When the citizens pressed to mark their liberation by demolishing Ortygia's fortifications, he forbade it. Equally, he refused to permit the introduction of democracy in any form, or any redistribution of land or houses. His only concessions were to share supreme authority with Heraclides, and to call in constitutional advisers from Syracuse's mother-city, oligarchic Corinth. He soon became sufficiently disturbed by Heraclides' sympathy for a wider sharing of power to order his assassination; thereafter he occupied alone the special office of *strategos autokrator*. With this record, it comes as no great surprise that he was himself assassinated later in the same year, 354, by Callippus, one of the members of Plato's Academy who had accompanied him from Greece.

Callippus may once have wanted to do more for Syracuse than just replace one tyrant by another, but he now unashamedly behaved as one himself in Dion's place. He lasted only a year. Then, while he was away leading an attack on Catane, Ortygia (only, and never the rest of the city) was retaken by Hipparinus and Nysaeus, the two sons of Dionysius I by his Syracusan wife Aristomache. They did this on their own behalf rather than for Dionysius II, and not surprisingly our sources represent them as a despicable pair. Hipparinus died by means unknown in 351, but Nysaeus continued to hang on to Ortygia till 346. That year he lost it, however, when Dionysius II finally mounted an expedition from Locri to recover it for himself. Such uncharacteristic success proved fortunate, because during his absence the Locrians expressed their revulsion at his rule by overpowering his mercenaries and butchering his wife and children. His only recourse, therefore, was to remain in Ortygia.

Syracuse was certainly unique in being fought over by so many claimants. But by the mid-340s the rest of Greek Sicily, too, had degenerated into a fragmented shambles, depopulated and exhausted by civil strife everywhere. Any sense of law or community had largely given way to the tyranny of whichever local boss could pay enough mercenaries to keep him in power. Only two of these men merit notice here – Andromachus (father of the future historian Timaeus), who controlled Tauromenium, and Hicetas, another of Dion's former followers, who had seized Leontini.

TIMOLEON AND THE REVIVAL OF GREEK SICILY

Meantime, the chilling appearance of a Punic fleet off eastern Sicily revived fears that had lain dormant for the previous twenty years and more. In alarm, therefore, an appeal for help was sent to Corinth at the instigation of certain Syracusan exiles who had fled to Leontini. On grounds of sentiment this was a logical enough choice, and Corinth had indeed maintained links with her illustrious colony Syracuse. On the other hand, Corinthian greatness had been ended by the Peloponnesian War, and she had no record of lavish response to appeals, however desperate.

Her decision in this instance thus seems at once typical and perfunctory. She commissioned one of her citizens, Timoleon, to intervene as best he could with a force of seven ships and 700 mercenaries, who most probably were offered rations, but no pay beyond whatever they could win in booty. Timoleon himself was elderly, tainted by involvement many years previously in the murder of a brother (who had been suspected of plotting tyranny) and, to cap it all, a stranger as much to western affairs as to the command of mercenaries. Whether this pathetic enterprise was intended by Corinth as a cruel joke on all those involved, or what other motives lay behind it, is now impossible to say. The surviving sources (none of them contemporary) see Timoleon only as a heaven-sent savior: in idolizing him, they obscure the background of his venture, and do even less to probe the means of its success.

There is no doubting the fact, however, that he did transform the fortunes of Greek Sicily. As his funeral decree sums it up, 'he overthrew the tyrants, subdued the barbarians [Carthaginians], repopulated the greatest of the devastated cities, and then gave back the people of Sicily their laws' (Plut. *Tim.* 39.5). All this moreover he achieved within as little as about eight years from 344.

The outline is clear enough, as is the fact that time and again he proved able to match a latent talent for leadership with the most amazing lucky streak. Held up at Rhegium by a large squadron of Punic ships, he should never have reached Sicily at all, but managed to outwit them, and (for whatever reason) was welcomed to Tauromenium by Andromachus. His chances of making further headway from there seemed slim, the more so as Hicetas by now held Syracuse (but not Ortygia) and had become a Carthaginian ally. However, rival factions at Adranum called upon both Hicetas and Timoleon for help. When both chose to respond, and arrived almost simultaneously, Timoleon seized the initiative by ordering his much smaller force to attack Hicetas' army during dinner-time, a complete surprise that turned into a rout and won him more allies, in particular Mamercus, tyrant of Catane.

For the next vital stage it becomes impossible to unravel exactly how events unfolded, except that Timoleon, Hicetas, Dionysius II (in Ortygia) and the Carthaginians all fought over Syracuse, and Timoleon emerged in sole control, sending off Dionysius II under safe conduct to Corinth where he lived out his life as an exile and tourist attraction. Having been given no suitable preparation for maintaining his father's strong rule, he should not perhaps be blamed too severely for lacking the talent, quite apart from the temperament, to do so. The tragedy, however, was that by his neglect and ineptitude he opened the way to even more widespread suffering and strife.

Timoleon's next concern was to revive both Syracuse and Greek Sicily in general. He committed himself to removing every tyrant with as much force as was required in each instance, except for his loyal supporter Andromachus who was left undisturbed at Tauromenium. This purge was successfully carried through, although interrupted by the need to counter a major Punic offensive, probably in May/June 341. Rather than waiting for the enemy to advance far, Timoleon led an army by forced marches to the Punic side of the island, where he caught them crossing the River Crimisus, in all likelihood the modern River Belice. Although outclassed as usual in numbers and equipment, his onslaught turned into a massacre of the Punic army because it happened to coincide with a thunderstorm and flash flood. There had been no such decisive victory over the Carthaginians since the time of Dionysius I, and certainly none without any corresponding major defeat.

As a result, Timoleon once again removed fear of Carthage for the time being, and thus secured one of the essential foundations for the revival of Greek settlement in Sicily. He advertised the victory widely in mainland Greece (at Delphi and Corinth in particular)[9] as part of an appeal for new settlers, which proved exceptionally effective. The highest ancient estimate of the number who responded to his offer is an impressive 60,000, but even though it happens to be preserved from a contemporary (Athanis), the overwhelming testimony of modern archaeology raises the possibility that the figure may in fact be on the low side. Certainly there is no question that throughout the east and south of the island, in both town and country, there occurred extensive revival and expansion. Now at last several of the principal communities wrecked by the Carthaginians towards the end of the previous century – Acragas, Gela, Camarina – were rebuilt and refortified (see Plate 15).

Plate 15 Fortification walls at Capo Soprano, west of Gela. These superbly preserved walls were built in the third quarter of the fourth century to protect the city of Gela, refounded by Timoleon. The lower courses are ashlar blocks of sandstone, the upper ones bricks of unbaked mud. Rapid build-up of sand required the walls to be raised in height more than once before the city's destruction in 282 BC. Sand then buried them completely until they were excavated shortly after World War II. The mud brick is now protected by canopies and glass panes. These fortifications stand as impressive testimony to Timoleon's revival of Greek Sicily. Photo: R. J. A. Talbert.

At Syracuse Timoleon handled public opinion with all the astuteness that Dion had lacked. Rather than wait for any agitation to demolish Ortygia, he invited everyone to bring crowbars on a designated day in order to make a ceremony and a celebration of this communal act of liberation; subsequently he built lawcourts where the fortress had been. He was also willing to redistribute land and houses. It is not clear what Syracusan office he held, and under what arrangements, in order to exercise such sweeping authority: *strategos autokrator* is again the most likely possibility, but it can only be a conjecture. In any event it was always Timoleon's policy not to highlight his own position or authority, but rather to insist that he acted for the public good rather than for himself at all. This did not stop him inviting in more constitutional advisers from Corinth (like

Dion), and the likelihood is that, true to the convictions of his birth-place, he left Syracuse with an oligarchic constitution, while at the same time parading the democratic tendency of his reforms, and allowing the assembly of citizens to be very vocal.

Elsewhere in the island, too, his stress was upon freedom and autonomy, although we lack all knowledge of constitutional arrange-ments in detail. At least it is clear that his purpose was to revive or establish independent city-states on the model familiar to him and to the settlers he attracted. All these communities were linked by some form of loose league or alliance, in which Syracuse is not known to have been given any special prominence.

Greek Sicily, therefore, as miraculously revived by Timoleon, presented a striking contrast to the Sicily first forged, and then neglected, by Dionysius I and his son respectively. In Timoleon's Sicily there was no place for the tyrant or mercenary, and Syracuse did not dominate: rather, on all sides there was population growth, reconstruction, independence, prosperity, and, above all, peace. The tangible attraction for so many immigrants was that this Sicily could fulfil their ideals of community (and property-holding) in ways that now seemed as unattainable in mainland Greece or South Italy as they had been in Sicily itself under the Dionysii.

However, before endorsing too enthusiastically the uncritical ancient chorus of praise for Timoleon, it is as well to enter two notes of caution about his achievement. First, while the ends may have been admirable, the means were frequently not. In order to fulfil his vision, Timoleon tricked, bossed, butchered, and robbed just as his opponents did and as Dionysius I had done. He enjoyed as much luck at critical moments as Dionysius, but without also suffering his heavy defeats. He, too, sought to publicize his achieve-ments in mainland Greece, and perhaps in part because his efforts never attracted ridicule (as some of Dionysius' had), he was even able to exploit a claim to divine protection. Where he most differed from all the tyrants, however, was in emphatically and genuinely disclaiming any concern to create a personal domination, either for himself or his family.

The second note of caution about Timoleon's achievement inevitably concerns whether it was equipped with the strength to last. He himself, worn out and blind, retired about 337 (though he continued to live outside Syracuse), and died not many years after. His loose network of city-states may have fulfilled an ideal in welcome contrast to the experience of Greek Sicily during the previous half-century and more, but such an ideal was not necessarily well calculated to endure. In mainland Greece, city-states on the traditional pattern had suffered increasing strains during the fourth century. In Sicily, comparable difficulties had surfaced even earlier. By Timoleon's time, prior experience of such communities was practically lost there, and the time and stability to re-establish it securely were liable to be lacking. Discharged mercenaries were now a substantial, and notoriously volatile, proportion of the population, while the Carthaginians were only defeated, not expelled, and there could be no knowing how their policy might develop. Meanwhile, domination by any individual or city, with consequent potential for strong leadership and concentration of forces, was by definition discouraged under Timoleon's arrangements. Thus, despite all the promise that they held out, there was the serious prospect that his ideals were at the same time shortsighted ones, which left Greek Sicily vulnerable from both within and without.

AGATHOCLES

In fact, trouble began before Timoleon's death, and there are clear signs of it mounting over the next twenty years, even though our surviving sources become sketchier than ever. The strife seems to have been between oligarchs and democrats, old citizens and new, haves and have-nots. At Syracuse, by 330 or so, all power was effectively in the hands of a 'Council of Six Hundred,' although Agathocles made successive attempts to challenge its grip. His background, like Dionysius', is obscure. But we do know that his family gained Syracusan citizenship on moving to the city from the Punic part of the island after the battle of the Crimisus, when he was about twenty (thus born around 360). Subsequently he gained great wealth through marriage, and used not only it but also his exceptional military distinction (earned in Sicily and South Italy, in campaigns both for and against Syracuse) to try and oust the Six Hundred.

Throughout the 320s, despite attracting popular support, his attempts failed. He realized that he needed, first, to distance himself from the city, gathering support elsewhere, and then mounting an assault; second, that he had to break the ominous alliance which had developed between the Six Hundred and the Carthaginians. Both objectives he had achieved by about 319, clearing the way for his return as 'general and guardian of the peace until the time when harmony might be established among those who together had come back to the city' (Diod. 19.5.5). In practice, despite the parade of virtuous intentions, Agathocles merely pressed ahead to consolidate his own position: he followed the example of Dionysius I, not of Timoleon. By 316 thousands of oligarchs had been either massacred or driven out of Syracuse, and a unanimous vote of the citizen assembly had granted him full powers.

Agathocles was at once able to consolidate his position at home by canceling debts and redistributing land. But the oligarchs in exile were not to be thwarted so readily: Acragas, Gela, Messana, and the Carthaginians all proved willing to support their cause. Messana withstood two assaults in 315/14, and only capitulated after a third attempt in 312/11. In the meantime, however, a campaign against Agathocles coordinated by Acragas had collapsed through weak leadership on the part of the Spartan prince Acrotatus, and the Greek cities (except for Messana) were constrained to acknowledge Syracusan supremacy under an agreement mediated by the Punic commander Hamilcar.

Yet such evenhandedness on his part only led to an escalation of Punic policy, demanded by those who shared the fear of many Greeks outside Syracuse that Agathocles was all too liable to become another Dionysius I. Carthage now proceeded to send large forces against him, and by 311 these had achieved near-complete success – heavily defeating him in battle, wresting many Greek cities from his control, and finally surrounding Syracuse itself on both land and sea.

In this desperate predicament, Agathocles took an unprecedented risk that might have daunted even Dionysius I. He left his brother Antander in charge of beleaguered Syracuse and successfully mounted a secret invasion of North Africa, on the supposition that the enemy would be convulsed by such a totally unexpected diversion. In this he was quite right, and was thus able to cause widespread damage, to provoke bitter conflicts among Carthage's leaders, and to unsettle many Punic subjects and allies. He even attracted the support of Ophellas of Cyrene, the neighboring ruler to the east of Punic territory; and despite his assassination in 308 (on Agathocles' orders), the substantial reinforcements he had brought stayed on. On the other hand, however, Agathocles also suffered defeats and placed strains on his men that drove them to mutiny, while throughout he could not take Carthage itself any more than his Punic opponents could take Syracuse. Finally, in 307 he felt forced to disengage from Africa altogether, even treacherously leaving his two sons and large numbers of his men behind.

By then developments in Sicily had to command his full attention. The Punic land forces attacking Syracuse had, it is true, been decisively defeated by Antander in 308. But a campaign by Acragas to dominate Greek Sicily next proved sufficient threat for Agathocles himself to return there to halt it, and then go on to break the Punic naval blockade of Syracuse. Even so, a still greater threat remained from an old rival, the exiled oligarch Deinocrates, who attracted widespread support. It was above all to be sure of defeating him that Agathocles abandoned his African venture and offered peace terms to Carthage.

The decisive battle (at Torgium, another unidentifiable location) was indeed a victory for Agathocles, in which it would seem that he finally stamped out all active Greek opposition, leaving himself in control of approximately the same area of Sicily that Dionysius I had held. Like him, now that he was securely established there, he showed some enthusiasm for intervening in South Italy and beyond, though both his motives and many of the details are obscured by the loss of Diodorus' narrative beyond 302. At any rate, he intervened in Bruttium, twice responded to appeals for help from Tarentum, and took Corcyra (an island of obvious strategic value on the straits between Italy and Greece).

At the time of his death in 289/8, aged seventy-two, he was preparing a renewed offensive against Carthage, but nothing came of it. More than any of his Greek predecessors during the previous century he had shaken, but still not removed, the Punic presence in Sicily. In so doing, of course, he had once again inflicted endless suffering upon his fellow Greeks there.

No account of his handling of internal affairs at Syracuse survives, but certain features can be glimpsed and likenesses noted. Following the example of the successors to Alexander the Great in the east, he came to style himself King, and actually put the title on coins without mention of Syracuse. Even so, like Dionysius I, he appreciated how the 'common touch' could win support among ordinary people. To maintain a plain lifestyle may in fact have been his genuine preference, because he evidently did not also make himself a remote, heavily guarded figure; nor did he share Dionysius' cultural pretensions. Instead he dispensed with protection and regalia, and preferred to dress simply as a priest of the popular divinities Demeter and Kore (recalling Timoleon's stress on divine protection). Despite this identification with the people, however, there is no sign that he felt any deeper regard for their welfare than Dionysius I had done.

Their regimes were alike in being unashamedly secured by a tight personal grip on all authority, the employment of mercenaries, and the brutal elimination of opponents.

Both regimes, too, were reinforced by the family of the ruler, although Agathocles' attempt to found a dynasty proved even less successful than Dionysius' had done. He was married three times – to two Syracusan women in turn, and then to a daughter or step-daughter of Ptolemy I. His two sons by his first wife were killed by the men abandoned with them in Africa (307). By his second wife he had a daughter, Lanassa, and a son, called Agathocles after his father. The elder Agathocles, strikingly, had gained sufficient standing in the wider Greek world to marry Lanassa first to Pyrrhus, King of Epirus, and then (after a separation) to Demetrius Poliorcetes. Agathocles' plan was for his one surviving son to succeed him, but shortly before his death the younger Agathocles was assassinated by Archagathus, a grandson of the king's first marriage. Rather than then make Archagathus his successor, he preferred to 'restore power to the people' (Diod. 21.16.4): as a result, the accumulated strength of the regime was quickly dissipated in the confusion following his death. The Syracusans wasted no time in furiously wiping out all trace of his memory. Like Dionysius I, he had given them a certain stability, but at a terrible price. Elsewhere, too, in Greek Sicily he had inflicted deep wounds. Surprisingly, however, none of this brought to an end the prosperity initiated by Timoleon (see Plate 16). In particular, Greek Sicily beyond Syracuse did not revert to the depopulated wasteland that it had been throughout the first half of the fourth century.[10]

THE GREEKS OF SOUTH ITALY

Last but by no means least, the twenty or so widely scattered Greek communities of South Italy (the general term Megale Hellas, Magna Graecia is more or less accurate) merit attention in their own right, certainly as more than just an appendage to Sicilian affairs. As usual, the problem lies in the lack of adequate source material: no connected narrative survives, and there were hardly even outstanding figures here to attract ancient biographers. As a result, it is all too easy to overlook, and certainly impossible to penetrate, this strate-gically located part of the Greek world with its multiple links east-ward to mainland Greece, south-west to Sicily, and northwards up the Italian peninsula.

Throughout the fourth century its principal community was Taras (Tarentum), which in a major shift for the region seems to have assumed the leadership of the century-old Italiote League (loosely linking all the Greek cities of Magna Graecia), once Croton was weakened by Dionysius I and finally fell to him early in the 370s. At least during the second quarter of the century, if not earlier too, Taras enjoyed firm leadership exercised by the mathematician and follower of Pythagoras, Archytas. The nature of the city's relations with Syracuse is the main puzzle, and insoluble on present evidence. Each seems to have left the other well alone. Perhaps this was by mutual agreement, though that is hardly what might be expected of Dionysius I, with his ambitions as far distant as the Adriatic and beyond. Just conceivably the link that he and Taras had in common with Sparta helped to restrain him.

Elsewhere, Dionysius' impact upon the Italiotes was doubly serious: he not only weakened them by his interference, he also diverted them from guarding against the growing menace of south-ward migration by Oscan peoples (Bruttians, Lucanians, Messapians) which dated back to the mid-fifth century. The Italiotes for their part could never summon up the strength and unity to fend him off, let alone strike back at him. Even after the collapse of his empire by mid-century, for their cities there was no recovery and repopu-lation to match what Timoleon achieved so unexpectedly in Sicily. The Italiotes' once-fabulous wealth from agricultural exports, timber and manpower took much longer to recover. Except at Taras (which at least strove repeatedly for greatness without ever quite attaining it), the outlook grew bleaker at first. In 356, for example, Meta-pontum and Heraclea were looted by Messapians, and Terina by Bruttians; the latter peoples also came to form their own league.

Resources were not the Italiotes' only problem; they also had no champion with the charisma of a Timoleon. Their solution was therefore to invite in what became an intermittent succession of leaders to take the initiative against the Oscan peoples. Each one was offered some citizen forces and some money, but otherwise was left to rely on mercenaries. With such poor terms it was necessary to offer considerable freedom of action, and inevitably the leaders' exercise of this became a source of tension. In addition, how far the Italiotes' policy consistently reflected the wishes of just Taras, as opposed to the entire League, remains obscure.

Several leaders, at least, came from the mother-city of Taras, Sparta. The first was Archidamus, who campaigned successfully against the Messapians for a few years until he was killed in battle at Manduria in 338, the same year that Athens and Thebes were defeated by Philip of Macedon at Chaeronea.[11] Alexander of Epirus, who followed Archidamus in 334, was particularly effective, expelling the Oscan occupiers of many Greek cities and winning back territory as far north as Campania. However, he was killed fighting the Lucanians in 331, and much of what he had gained came to be lost again. In the mid-320s Agathocles, while still bidding for power at Syracuse, was employed for a time by Taras, but soon dismissed as rash and unreliable. In 314, once he had become tyrant, Taras did briefly send ships to support Acragas' campaign against him, but withdrew it when Acrotatus, the unsatisfactory Spartan commander called in by the Acragantines, was ousted.

Near the end of the century (303/2) the Italiotes again found it necessary to invite in a leader, in this instance Acrotatus' brother Cleonymus, who (in the typical way) proved successful at first, but then preferred to pursue his own ambitions, and so was ousted. During the 290s it was Agathocles that the Italiotes appealed to in their desperation, and although anywhere near a full picture is lacking, it is clear enough that he did bring much of South Italy under his control. His death, and the decline of Syracusan power thereafter, were bad blows to the Italiotes. So it was logical enough that when they next sought a leader (in 281), they should turn to King Pyrrhus of Epirus.

His intervention was to provoke a full-scale clash between Taras and the Italiotes on the one hand, and the Romans on the other. Rome had had relations with Carthage which probably went back to the sixth century, and were certainly cemented during the fourth. There seems to have been no comparable contact with Greek rulers in Sicily, however, not even Agathocles. In Italy, on the other hand, Rome's interests extended southward to an increasing extent, especially during the latter part of the fourth century, when the first treaty with Taras was concluded (303/2, and possibly 332/1). Moreover, Roman society had increasingly been open to many different kinds of Greek cultural influence.

Although few Greeks in Sicily or South Italy would have predicted it in 300, over the next century Rome was in fact now to emerge as their long-term protector and ruler. Rome, with its incomparable reserves of manpower, would at last permanently remove the threats from Carthaginians and Oscans in a way that had proved beyond even the strongest Greek rulers. At the same time the Roman Republic was sufficiently stable to maintain a continuity of rule which had eluded the Greek communities in the West as much when they were ruled by tyrants as when they were not. At peace neither within themselves, nor with their neighbors, they were no longer able to fend for themselves amidst the many shifts and pressures of the period. As it turned out, their situation by 300 could have brought them many worse fates than to come under the control of Rome.

A postscript on coinage

Adoption of Corinthian coin-types and weight-standards by Syracuse seems to coincide with Timoleon's revival (see Plate 16). In due course, as many as fifteen Corinthian dependencies in Western Greece likewise issued silver 'Pegasi' almost indistinguishable from Corinth's own (an unprecedented step for the great majority of these communities), as did two more cities in Sicily itself, and six in South Italy. Hoard evidence indicates that, while the level of output must often have been modest, in some places (Leucas, for example) it was considerable. What steps Corinth or Syracuse took to introduce Pegasi thus, and precisely why, remains puzzling; but there is no question that Pegasi remained the dominant trading currency throughout the entire region into the 290s.

Key to the mints of the Pegasi illustrated:

1 Corinth

In Western Greece:

2 Leucas
3 Dyrrhachium
4 Apollonia
5 Corcyra
6 Anactorium
7 Argos Amphilochicum
8 Alyzia
9 Astacus
10 Stratus

In Sicily:

11 Syracuse
12 Leontini

In South Italy:
13 Locri

Plate 16 Corinthian coinage in Sicily and the Greek West. Reproduced from C. M. Kraay, 'Timoleon and Corinthian Coinage in Sicily,' in *Actes du 8ème Congrès International de Numismatique* [1973] (Paris, Bâle, 1976), pp. 99–105, Plate 8, by permission of Dr A. Burnett, British Museum, and Mrs M. Kraay.

NOTES

1 Left out of account in this chapter, regrettably, are those Greeks who settled even further west in France and Spain. For them, see A. J. Graham, 'The Colonial Expansion of Greece,' *CAH*² 3, 3: 139–43 (background); R. J. Harrison, *Spain at the Dawn of History*, London, Thames and Hudson, 1988, chap. 5; M. Blech, *Historia de España* vol. 1, Barcelona, Planeta, 1990, chap. 7; and, for France, G. Pugliese Carratelli, ed., *The Western Greeks*, Venice, Bompiani, 1996, esp. pp. 577–84 (by M. Bats).

2 To identify the disease with any precision is impossible. Diodorus (14.70.4–71) at least offers a graphic description of the symptoms which later devastated the Carthaginian besiegers of Syracuse in 396.

3 These men returned to the west and settled at Entella, where remarkable inscriptions found within the past twenty years show their descendants were still present over a century later. These are listed in D. M. Lewis, 'Sicily, 413–368 B.C.,' *CAH*² 6: 153, but no translation or discussion of them has yet been published in English.

4 The major advances in siege engines and weaponry made by Dionysius were slow to spread to mainland Greece. Philip II of Macedon, however, appreciated their importance. See further Y. Garlan, 'Warfare,' *CAH*² 6: 678–92.

5 Tod 108 (393 BC), 133 (369/8 BC), 136 (368/7 BC).

6 In particular, between about 402 and 397, the heights of Epipolae which command Syracuse to the north and east were enclosed with perimeter walls more than 16 miles in length. A formidable complex of fortifications is visible today at the highest point to the east, Euryalus, but subsequent modifications make it impossible to isolate the elements dating to Dionysius' time: see R. Stillwell, *et al.* (eds). *The Princeton Encyclopedia of Classical Sites*, Princeton, Princeton University Press, 1976, p. 873.

7 Tyndaris, founded on the north coast of the island in 396, is a fine example. A visit there confirms Dionysius' excellent choice of a commanding, defensible site, even if many of the visible remains date to later periods. See *Princeton Encyclopedia*, p. 943.

8 There is no hope of resolving the controversies over what to believe concerning any of Plato's visits to Sicily, or their impact upon his writings (especially the *Republic* and the *Seventh* and *Eighth Letters*). Among the many discussions, note P. A. Brunt, *Studies in Greek History and Thought*, Oxford, Clarendon Press, 1993, chap. 10, 'Plato's Academy and Politics.'

9 For the epigraphic evidence, see R. J. A. Talbert, *Timoleon and the Revival of Greek Sicily*, Cambridge, Cambridge University Press, 1974, pp. 49–51, 76–7.

10 It is striking that Diodorus (16.83.2–3) documents his account of

Timoleon's achievement by reference to construction undertaken in Agathocles' time and even later.

11 A coincidence which did not escape ancient observers, who were even tempted to claim that the day and hour of the two battles were identical (cf. Diod. 16.88.3).

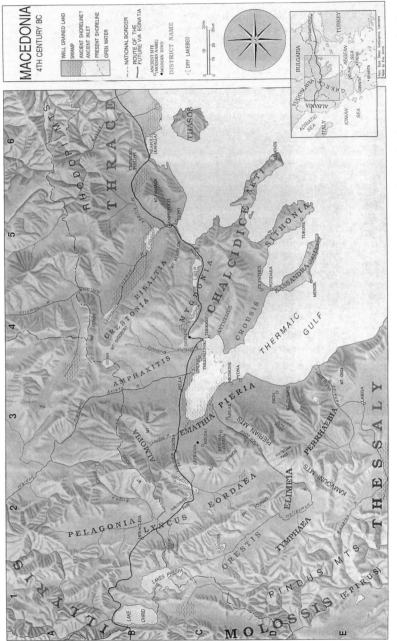

Map 5 Macedonia, from Eugene N. Borza, *In the Shadow of Olympus: The Emergence of Macedon* (Princeton University Press, 1990). By permission of the author.

7

MACEDONIA AND THE NORTH, 400–336

Julia Heskel

Fourth-century Macedonian history before the reign of Alexander the Great is especially difficult to reconstruct because of the nature of the ancient evidence. We must rely to a great extent on the universal histories of Diodorus (*c.* 60–30 BC) and Justin (third century AD), which are brief summaries of various accounts that do not survive. Although Diodorus' *Library of History* is by far the superior of the two, his tendency to group too many events under the heading of a single year often makes interpretation of those events difficult. We need to read his account in conjunction with occasional references in the *Hellenica* of Xenophon (which ends with the Battle of Mantinea in 362), in speeches of the Attic orators, and in the *Philippica* of Theopompus, to name only the most important sources.

The geography of ancient Macedonia played an extremely important role in the history of the region (see Map 5). Macedonia consisted of two distinct topographical areas, Upper and Lower Macedonia. Upper Macedonia was a plateau divided by impassable mountain chains and rivers into a number of districts: Tymphaea, Elimea, Orestis, Eordaea, Lyncus, Pelagonia, and Derriopus. Lower Macedonia consisted of the regions to the south, which were adjacent to the Thermaic Gulf: Pieria, Bottiaea, Amphaxitis, Crestonia, Mygdonia, Bisaltia, Crousis, and Anthemus. Though less mountainous than Upper Macedonia it, too, was divided into a number of districts by untraversable mountains and rivers. Moreover, in the middle of Lower Macedonia lies the Emathian plain, a marshland created by the seasonal flooding of rivers and their tributaries; plagued by mosquitoes from the fifth century on, it was possibly as difficult to cross as the mountain ranges. The lack of routes between the different districts meant that there was little mixing of the different populations, other than intermarriage of the aristocracy. As

167

a result of such isolation, each of the many districts developed its own tribal traditions. The topographical factors that isolated the various Macedonian districts from each other also served to isolate Macedonia from the outside world.

In contrast with Greece, both Upper and Lower Macedonia were rich in natural resources. The land of Macedonia was better for cultivation and pasturage because of the continental climate, with more moderate temperatures and more rainfall than the hot and arid Mediterranean climate of mainland Greece. In addition, Macedonia was richly forested, yielding the best timber in the Mediterranean world (Theoph. *Hist. Plant.* 5.2.1). It was also renowned for its mineral wealth. The gold and silver mines of Bisaltia were probably the reason for the Argead king Alexander I's expansion eastward (Thuc. 2.99.4, 4.109.4; Strab. 7 fr. 36). The abundance of Macedonia's natural resources allowed the peoples of the various districts to stay within their respective areas. Thus, like the topography, it encouraged isolation within Macedonia.

Virtually devoid of contact with the outside world, Macedonian political and social institutions remained relatively primitive. Shielded from the influences which played a role in the development of the Greek city-states, the various districts retained tribal monarchies, much like those of late Dark Age Greece. The Argead dynasty held Lower Macedonia from the late Archaic Period on, and the various districts of Upper Macedonia were ruled by other dynasties, some of whom had marriage ties to the Argeads. These kingdoms were each ruled by a personal monarchy, in which the king made all policy decisions, both foreign and domestic. Unlike the Greek city-states, there was no sort of constitutional framework. The case of the Argead dynasty is probably typical of the way things operated. In the absence of primogeniture, anyone in the royal family had a legitimate claim to rule. It was a case of the survival of the fittest: whoever was able to seize the throne reigned, and he remained king for as long as he could hold on to his throne, i.e., while he had sufficient support from the nobility. There was no formal council or assembly that took part in the decision-making process. Rather, the king was advised by his chief associates, the Companions, or *hetairoi* – select Macedonian nobles who fought, hunted, and drank with him.[1] They met informally, at the symposium, where they feasted and discussed matters of political and military significance.

It was no doubt because of these vast cultural differences that the Greeks believed the Macedonians were barbarians, and were reluctant to have dealings with them. This fact helps to explain the policies of Alexander I (*c.* 498–452). During the height of the Persian Empire in the early fifth century, he profited from his loyalty as a satrap of the Great King. After the Persian Wars, however, Alexander realized that Macedon's future lay with Greece, and wished to convince the Greeks that he was one of them. He claimed Greek descent in order to be allowed to compete in the Olympic Games, which were open only to Greeks. Tracing his dynasty's lineage back to Heracles, he convinced the judges that he was a Greek of the highest extraction. The Argeads henceforth portrayed themselves as Greeks ruling Macedonians. Although some Greeks continued to be reluctant to have dealings with the Argeads, commercial necessity – in particular, the need for Macedonian timber – prevailed.[2]

Perdiccas II (*c.* 452–413), Alexander's son and successor, was less successful in his dealings with the Greeks during his reign. Although he, too, wished to expand Macedonian influence in the north, dynastic turmoil made it impossible for him to compete with the great Greek powers. He was compelled instead to follow a defensive strategy that aimed to keep the Greeks out of Macedonia. As a result, he alternated between supporting Athens and Athens' enemies in the Peloponnesian War, and was depicted by Thucydides as perfidious.[3]

Archelaus (413–399), the son and successor of Perdiccas, made great strides for Macedonia. He established the road system and moved the administrative capital from Aegae to Pella, which is located at the crossroads of the main routes north–south and east–west (Aegae remained the sacred capital, where kings married and were buried).[4] Clearly, Archelaus was greatly interested in improving the communications between the different regions of Macedonia as well as between Macedonia and the outside world. He aimed to bring an end to the regionalism that divided Macedonia and strengthen ties with the Greeks. Archelaus invited major Greek artists to his court, among them Euripides and Zeuxis. This patronage reflects his concern to demonstrate the Greekness of the Macedonian nobility.[5] Plato's Socrates, however, would not have anything to do with Archelaus because he ruled by tyrannical methods (Pl. *Grg.* 471a–c, 525d; Arist. *Rh.* 2.1398a). After Perdiccas' troubles with rivals, it was surely the only way to maintain control of the throne.

Despite this interest in things Greek, Archelaus did not introduce one other reform necessary for success in the Greek world – hoplite tactics. The reason is apparent: the creation of the hoplite phalanx in Archaic Greece more than two centuries earlier had undermined the power of the aristocracy. It might have the same effect in Macedonia. Given the inherent instability of the dynasty, that was a risk Archelaus could not afford to take. It would not be until the reign of Philip II that a hoplite army was fully developed, and with it, the means to improve Macedon's position in the Aegean world.

The problems that Archelaus had tried to solve resurfaced after his death. For the first forty years of the fourth century, Macedonia was plagued by instability. Periods of dynastic turmoil were frequent, as various members of the royal house asserted their rightful claims to the throne. Neighboring barbarian tribes, especially the Illyrians, would often invade during these periods in the attempt to annex Macedonian territory. Greek states interested in expansion in the North also used such opportunities to intervene. The inadequacy of the Macedonian army made it practically impossible for the Argeads to defend their borders against such invasions, let alone extend their control beyond those borders.

THRACE AND ILLYRIA

We turn now to the neighboring tribes of Thrace and Illyria, which played extremely important roles in the history of the north in the fourth century. Politically, these regions had much in common with Macedonia. They were each inhabited by a number of tribes – e.g., the Odrysians, Triballi, Moesians, and Edoni in Thrace, and the Dardanii, Taulantii, and Grabaei in Illyria. The political institutions were similar to Macedonia's. Each of these people was ruled by its own king, whose rule was dependent on the support of the nobility. The throne was probably restricted to the members of the royal house. There were no rules of succession; all that mattered was the ability to obtain and retain control of the throne. As a result, dynastic struggles were a frequent occurrence. The strength of the kingdom depended on the king's ability to deal with his rivals.

In the early fourth century, the Odrysian dynasty of Thrace was by far the greatest power in the north. During the third quarter of the fifth century, Sitalces (d. 424) had built the kingdom into an enormous empire: it was larger than mainland Greece, extending as far north as the Danube and as far east as the Black Sea (Hdt. 4.99; Thuc. 2.96; Diod. 12.50). Sitalces died while making an expedition against the Triballi, and was succeeded by his nephew, Seuthes (Thuc. 4.101.5). During Seuthes' reign (424–c. 405), the kingdom reached the height of prosperity. He increased the tribute imposed on the possessions of the empire, bringing revenues to their maximum (Thuc. 2.97, 4.101.5).[6] Upon Seuthes' death, the empire began a period of decline that lasted nearly twenty years. Dynastic struggles were frequent: two of the next three kings gained the throne by assassination. This turmoil led to the dividing of the kingdom into two parts, with rival kings ruling the interior and the coast (Xen. *Hell.* 4.8.26; Arist. *Pol.* 1312a; Diod. 13.105.3, 14.94).

It was not until the reign of Cotys (*c.* 384–360) that the Odrysian kingdom returned to the position it had known in the fifth century. Upon his accession, Cotys established ties with major powers to protect his kingdom from their expansionist aims. Most important of these was Athens, which had interests in the area because of its timber (Thuc. 4.108.1). The king then spent the next twenty years reuniting Thrace under his control. In the late 360s, Cotys turned his attention to expansion, gaining possession of the adjacent region of the Chersonesus, which had been freed of Athenian control during the Peloponnesian War. This policy brought on war with the Athenians, who had recently decided to recover the Chersonesus for themselves. By the end of the decade, Cotys had succeeded in gaining control of most of the peninsula, thus making the Odrysian kingdom once again the greatest power in the North. In 360 he was assassinated, leaving the kingdom to disintegrate in dynastic struggles. Had he lived longer, he would have posed a serious threat to Philip, who came to the Macedonian throne in that year. The Athenians immediately took advantage of the turmoil in Thrace, and encouraged the division of the kingdom into three parts among Cotys' sons, with Amadocus, Berisades, and Cersebleptes ruling the western, central, and eastern regions respectively. Of the three kings Cersebleptes was the most powerful, and was the major obstacle to Philip's gaining control of Thrace during the first decade of his reign. It was, in fact, only after Philip had established himself as the greatest power in Greece and the North Aegean that he was able to defeat Cersebleptes.[7]

We know far less about the Illyrians who lived northwest of Macedonia, in what is now considered central Albania. These tribes were very warlike and raided many parts of the Mediterranean. Macedonia faced Illyrian invasions a number of times, usually when there was a change in Argead rule (Diod. 14.92.3; 16.2.5–6). As a result of these incursions, the Illyrians had acquired control of a substantial amount of territory in Upper Macedonia by the time of Philip's accession in 360 (Diod. 16.8.1).[8]

THE REIGN OF AMYNTAS III, 393–370

The fourth century began in Macedonia with a pattern that was to become all too familiar: the death of a king and dynastic turmoil. After Archelaus died in 399, the stability that he had created was greatly undermined, as in the next six years five kings from different branches of the Argead royal family held the throne (Diod. 14.37.6; Sync. 482, 498, 500). The last in this series, Amyntas III, followed his predecessors' pattern and gained the throne through assassination (Diod. 14.89.2).

Because of the lack of datable evidence, the reign of Amyntas can be sketched only in rough outline. It is abundantly clear from what little is known, however, that he was continually forced to defend his throne from the threats of invasions by his neighbors and challenges by rival claimants. Soon after Amyntas' accession, the Illyrians attacked and defeated him in battle. Consequently, the king was expelled from the throne, probably by Macedonian nobles disenchanted with his failure to protect the kingdom from invasion (Diod. 14.92.3, 15.19.2; Porphyr. *FHG* 3.691 F1). After three months, however, Amyntas managed to return to power with Thessalian aid.[9] To strengthen his throne and his borders, he formed an alliance with the Illyrian king Sirras, marrying his daughter, Eurydice.[10] They had three sons, Alexander, Perdiccas, and Philip, and one daughter, Eurynoë (Just. 7.4.5). Despite Amyntas' attempt to strengthen his throne, he was driven into exile again in the mid-380s by Argaeus, probably a member of the Argead dynasty, who ruled for two years.[11]

Amyntas managed to recover his throne again, this time probably with the aid of the Olynthians, with whom he formed a defensive alliance. Olynthus, as the head of the Chalcidian League, had emerged as one of the major powers in Greece in this period. The rise of Olynthus can be traced to the period of the Peloponnesian War. Since the mid-fifth century, Olynthus and the other major Chalcidian cities had been members of Athens' Delian League. On the eve of the Peloponnesian War, Potidaea, Olynthus' neighbor to the south, revolted from the League. Perdiccas II, trying to forestall Athenian efforts against his throne, incited a general revolt among the cities of Chalcidice and persuaded the Chalcidians on the coast to relocate at Olynthus. These actions led to the formation of the Chalcidian League and the establishment of Olynthus as a major power in Greece (Thuc. 1.58.1–2).

The support of Olynthus secured Amyntas' position, but at a cost. He was forced to hand over a large amount of territory, including Pella, the royal capital. No doubt he viewed this as a temporary solution that would allow him to rebuild his position. When, however, he later wished to recover the territory he had given up, the Olynthians refused. Amyntas once again sought aid from a Greek state, this time from Sparta, the leading power in Greece.[12] Alarmed at the growth of Olynthian power, the Spartans invaded Chalcidice in 382 (Xen. *Hell.* 5.2.24; Diod. 15.20.2f. (see above, p. 54)). After a long siege they defeated Olynthus and dissolved the Chalcidian League in 379 (Xen. *Hell.* 5.3.26; Diod. 15.23.3).

With the waning of Olynthian power in the early 370s, a new threat emerged in Jason, tyrant of Pherae, who aimed to subdue Macedonia as a step toward gaining hegemony over Greece (Xen. *Hell.* 6.1.11; Diod. 15.60.1). Amyntas again followed a defensive strategy. Since the Spartans were occupied in the Peloponnese, he sought an alliance with the Athenians, who had recently formed the Second Athenian League in the attempt to rebuild their Aegean empire. In the mid-370s, the two powers made a treaty (Tod 129). Amyntas thus acquired support against the ambitions of neighboring powers; in return he supplied the Athenians with timber for their fleet and supported their expansionist aims in the north (Aeschin. 2.32).

Bolstered by the alliance with Athens, Amyntas was now in a stronger position *vis-à-vis* his neighbors. It was probably at this time that he formed an alliance with the Olynthians (Tod 111). The inscription indicates that Amyntas had the upper hand and dictated the terms of the treaty.[13] His power, however, lasted only as long as the Athenians were actively engaged in expansion in the North Aegean. When their attention was diverted to western Greece in the late 370s, the king was again virtually defenseless (Xen. *Hell.* 6.2.31–8, Diod. 15.47.7). When the threat of Jason reappeared, Amyntas had no choice but to become his subject–ally, and they made a treaty.[14] Amyntas' problems with Thessaly were to leave their mark on the policies of his sons. Alexander II would make intervention in Thessalian affairs the mainstay of his foreign policy. Philip would go even further, gaining influence in Thessaly to facilitate his hegemony over the Greeks.

In 370 Amyntas died of old age, one of the few kings in Macedonian history to do so; Jason died in this year as well (Isoc. 6.46; Diod. 15.60.3; Just. 7.4.8). Amyntas' defensive strategy had enabled him to survive dynastic struggles and keep foreign powers out of Macedonia.

It succeeded, however, only when he found a sufficiently strong ally like Sparta or Athens to back him up. At other times Amyntas was forced to form compromising alliances with neighboring powers that prevented him from conducting an independent foreign policy. Without a strong army, it was all he could do to hold onto his kingdom. Expansion beyond Macedonia was an impossibility.

THE REIGN OF ALEXANDER II, 370/69–368/7

Amyntas was succeeded by Alexander, his son and heir-designate (Diod. 15.60.3; Just. 7.4.8). Like his father, Alexander had inherited both domestic and foreign problems that endangered his throne. Ptolemy of Alorus, who had been Amyntas' adviser as well as his son-in-law, was a powerful adversary who wanted the throne for himself. Moreover, Alexander faced threats from two neighbors of Macedonia – not only the Illyrians but also the current tyrant of Pherae, Alexander, who had inherited Jason's aims of Macedonian conquest.

The king dealt with these crises in order. After exiling Ptolemy and his followers (Plut. *Pel.* 26.5), he turned his attention to affairs in Thessaly. At this time, the Aleuads of Larissa were embroiled in a struggle with Alexander of Pherae over control of the Thessalian League. The Aleuads asked King Alexander for aid on the basis of their traditional friendship with the Argeads. Alexander saw the civil war as an opportunity to aid friends while extending his own influence into Thessaly (Diod. 15.61.3–5, 15.67.3; Plut. *Pel.* 26.1). He captured two cities but could not maintain control of them because his troops were insufficiently trained (Diod. 15.62.4). His position was further weakened by the fact that, during his absence, Ptolemy had returned to Macedonia in the hope of seizing the throne. The king made an alliance with the Thebans, whereby he handed over the Thessalian cities to Pelopidas in exchange for support against Ptolemy (Diod. 15.67.4; Plut. *Pel.* 26).

Alexander returned to Macedonia to reassert his right to rule. Realizing, however, that he lacked the forces necessary for dealing with rivals or foreign invaders, he initiated important military reforms. No doubt influenced by the Sacred Band, Pelopidas' crack Theban force, the king created and organized Macedonia's first heavy-armed infantry, the *pezhetairoi* or Foot-Companions (Anax. *FGrH* 72 F4). He did not, however, have much time to train his new army, for war with Ptolemy broke out almost immediately. Both sent ambassadors to Pelopidas requesting aid (Plut. *Pel.* 26.4). Arbitrating the dispute, Pelopidas reaffirmed Alexander's right to rule, but took steps to thwart his power. He restored Alexander's exiled opponents and demanded hostages – the young prince Philip and thirty sons of Macedonian nobles (Diod. 15.67.4; Plut. *Pel.* 26.5). With these measures, Pelopidas effectively reduced the king's power within Macedonia and forced him to conduct foreign policy that was pro-Theban. In late 369, Philip went to Thebes, where as a royal hostage he was to spend the next three years forming ties with prominent politicians and learning about the Greek city-state (see above, pp. 90–2).[15]

Despite Pelopidas' pledge of support, Alexander's position in Macedonia remained precarious. In the summer of 368, Ptolemy assassinated him and seized the throne (Diod. 15.71.1). Alexander's weakness was due to two major errors in policy. First, by exiling his rivals rather than executing them, he failed to secure his throne sufficiently. Second, he attempted to expand beyond the borders of Macedonia before stabilizing his throne and creating a strong infantry. Solving these problems was essential for building a strong Macedonia.

THE REIGN OF PTOLEMY OF ALORUS, 368/7–365/4

At the time of Alexander's death, both of Eurydice's surviving sons were minors, and so Ptolemy became regent, that is, an acknowledged ruler (Aeschin. 2.29). As was usual in Macedonia, the change in rule presented an open invitation to foreign powers to intervene. This time three major Greek states – Olynthus, Athens, and Thebes – took advantage of the opportunity to expand their influence at Macedonian expense.

The Olynthians, the leaders of the Chalcidian League, were the first to act. After the defeat of Sparta at Leuctra in 371, they began rebuilding their League and their hegemony in the north. This policy of expansion put them in direct conflict with the Athenians, who also wished to extend their influence in that region. The two powers became involved in war over Amphipolis, situated near the mouth of the Strymon River in Thrace. This city, a strategically and economically important colony founded under Pericles, had been freed from Athenian control during the Peloponnesian War (Thuc. 4.102–6). In 371 the Athenians decided to regain possession of Amphipolis and shortly thereafter launched a major expedition there (Aeschin. 2.27, 32). The Olynthians in response sent forces to Amphipolis. At this time, they decided to expand into Macedonia as well. In 368 they lent military support to Pausanias, an Argead who wished to challenge Ptolemy's rule (*sch. Aeschin.* 2.27). Ptolemy, realizing that his forces were no match for the Olynthian army, called on the Athenians for aid. They formed an alliance, and the Athenian general Iphicrates defeated Pausanias and expelled him from Macedonia (Aeschin. 2.27–9). Soon afterwards Pelopidas, determined to preserve Theban influence in Macedonia, went to Pella and forced Ptolemy to make an alliance that involved hostages (the king's son and fifty sons of the Companions) and a garrison (Plut. *Pel.* 27.2–3). Thus Ptolemy, like his predecessors, formed alliances with different Greek powers in order to stay on the throne.[16]

With his position secure, in 366 Ptolemy began to look beyond his borders, in particular, at Amphipolis, where Athenian military efforts were making some progress. The Amphipolitans, worried they would soon be forced to surrender to the Athenians, sent ambassadors to Ptolemy asking for an alliance; he agreed, demanding hostages (Dem. 23.149). The Athenians regarded Ptolemy's actions as a betrayal of their alliance (Aeschin. 2.29). His policy was frustrated, however, because the Amphipolitan hostages never reached Macedonia (Dem. 23.149). Shortly thereafter, in another attempt to avoid Athenian domination, the Amphipolitans handed control of their city over to the Olynthians. No more is heard of Ptolemy after this; he became embroiled in a struggle over the throne with Perdiccas and was assassinated (Diod. 15.77.5; see below). Thus Ptolemy, like Alexander, tried to pursue an aggressive foreign policy in the north. He, too, did not get very far, because he had not solved the two problems endemic to Argead rule: dynastic turmoil and an insufficiently trained infantry.[17]

THE REIGN OF PERDICCAS III, 365/4–360/59

When Perdiccas had come of age and wanted the throne that was rightfully his, Ptolemy refused to abdicate. Perdiccas assassinated him and made himself king in 365 (Diod. 15.77.5; *sch. Aeschin.* 2.29). The new ruler, keenly interested in philosophy, had as one of his chief advisers Euphraeus of Oreus, a former student of Plato. Perdiccas' enthusiasm for philosophy could not have been very popular among a nobility accustomed to hunting and drinking, and no doubt was a source of friction at court. Only Philip, who had recently returned to Macedonia from Thebes, is mentioned as a possible source of trouble, but apparently there were others who were dissatisfied with Perdiccas' rule (Diod. 16.2.4; Speus. *Epist. Socrat.* 30.12; Caryst. Perg. *FHG* 4.356 F1).

The fear of dynastic turmoil clearly influenced Perdiccas' early foreign policy. Like Ptolemy, he formed an alliance with the Athenians soon after his accession to strengthen his throne; in return, he agreed to support them against the Chalcidian League in the war over Amphipolis (Dem. 2.14; sch. *ad loc.*).

This arrangement did not last long, however. The Athenians, led by their general Callisthenes, began to enjoy success at Amphipolis. Fearful of Athenian domination, the Amphipolitans turned again to the Macedonian throne for alliance and protection. Perdiccas, like Ptolemy, seized the opportunity to gain control of Amphipolis; unlike Ptolemy, he actually succeeded, installing a garrison (Aeschin. 2.29; Diod. 16.3.3). This move brought on war with Athens, and Callisthenes led forces against Macedonia. During this phase of the war, the Athenians also became engaged in the Chalcidice, where their general Timotheus seized a number of cities, the most important being Potideia (Diod. 15.81.6; Isoc. 15.113). Timotheus' operations were far more successful than those of Callisthenes, who, unable to win a decisive victory, concluded a truce with Perdiccas (Aeschin. 2.30). Soon afterwards, Timotheus campaigned along the Macedonian coast and captured the key cities of Pydna and Methone (Din. 1.14; Dem. 4.4; Tod 143). Yet he could not force Perdiccas to surrender, and the king managed to recover Methone ([Dem.] 50.46). More importantly, Perdiccas held onto Amphipolis, which he controlled for the rest of his reign (Diod. 16.3.3).[18]

Perdiccas thus managed to expand Macedonian influence in the north, despite the efforts of two major Greek powers. This was no small achievement. Although the Amphipolitans' efforts to defend themselves certainly played a role, he was truly the first Argead to pursue an aggressive foreign policy with any success. But there was a limit to what any king could do without a strong infantry. In the summer of 360, the Illyrians invaded Macedonia, killing Perdiccas and decimating his army (Diod. 16.2.4–5). Macedonia again lay open to her enemies.

THE REIGN OF PHILIP II, 360/59–336/5

Upon the death of Perdiccas, Philip II came to the throne, and in the course of his reign transformed Macedon from a divided and defenseless kingdom into the most powerful state in the Greek world. To understand why he was so much more successful than any of his Argead predecessors, we need to examine his career from its very beginning.

Philip's youth

Philip's experiences during his youth provided unique preparation for the throne. The period in which he grew up was an especially turbulent one in Macedonia. Amyntas' difficulties in strengthening his kingdom, as well as the dynastic turmoil of the 360s, cannot have failed to make an impression on the young prince. These were problems that he would make a point of dealing with as soon as he took the throne.

More important, however, Philip had one experience which no Argead before him had ever had. As noted earlier, for over three years (369–365) he was a hostage in Thebes, which was the leading power in Greece at this time. Philip lived at the house of Pammenes, an important politician and general; as a royal hostage, he was treated well, and developed close ties with the Theban aristocracy (Plut. *Pel.* 26.5). While living in Thebes the young prince learned military, political, and social lessons that were to prove extremely useful during his reign.

Philip alone had the opportunity to observe the training of the Sacred Band, thus learning military tactics that he would later use when training his own heavy infantry. He would make military reforms his first major undertaking after securing his throne. Philip also witnessed firsthand how a Greek government, in particular a hegemonial democracy, functioned. This insight would later enable him to deal more effectively with the Greek states, especially Athens. The young prince learned a great deal about international relations as well, for he was in Thebes when at least one major congress was convened there.[19] He thus had the opportunity to see how a Greek international congress operated; this knowledge would prove quite useful later when he himself participated in such congresses. Finally, Philip's Theban stay gave him insight into Greek values, which he used to convince the Greek world that he was a Greek of the highest international prestige. Clearly, the lessons he had learned as a hostage in Thebes greatly contributed to the success of his reign.

Philip's accession

Philip came to the throne in the autumn of 360, immediately after the death of Perdiccas. Most likely during the first years of his reign he ruled as regent for Perdiccas' son, Amyntas, and then declared himself king once he had a legitimate heir, after the birth of Alexander in 356.[20] There was, however, no discernible difference in Philip's powers during his regency and his reign. Like his predecessors, he singlehandedly made all decisions concerning domestic and foreign policy.

Philip's accession, like those of his predecessors, was attended by crises. He faced invasions by the Illyrians and the Paeonians. At the same time, a number of rivals claimed their right to the throne: his three half-brothers, Archelaus, Arrhidaeus, and Menelaus; Pausanias, supported by a king of Thrace; and Argaeus, supported by the Athenians.[21] Unlike his predecessors, however, Philip succeeded in eliminating the various threats to his rule, clearly because of his pragmatic approach to his problems. He immediately had Archelaus executed, although the two younger brothers, Arrhidaeus and Menelaus, managed to escape.[22] He gave lavish gifts to the kings of Paeonia and Thrace and dissuaded them from invading (Diod. 16.3.4). To placate the Athenians, he immediately removed the Macedonian garrison from Amphipolis. Dissatisfied with the terms the king offered, they sent Argaeus with forces to Macedonia. Philip easily defeated his rival. Knowing, however, that his throne was too fragile to risk a protracted war with Athens at this time, he withdrew his claim to Amphipolis. With this move he convinced the Athenians to make peace and alliance (Diod. 16.2.6, 3.3–6, 4.1). The Athenians tried to seize control of Amphipolis, but were defeated once again (*sch. Aeschin.* 2.31).

Military and political reforms

While dealing with these different crises, Philip initiated military reforms, in the realization that a strong army was crucial to preserving his throne and expanding the power of Macedon. Diodorus, our chief source on this matter, speaks about these reforms only in a very general way in his discussion of Philip's accession (Diod. 16.3.1–3). Our knowledge of the details comes mostly from sources on the reign of Alexander the Great.

The best known of Philip's military reforms is his formation of the great Macedonian phalanx, developed from the Foot Companions that Alexander II had created. Philip made tactical innovations that gave his infantry distinct advantages on the battlefield. Most important of these was the *sarissa*, a pike up to 18 feet long.

This weapon, twice the length of the Greek hoplite's thrusting spear, enabled the Macedonian soldier to strike the enemy from a distance, before the enemy could strike him. To compensate for the size and weight of this weapon, Philip reduced the size of the body armor and shield. As a result, the Macedonian phalanx could maneuver far more easily than its Greek counterpart. The reduction in armor had another advantage. In an age when men provided their own armor, this equipment was far less expensive, thereby making it possible to recruit great numbers of soldiers. Famous for their rigorous training and discipline, Philip's infantry were practically professional soldiers.

Philip also made improvements in the cavalry, which consisted of two types of units. The Companions were an elite corps of heavy-armed cavalry drawn from the Macedonian nobility (Anax. *FGrH* 72 F4). These were large landowners who provided their own armor – a helmet, breastplate, shield, greaves, spear of cornel-wood (the strongest wood available), and short sword. A select number fought under the king personally as a Royal Bodyguard, the *Somatophylax*. The rest of the cavalry, the Sarissa-bearers or Scouts, were light horse who came from the class of less wealthy landowners. Most likely Philip organized them into squadrons on a regional and ethnic basis, for that is how they were organized in Alexander's day. Their weaponry was lighter than that of the Companions, since they probably did not wear a breastplate. Like the infantry, they carried a *sarissa* (or a cavalry version of the weapon) rather than the shorter lance of the Companions. The cavalry, trained to work in conjunction with the infantry, was used primarily to exploit gaps in the enemy phalanx.[23]

Philip was responsible for one other important military reform, the improvement of the siege engine first used in Greek warfare by Dionysius I of Syracuse in the early 390s (Diod. 14.41–2). His engineers succeeded in adding torsion to the catapult, thus making it possible to hurl large stones against city walls. Philip's first use of the torsion-catapult, at Byzantium and Perinthus in 340/39, was unsuccessful (Diod. 16.74.2–76.4). Alexander would, however, later use it with greater success.[24]

The ancient evidence makes it clear that Philip devoted much attention to expanding the size of the army. In 358, the infantry available for battle numbered 10,000 and the cavalry 600 (Diod. 16.4.3); by the time of Alexander's departure for Asia in 334, the infantry ready and mobilized had grown to 30,000 and the cavalry to 4,000 (Diod. 17.17.3–5). This manpower when mustered must have been truly overwhelming.

Aware that the creation of a strong infantry could undermine the position of the Macedonian nobility, Philip took steps to counteract this possibility. By giving them gifts – in particular, land from newly conquered territory – he ensured that they would be loyal to him alone (Diod. 16.3.3; 34.5; 53.3). During his reign the infantry became an important political force. As the evidence for the capital trials held under Alexander shows, the king regularly tested out his influence and prestige among the soldiers before he took important action. The infantry did not take part in judicial decision-making; rather, the king wished to ascertain that his personal political position in the army remained pre-eminent.[25]

Philip took other steps to enhance the power of the monarchy. As noted earlier, he established the Royal Bodyguard, which provided personal protection. In order to ensure the loyalty of the Macedonian nobility, he instituted the Royal Pages, sons of friends and relatives (Arr. *An.* 4.13.1). In addition, he established the Royal Secretary and Archive (Plut. *Eum.* 2.6). One scholar, noting also Philip's polygamy, has suggested that the king borrowed these ideas from Achaemenid practice.[26] Although this view may be exaggerated, the increasingly autocratic nature of Macedonian kingship did in some respects come to resemble its Persian counterpart.

One other political innovation deserves mention here. Philip founded a number of cities, most in Thrace, for the purposes of pacifying and maintaining control of the region (Diod. 16.71.2). These cities were also intended to develop the agricultural and commercial potential of the area. Their populations were mixed, comprising Macedonians, Greeks, and some local inhabitants (Plut. *Alex.* 9.1). Philippi is the best known of the cities he founded (Diod. 16.8.7).[27]

Foreign policy

Philip's greatest achievements no doubt lie in the realm of foreign policy. He remains one of the great figures of classical antiquity because he created a long-lasting hegemony over all the Greek states in the peninsula when no individual or state had ever succeeded in doing so before. The reasons for his success can be found in his pragmatism, seen not only in his approach to the problems that had been chronically ailing Macedonia, but also as in his methods of dealing with the Greeks and non-Greeks of the Aegean world.

Early reign

Once Philip had freed his throne of pretenders, he turned his attention to his neighbors in the north, whose invasions had repeatedly threatened Argead rule. Defeating the Illyrians in his first major battle, Philip regained control of Upper Macedonia and incorporated it into his kingdom (Diod. 16.4.3–7, 8.1). He turned his attention to expanding Macedonian influence elsewhere in the North Aegean. In 357 he captured Amphipolis (Diod. 16.8.2). The Athenians were outraged, but did nothing to stop the king while the siege was in progress because they had been led to believe he would give them Amphipolis after he captured it. And so they turned down requests for aid, first from the Olynthians and then from the Amphipolitans themselves, who had offered to hand over their city (Dem. 1.8–9; Dem. 2.6; [Dem.] 7.27). Ironically, after trying for so long to recover control of Amphipolis, the Athenians thus passed up the one sure chance that came their way. After capturing Amphipolis, Philip acquired the plentiful gold and silver mines of Pangaeum, and thus established the financial means for hegemony (Diod. 16.8.2, 6–7). He never did give Amphipolis to the Athenians.

During this period Philip achieved two other important successes. In July 356, his wife Olympias gave birth to his first son, Alexander (Plut. *Alex.* 3.5). With the birth of a legitimate heir, Philip strengthened his hold on the throne. He carefully groomed Alexander for the throne, appointing Aristotle as his tutor in 342 (Plut. *Alex.* 7). Two years later the crown prince would govern Macedonia, while Philip was away in Thrace (Plut. *Alex.* 9.1). In 338 Alexander was to play a major role at the battle of Chaeronea (Diod. 16.86.3–4; Plut. *Alex.* 9.2).

In the same month as Alexander's birth, Philip also achieved a major diplomatic success. He entered the Olympic Games at this time, the first possible opportunity since his accession. This was, as far as we know, the first time since the reign of Alexander I that an Argead competed in the Games. Philip took first place in the four-horse chariot race (Plut. *Alex.* 3.8). As a result of this victory, he was considered a Greek of the highest international prestige and could intervene in Greek affairs with considerable authority.

Expansion, 356–346

Shortly after Philip's capture of Amphipolis, a conflict erupted that would enable him to expand his hegemony into central and southern

Greece. The Third Sacred War began in 356 when the Amphictyonic Council decided to punish the Phocians for their sacrilege of the shrine at Delphi (Diod. 16.23–31.5). Philip's entrée to the conflict was provided by the civil war which had broken out again in Thessaly between Lycophron, the current tyrant of Pherae, and the Aleuads of Larissa. Intervening on behalf of the Aleuads, Philip was made *tagos*, leader of the Thessalian League and commander of its forces. The Phocians and Athenians came to Lycophron's aid, thus transforming the civil war into a front of the Sacred War. In 352 Philip defeated his enemies decisively and consolidated his control over Thessaly (Diod. 16.35; Just. 8.2.1–7). He then returned to the north to expand his hegemony there, while the Sacred War continued in central Greece (see above, pp. 94–8).

A second major war broke out in the year 356. The Athenians, realizing that Philip was not going to hand Amphipolis over to them after all, decided to take steps to recover it. So began the last phase of the war between Athens and the Argeads over Amphipolis. In the first three years of this conflict, Philip appreciably extended his hegemony in the north, forming an alliance with Olynthus and capturing a number of Athenian-held cities (Dem. 1.9, Diod. 16.8.3, 31.6, 34.4–5). But in the late 350s, Olynthus, fearing the growth of Philip's power, turned to Athens for aid and took in his half-brothers with a view to making them candidates for the throne (Dem. 23.108–9; Just. 8.3.10). The king responded to the betrayal by mounting massive expeditions against the Chalcidian League, operations made famous by the three *Olynthiacs* of Demosthenes (Diod. 16.52.2). At the orator's urging, the Athenians sent aid to Olynthus but to no avail (Philoch. *FGrH* 328 FF49–51; Suda, s.v. *Karanos*). In 348 Philip took the city by treason (Dem. 19.192; Diod. 16.53.2, 55.1).

The fall of Olynthus signalled that Philip was now the greatest power in the Aegean Greek world. In 346 he convinced the Athenians to make peace and alliance and give up their claim to Amphipolis; this treaty is known as the Peace of Philocrates after the Athenian who brought it about (Aeschin. 2.13, 82; Dem. 19.150). In the same year, Philip brought an end to the Sacred War. He presided over the next meeting of the Amphictyonic Council, which meted out a severe punishment to the Phocians (Diod. 16.60.1–3; Dem. 5 *Hyp.*; Dem. 19.325; Paus. 10.3.1–3, 8.2). Philip thus avenged the Phocian sacrilege and established himself as *hegemon* over Greece.

Hegemony threatened, 345-338

In the years that followed, Philip lost nearly everything that he had achieved so far, as his hegemony began to unravel in Greece.[28] In 344 he began intervening actively in the Peloponnese to prevent the re-establishment of Spartan hegemony there (Dem. 6.15). Increasingly dissatisfied with the terms of the Peace of Philocrates, the Athenians made the first in a series of attempts to rouse opposition among the Greeks to Philip's hegemony (Dem. *Hyp.* 6). In 343 the king offered to make amendments to the Peace, but negotiations broke down over the Athenians' demand that Amphipolis be returned to them.[29] During this period Philip was also having trouble in Thessaly, where his position had been strongest.

In the late 340s Philip continued to intervene in affairs in southern Greece. Moreover, he intervened in Thessaly, where he revived the ancestral form of government, with the aim of tightening his control on the region (Dem. 6.22; 9.26). Although these actions strengthened the king's position, they exacerbated the fears of many Greeks. As a result, the Athenians, led by Demosthenes, succeeding in winning over a number of Peloponnesian states to their cause (Dem. 9.72; *sch. Aeschin.* 3.83; *IG* II^2 225).

During this period Philip began making diplomatic and military preparations for expansion into a new region altogether, the Persian empire. By 342 he was conspiring with Hermias, tyrant of Atarneus and father-in-law of Aristotle, against the Great King (Dem. 10.32; *sch. ad loc.* 10.32). He then mounted a large expedition to Thrace to consolidate control on his eastern flank and to create a secure land route to the crossing points for Asia.[30]

Meanwhile, the Athenians continued to rouse opposition to Philip in southern Greece. They also tried to curtail his expansion in Thrace and the Chersonesus.[31] Alarmed at growing opposition in the Hellespont, Philip cut short his Thracian campaign, and in 340 besieged Perinthus and Byzantium (Diod. 16.74.2–76.4; Philoch. *FGrH* 328 F54; [Dem.] 11.5; Arr. *Anab.* 2.14.5; Paus. 1.29.10). Realizing that war with the Athenians was inevitable, he captured their corn fleet on its way from the Bosporus.[32] The Athenian Assembly declared war and broke down the stele recording the Peace of Philocrates ([Dem.] 11. Hyp., *sch. Dem.* 18.76).

In 339 the Fourth Sacred War began in central Greece when the Amphictyonic Council declared war on Amphissa for cultivating the sacred plain of Cirrha near Delphi. Two states abstained: the

Thebans, allies of Amphissa, and the Athenians, who hoped to improve relations with their inveterate enemy Thebes. In the second year of the war, the Amphicytons called on Philip to lead their army against Amphissa. Marching at once into central Greece, the king seized Elatea in Phocis and asked the Thebans for free passage through Boeotia. When the news reached Athens, Demosthenes convinced the panic-stricken Assembly to ask the Thebans for an alliance. The Thebans agreed, thus choosing Athens over their ally Philip. After capturing Amphissa in 338, Philip headed for Boeotia. The culmination of the hostilities took place in August at Chaeronea, where he decisively defeated his enemies, despite their advantage in numbers and battle position. The credit for his success belongs to the superior training and tactics of the Macedonian army and to Alexander's command of the cavalry (see also above pp. 100–02).[33]

After the battle, Philip arranged settlements with the participants. In general, he rewarded his friends and punished his enemies. The Athenians were the exception to the rule. Although they had led the resistance movement, the king treated them well because he needed their fleet for his Persian expedition and was unlikely to take their well-fortified city. By contrast, of his enemies he punished the Thebans most severely, because they had betrayed their long-standing friendship and alliance with him.[34] Having thus tightened his control on the major cities in Greece, the king was ready to turn his full attention to Persia.

The final years, 338–336

After completing his settlements with the Greek states, Philip began laying the groundwork for his Persian crusade. Calling upon the Greeks to join him in avenging Xerxes' invasion of 150 years earlier, he convened a congress to found a new league, the Hellenic League, which met at Corinth in 338/7. After forming a Common Peace, the League appointed Philip *hegemon* or commander of its forces and declared war on Persia.[35]

In the spring of 336, Philip sent an advance force under Attalus and Parmenion to Persia (Diod.16.91.2, 17.2.4; Just. 9.5.8–9). The king, however, never got there himself, for he was assassinated at his daughter's wedding in the autumn of that year. The circumstances of the murder reveal much about Philip's attitude at this point in his career. On the second day of the festivities, when a great procession made its way into the theater, he had a statue of himself carried along with those of the twelve Olympian gods. In an effort to show that he was protected by the goodwill of the Greeks, he refused to let his guards stand near him as he walked in the procession. Pausanias, a member of the Royal Guard, rushed up and stabbed him with a sword.[36]

Pausanias' motives were personal, arising from a grievance with Attalus that Philip had refused to address. But as the ancient sources themselves recognized, there was also a political element in the murder. Troubles in the Macedonian court had begun in 337, when Philip married Cleopatra, Attalus' niece. He had married his six other wives for political purposes (Sat. *FHG* 3.161 F5 = Athen. 13.557 B–D). Cleopatra, by contrast, he married for love. She thereby supplanted Olympias, who as the mother of Philip's firstborn son had previously enjoyed supremacy at the court. Olympias and Alexander did not take this lightly (Plut. *Alex.* 9.5–11). Rather than making greater efforts to guard his throne and provide for his succession, Philip abandoned the fiercely protective attitude he had displayed earlier in his reign. After establishing hegemony over all of Greece, he had apparently begun to regard himself as invulnerable, perhaps even divine. Forgetting the important lessons of survival he had learned as a youth, Philip, too, became a victim of dynastic turmoil.[37]

Despite the abrupt end to his career, Philip had without question done more to make Macedon a great power than any of his Argead predecessors. The reason for his success is quite simple. Utterly pragmatic, he made a concerted effort to solve the problems that had long plagued Macedonia: dynastic turmoil, invasions, and the lack of a viable hoplite army. By solving these problems, he could devote his attention to building his hegemony without fear of internal collapse. Philip was also pragmatic when it came to building that hegemony, seizing opportunities when they were presented to him and backing away from circumstances that were unfavorable. It can be no accident that he is responsible for making Macedon the greatest power in the Greek world in the fourth century.

NOTES

1 C. F. Edson, 'Early Macedonia,' *AM* 1 (1970), 2–24.
2 See E. Badian, 'Greeks and Macedonians,' in Barr-Sharrar, pp. 33–51; Edson, 'Early Macedonia,' pp. 25–44. On timber, see R. Meiggs, *Trees and Timber in the Ancient Mediterranean World*, Oxford, Clarendon Press, 1982, pp. 118–23, 325.

3 E.g., Thuc. 1.57.2–5, 62.2, 4.128.5. See Borza, pp. 133–60.
4 Thuc. 2.100.2; Hammond in Hammond–Griffith, p. 150.
5 See Badian, 'Greeks and Macedonians,' p. 35.
6 On the Odrysian kings of the fifth century, see A. Fol and I. Marazov, *Thrace and the Thracians*, New York, St. Martin's Press, 1977, pp. 150–2.
7 On Cotys' successors, see Dem. 23.163–80; E. Badian, 'Philip II and Thrace,' *Pulpudeva* 4 (1983), 54–69.
8 For discussion of the Illyrian tribes, see N. G. L. Hammond, 'The Kingdoms in Illyria circa 400–167 BC,' *ABSA* 61 (1966), 239–53.
9 Diod. 14.92.3. He was reportedly aided by the Thessalians (Isoc. 6.46); most likely the aid came from the Aleuads, the leading aristocratic clan in the city of Larissa, who had traditional ties with the Argeads.
10 E. Badian, 'Eurydice,' in W. L. Adams and E. N. Borza (eds) in *Philip II, Alexander the Great and the Macedonian Heritage*, Washington, DC, University Press of America, 1982, p. 103.
11 Diod. 14.92.4, 15.19.2; Beloch, *GG*,[2] 3.2.57–8; F. Geyer, *Makedonien bis zur Thronsbesteigung Philipps II*, Munich/Berlin, R. Oldenbourg, 1930, pp. 112–18; J. R. Ellis, 'Amyntas III, Illyria and Olynthos, 393/2–380/79,' *Makedonika*, 9 (1969), 7.
12 Diod. 15.9.3. At least two towns in Chalcidice seeking protection from Olynthus made similar requests (Xen. *Hell*. 5.2.11–19).
13 The date of this treaty is not preserved. Scholars have traditionally dated it to early in Amyntas' reign, when he needed support against the Illyrians. The terms, however, are clearly favorable to the king and indicate that he had the upper hand at the time the alliance was concluded. It is therefore more likely that the treaty belongs in the period after his alliance with Athens.
14 Diod. 15.60.2, dated to 371/0.
15 Diod. 16.2.2–3; Plut. *Pel*. 26.6–7; Just. 7.5.2–3. See discussion of Philip's youth below.
16 For discussion of Alexander's and Ptolemy's relations with Thebes, see J. Buckler, *The Theban Hegemony, 371–362 BC*, Cambridge, Harvard University Press, 1980, pp. 112–23.
17 For Ptolemy's foreign policy, see J. Heskel, *The North Aegean Wars, 371–360 BC*, Stuttgart, Franz Steiner Verlag, 1996, ch. 2.
18 For Perdiccas' war with Athens, see Heskel, ibid.
19 The chief source is Xen. *Hell*. 7.1.39–40. Philip may have been in Thebes when a second major congress was held there in the spring of 365 (Xen. *Hell*. 7.4.10–11; Diod. 15.76.3; Theop. *FGrH* 115 F239). For discussion of the two congresses, see Buckler, *Theban Hegemony*, pp. 158–60, 198–201.
20 Just. 7.5.10; Plut. *Pel*. 3.10; *IG* 7.3055; Beloch, *GG*,[2] 3.1.232 n. 3.
21 Diod. 16.2.5–6, 3.3–4; this king, not identified in the sources, is thought to be Berisades or Cersebleptes (Beloch, *GG*,[2] 3.1.225 n. 1; Badian, 'Philip II and Thrace,' p. 54).
22 Just. 7.4.5, 8.3.10; Theop. *FGrH* 115 F29; Beloch, *GG*,[2] 3.1.225, 2.67. Arrhidaeus and Menelaus later turn up at Olynthus. See discussion below.

23 For discussion of the Macedonian cavalry, see Griffith in Hammond-Griffith, pp. 408–14.
24 For discussion of Philip's innovation of the siege engine, see E. W. Marsden, *Greek and Roman Artillery: Historical Developments*, 2 vols, Oxford, Clarendon Press, 1969, 1:58–60.
25 See R. M. Errington, 'The Nature of the Macedonian State under the Monarchy,' *Chiron* 8 (1978), 86–112.
26 D. Kienast, *Philipp II. von Makedonien und das Reich der Achaimeniden*, Abhandlungen der Marburger Gelehrten Gesellschaft 1971, no. 6, esp. pp. 247–73.
27 See N. G. L. Hammond, *The Macedonian State*, Oxford, Clarendon Press, 1989, p. 183.
28 For a detailed account of these events with the ancient references, see Griffith in Hammond-Griffith, pp. 469–554.
29 [Dem.] 7.24–9. [Dem.] 7, Hegesippus' speech *On Halonnesus*, is the chief piece of evidence for the negotiations concerning the amending of the Peace of Philocrates. See E. M. Harris, *Aeschines and Athenian Politics*, New York, Oxford University Press, 1995, pp. 107–23, who argues that during this period Philip was concerned to preserve the *status quo* in Central and Southern Greece while strengthening his position in the North.
30 Sat. *FHG* 3.161 F5 = Athen. 13.557 D; Dem. 8.44, Theop. *FGrH* 115 F110; [Dem.] 12.8; Diod. 16.71.1–2.
31 Plut. *Dem.* 17.1; Philoch. *FGrH* 328 F 159; *sch. Aeschin.* 3.85, 3.103; Diod. 16.74.1; *IG* II² 230; [Dem.] 7.39–43; Dem. 8. *Hyp.*; Dem. 8.9, 16; [Dem.] 12.3, 11; Dem. 18.302.
32 Dem. 18.73, 139; *sch. ad loc.* 18.73; Theop. *FGrH* 115 F292; Philoch. *FGrH* 328 F 162; Front. *Strat.* 1.4.13; Just. 9.1.5–6.
33 For the evidence and a detailed discussion of the Fourth Sacred War, see Griffith in Hammond-Griffith, pp. 585–603.
34 For a list of the evidence for the various settlements, see C. Roebuck, 'The Settlements of Philip II in 338 B.C.' *CP* (43) 1948, 73–92.
35 Tod no. 177; Diod. 16.89.3; Just. 9.5.1–7; Dem. 18.201; Aeschin. 3.132; Ox. Chron. *FGrH* 255 F5; Polyb. 9.33.7; Plut. *Instit. Lacon.* 42.240A.
36 Diodorus 16.91.4–95.1 provides the fullest account of the assassination. See also Just. 9.6.1–7.
37 For a discussion of the events leading to Philip' assassination, see E. Badian, 'The Death of Philip II,' *Phoenix*, 17 (1963), 244–50.

8

RESISTANCE TO ALEXANDER THE GREAT

Waldemar Heckel

The assassination of Philip II in October 336,[1] placed in jeopardy not only the settlement of Greece effected in 337 and the war with Persia, inaugurated by Parmenion and Attalus in the spring of 336, but the security of the Macedonian kingdom itself. If not, in fact, symptomatic of political dissatisfaction at home,[2] Philip's death was the signal for rebellion, an irresistible invitation to test the stability of the kingdom and the mettle of its new king. For the neighbours of Macedon, Alexander was an unknown quantity, despite Plutarch's portrait of the precocious youth who had interrogated Persian envoys on points of strategy and logistics, campaigned against the Maedi at sixteen, and commanded the Macedonian right at Chaeronea two years later (*Alex.* 5.1–3; 9.1–2). Demosthenes soon learned to regret calling him 'a child and Margites,'[3] but he was not alone in undervaluing Alexander; at home as well as abroad there were those who despised him (Diod. 17.2.2). The brush-fires of rebellion foreboded greater conflagration (see Plate 17 and above p. 35).

EUROPE

On the northern marches, the influence of Pella was new and intrusive. Those Illyrian campaigns of the fourth century that have found their way into our historical accounts are highlights of a perennial struggle. Illyrian forces drove Amyntas III temporarily from the throne (393/2–391/0) and in 360 terminated the brief reign and life of Perdiccas III; as late as 344/3 and 337/6 they were inflicting serious casualties on Macedonian armies.[4] Political marriage, both on a dynastic and aristocratic level, provided some stability, but the frontiers were rugged and without permanent military presence, and the temptation to challenge Macedonian *imperium* great. Bardylis

Plate 17 Head of Alexander the Great, from Megara(?), *c.* 310 BC. Artist unknown. Marble, height 0.28m. Collection of the J. Paul Getty Museum, Malibu, California, 73.AA.27. Photo: J. Paul Getty Museum.

had indeed been brought into closer alliance in 359/8 by Philip's marriage to Audata (renamed Eurydice, perhaps in honour of her mother-in-law), but the dynastic links between Illyrians and Epirots appear to represent an alliance of the barbarous west against the emerging champions of 'Hellenism.' When Alexander's Persian adventure began in 334, the army contained few attested Illyrians and no Epirots; the commanders of the Thracian 'allies' provided useful hostages.[5]

To the south, Philip had lacked sufficient time 'to tame Greece and put it under the yoke' (Plut. *Alex.* 11.2). 'Alexander's Ladder' at Mt. Ossa (Polyaenus, *Strat.* 4.3.23) cut a path around Thessalian resistance in 336, and the rapid election of the king as *archon* of the Thessalian League and his recognition by the Amphictyones at 'the Gates' were gestures of contrition and military impotence. Further south the Thebans, Athenians and Spartans all made noises, only to be silenced by the speed of the new king's arrival in Greece. At Corinth they elected him Philip's successor as *hegemon* and *strategos* of the 'Panhellenic Crusade' – though Sparta, from a mixture of arrogance and petulance, held aloof, a foreshadowing of Agis' ill-fated 'war.' The concerns of central and southern Greece were, however, different from those of the Thessalians, whom events since the death of Jason of Pherae had moved out of the political orbit of Thebes and into that of Macedon. For the moment, Greece stood still, incapacitated by internal divisions and fear of Macedonian arms.

Alexander may, nevertheless, have under-estimated the extent of Greek opposition. Arrian (1.1.4) depicts his campaigns against the Triballians and Illyrians as pre-emptive, in preparation for his Asiatic expedition, so that he would leave behind borders that were secure. This implies that he would turn his attention to Persia in 335 and expected no further trouble from the south. Overpowering the barbarians, including the 'independent Thracians' in the hill country northeast of Amphipolis, Alexander invaded the territory of the Triballians. Their king, Syrmus, withdrew to the Danube, leaving the non-combatants on the island of Peuce, before succumbing to the destructive Macedonian phalanx. The expedition did more than merely bring the Triballians into submission: it served as a warning to the dependent kings in Thrace, and established the Danube as the northern frontier. To the west, the menacing gestures of the Autariatae were derided by Langarus, king of the Agrianes, a stout ally who called them 'the least warlike tribe in those parts' (Arr. 1.5.3) and kept them in check while Alexander moved to the region south of Lake Ochrid to confront a rising by the Dardanian chieftains, Glaucias and Cleitus.[6]

By spring 335 Alexander's lengthy absence in the north spawned rumors that he had been killed in Illyria. Whether such reports had actually reached Athens or were invented there by the anti-Macedonian party, we cannot be sure, but in the latter case Demosthenes and his supporters must shoulder a greater share of the blame for the fate of the Thebans, whose attempt to oust the Macedonian garrison from the Cadmea was prompted by the report. For Thebes there was also the bitter legacy of Chaeronea. Philip's treatment of the city, the scene of his early years of political captivity, had been comparatively harsh: the opponents of the king were executed and the government entrusted to an oligarchy of 300, supported by a Macedonian garrison. The 'Boeotian League' continued to exist, but the reconstitution of Thespiae, Plataea, and Orchomenus subverted Thebes' ability to dominate. Confident of Athenian, and apparently Persian (cf. Just. 11.3.9) support, the anti-Macedonian party, led by Phoenix and Prothytes and armed in exile by Demosthenes,[7] besieged the garrison on the Cadmea and proclaimed their intention to liberate Greece from Macedonian control with the help of Persia (Diod. 17.9.5).

Alexander moved from western Macedonia to Boeotia in less than two weeks. The suddenness of his arrival stunned even those who had treated the rumors of his death with skepticism. Demosthenic Athens, which had voted military aid, now prevaricated; reinforcements from the Peloponnesus likewise delayed, perhaps restrained by the diplomacy of Antipater.[8] Their inaction proved fatal for Thebes. Alexander needed to make an example of an important Greek polis, and found a convenient target: in addition to a long history of Medism, the city had won few allies despite its comparatively benign hegemony of the 360s. Alexander could destroy Thebes, claiming to fulfil the infamous 'Oath of Plataea,' and set an example for the rest of Greece without striking out 'one of its two eyes.' It was an act of terror that carried with it the message of the Panhellenic crusade: this was the beginning of the war on Persia. On a less elevated plane, responsibility for razing the city and enslaving its population could be fobbed off on the Phocians and disaffected Boeotians, whose more immediate grievances demanded the destruction of an ancient enemy. Even among compatriots, bonds of kinship and ethnicity meant little as the pro-Macedonian party drove up the price of captives in their zeal to enslave political enemies

(Just. 11.4.8). Athens could bemoan the Thebans' fate, but the hypocrisy is brought home by the story that the orator Hypereides purchased a Theban captive named Phila for 20 minae and kept her as his mistress in Eleusis.[9] In all, some 6,000 Thebans fell in battle and another 30,000 were auctioned off, netting a sum of 440 talents.

Predictably, Athenian opposition melted away, as the *demos* pondered Chaeronea, its worst disaster since the Peloponnesian War. Bellicose oratory, and resolutions passed on emotion, gave way to prudence and fear of the Macedonian juggernaut. Persuaded by Demades, the city sent an embassy to Alexander congratulating him on his victories in the north and seeking forgiveness for its own part in the uprising. The king at first demanded the surrender of ten prominent orators and generals, but in the end insisted on only one intractable enemy – Charidemus of Oropus, who promptly sought refuge at the court of Darius III.[10] Military action against Athens would have been costly and counter-productive. Not only did Alexander have to consider, as Philip II did in 338, the ancient reputation of Athens, but he needed the city's naval strength for the impending war in the east. In the event, the role of Athenian sea power was negligible, but Alexander's clemency had served its purpose. For the duration of his reign, the Athenians remained idle, refusing to join in Agis' war and rebuffing Harpalus in 324. When they did finally join the Hellenic uprising against Antipater in the following year, taking a lead in the so-called 'Lamian War,' the results were tragic. But for the moment, Athens had gained by not putting her military strength to the test.

For the Greek world in general, the winter of 335/4 must have been one of bitter disappointment. But the leading states had only themselves to blame: the pernicious struggle for hegemony that followed the Peloponnesian War had debilitated Athens, Sparta, Thebes, and their adherents. The Third Sacred War, which had opened the door to central Greece for Philip II, had divided Thebes from Athens and Sparta. When Thebes and Athens combined to resist Philip in 338, Sparta held aloof. And so it was to continue, through the war of Agis, and later the Lamian war. Secretly, opposition continued in the form of embassies to the Great King, but officially there was support for Macedon and the expedition.

ASIA MINOR

The army that crossed into Asia included 600 allied cavalry from states south of Thessaly (Diod. 17.17.4) and numerous Greek mercenaries, but the number of Greeks who took service with the Persian king and his satraps was far greater, and the early years of the campaign saw ambassadors from various states in the Persian camp. The Greeks of Asia Minor too resisted the Macedonian invasion, partly in opposition to the growing Macedonian empire, but mainly because they had been schooled in the facts concerning 'liberation' from Persia by Athens and Sparta. Many cities and villages had found Greek armies a greater burden on their economies than Persian rule. In truth, Persian domination had been relatively benign and, for the ruling aristocratic oligarchies, essential. Thus, for the modern reader, Alexander's instructions to Alcimachus to establish democracies in Aeolia (Arr. 1.18.1), and the efforts of Hegelochus and Amphoterus to remove the tyrannies from the coastal islands, appear misleadingly as noble actions which the local populations ought to have welcomed (see also above pp. 125–6).[11]

Before Alexander's arrival, there had been grounds for optimism in the Troad, where the Macedonian expeditionary force under Parmenion and Attalus had stalled.[12] The Macedonians had taken Cyzicus – some 190 stades from Zeleia (Strab. 13.1.10) and thus dangerously close to Dascylium – but were checked when they pushed south to Magnesia by Memnon, a Rhodian adventurer (and son-in-law of Artabazus) who had estates in the Troad.[13] Memnon then crossed the range of Ida and fell just short of retaking Cyzicus. The Macedonian forces, weakened by internal dissension and the execution of one of their generals, Attalus, soon found themselves driven back to the Hellespontine coast. Parmenion, indeed, had taken Grynium, sacking the town and enslaving its inhabitants, apparently on the pretext of punishing 'Medisers,' but was driven off when he attempted to besiege Pitane. Elsewhere, Persian forces outnumbered Calas son of Harpalus, Parmenion's colleague and, perhaps, Attalus' replacement,[14] driving him back to the peninsula of Rhoeteum (Diod. 17.7.10). By the time the 'Panhellenic army' arrived at Sestus, the advance party had managed to retain only a toe-hold in Asia.

For the defenders of Asia, namely the western satraps, Alexander's crossing with a force in excess of 40,000 constituted a state of emergency. Satrapal levies converged on Zeleia in Hellespontine Phrygia where their leaders held a council of war. It was determined, despite the advice of Memnon, who advocated a 'scorched-earth' policy, to confront the invader at the Granicus river to the west. And here, although it was a popular motif in the Greek historians to depict the Persian court as faction-ridden, the self-interests of the satraps clearly outweighed the needs of the Empire, and the paladins of Asia Minor were reluctant to destroy their own lands – thus decreasing their own revenues, or incurring the expenses of such a policy – for the sake of the Great King. But the seriousness of the threat had not escaped them. At Zeleia, the local satrap Arsites was joined by Arsames of Cilicia, Spithridates (and his brother Rhoesaces) of Lydia and Ionia, Atizyes and Mithrobuzanes of Phrygia and Cappadocia respectively, as well as Mithridates, Arbupales and Pharnaces, all prominent adherents of the royal house.[15] Concerted action on such a scale had not been taken since the so-called 'Great Satraps' Revolt' of the 360s. Clearly, the satraps regarded Alexander's landing as a threat to Anatolia as a whole, and not a limited danger like that posed by Agesilaus at the beginning of the century.

Memnon's role is difficult to assess. His scorched-earth policy made little sense in northwestern Asia Minor, which offered the enemy too many military options. For an army retreating before another, intent on a specific goal and without an alternative route, the strategy had its merits. But even Arsames' decision to adopt it in 333 in Cilicia proved futile; for it was negated by the misapprehensions of his own soldiers and the speed of Alexander's march.[16] In truth, Memnon's advice required the amputation of a significant portion of the Empire in an attempt to save the remainder. Persian resistance to the plan was stiffened further by a natural distrust of a Greek mercenary leader. The security of Asia Minor had been entrusted, in no small way, to a sizable force of Greek mercenaries, whose interests on this occasion at least extended beyond the benefits of regular pay. Many, no doubt, regarded their fight with Alexander as beneficial to their compatriots at home. Indeed, Alexander's harsh treatment of Greeks captured in battles makes it clear that he regarded them as traitors to the Panhellenic cause. But the Persian commanders, who showed similar distrust of the Greek mercenaries and their leaders on the eve of Issus, may have viewed Memnon with suspicion and negated the effectiveness of the mercenary infantry.[17]

For Alexander, who had crossed the Hellespont and sacrificed at Troy as a new Achilles, the Granicus was indeed a mere trickle, and the Persian cavalry who occupied its banks proved no match, in tactics or hand-to-hand combat for their European counterparts. Two would-be champions were felled by Alexander's *sarissa*, a third by the protecting sword of 'Black' Cleitus. And, in the event, the Persian suspicions of the Greek infantry played no small part in the defeat of the satrapal coalition. Of the territorial rulers, Mithrobuzanes and Spithridates were among the dead;[18] Arsites escaped the battlefield, only to die by his own hand; Arsames fled to his own satrapy, to fight and die at Issus.

The defeat left western Asia Minor vulnerable, but not entirely defenseless. Mithrenes, who commanded the citadel of Sardis, was the first Persian to submit to Alexander – an opportune defection in view of the city's natural defenses.[19] Dascylium too was easily occupied in the absence of its ruler. For a third time, Ephesus found itself in the grip of *stasis*, reverting once again to Macedonian control. In anticipation of Philip's war on Persia, Ephesus had not only undergone a change of government but had even erected a statue of Philip II in the temple of Artemis. But the anti-Macedonian (oligarchic) faction, incited by the news of Parmenion's defeat at Magnesia-on-the-Maeander (cf. Polyaenus, *Strat.* 5.44.4), with the support of Memnon, overthrew the democracy. Memnon may have sent to them Amyntas son of Antiochus, who had fled the Macedonian court after Philip's assassination (Arr. 1.17.9). But now the defeat of the satrapal coalition at the Granicus, and the surrender of Sardis, encouraged counter-revolution: Amyntas abandoned the city with two Ephesian triremes, no doubt accompanied by some of the prominent oligarchs. Those who remained, like Syrphax and his relatives, were dragged from the unavailing shelter of the temple and stoned to death.[20]

Other Greek cities of the coast and the islands proved more stubborn. As in European Greece, the coastal population recognized the Panhellenic Crusade as the thin veil of Macedonian imperialism. Miletus and Halicarnassus resisted fiercely. The former, supported by the Persian fleet, was soon overwhelmed by Macedonian power and Philotas' occupation of Mycale; the latter, despite desperate counter-attacks by the exiles Ephialtes and Neoptolemus, was eventually abandoned by its leaders, Memnon and Orontopates.[21] In Halicarnassus, the resistance to Alexander was compounded by factional strife. After the death of Mausolus, the rule of Caria had passed to his brother, Idrieus. When the latter died of illness, Pixodarus, the third son of Hecatomnus, swept aside the claims of Idrieus' wife, Ada, and seized power (Strab. 14.2.17). In 337/6 he had offered the hand of his daughter, also called Ada, to a son of Philip II, but when the negotiations were disrupted by Alexander's intervention[22] he gave her to Orontopates, who ruled the satrapy after Pixodarus' death (335/4). Hence, Alexander in 334 restored the elder Ada to the throne and allowed her to become his adoptive mother – in effect, reserving for himself hereditary claim to Caria. A metaphorical wave of Macedonian success thus surged over the coastal region. By the winter of 334/3, the actual sea would be said by Alexander's 'official' historian to have withdrawn, performing *proskynesis* as to one destined to rule Asia.[23] But the conquest was far from complete and the Macedonian army, reunited at Gordium and augmented by reinforcements, advanced into Cappadocia with considerable anxiety about Persian recovery on the Aegean littoral.[24] There, in 333, Memnon had launched a successful counter-offensive before succumbing to illness. Miletus and Halicarnassus quickly reverted to Persian control; Lesbos was recaptured (Arr. 2.1.1). The pro-Greek sources, however, over-estimated the impact of Memnon's death: his successors, Pharnabazus and Autophradates, showed that they could manage affairs effectively, but in the end Persian resources proved inadequate for the undertaking (see also above pp. 127–8).[25]

BEYOND THE HALYS

The failure of the satrapal coalition in the west forced Darius III to take the field in person. It was an unwelcome task, not just on account of the threat posed by the Macedonian army, but because the Great King had had only a brief respite from the chaos that attended his accession. Darius' rise to power had been sudden, and in dangerous circumstances. Early in 338, Artaxerxes III Ochus, the ruthless successor of Artaxerxes II, fell victim to court intrigue and the poison of his chamberlain, Bagoas. This figure, possibly a eunuch, appears to have been the most powerful individual at the Achaemenid court in the 340s and early 330s. Not content with the elimination of Ochus, he murdered also the brothers of the new king, Arses (who reigned briefly as Artaxerxes IV),[26] and then the king himself. The kingship devolved upon Artasata, whom Greek writers incorrectly called Codomannus and who took the dynastic name Darius (III).[27] Unlike the unsuspecting children of Ochus, Darius was an experienced warrior – he had defeated a Cadusian champion in one of Artaxerxes' campaigns and was forty-four or forty-five at the time of his accession (cf. Arr. 3.22.6) – who saw through the machinations of Bagoas, forcing him to drink his own poison. But Darius had little time to enjoy his freedom at the court before he was called away to deal with yet another uprising in Egypt. It was fresh from this campaign that he was drawn into the life-and-death struggle with Alexander.

In retrospect, it is easy to dismiss Darius' chances at Issus, and to regard his alleged boasting before the battle as vainglorious delusion. Curtius writes:

Furthermore, Darius continued, this king [sc. Alexander] who had formerly been a fearsome figure and who had been elated to groundless self-confidence by his enemy's absence – on hearing of Darius' approach, this man's presumption had given way to caution and he had taken to a hiding-place in the narrow parts of a mountain valley, just like the lowly animals that lurk in their woodland lairs at the sound of people passing. Now he was even deceiving his own soldiers with a feigned illness. But he, Darius, was not going to let him put off the fight any longer; he was going to crush the Macedonians as they hung back in that lair into which they had retreated in fear.[28]

But, in fact, Persian prospects were good, at least when the king set out from Babylon. At that time, the counter-offensive in the Aegean, and the anti-Macedonian forces had regained lost ground on Lesbos and at Halicarnassus. Memnon's sudden death from illness was a blow to their fortunes, but nevertheless the Persians had found a competent successor in Pharnabazus, who met with the Spartan king, Agis, near Siphnus in the hope of encouraging revolt in the Peloponnesus. Certainly, there were many in the Macedonian army who had their misgivings: Alexander had been struck down by fever after bathing in the Cydnus river, and it was not at all certain that he would survive. It has been suggested that Alexander's friend and treasurer, Harpalus, defected at this time because 'he had decided that Cilicia was a most undesirable place to be if his king died.'[29] Furthermore, Darius had attracted to his cause the largest force of Greek mercenaries employed by a Persian king in the history of Achaemenid rule. The figure given by Callisthenes (*FGrH* 124 F35) is doubtless exaggerated; for 30,000 Greeks, by themselves, would have come close to matching the entire Macedonian force. But there is no doubt that the mercenary totals were substantial, and thus a serious concern to the Macedonian military staff. Plus, the mercenary forces were led by an experienced opponent of Macedon, Charidemus, and a high-ranking Macedonian defector named Amyntas son of Antiochus. In the event, Charidemus fell victim to court intrigue, but Amyntas gave a good account of himself and made good his escape from the battlefield with some 4,000 mercenaries.[30]

Darius had moved with an army, numbered by the Alexander historians between 300,000 and 600,000, from Babylon to Sochi, where he encamped in September/October 333.[31] Alexander had, by this time, reached the coastal plain of Cilicia and marched past the Pillar of Jonah (the so-called 'Syrian' or 'Assyrian' Gates) south of modern Iskenderun (medieval Alexandretta). The Persians saw the danger of forcing the Belen Pass, which separated the two armies – though Alexander was surprisingly ignorant of the enemy's presence at Sochi – and invaded Cilicia via the Amanic Gates (the Bahçe Pass), arriving at Issus through Toprakkale. Darius' appearance north of the Pinarus river sent the Macedonians back in alarm to deal with an enemy that sat astride their lines of communication.[32]

But the Persian army had committed a grave error in abandoning the plains of Mesopotamia, where their numerical superiority and powerful cavalry could be deployed most effectively, in favor of the cramped confines of the Cilician coastal plain. Here the topography served to prevent the smaller Macedonian force from being outflanked. That Alexander, in imitation of the younger Cyrus at Cunaxa, charged directly at the Persian centre where Darius himself was positioned, may be more than mere fiction – though admittedly it served Alexander's propagandists to depict the young king in single combat with his enemy.[33] But the Persian ranks broke, and Darius fled, long before the protagonists could come to blows, leaving some 100,000 to be killed or captured. Among the captives, the mother, wife, and children of Darius himself.

PHOENICIA AND EGYPT

Defeat at Issus staggered the Persian colossus. For the moment, it looked as if Achaemenid power had been broken, and it remained only for the conqueror to reassemble the fragments of the empire under his own control. In Asia Minor, remnants of Persian resistance were mopped up by Antigonus the One-Eyed, Ptolemaeus, and Balacrus. In Phoenicia, the news of Issus and Parmenion's capture of Damascus caused delegations, armed with congratulations and crowns of gold, to issue forth from the coastal cities: Aradus, Marathus, Sigon, Marianne, and Byblus submitted to the Macedonian conqueror.[34] Abd-astart, the son of Tabnit and the king of Sidon, also surrendered, only to be deposed; his record of collaboration with Persia made him unpopular with a Sidonian population that looked upon Alexander as liberator.[35] Like Egypt, which had asserted its independence between 405 and 343,[36] Phoenicia had experienced the loss of a brief period of freedom in the form of brutal reprisals against Sidon by Artaxerxes III.[37] Now the collapse of the Persian power west of the Euphrates left the Phoenicians and the Cypriots in a precarious situation: whether they welcomed liberation from the Achaemenid yoke, or recognized that they would be forced to accept a new master in the place of the old one, the uncomfortable fact was that large numbers of their countrymen, and among them numerous local dynasts, served with the Persian fleet.

Of the Cypriot rulers, Androcles of Amathus sailed with the Aegean fleet of Pharnabazus and Autophradates in 334, but defected soon after Issus to join Alexander at Sidon in 332 (Arr. 2.20.3). Thereafter, he took part in the final assault on Tyre, though his own quinquereme was destroyed (along with those of Pnytagoras of Salamis and Pasicrates of Curium) by a Tyrian attack as it lay at anchor in the harbor (Arr. 2.22.2). Pnytagoras, who had earlier rebelled from Artaxerxes III in concert with the Sidonians, was richly rewarded: Tamasus in the territory of Citium, which had formerly belonged to Pymiathon's realm. But he appears not to have lived long to enjoy his reward, for in spring 331 we find his son Nicocreon ruling in Salamis; a second son, Nithaphon, is named as one of the trierarchs of Alexander's Hydaspes fleet.[38]

Many of the 'Syrians,' however, remained steadfast in their loyalty to Darius and their satrap, Mazaeus, whom we find leading contingents from Coele Syria and Syria Mesopotamia at Gaugamela (Arr. 3.8.6; cf. Curt. 4.16.1). Mazaeus, now satrap of Mesopotamia, thus retained the 'Syrians' of Abarnahara ('the land beyond the river') who remained loyal to Darius.

For Darius, the interval between his escape from Issus and the arrival of the first reports that Alexander had turned south to detach Phoenicia and Egypt, must have been particularly trying. He now resorted to diplomacy in an effort to free his captured relatives and call a halt to the Macedonian advance. But the exchanges between the two parties were marred by the Persian king's refusal to recognize the gravity of the danger to the Empire. Darius persisted in treating Alexander as an upstart, an inferior who could, as he thought, be bought off with the cessation of Asia Minor and 10,000 talents. Alexander soon made it clear to him that he was neither venal nor prepared to accept a subordinate role. And although the negotiations continued for almost two years, with the escalation of the terms – Darius was eventually to offer Asia west of the Euphrates, 30,000 talents and the hand of his daughter in marriage – the Persian offer contained little that Alexander did not already possess by right of conquest. Darius no longer had the authority to dispose of Alexander's 'spear-won land.' And so diplomacy failed.[39]

Tyrian opposition to Alexander, on the other hand, may be seen as a careful attempt to exploit the situation. As long as the issue had not been resolved at sea, there was danger of reprisals from Persia. But a collapse of Persian power east of the Euphrates might mean the disintegration of the fleet and the prospect of real independence. For the moment, there was the vain expectation that Alexander might be prepared to accept Tyrian neutrality. But such a proposal suited neither Macedonian grand strategy nor the mentality of the young king. The Tyrians would hold out for seven months, disappointed in the hope of succour from their colonists in the west, the Carthaginians. Eventually they were overcome by the tenacity of Alexander, the innovation and industry of his troops, and the gradual disintegration of the Persian fleet. Vital support for Alexander came from Cypriots and Phoenicians, many of the latter inspired by jealousy of Tyrian prosperity and pre-eminence – though in the end bonds of ethnicity saved many Tyrians from the blood-lust of the enemy once the walls had been breached.[40]

Gaza's two-month resistance of Alexander is more difficult to explain. Ethnicity bound the Gazans to neither Phoenicia, which had fallen, nor Egypt which showed no intention of resisting. The area was originally Philistine – Gaza was but a short sail down the coast from Ascalon – and Gaza's Persian garrison had probably been strengthened during the reign of Artaxerxes III, on account of its strategic location near the entrance to Egypt. The citadel was now manned by Nabataean Arabs under the command of the eunuch, Betis, and it may have been the ethnic factor that kept the Arabs faithful to Persian rule. Similarly, in Samaria, which had surrendered during the siege of Tyre, the inhabitants rebelled against Macedonian authority in the spring of 331, burning alive Alexander's governor, Andromachus.[41]

Egypt, by contrast, welcomed Alexander with open arms. Only recently had Persian occupation of the Delta been reinstated, after more than a half-century of independence. But the satrap Sauaces had fallen at Issus,[42] and his subordinate, Mazaces, had neither the ability nor the resources to continue the struggle.[43] Weakened by the attempt of Amyntas son of Antiochus to exploit the Persian loss in Cilicia, Mazaces bowed to fortune and surrendered to Alexander. In Memphis, the legitimacy of Alexander's kingship was recognized, but further support was sought and obtained when the army advanced to Siwah and the oracle of the Libyan Zeus, Amun. But the accompanying recognition of Alexander as 'son of Amun'[44] was to have a negative impact on the Macedonians themselves, particularly upon many officers (see below, p. 217).

MESOPOTAMIA

Further east Darius III was returning to the offensive, frustrated in his attempts to control the damage through diplomacy and secure the return of his family, captured at Issus. The counter-offensive in the Mediterranean was now dead; for the fall of Tyre and Gaza, and the loss of the Nile Delta, had left Persia not merely without bases for the fleet, but without the fleet itself. It was a fundamental weakness of the Persian empire that the security of the west depended to such a large extent on a navy composed entirely of subject nations. Only the prospect of Agis' war in the Peloponnesus kept alive the hope of distracting Alexander from the heart of the empire.

It was, in fact, on his second visit to Tyre that Alexander first learned of the unrest in the Peloponnesus (Arr. 3.6.3). In 331 Agis and his allies defeated Antipater's general, Corrhagus, in the Peloponnesus, an auspicious beginning considering that Persian support had collapsed and Athens had chosen to remain aloof. With a force that numbered in excess of 22,000, drawn from Elis, Arcadia, and Achaea, Agis besieged Megalopolis. The news of these activities reached Antipater at a time when he was distracted by the rebellion of Memnon, Alexander's *strategos* of Thrace, an uprising so opportune that many scholars have suspected collusion between Memnon and Agis. Against this view is the fact that Antipater was able to reach an agreement with Memnon, which allowed the latter to remain in power in Thrace, soon enough to allow for the decisive defeat of Agis in the south in the same campaigning season. The engagement at Megalopolis was bloody: 3,500 lay dead on the Macedonian side; of the rebels, 5,300 had fallen, including Agis himself.[45]

Darius, meanwhile, had assembled an even larger army than that which he had brought to Cilicia. For if there was anything that the empire had no shortage of, it was manpower. Syrians, defeated at Issus but steadfast in their loyalty to Persia, were included in the troops that fought at Gaugamela, along with the Persians, Babylonians, and Medes who formed the nucleus of the Great King's forces.[46] But, despite Alexander's boast that his men would be facing the same men they had defeated twice before in battle, the fact was that the composition of the army at Gaugamela was radically different, including some rather potent contingents – particularly amongst the cavalry – from the eastern satrapies, which Darius had either been unable to mobilize or thought unnecessary in 333.[47] Like Issus, the Gaugamela campaign offered reasonable expectation of success. And, for the first time, the terrain would be selected by and beneficial to the Persians.[48]

With vastly superior numbers deployed on the plain beyond the Tigris, Darius had every hope of outflanking and enveloping the Macedonian army, which must have seemed miniscule by comparison.[49] To this numerical superiority was added the terror of scythe-chariots and elephants, the latter so far unknown to the Macedonians. But Alexander seized the initiative by driving with the right wing hard into the Persian left, which broke before the battle could be won on the Macedonian left and centre. Scythian and Indian horsemen had, indeed, exploited a gap in the line of the *pezhetairoi*, which surged ahead to keep contact with Alexander's cavalry and the hypaspists. But the barbarian riders directed their attention to the baggage, eager for plunder and assured that the victory had been won. Their presence on the Macedonian left, where Mazaeus had put fearful pressure on Parmenion, might have turned the tide of battle. Had they not turned prematurely to pillaging the baggage camp, Alexander's victory on the right might have been as illusory as that of Demetrius at Ipsus in 301 (Plut. *Demetr.* 29). But fortune and the leadership of Parmenion and Craterus would save Alexander's reputation, turning youthful folly into military brilliance.

THE HEART OF THE EMPIRE

Darius' hopes collapsed with the complete defeat of his forces at Gaugamela. He himself, with the shattered remnants of his army, fled first to Arbela and thence to Ecbatana in Media, leaving Babylon, Susa and Persepolis to the enemy. Mazaeus withdrew into southern Mesopotamia and occupied Babylon. But prudence dictated that he should come to terms with the conqueror, and, together with Bagophanes, the guardian of the city's treasure, Mazaeus made a formal surrender of the city.[50]

A large number of the Babylonians had taken up a position on the walls, eager to have a view of their new king, but most

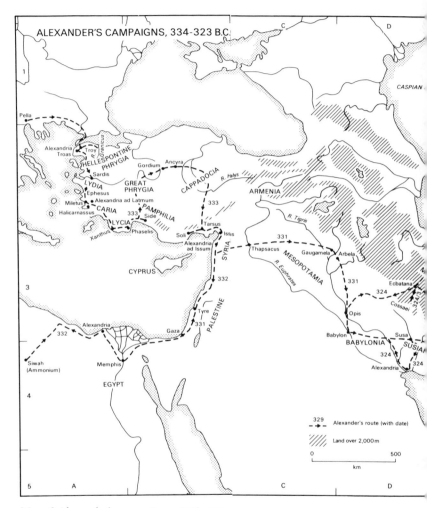

ALEXANDER'S CAMPAIGNS, 334–323 B.C.

Map 6 Alexander's campaigns, 334–323 BC

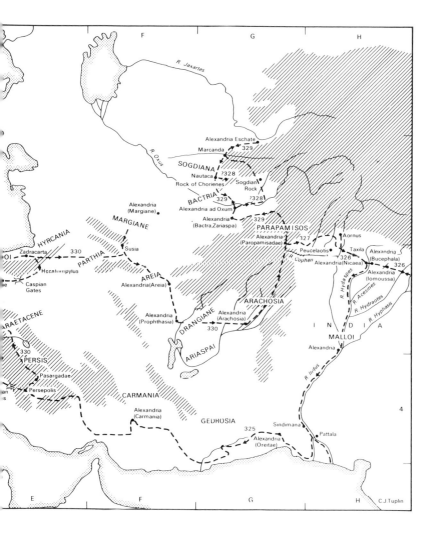

F   G   H

R. Jaxartes

Alexandria Eschate
Marcanda 329
SOGDIANA
Nautaca ?328
Rock of Chorienes Sogdian
 Rock
BACTRIA 329 ?328
Alexandria ad Oxum
Alexandria
(Bactra,Zariaspa) 329

Alexandria
(Margiane)

MARGIANE PARAPAMISOS

Alexandria 327 Aornus
(Paropamisadae)
Peucelaotis Taxila Alexandria
HYRCANIA R. Cophen (Bucephala)
Zadracarta 330 Susia Alexandria(Nicaea) 326
PARTHIA
Hecatompylus Alexandria
Caspian AREIA (Iomoussa)
Gates Alexandria(Areia)

ARACHOSIA

Alexandria Alexandria MALLOI
(Prophthasia) DRANGIANE (Arachosia) Alexandria
 330
ARAETACENE ARIASPAI

330 PERSIS
Pasargadae
Persepolis CARMANIA

Alexandria GEDROSIA Sindimana
(Carmania) 325 Pattala
 Alexandria
 (Oreitae)

R. Oxus

I N D I A

R. Hydaspes
R. Acesines
R. Hydraotes
R. Hyphasis
R. Indus

4

E   F   G   H C.J.Tuplin

went out to meet him, including the man in charge of the citadel and royal treasury, Bagophanes. Not to be outdone by Mazaeus in paying his respects to Alexander, Bagophanes had carpeted the whole road with flowers and garlands and set up at intervals on both sides silver altars heaped not just with frankincense but with all manner of perfumes. Following him were his gifts – herds of cattle and horses, and lions, too, and leopards, carried along in cages. Next came the Magi chanting a song in their native fashion, and behind them were the Chaldaeans, then the Babylonians, represented not only by priests but also by musicians equipped with their national instrument. (The role of the latter was to sing the praises of the Persian kings, that of the Chaldaeans to reveal astronomical movements and regular seasonal changes.) At the rear came the Babylonian cavalry, their equipment and that of their horses suggesting extravagance rather than majesty.

Surrounded by an armed guard, the king instructed the townspeople to follow at the rear of his infantry; then he entered the city on a chariot and went to the palace.[51]

What Curtius depicts as spontaneous behavior was, in fact, ritual surrender, enacted so many times in the past – in ceremony for the legitimate heir to the throne, as well as in earnest for a conquering king.[52] Mazaeus had made a virtue of necessity: for his expedient act he was rewarded with the satrapy of Babylonia, though Alexander was careful to install a Macedonian garrison commander and military overseers (*strategoi*).[53] The resources of Babylon which had once been drawn upon to resist the invader now feted him, for thirty-four days, and the lewd entertainment that has become synonymous with the city's name corrupted the conquering army. Lax discipline took its toll, and Alexander turned to the refreshment of military drill and hunting in Sittacene.

Without direction from the Great King,[54] the ancient centre of the empire submitted without a fight: Susa in its turn embraced the conqueror. Darius' satrap of Susiana, Abulites, surrendered the city and himself to Philoxenus, whom Alexander had sent to him after the battle of Gaugamela (Arr. 3.16.6). Its commandant had perhaps been a certain Mazarus, whom Alexander relieved of command in favor of Xenophilus – but Abulites, like Mazaeus, was retained.[55] Here again, Alexander was careful to combine a show of native rule with the fetters of military occupation. In the closing months of

331, anxiety about Agis' war in the Peloponnesus helped to buy the Persians time. The need to await news of events in the west kept Alexander in Babylonia and Elam longer than usual, a delay exploited by Ariobarzanes, satrap of Persis.[56] This Persian notable was able to equip an army of perhaps 25,000 men and occupy the so-called Persian or 'Susidan' Gates.[57] But his efforts, like those of the Uxian leader, Madates (an adherent of the royal house),[58] did little more than harass the advancing army. The best Ariobarzanes' blockade could do was to delay the Macedonians, or rather Alexander's select force; for the wagon road to the south offered no natural barriers and was already bringing Parmenion, with the heavy infantry and the baggage train, toward the Persian capital. If the delay was intended to facilitate the removal or even the destruction of the treasure in Persepolis, there is no indication that such measures were taken. Instead, attention was given to the destruction of the bridges on the Araxes. Perhaps, too, there was the vain expectation that Darius with a refurbished army would come to save the city of his ancestors.

In fact, nothing of the sort happened. Ariobarzanes' force was easily circumvented, despite the perils of terrain and winter snow, with the help of captive informants. With military efficiency the Araxes was bridged, and Tiridates surrendered the city,[59] which paid for its symbolic importance as the seat of Persian power the very real penalties of pillage, rape and destruction. Soon the palace fell victim to the victor's wrath – whether by design or through a spontaneous urge for revenge. In the long term, the act was detrimental to the cause of Hellenic rule in Asia, but it served the needs of the moment.[60] For all intents and purposes, the Panhellenic war had drawn to an end. The empire was lost.

CENTRAL ASIA

Of the four Achaemenid capitals, only Ecbatana (modern Hamadan) remained in Persian hands. Here Darius monitored Alexander's intentions, awaiting also the arrival of reinforcements from the Upper Satrapies, Scythians, and Cadusians. But with the news that Alexander had crossed the Zagrus into Media, and the failure of reinforcements to materialize, Darius placed his hopes in flight and the solitudes of Central Asia.[61] From Ecbatana, Darius travelled the caravan route, leading from Rhagae through the Sar-i-Darreh pass and skirting the Great Salt Desert. To the north lay the Elburz mountains, beyond which the fertile satrapy of Hyrcania slopes gently towards the Caspian. But it was the hard road into Parthiene that vexed Darius, under the relentless pressure of Alexander's pursuit. The covered wagons (*harmamaxai*) which carried the women, and *impedimenta* of royalty, made the Great King's escape into Bactria impossible, given the speed of Alexander's column. Darius thus felt compelled to decide the matter in battle, even though his army had dwindled to fewer than 40,000 barbarian troops and 4,000 Greeks (Curt. 5.8.3).

That decision proved fatal. The rulers of the Upper Satrapies and the *chiliarch* Nabarzanes were convinced that there could be no hope of safety unless the army reached Bactria, where it could regroup to meet the enemy. They now demanded the king's abdication in favor of Bessus, a proposal that Darius, understandably, rejected. Ultimately, it was decided to arrest him and abandon his murdered body by the roadway in the hope of buying time for their own escape or, possibly, winning Alexander's goodwill. Already before Darius' murder there had been defections as the party loyal to the king, but powerless to deal with Bessus and Nabarzanes, abandoned the Persian column. Bagisthanes and Mazaeus' son, Antibelus, had been among the first to surrender to Alexander, along with Melon the king's interpreter.[62] Once Bessus had seized power, the number and importance of the defectors increased: Phrataphernes, Autophradates, Artabazus, and his sons, all preferred to seek accommodation with Alexander than to support the usurper and regicide. Bessus, meanwhile, fled with 600 horsemen, assigning Parthia and Hyrcania to Nabarzanes, and relying on Satibarzanes and Barsaentes to preserve Areia and Arachosia respectively.

Of the leading Persians who submitted, Alexander installed Phrataphernes in Parthia and Autophradates amongst the Tapurians.[63] Artabazus and his sons remained in the king's entourage and soon reaped suitable awards. But Nabarzanes, who had been induced to surrender through the agency of the younger Bagoas, was disappointed. Under the circumstances, he ought to have been content with a pardon, but there was no honor without political or military office. He appears to have deserted Alexander soon afterwards in an attempt to regain control of Parthia and Hyrcania. Eventually, he was captured and presumably executed.[64]

A similar act of perfidy was committed by Satibarzanes. At Susia (Tus), Satibarzanes surrendered to Alexander and was confirmed as satrap of Areia.[65] But he soon betrayed Anaxippus and the forty javelin-men sent with him (Arr. 3.25.2), butchering them once Alexander had set out for Margiana (Merv), intent on Bactria where Bessus had assumed the upright tiara and the dynastic title 'Artaxerxes' (V). Satibarzanes assembled the rebellious Areians at Artacoana, the satrapal capital (probably in the vicinity of modern Herat).[66] Within two days of receiving the news of Satibarzanes' treachery, Alexander appeared at Artacoana, from which the satrap fled to Bactria with 2,000 horsemen. Replaced by the Persian Arsaces, he soon returned to his satrapy with his horsemen to incite rebellion, whereupon he was killed in single combat by Erigyius.[67] For Bessus, there remained only the nomadic tribesmen of Margiana, Bactria, and Sogdiana, as well as the allied Scythian tribes of Dahae and Massagetae.

Alexander himself had moved along the Helmand river valley, which curved eastward into Arachosia. The Ariaspians, who had aided Cyrus the Great in the 530s and earned the sobriquet 'Benefactors' (*Euergetai*), now supplied Alexander over the winter of 330/29. Alexandria-in-Arachosia, in the vicinity of modern Kandahar, was established in the satrapy abandoned by the regicide Barsaentes, whom Sambus now sheltered.[68] The Parapamasidae offered no resistance, but the Macedonians, expecting that the main passes into Bactria would be guarded, entered the satrapy via the Khawak Pass which led to Drapsaca (Qunduz). Once again the barbarians sought reprieve by surrendering the author of their mischief: Bessus was arrested, stripped naked and left in chains to be taken (by Ptolemy) to Alexander.

The punishment of the usurper, whom Alexander sent back to Ecbatana to be tortured and executed in Persian fashion, should have ended the affair. But Alexander's campaign to the Iaxartes, and the establishment of Alexandria–Eschate, to replace the old outpost of Cyropolis, threatened the old patterns of life in Sogdiana and incited further rebellion. Now the local dynasts, Spitamenes, Sisimithres, Oxyartes, and Arimazes, took up the fight, and three years of guerrilla warfare followed before the political marriage of Alexander and Oxyartes' daughter, Roxane, could bring stability to the region.

Alexander's treatment of Bessus had perhaps sent the wrong message: the rebels should expect no clemency from the conqueror. Invited to a council at Bactra (Zariaspa), the chieftains of Bactria and Sogdiana suspected treachery and renewed their opposition (Arr. 4.1.5, cf. Curt. 7.6.14–15). Spitamenes, perhaps an Achaemenid,[69] emerged as the leader of the resistance, striking at Maracanda while

Alexander carried the war beyond the Iaxartes. Next he caught the force sent to relieve the town in an ambush at the Polytimetus, inflicting heavy casualties and inspiring the natives' hopes. But the following year, he was hemmed in by the contingents of Craterus and Coenus and eventually betrayed by his Scythian allies, who sent his head to the Macedonian camp while they themselves made good their escape into the desert.[70]

In late autumn 328, Sisimithres took refuge, along with the other hyparchs of the region, on the so-called 'Rock of Chorienes' (Koh-i-nor), some 20 stades high and 60 stades in circumference[71] and surrounded by a deep ravine. But Alexander induced his surrender through the agency of Oxyartes.[72] This voluntary act probably saved Sisimithres' life (cf. the punishment of Ariamazes), and he was allowed to retain his territory (probably the region of Gazaba), although his two sons were retained as hostages in Alexander's army.[73] In early 327, Sisimithres was able to provision Alexander's army (which had suffered from adverse weather in the region) with supplies for two months: 'a large number of pack-animals, 2,000 camels, and flocks of sheep and herds of cattle.'[74] Not to be outdone in generosity, Alexander plundered the territory of the Sacae and returned to Sisimithres with a gift of 30,000 head of cattle. This was almost certainly the occasion of the banquet given by Chorienes, at which Roxane was introduced to Alexander, along with the host's own unmarried daughters, and Alexander took his first oriental bride.[75]

Military outposts dotted the satrapy, and not fewer than 10,000 Greek mercenaries were abandoned in Central Asia. Ultimately, it proved to be an unshakeable outpost of Hellenism, despite attempts in 325/4 and 323 to uproot the population.

INDIA

The guerrilla war in Bactria and Sogdiana gave only temporary relief to Gandhara. In spring 327, Alexander crossed the Hindu Kush and made short work of the natives of Bajaur: in the Kunar or Chitral valley, the Aspasians fled to the hills, abandoning and burning their chief city, Arigaeum (Nawagai). Ptolemy, who distinguished himself in this campaign, reports the death of one of their leaders and the capture of 40,000 men and 230,000 oxen. But a more serious threat was posed by the Assacenians, who prepared to resist the invader with 2,000 cavalry, 30,000 infantry, and thirty elephants. Their chief city, Massaga in the Katgala pass, was defended by Cleophis, the mother (or possibly widow) of Assacenus, who had died only shortly before the advent of Alexander.[76] The actual operations appear to have been managed by Assacenus' brother, known in the *Metz Epitome* as Amminais, and 9,000 mercenaries. After a valiant defense, in which the commander of the place (Amminais? or the commander of the mercenaries?) was killed, the Assacenians sent a herald to Alexander to discuss terms of surrender.[77] The story of Cleophis' relations with the Macedonian king is heavily romanticized, and her reputation in the area was that of the 'royal whore;' for she was said to have retained her kingdom through sexual favors (cf. Just. 12.7.9–11). The other strongholds of the Assacenians, Ora (Udegram) and Beira or Bazeira (Bir-kot), soon fell to the European army, which took the seemingly impregnable rock of Aornos (Pir-sar or Mount Ilam?).[78] Some of the Assaceni took refuge in the Buner region, where Aphrices, another kinsman of the notorious queen of Massaga, attempted to hold the passes (Diod. 17.86.2; Curt. 8.12.1). But he was killed by his own men, leaving the road clear for Alexander to move south.

In the Kabul valley, the dynast of Peucelaotis,[79] Astis, was besieged for thirty days by Hephaestion and Perdiccas in an unnamed city (probably his own capital, Pushkalavati, modern Charsadda). Astis himself perished in the defense and his territory was handed over to Sangaeus, apparently a local rival. Peucelaotis, upon formal surrender to Alexander, accepted a Macedonian garrison under the command of Philip, probably the son of Machatas.[80]

For the rajahs of the Punjab, their decisions to make peace with or wage war on Alexander were, in many cases, made for them by the actions and affiliations of the dynasts on their borders. Ambhi, ruler of the region between the Indus and the Hydaspes, with his capital at Taxila (near modern Islamabad), welcomed Alexander's army in the hope of gaining relief from his enemies, Abisares to the north,[81] and Porus, Rajah of the Paurava, to the west. Against them he did, indeed, win Macedonian support, but the cost was the same as in the Persian strongholds: Philip son of Machatas was appointed as overseer of the region, with Ambhi (= Omphis, with his official name 'Taxiles') as nominal head of the kingdom.

Abisares had known of Alexander's advance since, at least, winter 327/6; he sent troops to bolster the defence of Ora (Udegram). After the fall of Aornos in 326, natives from the region between Dyrta and the Indus fled to him, and he renewed an old alliance with Porus. Although inferior in authority, Abisares could muster an army comparable in size to that of Porus; hence Alexander planned to attack the latter before Abisares could join forces with him. Abisares did not, in fact, act in time to aid Porus, who looked in vain for reinforcements. Instead, he made (token?) submission to Alexander, content to await the outcome of events.[82] After the defeat of Porus, Abisares sent to Alexander a second delegation, led by his own brother and bringing money and forty elephants as gifts.

Abisares declined to come to Alexander in person, a condition upon which the latter insisted, but sent his brother once again, in concert with Arsaces and the envoys whom Alexander had sent to Abhisara. The Indian brought an additional thirty elephants and offered the excuse that Abisares was too ill to present himself to Alexander, a fact verified by Alexander's own agents. The king allowed Abisares to retain his kingdom and included in his administrative sphere the hyparchy of Arsaces;[83] Abisares was, however, assessed an annual tribute, which was probably due to the satrap of India between the Jhelum (Hydaspes) and the Indus, Philip son of Machatas. Although Abisares is referred to as 'satrap' by Arrian, his son doubtless followed an independent course of action after Alexander's return to the west.[84]

For his part, Porus was determined to face the invader and his traditional enemy, Taxiles, at the Jhelum. Here, after much feinting, Alexander eventually managed to ford the river some 17½ miles north of the main crossing point, catching Porus' son, who had been posted upstream, off his guard.[85] The main engagement was a particularly hard-fought and bloody one, in which the Indian ruler distinguished himself by his bravery. The valiant enemy earned Alexander's respect, and was allowed to retain his kingdom. It had not always been so: Alexander had not always been so generous in his treatment of stubborn adversaries. The greater challenge lay, however, in the attempt to bring about lasting peace between the Indian rivals. Curtius claims that an alliance between Taxiles and Porus was sealed by marriage,[86] the common currency of such transactions. But the arrangement was never entirely satisfactory. Though Taxiles was perhaps more trustworthy than Porus, Alexander needed the latter for his upcoming campaigns in the Punjab.

Farther east, opposition was less intense. The lesson of Porus' defeat was not wasted on neighboring dynasts, whose opposition was generally defensive rather than proactive. The Glausae were reduced by Alexander, while Hephaestion annexed the kingdom of the so-called 'cowardly' Porus, between the Chenab (Acesines) and Ravi

(Hydraotes) rivers.[87] During the campaign against the Glausae, Phrataphernes arrived with Thracian reinforcements. They had no doubt traveled via Merv to Bactra, reaching the Punjab through the Swat region, where, it was reported to the king, the Assacenians had killed Alexander's administrative officer, Nicanor. It was an all-too-familiar pattern, and Alexander instructed Philip son of Machatas, who was resident at Taxila, and Tyriespes, ruler of Parapamisadae, to conduct a punitive expedition. The Assacenians were henceforth attached to Philip's satrapy.

Beyond the Ravi, Macedonian arms carried the day: the Adrestae surrendered at Pimprama, though at Sangala the Kshatriyas resisted bitterly, particularly when Porus arrived with elephants and 5,000 Indian reinforcements.[88] By contrast, Sophytes (Saubhuti) made peace with the European invader, providing an intimidating display of his kingdom's wealth; for Sophytes the suppression of the Kshatriyas was no doubt welcome news. More serious was the effect of the elements. For the monsoons and the prospect of greater rivers and deserts, to say nothing of hostiles beyond number,[89] deterred the invader. The troops themselves proved the greatest obstacle in Alexander's path: at the Beas (Hyphasis) the Macedonian army, now virtually in rags and demoralized by battle fatigue and illness, handed Alexander his only defeat. The camp and altars erected at the Beas, designed to cheat posterity with the illusion of invaders larger than life, were monuments to Alexander's failure. Returning to the Jhelum, they discovered that the monsoons had washed away Nicaea and Bucephala, cities which Alexander had built on opposite banks of the river to commemorate the victory over Porus.[90] It was an ominous sign: India could be defeated, but not governed, by the European invader. Soon these regions were incorporated into the Mauryan empire of Chandragupta, who reaped the political rewards of Macedonian blood and conquest.[91] But for Alexander, the path to Oceanus now led south, along the Indus river system.

For a time, Alexander had been deflected from his goal rather than turned back completely. The descent of the Indus waterway, conducted by land as well as on the river, shows that Alexander intended a systematic reduction of the area which would ensure Macedonian rule in the Punjab. *En route*, the Sibae, whom the Europeans considered descendants of Heracles' companions, were subdued. But fierce resistance from the Kshudrakas (Sudracae or Oxydracae) and Malavas (Mallians) jeopardized the future of the entire expedition; for it was in the attack on a Mallian town that

Alexander received a near-fatal wound. From here Alexander was conveyed downstream by ship and displayed to the troops in an attempt to stifle rumors that the generals were keeping his death secret.

Further south, beyond the confluence of the Chenab and the Indus, lay the kingdom of Musicanus – probably ancient Alor, near Rohri and Sukkur – and Sind. Here Alexander was forced to deal with a succession of recalcitrant dynasts, as well as the troublesome Brahmans. Musicanus himself was caught off guard by the speed of the fleet's progress.

> Alexander's voyage down river was so swift that he arrived at the borders of Musicanus' territory before the latter learned that he was advancing against him. Seized by panic, he met Alexander in haste, conveying gifts that have the greatest value amongst the Indians, leading elephants, and surrendering his people and himself; he also admitted his mistake [in not surrendering earlier], which was the surest way of getting from Alexander what one might desire. And indeed Musicanus was granted a pardon by Alexander, who marvelled at his city and country and granted the rule of it to Musicanus (Arr. 6.15. 6–7).

In keeping with the now well-established practice, Musicanus' city was garrisoned by the conqueror.[92] Much less amenable was Oxicanus, a nomarch of upper Sind, based perhaps at Azeika (Ptol. *Geog.* 7.1.57). Alexander took his two largest cities by assault, capturing him in the second of these. His fate is not recorded, but it is likely that he was executed. A similar fate awaited Porticanus, ruler of Pardabathra, but there is no good reason for identifying the two rulers.[93] At Sindimana, the capital of Sambus, whom Alexander had appointed satrap of the hill country west of the Indus, the gates were opened to receive the Macedonians, though Sambus himself had fled, allegedly out of fear and pique, because of the friendly reception of his rival Musicanus (Arr. 6.16.4). In the event, his actions were premature: Musicanus, on the advice of the Brahmans, had revolted soon after the king's departure. He was now captured by Peithon son of Agenor and brought to Alexander, who crucified him and the Brahman instigators.[94] Sambus' fate is unknown, but it appears that Craterus' return to the west via the Bolan pass may have been intended to root out the remaining insurgents; for it appears that Sambus controlled the profitable trade route between Alor and Kandahar.

FROM CONQUEST TO CONSOLIDATION: THE 'INTERNAL ENEMY'

From Sind, the exploration of Patalene and the founding of Xylinepolis were comparatively simple, but what followed was far from routine. The first view of the Indian Ocean could scarcely fail to impress upon commander and soldier alike the magnitude of the accomplishment. Sailing into the open sea, Alexander sacrificed to the same sea deities he had propitiated at the Hellespont. For the common soldier, the prospect was tempered by an awareness that the whole of the known world was at his back, and the road to the fatherland as distant as the one already traveled. The return to the west, through the land of the Oreitae and the Gedrosian desert, is famous for the hardships endured by the army – though it was the camp-followers who suffered most.[95] But, by the time the king reached Carmania and reunited with Nearchus, who had completed a hazardous, if not unprecedented, journey by sea from the Indus delta to the straits of Hormuz,[96] the major concern was no longer conquest but consolidation and the exercise of central authority.

Ever since Alexander's decision to retain native administrators, disturbing as little as possible the traditional patterns of rule and tribute collection, there had been – as indeed had been the case in the Persian empire – insubordination and maladministration on an alarming scale. In some cases, it was a continuation of resistance to the invader: Macedonian 'watch-dogs' like Anaxippus, Nicanor, and Philip were murdered by native rulers or their subjects; rebel leaders, like Haustanes, Autophradates, Ordanes, and others, were arrested and executed.[97] Elsewhere, barbarian officials had been slow to respond to Alexander's orders: thus Oxydates and Arsaces were removed from office for deliberately shirking their responsibilities,[98] and Tyriespes, ruler of Parapamisadae, was deposed during the Sind campaign. The latter's territory was reassigned to Oxyartes, though even he was implicated in some mischief.[99] The king's father-in-law, at least, could expect a measure of leniency. Farther west, the Persian noble, Orxines, was replaced as satrap of Persis by Peucestas, the man who saved Alexander's life in the Mallian town.[100] In Susiana and Paraitacene, Abulites and his son, Oxathres, were punished for their failure to supply the army during the Gedrosian march;[101] in Media, Atropates the satrap (and future father-in-law of the marshal Perdiccas) arrested Baryaxes, who had assumed the upright tiara and sought to rally the Medes and Persians to his side.[102]

But it was not merely the barbarians who proved unreliable. In Bactria and Sogdiana, the false report of Alexander's death in the Mallian campaign had precipitated an uprising of the Greek mercenaries, which, although suppressed at the time, resurfaced in the months after the king's death in Babylon (Curt. 9.7.1–11).[103] Harpalus, Alexander's friend and imperial treasurer, had indulged his luxurious tastes and used the resources of the empire to finance his debaucheries.[104] In this he had been abetted by his military colleagues, Cleander, Sitalces, Agathon, and Heracon. Harpalus, indeed, made good his escape to Athens, where he attempted to pre-empt just punishment by raising the standard of war in Europe. Cleander and the others were less fortunate. Lesser individuals, like Poulamachus, who was found guilty of plundering the tomb of Cyrus the Great, were elevated in death; for it appears that Alexander now favored the barbarian methods of execution by impalement or crucifixion over the traditional Macedonian practice of stoning.[105] Corruption and mismanagement had taken place on an unprecedented scale during the king's absence, encouraged by rumors that the king had been killed in the east, or the belief that, if he did return, it would not be for a long time. Hence, the purge which accompanied Alexander's return from Carmania to Babylonia corresponded to both the magnitude of the crimes and the depths of the king's anger.

And, for the king, there was yet another factor, which can receive only brief notice here: the internal enemy, the disaffected Macedonian nobility. Alexander's succession had been anything but certain in 336. Despite the Crown Prince's exemplary showing at Chaeronea, the rival claims of Amyntas son of Perdiccas and the sons of Aëropus, as well as the aspirations of the powerful 'Attalus faction,' threatened to put Alexander and his Epirot mother in the political shade. Suspicions of regicide would have intimidated some but alienated others. The son may have protested his innocence and affected filial piety. Not so his 'terrible mother' (to use W. W. Tarn's now famous phrase). There was, however, the support of Antipater, perhaps all that was needed: after that, the prompt recognition of the new king by Alexander the Lyncestian. The latter was a transparent act of self-preservation; for two of the Lyncestian's brothers had been arrested as accomplices of the assassin Pausanias.[106] But Alexander was married to a daughter of Antipater, and the king cared more for his public actions than his private thoughts. Parmenion, too, declared himself for Alexander by sacrificing his son-in-law

Attalus,[107] but the cost of his support was high. On the eve of the Asiatic campaign, Parmenion's family was firmly entrenched in the command structure of 'Alexander's army.' The purge of the aristocracy, which followed Philip's murder, was surgical rather than sweeping. Hostile factions survived even the loss of powerful adherents.

Most difficult for the king was the fact that political opponents were often the commanders of contingents recruited on a territorial basis.[108] Alexander's own friends were too young, and predominantly from Upper Macedonia. In time, it would be possible to integrate these men into the hierarchy of command. The campaign itself and the burden of empire would decimate the old guard: some would die in battle or of illness, others would be distributed among the satrapies. But, for the present, the king would have to make peace with Philip's generals if he wanted the loyalty of their troops.

In the winter of 334/3, Alexander Lyncestes was arrested on information divulged by a Persian agent, Sisenes. That he had been in treasonous contact with the *chiliarch* Nabarzanes and the exile, Amyntas son of Antiochus, appears virtually certain. But, although Alexander could trust Parmenion to carry out the arrest, the Lyncestian's connections with Antipater meant that a capital sentence would have to be commuted to imprisonment. Lyncestes' nephew Amyntas, however, soon vanishes from our records.[109]

Further dissatisfaction resulted from the king's acceptance of his 'divine birth' at Siwah. For the conquest and administration of the satrapy, Alexander's recognition by the priests of Amun was a political expedient. But the subtleties of politics were wasted on the conservative Macedonian aristocracy, which had grown to regard its king as *primus inter pares*. Like the king's later orientalisms, the decision to exploit native sentiment was regarded by the conquerors as a demotion of the victors and their practices. Hegelochus, perhaps a relative of Philip's last wife, Cleopatra, appears to have plotted against the king in Egypt, but the plan came to nought and was disclosed only in 330, more than a year after the conspirator's death at Gaugamela. Philotas had also voiced his displeasure in Egypt – treasonous activity for a lesser man. His claim that Alexander's military success was due to Parmenion's generalship did not sit well with the son of Philip of Macedon, perhaps because there was some truth in it.[110] Before the final decision at Gaugamela, the remark was ignored but not forgotten. The echo of Philotas' boast would resound in Phrada (Farah) in 330, when Parmenion had been left behind in Ecbatana.

Whether Philotas was involved in the conspiracy of the obscure Dimnus or merely favored it is unclear. In either case, unless Dimnus' conspiracy was an utter fabrication intended to entrap Philotas,[111] his failure to report the news of the affair, once it had reached his ears, *was* treasonous. The entire process, however, exposed deep-rooted problems at the court and within the army. The trial itself was largely for show: the verdict was never in doubt, and the consequences of Philotas' conviction went beyond the issue and the camp. In a short time, Philotas, Parmenion, Alexander Lyncestes, and Demetrius the *Somatophylax* were dead; by comparison, the execution of Dimnus and his band of non entities was hardly front-page news. Whether it was a victory for justice or political intrigue cannot be known. But the political after-shocks were felt in late summer 328 at Maracanda, where Alexander silenced his most outspoken critic 'Black' Cleitus, and in the Hermolaus conspiracy, which showed how feeble the old guard had become and evinced the triumph of the 'New Men.' The common soldier vented his displeasure at the Beas, where the army refused to advance farther east, and at Opis, where Alexander's vision of the new empire was seriously challenged.[112] But the fear of Alexander can be seen clearly in Antipater's unwillingness to report to the king in Babylon. His inertia gave rise to rumours that the regent of Macedon contrived to murder the king in Babylon. And, even if this too can be dismissed as propaganda, it is clear evidence that resistance to Alexander continued, on many fronts, even that of the pamphleteers and historians. The resistance of the conquered peoples and the divisions of the aristocracy were inherited by Alexander's 'Successors' (*Diadochoi*), whom history remembers, with some injustice, as shadows of the Great Man.

NOTES

1 For date see N. G. L. Hammond, 'The Regnal Years of Philip and Alexander,' *GRBS* 33 (1992), 359–61.

2 A. B. Bosworth, 'Philip II and Upper Macedonia', *CQ* 21 (1971), 93–105, argues that Philip's death was instigated by disaffected Upper Macedonians.

3 Plut. *Demosth.* 23.2; cf. Aesch. 3.160. Cf. also Plut. *Alex.* 11.6, with J. R. Hamilton, *Plutarch's Alexander: A Commentary*, Oxford, Clarendon Press, 1969, p. 29.

4 Diodorus calls Philip's campaign of 344/3 'ancestral hatred' (16.69.7); for 337/6 see Diod. 16.93.6 and Curt. 8.1.25.

5 Frontin. *Strat.* 2.11.3; cf. Just. 11.5.3. These included the Odrysian prince, Sitalces: H. Berve, *Das Alexanderreich auf prosopographischer*

Grundlage, 2 vols, Munich, Beck, 1926, 2: 357, no. 712; W. Heckel, *The Marshals of Alexander's Empire*, London, Routledge, 1992, p. 334 and the Paeonian Ariston (Berve, ibid., 2: 74–5, no. 138; Heckel, ibid., pp. 354–5).

6 For the Illyrian campaign see Arr. 1.5–6; cf. Hammond in Hammond–Walbank, pp. 56–66; A. B. Bosworth, 'The Location of Alexander's Campaign Against the Illyrians,' in Barr-Sharrar, pp. 75–84; also J. F. C. Fuller, *The Generalship of Alexander the Great*, London, Macmillan, 1958, p. 85.

7 Prothytes and Phoenix: Plut. *Alex.* 11.7; cf. Berve, *Alexanderreich*, 2: 328 (no. 661), 2: 399 (no. 809). Demosthenes: Plut. *Demosth.* 23.1.

8 Diod. 17.8.5–6; cf. Frontin. *Strat.* 2.11.4; Din. 1.18.

9 Idomeneus, *FGrH* 338 F 14 (= Athen. 13.590D).

10 Arr. 1. 10. 6; Just. 11.4. 11–12; Curt. 3.2.10; Diod. 17.30.2; cf. D. Kelly, 'Charidemos' Citizenship: The Problem of *IG* II² 207', *ZPE* 83 (1990), 96–109.

11 Cf. E. Badian, 'Alexander in Iran', in *The Cambridge History of Iran*, ed. I. Gershevitch, Cambridge, Cambridge University Press, 1985, 2: p. 427: 'The Greeks clearly showed no hatred for their overlords . . .. But they felt strongly about the collaborating oligarchies and tyrannies supported by the Persians. . . .'

12 For Parmenion's expedition see Diod. 16.91.2, cf. 93.9; 17.5.1–2, 7.1–10; Just. 9.5.8 (cf. Trogus, *Prol.* 9); Polyaenus, *Strat.* 5.44.4-5. Polyaenus gives 10,000 men for the Macedonian force and 4,000 to Memnon.

13 Polyaenus, *Strat.* 4.3.15; cf. A. B. Bosworth, *A Historical Commentary on Arrian's History of Alexander, I–III*, Oxford, Clarendon Press, 1980, p. 131. But see also W. Heckel, 'Kalas son of Harpalos and "Memnon's Country",' *Mnemosyne* 47 (1994), 93–5.

14 Thus W. Judeich, *Kleinasiatische Studien*, Marburg, Elwert, 1892, p. 305; cf. Berve, *Alexanderreich*, 2: 188.

15 Mithridates was son-in-law of Darius III (Arr. 1.15.7, 16.3); Arbupales, son of Darius, was a grandson of Artaxerxes II (Arr. 1.16.3); Pharnaces is described as the brother of Darius III's wife (Arr. 1.16.3; Diod. 17.21.3), that is, the brother of a wife other than Stateira.

16 Arr. 2.4.5–6, 10.8; cf. Curt. 3.4.14.

17 J. W. McCoy, 'Memnon of Rhodes at the Granicus,' *AJP* 110 (1990), 413–33 makes a good case for Persian distrust of Memnon and the Greeks. For Persian suspicions regarding the Greek mercenaries in Cilicia see Arr. 2.6.3–6, Curt. 3.8.1–9, Diod. 17.30.1–4.

18 The deaths of these prominent Persians, together with the exemplary bravery of Oxathres (the king's brother) at Issus, dispels the common misconception of Persian cowardice (cf. A. T. Olmstead, *History of the Persian Empire*, Chicago, University of Chicago Press, 1948, p. 497: 'Persians could yet sacrifice themselves for their king').

19 For discussion of the site see G. E. Bean, *Aegean Turkey*,² London, John Murray, 1979, pp. 217–29. Evidence of Demosthenes' negotiations with the Persians came to light at Sardis (Plut. *Demosth.* 20.5).

20 For events in Ephesus see Arr. 1.17.9–12, with Bosworth, *Arrian's History*, pp. 131–3.

21 Ephialtes (Diod. 17.25.6–27.3) was one of the Athenians whose extradition Alexander had demanded after the sack of Thebes. Though the king had relented and required only the surrender of Charidemus, Ephialtes joined Alexander's enemies in Asia Minor. Neoptolemus was the son of Arrhabaeus (apparently the regicide). He was probably the brother of Amyntas son of Arrhabaeus (see Heckel, *Marshals*, p. 352) who commanded the cavalry 'Scouts' in Alexander's army. Diod. 17.25.5 says he died fighting on the Macedonian side, but Arr. 1.20.10 is probably right in treating him as a defector.

22 Plut. *Alex.* 10.1–5. Cf. V. French and P. Dixon, 'The Pixodaros Affair: Another View,' *AnW* 13 (1986), 73–86. For the younger Ada see Berve, *Alexanderreich*, 2: 12, no. 21.

23 Callisthenes, *FGrH* 124 F31 (reminiscent of Xen. *Anab.* 1.4.18).

24 For the view that Memnon's death relieved Alexander of anxiety about the Aegean campaign: Curt. 3.1.21, 2.1; Diod. 17.31.4. More harmful was Darius' decision to call the Greeks serving with Thymondas east to fight at Issus (J. Seibert, 'Dareios III,' in *Zu Alexander d. Gr.*, vol. 1, eds W. Will and J. Heinrichs, Amsterdam, Hakkert, 1987, pp. 445–6).

25 Arr. 3.2.4–5, 7; cf. Curt. 4.5.19–21, 8.11.

26 See E. Badian, 'A Document of Artaxerxes IV?' in *Greece and the Early Mediterranean in Ancient History and Prehistory*, ed. K. H. Kinzl, Berlin, de Gruyter, 1977, pp. 40–50.

27 A. Sachs, 'Achaemenid Royal Names in Babylonian Astronomical Texts,' *AJAH* 2 (1977), 143. For the form Codomannus see Just. 10.3.3; his accession: Diod. 17.5.3–6.

28 Curt. 3.8.10–11, in Quintus Curtius Rufus, *The History of Alexander*, trans. J. C. Yardley, with introduction and notes by W. Heckel, Harmondsworth, Penguin, 1984, p. 38.

29 A. B. Bosworth, *Conquest and Empire: The Reign of Alexander the Great*, Cambridge, Cambridge University Press, 1988, p. 57.

30 Other mercenaries also escaped from Issus to join Agis in the Peloponnesus, but it is doubtful that these numbered 8,000 as suggested by Curt. 4.1.39 and Diod. 17.48.2 (but see the comments of P. Brunt, *Arrian*, vol. 1, Cambridge, Harvard University Press, 1976, pp. 481–2).

31 Persian totals: 400,000 infantry, 100,000 cavalry (Diod. 17.31.2; Just. 11.9.1; but only 300,000 infantry in Oros. 3.16.6); 250,000 infantry, 62,200 cavalry (Curt. 3.2.5–9); 600,000 men in all (Arr. 2.8.8; Plut. *Alex.* 18.6; *P Oxy.* 1798 44, col. 2 = *FGrH* 148).

32 For the location of the Pinarus see D. W. Engels, *Alexander the Great and the Logistics of the Macedonian Army*, Berkeley, University of California Press, 1978, pp. 131–4 and N. G. L. Hammond, 'Alexander's Cavalry Charge at the Battle of Issus in 333 BC,' *Historia* 41 (1992), 395–6.

33 Chares of Mytilene, *FGrH* 125 F6 (= Plut. *Alex.* 20.9), went so far as to claim that Alexander's thigh wound (mentioned also by Curt. 3.11.10; Diod. 17.34), was inflicted by Darius himself.

34 Arr. 2.13.8, 15.6; Curt. 4.1.5–6, 15; cf. Just. 11.10.5; Diod. 17.40.2. Straton, son of Gerostratus, surrendered Aradus and Marathus though

his father and a large proportion of the citizen population were still serving with the Persian fleet. It is doubtful that the defection of the Phoenician contingents, which later joined Alexander, occurred before the surrender of their home bases.

35 Straton son of Tennes in Greek texts (Berve, *Alexanderreich*, 2: 365–6, no. 728). Straton was replaced by Abdalonymus (Abd-elonim; cf. Berve, ibid., 2: 3, no. 1), an impoverished scion of the royal house. For his story see Curt. 4.1.16–26; Plut. *Mor.* 340D; Diod. 17.47. Athen. 12.531D–E may indicate that Straton was executed.

36 Cf. Diod. 16.51.3, under the year 350/49! But Diodorus' chronology for the suppression of the rebellions in Phoenicia and Egypt is hopeless. See, e.g., N. Grimal, *A History of Ancient Egypt*, trans. I. Shaw, Oxford, Basil Blackwell, 1992, p. 380–1.

37 Diod. 16.43–5. In the capture of the city some 40,000 Sidonians perished.

38 Tamasus: Duris, *FGrHist.* 76 F4 (= Athen. 4.167C). Nicocreon: Plut. *Alex.* 29.3; cf. Diog. Laert. 9.58. Nithaphon: Arr. *Ind.* 18.8.

39 For the diplomatic negotiations, see Arr. 2.14, 25.1–3; Diod. 17.39.1–3, 54.1–6; Curt. 4.1.7–14, 5.1–8, 11.1–22; Just. 11.12.1–16; Plut. *Alex.* 29.7–8.

40 Curt. 4.4.15–16 claims that the Sidonians saved some 15,000 fellow Phoenicians.

41 Curt. 4.8.9 (cf. 4.5.9). See also A. B. Bosworth, 'The Government of Syria under Alexander the Great,' *CQ* 24 (1974), 46–64.

42 Arr. 2.11.8; Diod. 17.34.5; Curt. 3.11.10; 4.1.28.

43 Arr. 3.1.2; cf. Curt. 4.1.32, 7.4.

44 For Alexander at Siwah see Plut. *Alex.* 27; Arr. 3.3–4; Diod. 17.49.2–51.4; Curt. 4.7.5–32. On a wall of the temple of Amun at Luxor, Alexander is shown in Egyptian dress, with the titles 'Beloved of Amun' and 'Chosen by Re'.

45 Diod. 17.63.3; Curt. 4.1.16. The date of Antipater's victory over Agis at Megalopolis is a notorious crux in Alexander studies. I believe, however, that there is no good evidence to refute Curtius' claim that the war began suddenly and ended quickly, 'before Darius' defeat by Alexander at Arbela' (6.1.21). More difficult is to determine when Alexander received the news that Agis' war was over.

46 The Carians at Gaugamela are not from Asia Minor, but rather Carians who had been transplanted to Babylonia, the so-called 'Carian villages' (Arr. 3.8.5; cf. Diod. 17.110.3; 19.12.1). Hence they fight under the command of Bupares, satrap of Babylonia (Arr. 3.8.5).

47 Details of the composition of Darius' army come from an official document captured in the Persian camp after the battle and transcribed by Aristobulus (*FGrH* 139 F17 [= Arr. 3.11.3–7]); cf. Curt. 4.12.6–13.

48 Darius had not left the river crossings unopposed. see Curt. 4.9.7, 12, 14; Diod. 17.55.1–2; Arr. 3.7.1, for Mazaeus and Satropates at the Euphrates and Tigris.

49 The figures are, again, grossly exaggerated, but the Persian army at Gaugamela was certainly larger than that at Issus. Arr. 3.8.6 says there were 1,000,000 infantry, 40,000 cavalry, 200 scythe-chariots; Diod.

17.53.3 reports 800,000 infantry, 200,000 cavalry (cf. Plut. *Alex.* 31.1: one million in all); only Curt. 4.12.13 gives very low figures: 200,000 infantry and 45,000 cavalry. By contrast, Alexander had 40,000 infantry and 7,000 cavalry (Arr. 3.12.5; cf. Brunt, *Arrian*, 1976, pp. 509–14).

50 Mazaeus' official position is unclear. The satrap of Babylonia at Gaugamela had been Bupares (Arr. 3.8.5), who perhaps fell in the battle.

51 Curt. 5.1. 19–23, trans. by J. C. Yardley in Curtius Rufus, *Alexander*, pp. 93–4.

52 Cf. A. Kuhrt, 'Usurpation, Conquest, and Ceremonial: From Babylonia to Persia,' in *Rituals of Royalty. Power and Ceremonial in Traditional Societies*, eds D. Cannadine and S. Price, Cambridge, Cambridge University Press, 1987, pp. 48–52.

53 Mazaeus was satrap (Arr. 3.16.4; Curt. 5.1.44; cf. Diod. 17.64.5–6) until his death in late 328, whereupon he was replaced by Stamenes (Arr. 4.18.3; cf. Curt. 8.3.17 'Ditamenes'). For the Macedonian appointments see Curt. 5.1.43; Diod. 17.64.5; cf. Arr. 3.16.4.

54 I regard as fanciful the suggestion of some unnamed authors, recorded by Diod. 17.65.5, that Abulites surrendered Susiane on the king's instructions, in order to preoccupy the Macedonian ruler while Darius prepared to renew the war.

55 Abulites made his official surrender in person to Alexander and was allowed to retain his satrapy, which he enlarged at the expense of Madates (Curt. 5.2.9–10, 16). See Curt. 5.2.16–17 for Macedonian appointments.

56 Identification with the son of Artabazus (Arr. 3.23.7) is ruled out by Curtius' claim (5.4.34) that the satrap of Persis died before Alexander's capture of Persepolis (cf. Bosworth, *Arrian's History*, 1980, p. 325).

57 Curt. 5.3.1; Diod. 17.68.1; Arr. 3.18.2. See W. Heckel, 'Alexander at the Persian Gates,' *Athenaeum* 58 (1980), 168–74, with additional literature. For the location see A. Stein, 'An Archaeological Journey in Western Iran,' *GJ* (1938), 314–18; but Bosworth, *Conquest and Empire*, p. 90, suggests Tang-i Mohammed Reza.

58 See Curt. 5.3.12; Diod. 17.67.4; for Madates see also Berve, *Alexanderreich*, 2: 243, no. 483. Curt. 5.3.15 says that Alexander left the Uxians free from taxation, but the fact is clearly that he, like the Achaemenid rulers, was unable to impose tribute upon them (cf. J. M. Cook, *The Persian Empire*, New York, Schocken, 1983, pp. 182, 184–5). Arrian's claim (3.17.6) that they paid a substantial tribute to Alexander is probably face-saving propaganda.

59 Curt. 5.5.2; Diod. 17.69.1. For Tiridates see Berve, *Alexanderreich*, 2: 374–5, no. 754. The treasure amounted to 12,000 talents (Curt. 5.6.9; Diod. 17.71.1)

60 For the long-term impact see J. M. Balcer, 'Alexander's Burning of Persepolis,' *Iranica Antiqua* 13 (1978), 132. Omitted here is discussion of Alexander's motives (and timing) for the destruction of the palace, which have little to do with the question of Persian resistance, being instead connected with the 'Panhellenic Crusade' and public opinion in European Greece. See further E. Badian, 'Agis III: Revisions and

Reflections,' in *Ventures into Greek History*, ed. I. Worthington, Oxford, Clarendon Press, 1994, pp. 289–92.

61 Arr. 3. 19. 4. The road from Arbela to Ecbatana, depending on the route taken, was about 600 km (J. E. Atkinson, *A Commentary on Q. Curtius Rufus' Historiae Alexandri Magni, Books 5–7.2*, Amsterdam, Hakkert, 1994, p. 136). Darius had been in Ecbatana from November until the news of Alexander's approach reached him in May (?) 330.

62 Arr. 3.21.1 (Bagisthanes, Antibelus); Curt. 5.13.3 (Bagisthanes), 13.7 (Melon), 13.11 (Brochubelus). Curt. 5.13.9 mentions also Mithrazenes and Orsillus as supporters of Darius who defected from Bessus' camp.

63 Curt. 6.4.24–5, 5.21. Autophradates surrendered to Alexander in Zadracarta (Sari, or Asterabad?), the capital of Hyrcania (Arr. 3.23.7; Curt. 6.4.24–5).

64 The 'Brazanes' (sc. Barzanes) arrested by Phrataphernes (Arr. 4.7.1, 18.1) is probably Nabarzanes. Cf. W. Heckel, 'Some Speculations on the Prosopography of the *Alexanderreich*,' *LCM* 6 (1981), 66–9; but see Bosworth, *Conquest and Empire*, p. 236.

65 Arr. 3.25.1; Curt. 6.6.20; he brought news that Bessus had assumed the upright tiara and title of 'Artaxerxes' and was mobilizing the Scythians, Curt. 6.6.13.

66 For the location of Artacoana see Olmstead, *Persian Empire*, p. 46, n. 55; J. Seibert, *Die Eroberung des Perserreiches durch Alexander den Grossen auf kartographischer Grundlage*, Wiesbaden, Reichert, p. 120. Engels, *Alexander the Great*, pp. 89–90, puts Artacoana north and east of Kalat-i-Nadiri. For Artacoana as satrapal capital see Arr. 3.25.5; Curt. 6.6.20; Diod. 17.78.1.

67 Satibarzanes: Arr. 3.25; 3.28.2–3; Diod. 17.78.1, 81.3, 4–6; Curt. 6.6.13, 20, 22; 7.3.2, 4.33–40. Cf. Heckel, *Marshals*, p. 210. News of Erigyius' victory reached Alexander in Bactria.

68 P. H. L. Eggermont, *Alexander's Campaigns in Sind and Baluchistan and the Siege of the Brahmin Town of Harmatelia*, Louvain, Louvain University Press, 1975, p. 18, identifies the 'Samaxus' of Curt. 8.13.3–5 with Sambus.

69 For his career see Berve, *Alexanderreich*, 2: 359–61, no. 717. 'Spitamas' had royal, and Zoroastrian, connexions; Spitamenes' daughter was called Apame (Arr. 7.4.6; Strab. 12.8.15; cf. App. *Syr.* 57; the other known Apame of this period was Artabazus' daughter, named for her grandmother, the daughter of Artaxerxes II). Spitamenes, though once a supporter (Curt. 7.5.20), had joined Catanes and Dataphernes in arresting Bessus and extraditing him to Alexander (Curt. 7.6.14; Arr. 3.29.6).

70 The barbarians had put Alexander's garrison troops to the sword (Arr. 4.1.4; Curt. 7.6.13–15). Attack on Maracanda: Arr. 4.3.6; Curt. 7.6.24. A relief force ambushed at the Polytimetus (Zeravshan) river: Arr. 4.3.7, 5.2; Curt. 7.7.31–9; cf. *Metz Epitome* [hereafter *ME*] 9, 13. Attack on Zariaspa (328): Arr. 4.16.4–7. Defeated by Craterus and Coenus: Arr. 4.17.1–2, 4–7. Death of Spitamenes: Arr. 4.17.7; but see Curt. 8.3.1–15; *ME* 20–3).

71 Arr. 4.21.2; cf. Strab. 11.11.4, who says it was 15 stades in height with a circuit of 80.

72 Arr. 4.21.6–8; Curt. 8.2.25–31; W. Heckel, 'Chorienes and Sisimithres,' *Athenaeum* 64 (1986), 223–6; A. B. Bosworth, 'A Missing Year in the History of Alexander the Great,' *JHS* 101 (1981), 17–39.

73 Curt. 8.4.1; cf. *ME* 28, Gazabes. Curt. 8.2.33 is corrupt: *cohortandus* appears to refer to Chorienes.

74 Curt. 8.4.19. Arr. 4.21.10 says that they experienced heavy snowfall *during the siege*; Curt. 8.4.2–18 and *ME* 24–7 claim the privations occurred after the capture of the Rock.

75 Curt. 8.4.22–30; *ME* 28–31; Strab. 11.11.4; but Arr. 4.19.4–6 places the marriage after the capture of the Sogdian Rock.

76 See Curt. 8.10.22 for the death of Assacenus. Cleophis as mother of Assacenus: Curt. 8.10.22; *ME* 39; cf. Arr. 4.27.4. Massaga: Curt. 8.10.22; Strab. 15.1.27; Arr. 4.26.1. Assacenus' kingdom was located between the Panjkora (Guraeus) and Swat rivers. Arrian distinguishes the Aspasians (4.24.1) from the Guraeans (4.25.7) and Assacenians (4.25.5; 4.26).

77 Arr. 4.27.3–4. Curt. 8.10.34–5 writes that Cleophis and the noble-women came in person to surrender to Alexander (cf. *ME* 45), that Cleophis placed *her own son* (Assacenus' son in *ME* 39, 45) on the king's knee and thereby won his pardon and retained her position as queen. Curtius adds that she subsequently bore a son, named Alexander (8.10.36), but stops short of Justin's affirmation (12.7.10) that Alexander himself was the father.

78 On these sites see A. Stein, *On Alexander's Track to the Indus*, London, Macmillan, 1929, pp. 53–61 (Udegram and Bir-kot) and 128–34 (Pir-sar). Recently, Stein's identification of Aornus with Pir-sar has been challenged in favour of Mount Ilam, which separates Swat from Buner), and is situated south of Udegram and in the vicinity of Bir-kot (P. H. L. Eggermont, 'Ptolemy the Geographer and the People of the Dards,' *OLP* 15 (1984), 191–200). Mount Ilam better suits Arr. 4.28.1, which puts the rock in the country of the Bazirans.

79 Peucelaitis, Strab. 15.1.29, that is, the territory of Gandhara, of which Pushkalavati was the capital; it had replaced Peshawar as the capital of Gandhara (O. Caroe, *The Pathans*, London, Macmillan, 1962, p. 48). See now E. Badian, 'Alexander at Peucelaotis,' *CQ* 37 (1987), 123–6.

80 Arr. 4.28.6. Astis was originally among the hyparchs who submitted to Alexander along with Taxiles (Arr. 4.22.6), but it appears that Taxiles was accompanied by Sangaeus, a rival of Astis, who sought, with Taxiles' aid, to win Macedonian backing for his cause. Hence Astis' opposition to the forces of Hephaestion and Perdiccas.

81 Curt. 8.12.13; cf. *ME* 53. Wrongly identified by Berve *Alexanderreich* 2: 3 as Hazara, which corresponds to Urasa, the kingdom of Arsaces; Abhisara belongs to the Kashmir. Megasthenes (*FGrH* 715 F9 [= Arr. *Ind.* 4.12) mentions the Abissarians, who are mountain-dwellers, in whose territory the Soanus, a tributary of the Indus, rises.

82 Curt. 8.13.1; Arr. 5.8.3; *ME* 55. See Curt. 8.14.1 for Abisares' failure to aid Porus.

83 This was, in fact, a confirmation of Abisares' authority over Urasa (or Hazara), since the fugitives from Aornus sought refuge with Abisares,

i.e., across the Indus (Arr. 4.30.7). For Arsaces see Berve, *Alexanderreich*,
2: 81, no. 147. Alexander's envoys to Abisares included a certain
Nicocles (*ME* 55–6), whom the ruler was reluctant to send back.
84 Arr. 5.29.5. Unlike Porus and Taxiles, there is no reference to an Abisares
in the satrapal allotments of 323 or 320 BC (cf. P. A. Brunt, *Arrian*,
vol. 2, Cambridge, Harvard University Press, 1983, p. 474). In 325,
Alexander received word that Abisares had died of illness, and he
approved the accession of his son, who also took the dynastic name
(Curt. 10.1.20–1).
85 The point of Alexander's crossing and the site of the battle with Porus
have been fiercely debated. Lately there is considerable support for A.
Stein's view ('The Site of Alexander's Passage of the Hydaspes and the
Battle with Porus,' *GJ* 80 [1932], 31–46) that Alexander crossed at
Jalalpur, beyond the island of Admana, and that the main camp (opposite Porus) was at Haranpur. Cf. Fuller, *Generalship*, pp. 180–99;
Bosworth, *Conquest and Empire*, p. 126, n. 313. For Porus' son see Arr.
5.14.6 (= Ptolemy, *FGrH* 138 F20); Plut. *Alex.* 60.8. His contingent
is separate from that of Spitaces (Curt. 8.14.2, calling him Porus'
brother; cf. Arr. 5.18.2, an Indian nomarch).
86 Curt. 9.3.22 dates this marriage alliance to the time after Alexander's
return from the Hyphasis, by which time another dispute had broken
out between the two rulers (cf. Curt. 10.1.20). Curtius' claim (8.14.45)
that Porus was 'made one of Alexander's friends' (*amici*) probably means
that he was enrolled as one of the *hetairoi*. Philip had extended the
practice to include non-Macedonians; Alexander added men like
Abdalonymus, Oxathres (the brother of Darius) and now Porus. These
were 'political' rather than 'military' Companions.
87 The Glausae: Arr. 5.20.2–4; their territory was perhaps in the vicinity
of Bember (Brunt, *Arrian*, 2: 461). 'Cowardly' Porus: Diod. 17.91.1,
93.1; cf. Arr. 5.20.6, 21.2–3.
88 Pimprama: Arr. 5.22.4. Sangala (Lahore or Amritsar): Arr. 5.22.4–7;
Curt. 9.1.14–23; cf. Fuller, *Generalship*, pp. 255–8.
89 Sophytes: Diod. 17.91.4–92. 3; Curt. 9.1.27–35; *ME* 66–7. At the
Hyphasis a certain king Phegeus was said to have reported on the tribes
to the east, especially the kingdom of Xandrames (apparently of the
Nanda dynasty of Magadha). See also Arr. 5.25.1, Curt. 9.2.1; Diod.
17.93; *ME* 68–9; cf. Plut. *Alex.* 62; Just. 12.8.10 (corrupt).
90 Arr. 5.19.4; Diod. 17.89.6, 95.5; Curt. 9.1.6, 3.23; Strab. 15.1.29.
91 On Chandragupta see Plut. *Alex.* 62.4, 9; cf. Just. 15.4.12–20.
92 Arr. 6.15.7. The area came under the administrative control of Peithon
son of Agenor, whose satrapy must have included Sambus' kingdom as
well (Arr. 6.15.4; cf. Heckel, *Marshals*, pp. 324–5).
93 I see no good authority for Berve's (*Alexanderreich*, 2: 293, no. 587)
form 'Oxycanus', nor for the identification of Oxicanus and Porticanus
(Strab. 15.1.33; Curt. 9.8.11–12; Diod. 17.102.5). Their names and
the details concerning them are sufficiently different that we may suspect
conflation of two successive incidents, with Arrian preserving the name
Oxicanus, the Vulgate Porticanus. Porticanus in Pardabathra: Ptol. *Geog.*
7.1.58. For his fate see Curt. 9.8.11–12; Diod. 17.102.5.

94 If Cleitarchus (*FGrH* 137 F25 [= Curt. 9.8.15]) can be trusted, the slaughter of the natives in this district must have been extensive. The vulgate account of Alexander's dealings with Sambus and Musicanus differs substantially from Arrian's.

95 For the route see A. Stein, 'Alexander's Route into Gedrosia,' *GJ* 102 (1943), 193–227; Engels, *Alexander the Great*, pp. 135–43; see also J. R. Hamilton, 'Alexander Among the Oreitae,' *Historia* 21 (1972), 603–8.

96 For early travel from the 'Red Sea' (i.e., Persian Gulf) to India see L. Casson, *Travel in the Ancient World*, Baltimore, Johns Hopkins University Press, 1994, pp. 30–1, 45.

97 Haustanes (Arr. 4.22.2; Curt. 8.5.2); Autophradates (Arr. 3.23.7; 4.18.2; Curt. 6.4.24–5; 8.3.17; 10.1.39); Ordanes (Arr. 6.27.3; Curt. 9.10.19 [cf. 10.1.9] names Orzines and Zariaspes (see E. Badian, 'Harpalus,' *JHS* 90 [1960], 19).

98 Oxydates: Arr. 4.18.3; cf. Bosworth, 'A Missing Year,' pp. 21–3. Arsaces: Arr. 3.29.5; 4.7.1; Curt. 8.3.17.

99 Tyriespis (Arr. 4.22.5; 6.15.3). Curtius 9.8.9 calls the governor of Parapamisus 'Terioltes' and says that he was tried for greed and tyrannical acts and executed; he adds that Oxyartes was acquitted and given a more extensive territory (9.8.10).

100 Phrasaortes was appointed satrap in 330 (Arr. 3.18.11), replacing the dead Ariobarzanes; but, when he died of illness while Alexander was in India, Orxines, who had commanded the contingent from the Persian Gulf at Gaugamela (Arr. 3.8.5), took control of the satrapy (Arr. 6.29.2). But Orxines too proved corrupt and was replaced by Peucestas (Arr. 6.30.1–2).

101 Arr. 7. 4. 1; cf. Plut. *Alex.* 68.6–7, claiming that Alexander ran Oxathres through with his *sarissa*.

102 Arr. 6.29.3; cf. Berve, *Alexanderreich*, 2: 104, no. 207.

103 Curt. 9.7.1–11, naming Athenodorus, Boxus and Biton as leaders in the dispute; cf. Diod. 17.99.6. For the sequel see Diod. 18.7.1–9.

104 Details in Berve, *Alexanderreich*, 2: 75–80, no. 143; Heckel, *Marshals*, pp. 213–21.

105 Cf. Alexander's treatment of Hephaestion's physician Glaucus (or Glaucias) after the former's death in Ecbatana (Plut. *Alex.* 72.3; Arr. 7.14.4). For Poulamachus see Plut. *Alex.* 69.3, who does not specify the method of punishment. Since the crime was perpetrated against the tomb of Cyrus, it is likely that the form of punishment was 'oriental' (cf. the punishment of Bessus).

106 Arr. 1.25.1; cf. Just. 11.2.2.

107 Diod. 17.2.4–6, 5.2. Attalus' widow was probably soon married to Coenus son of Polemocrates (Curt. 6.9.30; cf. Arr. 1.24.1, 29.4).

108 Possibly there was also some geographical basis for the selection of the seven *Somatophylakes* (Heckel, *Marshals*, p. 261).

109 For the Lyncestian's connexions with Amyntas see Arr. 1.25.3; for Nabarzanes, Curt. 3.7.12, but the story is garbled. For Amyntas son of Arrhabaeus see Heckel, *Marshals*, pp. 352–3.

110 Philotas' Egyptian 'conspiracy': Arr. 3.26.1; Plut. *Alex.* 48.4–49.12.

Curt. 3.2.33 echoes Philotas' own assessment. It has, moreover, persuaded several modern scholars.

111 Thus E. Badian, 'The Death of Parmenio,' *TAPA* 91 (1960), 324–38; but see W. Heckel, 'The Conspiracy *against* Philotas,' *Phoenix* 31 (1977), 9–21.

112 For the Opis Mutiny see Diod. 17.109.2; Just. 12.11.5–9; Arr. 7.8; Curt. 10.2.8–30.

9

THE SUCCESSORS OF
ALEXANDER

W. Lindsay Adams

When Alexander died in Babylon in June of 323, he left behind
more questions than he had resolved; worse, he had failed to provide
for an heir. Half of the twenty provincial governors (satraps) had
either already been executed during the last year for treason and
malfeasance or were awaiting that fate, which gutted the normal
machinery of government. The leading figures of the previous decade
were all gone: Coenus, who had replaced the murdered Parmenion
as chief commander, had died in India; when Hephaestion, who had
served as *chiliarch* (for all intents and purposes 'Prime Minister'),
had died the year before (324), Alexander left the position officially
vacant; Harpalus, who had been the head of the central financial
office, had fled with his embezzled funds and would soon be dead;
Craterus, who succeeded Coenus, was leading 10,000 veterans back
to Macedonia with orders to replace (and possibly kill) Antipater, as
general for Europe. Only the second rank of officers were left in
Babylon, led by Perdiccas, who was carrying on the functions but
not the office of *chiliarch*.

Further, no permanent structure for the empire had been created;
rather, Alexander's initial tinkering with traditional Persian administration remained: civil functions in each satrapy had been split off
from military commands and finance, with the former in the hands
of a Macedonian or Greek commander, and the latter concentrated
at Alexander's court. The idea had been to lessen the chance of
revolt, and it would have been a good thing to keep in mind for
the future. The most pressing problem was that of a successor. A
decade of hard campaigning and Alexander's own jealousies had
eliminated most of the prospects. Alexander's first wife, Roxane, was
pregnant, which presented the possibility of a direct male heir; and
there was Alexander's half-brother, Arrhidaeus, who was reputedly

mentally incapacitated.[1] Beyond that, there were a host of potential usurpers.

Without a competent candidate from the Argead House, or for that matter without any figure with the stature of a leader, a power struggle was imminent. The one thing present in abundance at Babylon was a group of talented men with strong ambitions, no fewer than four of whom would become kings in their own right before the Wars of the Successors were over (Cassander, Lysimachus, Ptolemy, and Seleucus). The stage was set for over forty years of civil war among the Macedonians, at first for the regency of the empire itself, and then over the question of the very existence of the empire. It became the Great Game of Empire and Survival.

OPENING PLAY: THE STRUGGLE FOR THE REGENCY, 323–321

The continuity of the empire was not a foregone conclusion even at this point. Alexander had held together the disparate Macedonian and Persian elements that made up his army, officers and territories on the basis of his personal authority, the basis of Macedonian kingship. The council of officers which gathered within a few days of Alexander's death at Babylon did not even include the most experienced commanders (Antipater, Craterus, and Antigonus), let alone possess the authority for any settlement. Perdiccas claimed, conveniently, that Alexander had given him his signet ring and hence his authority (though there were no witnesses to that fact). Nevertheless, Perdiccas held the initiative and so called the meeting.

Ptolemy suggested that the council itself govern the empire, exercising royal authority without a king, and await the outcome of Roxane's pregnancy. The latter was the most popular position, supported by Alexander's Bodyguards, 'Friends,' and ultimately the Companion Cavalry, but Perdiccas wanted executive control himself. Nearchus proposed the alternative of choosing as king Heracles, the son of Barsine, who was reputedly Alexander's bastard, but that was never either a credible claim or a possible option. Ultimately, they chose a compromise of Ptolemy's solution for the succession and Perdiccas' political position, but events were already running ahead of them.[2] Almost imperceptibly the nature of kingship began to change and become institutionalized.

While the officers talked, the infantrymen of the Phalanx itself acted. They wanted a true Macedonian king, and proclaimed

Arrhidaeus (as a son of Philip II) to be king in fact. He was renamed Philip III to make the point. They found spokesmen in Meleager and Attalus, two of the Phalanx Brigadiers curiously left out of the council.[3] Meleager, who was named by the Phalanx as Philip Arrhidaeus' guardian, made it clear that they were willing to take up arms to force their case by actually storming the palace where the council was meeting. The stunned council was forced to accept a compromise: Philip III was recognized as king, but provision was made for a joint kingship should Roxane bear a son, with Perdiccas and Leonnatus as the infant's guardians. Meleager remained as Arrhidaeus' guardian, but now became second in command to Perdiccas as the confirmed *chiliarch*. A few months later Roxane would bear a son: Alexander IV.

The next order of business was to provide for administration of the empire. The council, under Perdiccas' direction as *chiliarch* (and a proclamation by Philip Arrhidaeus), named the satraps and army commanders. Pausing only briefly to murder Meleager (which preceded the proclamation), Perdiccas' goal was to secure his central position and this distribution of commands served both to reward supporters and to get potential rivals out of court. In doing so, the Alexandrian distinction between civil, military, and financial authority within each of the satrapies was conveniently forgotten. It is doubtful that this was either formal or intentional, just something which happened functionally, but it did not bode well for the future.

In the distribution of power, Antipater and Craterus were jointly named as generals for Europe, neatly settling that problem and seeing to it they would not be needed at court. The majority of satraps were reconfirmed, such as Antigonus Monophthalmus ('the One-Eyed') of Greater Phrygia, who was to prove a significant player but at this point was still only one of many, and Peucestas in Persis. More interesting were the new appointments, especially that of Ptolemy, who got Egypt; Lysimachus, who received Thrace; Leonnatus, who was appointed to Hellespontine Phrygia; Eumenes of Cardia, Alexander's Greek secretary, who was named to Cappadocia; and Peithon, who was to hold Media. In the case of Leonnatus, his departure was the occasion for Perdiccas to offer sharing the joint guardianship of the kings with Craterus (who was also conveniently far away, but a popular choice with the Phalanx). The chief army commands were given to Seleucus (the senior position: command of the Companion Cavalry) and to Cassander (command of the Hypaspists, including the Agema, which formed the Guards Brigade), both subordinate to Perdiccas himself, of course; and new commanders were detailed for the Phalanx brigades. Cassander's appointment was an opening gesture for the support of his father, Antipater, which was followed by negotiations for a marriage alliance between Perdiccas and Antipater's daughter, Nicaea.[4]

While Perdiccas was solidifying his position at court, the empire was crumbling at the periphery. The mercenaries in Alexander's multiple colonial foundations in Bactria mutinied in an attempt to go home. In the Aegean, Rhodes declared its independence while many of the poleis on the mainland, again led by Athens, initiated the Lamian War to free Greece of Macedonian control. Even the Aetolian League, stirred up against Antipater by Olympias, cooperated with the rebels. When Antipater moved to suppress the rebels, he was bottled up in the Thessalian city of Lamia (just north of Thermopylae) and had to send out an appeal for help. A Thracian rebellion under the chieftain Seuthes prevented Lysimachus (the nearest satrap) from sending any aid, though he did maintain both control of Thrace and open lines of communication. It was Leonnatus, from the satrapy of Hellespontine Phrygia, who ultimately broke Antipater out of Lamia in early spring of 322, but Leonnatus was killed in the process. Antipater withdrew to Macedonia to await the arrival of Craterus and the 10,000 veterans.

After a brilliant naval campaign by the Macedonian admiral Cleitus, which culminated in a victory over the Athenian fleet in midsummer of 322, Craterus crossed from Asia Minor to Macedonia and placed his forces under Antipater's command. The old general, with some 40,000 hoplites and 5,000 cavalry, moved back into Thessaly and at Crannon in late August of 322 won a hard-fought battle. The Greek alliance came apart. A Macedonian garrison took over the Munychia fortress in Athens in late September, while the Athenians had already condemned to death the rebellion's leaders (especially Demosthenes, who committed suicide rather than fall into Macedonian hands). Antipater, who had been using garrisons and pro-Macedonian oligarchies to control hostile areas of Greece following the rebellion led by Agis of Sparta in 331, now tightened that control and introduced more garrisons. Seuthes in Thrace, with Antipater's victory, also acknowledged Macedonian overlordship.

Meanwhile, the Greek mercenaries' mutiny in Bactria was roughly suppressed by Peithon, from Media, acting on Perdiccas' orders. Perdiccas first reinforced Peithon's satrapal forces (8,000 cavalry and 10,000 infantry) with 800 cavalry and 3,000 infantry drawn from the Royal Army itself, probably with the intention of both stiffening

Peithon's army and keeping an eye on the satrap. The combined forces defeated the mutineers, and then the Royal contingent massacred the survivors, under orders originally issued by Perdiccas.

In addition to these troubles, one native satrap (Ariarathes of Cappadocia) refused to accept the settlement at Babylon, since he was to be replaced in his hereditary satrapy by Eumenes of Cardia. Perdiccas decided to use this as a litmus test for the loyalty of all the satraps in Asia Minor. Perdiccas ordered Leonnatus (who was then later excused to aid Antipater), Antigonus the One-Eyed and the other satraps in Asia Minor to join the Royal Army under his command (and nominally Philip III) in order to punish Ariarathes. This was accomplished (with the conspicuous absence of Antigonus) in the summer of 322, even before the Battle of Crannon. If the nature of the price of defiance to Perdiccas had been unclear before, the fate of the Bactrian Greek mercenaries and of Ariarathes and his family (whom Perdiccas had tortured to death) ended any ambiguity. Antigonus was ordered to report to the court for trial before the Army Assembly (the 'Macedonians'); instead, he fled to Antipater and Craterus.

THE FIRST CIVIL WAR, 322–321

To Perdiccas' ruthless actions, were now added his unbounded ambition. Olympias sent her daughter, Cleopatra, on to Sardis and contacted Perdiccas to offer him a royal marriage. Being a royal uncle and regent was a possible path to kingship itself, but it was made clear to Perdiccas that the price for this was cancellation of his marriage to Antipater's daughter. Antipater was Olympias' old rival, who had forced her out of *prostasia* in Macedonia just as Craterus had now forced Cleopatra out.[5] Both wanted back in the game, and revenge. Antigonus' flight to his old friend and comrade, Antipater, made any connection there tenuous as well as impolitic for Perdiccas. To complicate matters further, another daughter of Philip II, Cynane, pushed her daughter Adea forward as a bride for Philip III Arrhidaeus. Perdiccas tried to prevent this by murdering Cynane, but a mutiny by the Phalanx (ever sentimentally attached to the descendants of Philip II) forced the marriage, and the bride took the name Eurydice to conjure up the proper royal connection. In the fallout from all this, the lines were drawn for the civil war.

During the winter of 322/1, Antigonus convinced Antipater and Craterus of Perdiccas' ambitions: the examples of his ruthlessness were self-evident, but the threatened re-emergence of Olympias on the scene and the marriage rejection played this up as well. The new coalition first made peace with the one still rebellious area, the Aetolians, who were reasonably safe in the mountain fastness of western Central Greece.

The ambitions of Ptolemy in Egypt also fell in with their plans. Ptolemy had secured his position in Egypt by driving out the corrupt satrapal financial officer Cleomenes (a vestige of Alexander's regime) and seizing the embezzled funds (some 8,000 talents) for his own use. Ptolemy had then annexed Cyrenaica to his satrapy. Both actions extended Ptolemy's power, but it was actually the next act which prompted the civil war. In a brilliant but risky propaganda ploy, Ptolemy ambushed the funeral cortège bearing Alexander's body back to Aegae in Macedonia for burial in the royal cemetery, and took it to Memphis.[6] There was no greater image with which to conjure legitimacy than Alexander's person, nor any more powerful symbol of the failure of Perdiccas' authority. Ptolemy, already married to Antipater's daughter, now rounded out the coalition, and Perdiccas was faced with a two-front civil war.

Rather than await an invasion of Macedonia by Perdiccas, who had the kings and the royal army to back his claim of legitimacy regardless of what his other ambitions may have been, Antipater and his allied commanders (Craterus and Antigonus) decided to invade Asia Minor. Perdiccas, rather than face a rebel army commanded by the most experienced generals in the empire, decided to knock off Ptolemy first and then deal with Antipater. He detailed Eumenes of Cardia to hold Asia Minor, which was tantamount to an admission that this was a lost cause. Though loyal to Alexander, Eumenes was neither a Macedonian nor had he ever before held a military command. But Eumenes could buy time (in fact, he did much more than that). The minor satraps in Asia Minor now began deserting Perdiccas.

By July of 321, Perdiccas brought the royal army to the frontier of Egypt. But in trying to force the Nile, Perdiccas proved an unlucky if not incompetent commander. More than 2,000 men (more than Alexander lost in all his major battles combined) were drowned in an abortive assault on Memphis. The royal army was used to better commanders. The result was that that very night some of his officers butchered Perdiccas in his tent rather than continue the civil war. The next day the army received Ptolemy, and in assembly it declared Peithon and one Arrhidaeus,[7] who were involved in the plot, to be the new guardians of the kings and hence joint commanders of the army. The assembly immediately condemned Eumenes and some fifty of his supporters, formally outlawing the remainder of Perdiccas' following.

In the meantime, Antipater and his army were marching through Asia Minor to attack Perdiccas, while Craterus took a portion of the allied force against Eumenes of Cardia to secure their flank. Craterus proved as unlucky as Perdiccas. Along with the rebel satrap of Armenia, Craterus was not only defeated but killed by Eumenes in Cappadocia. Antipater continued on into Syria, however, and the coalition forces met in midsummer at Triparadisus, in Syria. It proved to be the last meeting of Alexander's 'Grand Army.'

Things were still touch-and-go for a while. The army itself was in arrears for pay, and with Eumenes' victory it was probably feeling a bit ambivalent about events. Philip III's 16-year-old bride, Eurydice, took the opportunity to stir up the Phalanx, promising that Philip would pay them when given full authority. In the face of an ugly mood and possibly mutiny, Peithon and Arrhidaeus resigned their commands even before Antipater's arrival. By the time he got there, Antipater had already been chosen as the guardian of the kings and supreme commander, but he had no more funds than his predecessors, so Eurydice continued her campaign. With the backing of Antigonus and Seleucus, Antipater managed to restore discipline and suppress Eurydice.

Antipater, now fully in control, once again reordered the commands and satrapies. The members and supporters of the coalition, such as Ptolemy, were confirmed in their satrapies. Vacancies were equally filled with loyal officers, such as Seleucus' appointment as satrap in Babylon. The one remaining problem (Eumenes) was left to Antigonus, who was now named to command the reduced Asian field army and commissioned to hunt Eumenes down. To cement relations with Antigonus, Antipater appointed his own son, Cassander, as *chiliarch* for the Asian army and married off his daughter (the widowed Phila) to Antigonus' son Demetrius. With these safeguards in place (neither of which proved sufficient against Antigonus' growing ambitions), Antipater returned to Macedonia with both Philip III and Alexander IV in tow. The first struggle, which was fought over which generals would exercise power within the empire, came to a close. But the escalating scale of ambitions among the survivors assured that it was not the end but the beginning of a process of transition.

THE STRUGGLE FOR MACEDONIA

When Antipater returned to Macedonia, he was well into his eighties. Even before Perdiccas' death, the Athenian Demades expressed the idea that Macedonia and Greece were held only by an 'old and rotten thread [Antipater].' The settlement at Triparadisus even in the best of times could only have been temporary. In fact, Antigonus almost immediately began acting as an independent agent in his campaign against Eumenes, and Cassander returned to Macedonia in the winter of 321/20 to warn his father of Antigonus' ambitions. There Cassander found his father ailing, and he took over the running of affairs.

In the meantime, Antigonus defeated Eumenes and drove him out of Cappadocia. But Eumenes proved more ingenious and resilient than anyone could have expected. With some 600 supporters, he slipped into the fortress city of Nora (on the Cappadocian frontier) where he held out against Antigonus. While laying siege to Nora, Antigonus mopped up the rest of the Perdiccan faction (Alcetas and Attalus) in Asia, which left him a clear field. The rest of the commanders, even Ptolemy in Egypt, now consolidated their positions. It was not that they lacked ambitions beyond what they may have currently held, it was just not yet the time to foster them. Then Antipater died in early 319.

Antipater's last act was to name a successor as regent. This was unprecedented, but the Macedonians who had confirmed Antipater as regent were scattered into dozens of garrisons, satrapal armies, and Antigonus' Asian field force (never to be reassembled), so there really was no alternative. It was a careful choice, which fell on one Polyperchon, an old comrade in arms from among Alexander's original brigadiers. Polyperchon was both of undoubted loyalty to the Argead House itself, and was held in general high esteem by his fellow Macedonians. It was an attempt by Antipater to avoid another civil war, but in doing so Antipater passed over his own son, Cassander (now named *chiliarch* to Polyperchon), and ignored the ambition of Antigonus (who would accept no authority save his own).

Indeed, the plotting began even before Antipater was dead. Cassander had taken the precaution of changing the garrison commanders at key citadels in Greece, such as Athens, by putting in men loyal personally to him. Shortly after Polyperchon's appointment, Cassander laid the groundwork in Macedonia by urging friends to make common cause with him, in Greece by contacting the garrison commanders and poleis asking them to ally with him, and outside of the Aegean by appealing to both Ptolemy and Antigonus for support. As neither of the latter two wanted any rival to their own positions in Egypt and Asia, and were virtually already operating as if independent, Cassander's plans fell in with their own. For his part, Polyperchon tried to strengthen his position by sending to Olympias to offer her the guardianship of Alexander IV. She declined, but provided assistance in other ways. Late in 319, Cassander slipped out of Macedonia and went to Asia Minor where he raised a force (with Antigonus' backing) of thirty-five ships and 4,000 men to augment those garrisons already supporting him in Greece.

Polyperchon realized his vulnerability, and called a council of his own friends to assess the nature of the crisis. Assuming correctly that Cassander had support from Antigonus, Ptolemy and many of the Greek cities and Macedonian garrisons in the south, Polyperchon decided to use his chief asset (the kings) and Cassander's chief weakness: his power in Greece was predicated on maintaining Macedonian control over the cities. Philip III now issued a proclamation declaring 'freedom' for the Greek cities and the establishment of democracies (as opposed to the narrow oligarchies by which Antipater had governed Greece). It was an invitation to throw Cassander's people out with impunity, and its provisions called for the return of all exiles, restoration of their property and a general amnesty. Following the proclamation, Polyperchon wrote to specific cities such as Argos to demonstrate what was to be done to the previous regimes: all government leaders from the time of Antipater were to be exiled, their property confiscated and in some cases individuals were to be executed so as to prevent any future cooperation with Cassander.[8]

As for Athens, Polyperchon restored the island of Samos outright to Athenian sovereignty (so much for 'freedom to all the Greeks') but dangled the prospect of regaining Oropus as a further inducement. The Athenians, keeping first things first, wanted the Macedonian garrison removed from the Munychia and demanded this of the commander, Nicanor. His answer was to seize the harbor and walls of the Piraeus to insure holding it for Cassander. Polyperchon tried to bluff Nicanor into surrendering his position by having Olympias write to him to demand that the Munychia and Piraeus be turned over to the Athenians; an order Nicanor ignored. In the meantime, Polyperchon brought an army of 20,000 infantry, 4,000 allies, 1,000 cavalry and sixty-five war elephants south.

The Greek cities were caught between the warring factions, and there are no greater examples of this than the fates of Philip II's old friends Dinarchus of Corinth and Phocion of Athens. The former was executed out of hand by Polyperchon when he met him on the road south to Athens. At the same time, Phocion was caught up in a radical democratic return to power in Athens; he was accused and abandoned by Philip III (i.e., Polyperchon) and then finally condemned and executed by his rivals in Athens. It was at this point that Cassander sailed into the Piraeus. Polyperchon arrived shortly after that, but the reinforcements were such that all he could do was besiege Cassander. Greater damage might be done to Cassander's supporters elsewhere in Greece so, leaving an adequate force to continue the siege, Polyperchon moved on to the Peloponnesus to attack Megalopolis.

Things now began to go badly for Polyperchon. The siege of Megalopolis proved an unmitigated disaster. Though Polyperchon breached the walls, he failed to take the city and the losses were heavy. He sent Cleitus and the fleet to the Hellespont to interdict any more support from Antigonus to Cassander, but was defeated by Cassander's forces serving under Nicanor (from Athens). Following this, even the radical Athenian democracy opened negotiations with Cassander for a treaty of friendship and alliance. A moderate government under Demetrius of Phalerum was established, and though the Athenian Assembly tried and condemned those responsible for Phocion's death, there were no wholesale massacres or confiscations of property. Now those Greek cities that had been neutral came in on Cassander's side.

Antipater's death not only opened things up in Europe to conflict and ambition, but also in Asia. Ptolemy, with an eye to insulating himself further in Egypt, moved out to incorporate Coele Syria (Lebanon) into his holdings. It also changed the situation for Antigonus, who no longer had to mask his ambitions to control all of Asia. In that task, Eumenes could be a valuable asset, rather than a continued distraction held up in Nora. The result was that Antigonus offered Eumenes a place in his entourage, and for a time in the summer of 318 Eumenes accepted. In doing so, however, Eumenes pledged his oath to the kings, not to Antigonus; but by the time Antigonus found that out, Eumenes had already slipped away.

It was at this point that Polyperchon, through the good offices of Olympias, sought allies in the struggle with Cassander. They offered to Eumenes, on behalf of the kings, the title of General for Asia

(Antigonus' commission, if not his army), as well as the funds to recruit an army and conduct operations. Should Eumenes come to Europe, he would share in the guardianship of the kings. Satraps loyal to the king were to support Eumenes, who gained control of the Silvershields (the old Guards Brigade) by invoking Alexander's name and image (literally in the form of Alexander's armor). At the very least, Eumenes would keep Antigonus busy, which he indeed did until the winter of 317/16. Eumenes kept withdrawing further East, in search of loyal satraps, and Antigonus ultimately caught up with him in Media in 317. Following an indecisive battle at Paraecene, Eumenes was finally betrayed by the Silvershields at Gabiene and executed in 316.

Any claim by Antigonus to be operating under orders from here on would be idle, but the reality was that Antigonus controlled most of Asia and had a huge army of some 80,000 men. Taking advantage of the situation, Antigonus proclaimed himself 'Lord of Asia' and began hounding all potential rivals out: Peithon of Media was executed, Peucestas of Persis forced to flee and Seleucus in Babylon, feeling himself next on the list, took action first by fleeing to Ptolemy. Naked ambition ruled the day.

Eumenes' distraction of Antigonus proved of little advantage to Polyperchon back in Macedonia. The mismanagement of the war against Cassander reached a head by the spring of 317, when Cassander planned his first expedition to Macedonia from his secure base in Greece. Seeing the flood of Macedonian opinion swinging away from Polyperchon, and an opportunity to strike a blow for Philip III and herself, Eurydice now had Philip III issue a proclamation transferring the guardianship from Polyperchon to Cassander (which was fully within his legal rights). So Cassander returned to Macedonia in triumph, but his stay was brief since Polyperchon still had his independent forces operating in Greece.

In an atmosphere where Olympias already saw plots against her grandson everywhere, Cassander as guardian (even for just Philip III) was too much of a threat and Olympias now finally moved out of Epirus. With a combined force of Aetolians, Epirotes, and Macedonians, she invaded Macedonia in the autumn of 317. Philip III and Eurydice pulled together a force which met Olympias at Euia, but the army chose to lay down its arms. Olympias murdered Philip III and forced Eurydice to commit suicide. She then continued into Macedonia proper, where Olympias killed Cassander's brother, Nicanor, who had been left in charge in Cassander's absence, and some 100 other Macedonian nobles against whom she had collected grudges over the years. Even by Macedonian standards this was excessive, and to justify it Olympias also desecrated the tomb of Cassander's brother (Iollas), claiming that he had poisoned Alexander (a claim not taken seriously even in antiquity).[9]

Olympias' actions cost her most of whatever sympathy she might have expected among the Macedonians, and in the meantime Cassander rapidly brought his army back into Macedonia even before Olympias could make any preparations. The royal party took refuge in Amphipolis, Pella, and Pydna (where Olympias herself retreated). Cassander besieged these cities throughout the winter of 317/16, but otherwise held the rest of Macedonia. By spring, all three centers of opposition had surrendered to Cassander, who put Olympias on trial for murder; she was convicted and executed by the families of her victims.

By the spring of 316, then, Eumenes was dead, as were Philip III, Eurydice, and Olympias, not to mention a number of minor players such as Peithon. Antigonus had declared himself Lord of Asia and was consolidating his power. Alexander IV was in the hands of Cassander, and in fact in 'protective' custody at Amphipolis. Cassander capped his success by marrying another daughter of Philip II: Thessalonice. The field of contenders was narrowing.

THE END OF A DYNASTY, 316–311

Although Antigonus was acting as if independent, the overall authority of the monarchy was unchallenged and, so long as Alexander IV lived, the power struggles would take place in that context. The nature of kingship continued to change, with more reliance on authority than personality, as Alexander IV was invariably invoked in name but not present. Accordingly, Cassander's activities in 316, in addition to his marriage, were designed to establish his authority as Alexander IV's regent. At some point, soon after Olympias' end, Cassander buried not only Philip III and Eurydice, but also her mother Cynane (who had been killed at Perdiccas' orders six years before). The funeral rites were elaborate and Homeric in nature, both to display Cassander as the upholder of the Argead tradition and to be a counterpoint to Olympias' actions.[10] In the same vein, he also founded two cities (both actually refoundations: Thessalonica at the head of the Thermaic Gulf (named for his Argead wife) and Cassandreia on the old site of Potidaea (on the Pallene promontory), which was named after himself. Like royal burials, city foundations were royal acts, but Cassander went even further when he ordered the refounding of Thebes in Boeotia.

Thebes had been destroyed by Alexander the Great prior to the Persian expedition, so this was not only a popular act among the Greek cities, it pointed to a new beginning. Cassander still had to contend with Polyperchon in Greece itself and this was intended to clear the air there. Polyperchon held Corinth as a base of operations, under his son Alexander, and hoped to play on Cassander's weak points in Greece and his own popularity among elements in Macedonia in the hopes of changing popular opinion and regaining the regency. For the moment, however, he was operating outside the area of legitimate authority.

The situation now began to clarify. Antigonus, with a huge army and some 45,000 talents in his war chest, held virtually everything east of the Mediterranean littoral in Asia and clearly saw his chief rivals in front of him to the west: Ptolemy, Lysimachus, and Cassander. Ptolemy's position in Egypt was the most secure, and Lysimachus was marginalized in Thrace. Cassander had the weakest position of the three precisely because of Polyperchon, the Greek cities which wished to re-establish their independence, and the factionalism still evident in Macedonia itself. Also, Cassander held a dangerous card in Alexander IV, the theoretical source of all authority. Further, Antigonus' actions in killing Peithon and driving out Peucestus and Seleucus had alarmed all three rivals.

In the winter of 316/15, a joint embassy from Ptolemy, Cassander, and Lysimachus delivered an ultimatum to Antigonus: if he wanted peace, as surety of his goodwill, Antigonus would deliver Hellespontine Phrygia to Lysimachus, Cappadocia and Lycia to Cassander, Syria to Ptolemy, and restore Babylonia to Seleucus; otherwise it would be war. Antigonus' answer was to tell them to prepare for war and his first target was Cassander. Aristodemus, an agent, was dispatched with 1,000 talents to Sparta, where he recruited some 8,000 mercenaries and offered Polyperchon both the men and the money, along with Antigonus' commission as General for the Peloponnesus. Polyperchon needed all three, and so accepted. Antigonus also sent his nephew, Ptolemaeus, to push Cassander's forces out of Asia Minor (where they had been operating in Cappadocia). But it was what happened next that proved brilliant.

Antigonus called an Assembly of Macedonians to meet at Tyre (to which only Antigonus' supporters came) at which he denounced

Cassander for the murder of Olympias, the incarceration of Roxane and Alexander IV, the forced marriage of Thessalonice (by which he declared Cassander was laying claim to monarchy), the founding of Cassandreia, and the refounding of Thebes (which restored traditional Macedonian enemies at both places). Unless Cassander capitulated to Antigonus' authority and surrendered the royal family, he was to be declared a public enemy. It was a brilliant ploy by Antigonus, and his assembly boisterously endorsed it. The hope was to isolate Cassander, and towards that end the decree making this declaration also proclaimed 'freedom and autonomy' for the Greek cities (echoing Polyperchon's similar rescript in 319).

The coalition, however, was held together by their joint fear of Antigonus, which meant that the war would be fought on several fronts. Cassander brought an army almost immediately first into Boeotia, where he helped complete the new walls of Thebes (as a useful base) and then fought his way into the Peloponnesus past Corinth, where he used Argos as his base. Cassander's goal was to keep the action away from Macedonia itself, and in this Cassander was successful. His active campaigning in the Peloponnesus in 315 neutralized Antigonus' efforts, and even brought Polyperchon's son, Alexander, over to his side (though Alexander was soon afterwards assassinated). The following year, Cassander kept up the pressure in central Greece, while Ptolemy dispatched a fleet (one squadron of which was under Seleucus) for operations against Antigonus in the Aegean. By the end of 314, not only was the Ptolemaic fleet active, but Cassander sent forces to attack Antigonus' nephew (Ptolemaeus) in Asia Minor.

Antigonus, who had been planning operations against Ptolemy – first to take Coele Syria and then to invade Egypt itself – was totally caught off-guard. The next few years resemble a boxing match, with each side trading blows. Cassander and his allies kept up the pressure in Asia Minor, sending new commanders and widening the conflict in 313. Antigonus put his fleet into operation in the Aegean and stepped up pressure on Caria as defensive measures. Despite initial defections from his cause in the Peloponnesus, Antigonus finally found successful commanders in two of his nephews (first Telesphorus and later Ptolemaeus), who managed to free most of the Peloponnesus from Cassander's garrisons and then move into Central Greece in 313. By the end of 312, Cassander had suffered setbacks both in Greece itself and on his own Illyrian frontier to the northwest, where he was driven from Apollonia.

This was balanced by Ptolemy's defeat of Antigonus' army under Demetrius at Gaza, which crushed the Egyptian invasion plans. Neither side was doing well, nor had any front proved decisive, and so negotiations were opened up in the winter of 312/11, because all parties needed a respite. The Peace basically acknowledged the status quo: Cassander was confirmed as General of Europe; Lysimachus likewise kept Thrace; Ptolemy held Egypt and the adjacent areas of Libya and Arabia; and Antigonus was recognized as 'first' in Asia. All this would explicitly last, according to the Treaty, only until Alexander IV should reach his majority (sixteen years of age in Macedonian terms).[11]

It was clear from the settlement that the possibility of Alexander IV's majority (only five years away) loomed more and more important on the horizon. Indeed, the wording was practically an invitation to Cassander to insure that this would never happen. At some point, probably in the next year, Alexander IV was killed in secret on Cassander's orders, which brought the Argead Dynasty to end.[12] In doing so, Cassander was acting as the agent for all of them, but as yet none of them dared to claim kingship themselves. Instead, they maintained the fiction of ruling in the 'king's name,' which provided another step to the institutionalizing of that office.

THE GAME OF KINGS, 310–301

The political maneuvering and machinations, of course, were not ended by the treaty. Nothing had been resolved in terms of the supreme authority in the empire; it was only a matter of time before undeclared war broke out, to be followed by the real thing. The number of minor moves in fact increased, but it was the bolder strokes born of desperation which carried the game forward. This started in the spring of 310, when Antigonus' discontented commander in Greece, his nephew Ptolemaeus, went over to Cassander and was commissioned as Cassander's general in Greece. Ptolemy of Egypt also accused Antigonus of reneging on his promise of freedom for the Greek cites and began operations in the Aegean, presumably to correct that oversight. But the most daring move came from an unexpected source: Polyperchon.

Possibly with the backing of Antigonus (in an attempt to undermine Cassander), Polyperchon brought Heracles, the son of Barsine (and possibly the natural son of Alexander the Great), from Pergamum and championed his cause to be king (the precondition of which must have been the common knowledge of Alexander IV's death). The point was to capitalize on the discontent among Macedonian loyalists to the Argead House. Polyperchon was ready to strike by early 309, and moved into Epirus. Cassander had no desire to force things in Macedonia itself, and so marched into Epirus as well. Here Cassander opened negotiations in the hope of avoiding more civil war, offering Polyperchon the restoration of his estates and a commission as Cassander's general in the Peloponnesus (though this would infringe on Ptolemaeus). The price for this was the life Heracles. Polyperchon seized the opportunity to retire from the game with security if not honor, and Heracles along with his mother were killed and buried in secret.[13]

Polyperchon's appointment did upset Ptolemaeus, and he contacted Ptolemy of Egypt to offer him his forces and cities in Greece. Ptolemy of Egypt was clearly seeking to increase his position in Greece. His fleets were operating openly in the Aegean; he had begun challenging Antigonus on 'freedom for the Greeks,' then plotting with Cleopatra, and now thought of facing down Cassander in Greece on this same issue as well. Ptolemy was commanding his fleet in person, and wintered in 309/8 at the island of Cos (off the Asia Minor coast), where he now summoned Ptolemaeus to present his proposal. In the course of discussion, it became clear that Ptolemaeus could not be trusted, so Ptolemy forced him to commit suicide. That, of course, did not hinder Ptolemy's plans for Greece.

In the spring of 308, Ptolemy sailed to the Peloponnesus where he again proclaimed freedom for the Greeks, and possibly tried to revive the old League of Corinth (Philip II's instrument to unite Greece) with himself as *hegemon* (or leader). The Greeks had heard all of this far too often before, and Ptolemy was underwhelmed with support. As a result, he cut his losses and made his peace with Cassander (who had patiently awaited developments).

Ptolemy's withdrawal from the Aegean convinced Antigonus to make a major effort to dislodge Greece from Cassander's control, before someone else proved more successful. His previous attempts through agents and his nephews had been on a relatively small scale. In 307, Antigonus now sent his son Demetrius with a fleet of 250 ships and 5,000 talents to Greece. In May of 307, mistaking Demetrius' fleet for that of the now friendly Ptolemy, Cassander's garrison in the Piraeus permitted Demetrius to enter the harbor. Demetrius still had the city and fortress to win, but the Athenians welcomed him enthusiastically. Demetrius besieged Cassander's garrison in the Munychia, and then by assault took the whole city. The Athenians named two new eponymous tribes, after Antigonus and Demetrius respectively, and placed their names among the gods. Cassander responded by besieging Athens, but the damage was done.

Strangely, rather than pursue the game in Greece, Demetrius opened a second front when he took the fleet to challenge Ptolemy on Cyprus, besieging Salamis there, in the hopes of luring Ptolemy and his fleet into a major confrontation. This succeeded in 306, and a major naval engagement (the largest fleet action since the Peloponnesian War) was fought off Salamis, in which Demetrius destroyed the Egyptian fleet and nearly took Ptolemy. On hearing of the victory, Antigonus had both himself and Demetrius proclaimed kings by his Macedonians. Five years after the death of Alexander IV, Antigonus now fulfilled at least seventeen years worth of ambition to rule openly and independently. He was quickly copied by the other Successors.[14] Each proclamation was carefully timed and staged, again relying more on form and authority than personality to establish kingship.

Following the victory off Salamis, Demetrius joined his father for the planned invasion of Egypt, which failed miserably. Ptolemy was as tough and resilient on the Nile line as he had been against Perdiccas all those years before. Stung, Antigonus withdrew to Syria to recoup his losses, while Demetrius turned his attention to Rhodes. Oblivious to his declaration of freedom for the Greeks, Demetrius besieged and tried to force Rhodes into the Antigonid orbit. The siege, one of the most famous in antiquity, wasted a full year and was an utter failure. It was with considerable irony that Demetrius was taunted as the 'Besieger of Cities' by the Rhodians; he sailed back to Greece in 304. Kingship was not proving any kind of lucky talisman for the Antigonids.

Cassander's chief activity had been to maintain as much control in Greece as possible and press the siege of Athens, and it was this which brought Demetrius back to Greece. It also opened the final stages of the struggles of the Successors. Demetrius landed in Boeotia in Central Greece, attempting to cut Cassander (who was personally conducting the siege of Athens) off from Macedonia. The maneuver produced the expected result: Cassander broke off the siege of Athens and retreated into Macedonia itself.

Demetrius spent the next two years strengthening the Antigonid position in Greece. He drove out Cassander's garrisons in Central Greece, and assaulted Cassander's supporters in the Peloponnesus.

Demetrius wintered in Athens, taking up residence in the Parthenon as one of the city's gods. Come spring, Demetrius solidified his position in Greece by refounding the League of Corinth, with himself and Antigonus as *hegemones*. With Greece more or less secure, Demetrius was ready to move on Macedonia. The Antigonid force with Demetrius was immense, amounting to some 56,000 foot (including 8,000 Macedonians) and 1,500 horse. Demetrius now brought that army into Thessaly in the autumn of 302. Cassander had only an army of 29,000 Macedonian foot and 2,000 cavalry to face a spring invasion. The last round was about to open.

Opposed by these massive forces, over the winter of 302/1, Cassander sought to play an old hand by renewing the coalition of 315 with Ptolemy, Lysimachus, and Seleucus (who had again been driven out of Babylon). They all had as much reason to fear an Antigonid victory in Macedonia as Cassander, and what Cassander proposed was allied activity to draw Demetrius away from his upcoming invasion of Macedonia (taking a leaf from Demetrius' own book two years before). Lysimachus (already in Asia Minor) and Seleucus (who crossed from Iran into Asia Minor) gathered an army of 64,000 foot, 10,500 horse, 400 war elephants and 120 chariots to confront Antigonus in the early spring of 301. As Cassander expected, this too produced the desired effect. Antigonus recalled Demetrius and his forces to Asia Minor, removing the pressure from Cassander.

The combined Antigonid forces (80,000 foot, 10,000 horse and 75 war elephants) met the allies at Ipsus in southern Asia Minor in the summer of 301, in what they hoped would be the decisive battle. It opened with a successful cavalry charge led by Demetrius, which drew him from the battlefield itself. While Demetrius was thus engaged, the Antigonid center collapsed and Antigonus himself was isolated and killed. Demetrius returned to find both the battle and his father lost. With only 5,600 cavalry, Demetrius withdrew to what was left of Antigonid forces on the coast, where he joined the fleet and established a sea kingdom.

The Great Game was far from over, but the most successful bid to hold the empire together (even if under a new dynasty) had been crushed. From the dust of Ipsus, there emerged five kingdoms, each under its own dynasty. The wars of the Successors would continue for another twenty years, and only three dynasties would ultimately survive the struggle: the Antigonids in Macedonia, the Ptolemies in Egypt, and the Seleucids in Asia. Nevertheless, the pattern was now set for the next century: a balance of power between established kingdoms, each with their own advantages and disadvantages, but none with a clear superiority. That balance made possible the existence of smaller powers in the Hellenistic East: the commercial republic of Rhodes, the Attalid Kingdom of Pergamum, the Aetolian and Achaean Leagues in Greece itself. The old traditional polities of Athens and Sparta drop to third-rate powers, as the single polis becomes irrelevant to Greek politics. After three generations, that balance of power inevitably began to unravel (at the end of the third century), and those minor powers asked in Roman help to redress the situation and preserve their existence. Rome ended the game.

NOTES

1 The exact nature of Arrhidaeus' problem has never been satisfactorily explained. It is generally taken to be retardation because Plutarch refers to him as a 'half-wit' and acting childishly (*Alex.* 77.5 and *De Alex. fort.* 337 DE respectively). Nevertheless, Diodorus states that he had an incurable mental illness (18.2.2) and Plutarch also stated that he was of 'unsound mind' (*Alex.* 10.2). Judging from the few episodes where we see Arrhidaeus at least functioning at the court level (e.g., Curt. 8.1 and 10.7.13, or Plut. *Phoc.* 33.5–7), the problem may have been emotional instability.

2 The period from Alexander's death to the assembly at Triparadisus in 321 was particularly interesting to our ancient sources. Arrian, whose *Anabasis* of Alexander's campaigns covers a period from 336 to 323 in just seven books, recounts the period from 323 to 320, in the *ta meta Alexandron*, in much greater depth (ten books). It was a theme taken up later by the Athenian historian Dexippus, who abridged the work to four books and even later by the Byzantine Patriarch Photios, in his *Bibliotheca*. All of the accounts, theoretically, rely on the work of Hieronymus of Cardia (a cousin of Eumenes), a general and historian who became the Macedonian royal archivist under Antigonus Gonatas. Hieronymus survives only in fragments, but is the chief source for not only the authors mentioned above (who also survive only in fragments) but for our chief continuous source (Diodorus) and Q. Curtius Rufus (whose description of the events at Babylon is the most detailed). For a good modern commentary on the sources and events, see R. M. Errington, 'From Babylon to Triparadeisus: 323–320 B.C.' *JHS* 90 (1970), 49–77.

3 I have translated the term *taxiarchos* here as 'brigadier' rather than 'marshal,' simply because the latter has a tendency to convey a false and somewhat grandiose impression both as to the size of the command and its function. It does accurately convey the importance of the officer in Alexander's campaigns, but not in the Period of the Diadochi where they increasingly become minor functionaries.

4 A small marriage alliance competition began at this point which mirrors the political struggle and imperial ambitions. Alexander's sister, Cleopatra (the widow of Alexander of Epirus), who was serving as a royal figurehead in Macedonia (*prostasia*), offered herself in marriage first to Leonnatus (probably at the prompting of Olympias) and then after Leonnatus' death to Perdiccas (definitely at the suggestion of Olympias). The latter proposal precipitated the first of the civil wars. Another of Antipater's daughters, Phila, was given in marriage to Craterus to cement their friendship and a third, Eurydice, married Ptolemy.

5 Antipater and Olympias had quarreled all during Alexander's campaigns, probably because Antipater blamed her for Philip II's death (with considerable justification). What Olympias' official position had been is unclear, though she will later be offered *prostasia* by Polyperchon and one presumes that is what she had had earlier. Regardless, she was in a voluntary exile in Epirus, from which Olympias sought to stir up as much trouble as possible for Antipater, while securing as much power for herself and protection for her daughter and grandson.

6 The burial of a king, by Macedonian custom, was a royal act itself, so this could be interpreted as Ptolemy's first declaration of intentions. Regardless, the body never reached Aegae, but was eventually placed in a special temple in Alexandria (the Sema) and became a talisman for the Ptolemaic dynasty.

7 This Arrhidaeus should not be confused with Philip III, but is an otherwise unknown officer who had commanded Alexander's funeral cortège.

8 This is virtually a translation of Diodorus (18.57.1–2). The proclamation, in the form of a *diagramma*, constitutes one of the longest 'documents' in Diodorus (18.56). See K. Rosen, 'Political Documents in Hieronymus of Cardia,' *AClass* 10 (1967), 29–30.

9 The basic account is that Aristotle made up the drug; Cassander conveyed it to Babylon (in the hoof of a horse) and Iollas (Alexander's cup-bearer) administered it. It can be found in Curt. 10.10. 14–17; Just. 12. 14; Arr. 7.27; and Plut. *Alex*. 77. 1–3 and *X orat*. 849F. Arrian rejected the account out of hand (7.27.3) but Plutarch is even more explicit, stating that the story did not circulate until Olympias' episode with Iollas' tomb, i.e., it is part of the propaganda of the Wars of Succession (*Alex*. 77.1–2).

10 For the burial itself, see Diod. 19.52.4; and for the obsequies, Athen. 4. 155A. The spectacular archaeological discoveries of Manolis Andronikos relate, at least in part, to Cassander's burials (if only the later burial of Alexander IV in Tomb III). There is an extensive bibliography over which Philip (II or III) may be buried in Tomb II. For an excellent discussion of the material culture and a summary bibliography, see Borza, pp. 253–66 and 311–3 and below, pp. 000–00.

11 A careless reading of Diod. 19.105.1, where this phrase follows Cassander's name in the settlement, has led some to conclude that it applied only to him; but all four parties appear in the same sentence (a standard *men*, *de* construction in Greek) and the conditions logically must be applied to all. It is only that Cassander held the boy, and therefore only he could do anything about it.

12 As the deed was done in secret (Diod. 19.105.2–3; Paus. 9.7.2; and
    Just. 15.2.3) and kept so for an undetermined amount of time, dating
    is difficult. Most authorities place it in 310/09 (based on its listing then
    on the *Marmor Parium*, *FGrH*, 239 F B 18), but that may reflect the
    official announcement of Alexander's death. Arguments have been made
    for a later date. See Hammond in Hammond–Walbank, pp. 166–8.

13 This was not the only Argead death in 309. Cleopatra, Alexander the
    Great's sister, had been living quietly in Sardis since the outbreak of
    the wars in 322/1. She now quarrelled over the recent developments
    with Antigonus and planned to flee to safety with Ptolemy of Egypt.
    Her plans were discovered and she was killed on Antigonus' orders.

14 They could hardly do otherwise without acknowledging Antigonid supe-
    riority: first was Ptolemy, then Lysimachus and Seleucus (who had been
    restored to Babylon probably as a result of the Treaty of 311). Plut.
    Demetr. 18.2 states that Cassander did not use the title, but all the
    others referred to him as *basileus* anyway.

10

ART AND ARCHITECTURE

Steven Lattimore

The closing years of the fifth century witnessed jubilation such as had seldom if ever occurred among the Greeks. Sparta's naval victory over Athens at Aegospotami in 405 brought about the surrender, in the following year, of the 'tyrant city' which the victorious allies now voted to destroy. Through Spartan magnanimity and pragmatism, Athens was spared because of its past heroism against the Persians; the dismantling of its fortifications was believed to mark 'the beginning of freedom for Greece' (Xen. *Hell.* 2.2.23). The Spartan Lysander, who had commanded the allied fleet in 405 and presided over Athens' capitulation, commissioned a victory monument of appropriate size and novelty: not at Olympia, where the Panhellenic ideal had for some time discouraged displays of civic pride and especially of spoils taken by Greeks from other Greeks, but at Delphi (Paus. 10.9.7–11), where the confrontation with a mid-fifth-century Athenian monument commemorating Marathon could not be missed.[1] The Athenians had set up bronze statues by Phidias of Apollo and Athena, the general Miltiades, and the heroes of the ten Attic tribes. For Lysander a team of sculptors, mostly followers of Polyclitus from the Peloponnesus, executed at least thirty-seven figures, arranging them in two rows.[2] In front, presumably in the center, was Poseidon crowning Lysander: the first Greek general to receive divine honors during his lifetime. Previously, only athletes among living men had been likely to enjoy the honor of a commemorative statue and, much more rarely, cult status. The two-figure group was accompanied by statues of the Dioscuri, Zeus, Apollo, Artemis, and Lysander's soothsayer and helmsman. In the background stood a much longer row of admirals, representing twenty-two states in addition to Sparta. These were in varied stances which indicate interaction and probably contact (such as a hand on a

249

neighbor's shoulder) symbolizing the friendly relations among the allies. Many were separated by representations of marine spoils and trophies and in some cases probably rested on these. The admirals formed a more pictorial composition than the foreground figures, and the influence of painting as well as architectural sculpture is a distinct possibility. Like these, and in contrast to earlier free-standing groups, the Lysander monument, accessible for viewing only from the front, occupied the illusionistic space of the artistic composition rather than the actual space it shared with the beholder.

The Lysander monument foreshadows many developments in art throughout the fourth century; more specifically, it exerted great influence on subsequent sculptural groups, especially at Delphi. It was erected before 395, when Lysander died fighting against Boeotians who had been Sparta's long-term allies but became alienated immediately after the end of the Peloponnesian War. These events are indicative of the course of fourth century history. The period is a byword for turbulence and instability, shifting alliances and class conflict, growing inequality in the distribution of wealth, increased individualism and diminished civic loyalty, with Macedonian hegemony a natural if not inevitable culmination. The elements of continuity between the era beginning in 405 and the one beginning in 323 have often raised the question among both historians and art historians: when did the Hellenistic age actually begin? Perhaps, for example, with the King's Peace of 387/6?[3] Conversely, there is also significant continuity between the last third of the fifth century and the early decades of the fourth. The characteristic pictorial art of this period is flamboyant, decorative, and sensuous, highly skillful both in execution and in methods of display. A nineteenth-century reaction to the 'Sandalbinder' on the Nike parapet frieze is wholly appropriate.

> What breasts, my god, what a breast! It is round as an apple, full, abundant, well spaced from the other, a weight in the hand. There is the richness of maternity and enough of love's sweetness to die for. Rain and sun have turned the white marble a golden yellow; it is a tawny color that almost makes it seem flesh. It is so calm, so noble! One would say it is about to swell, the lungs beneath it about to breathe.[4]

Pollitt has explained this style as escapist, 'refuge in gesture:' a reaction to the ordeals of the Peloponnesian War and the concomitant turmoil within the city states.[5] While such an approach to stylistic phenomena in Greek art has formidable detractors,[6] I find it impossible to doubt that the basis of the late fifth-century 'rich style'[7] is escapism. There are parallels not only in the contemporary development of rhetoric (especially in the 'dazzling insincerity' of Gorgias),[8] but in the preserved plays of Euripides, which belong almost entirely to the war years and whose choral lyrics are often most beautiful when most irrelevant – and in which the note of escapism is constant.[9]

As Pollitt notes, religious expression becomes less civic and more personal. 'The great age of votive reliefs is the late fifth and fourth centuries,'[10] and these works are often dedicated to new or newly prominent divinities whose appeal was directed towards the individual. Increased individualism is recognized as a hallmark of fourth-century Greek society. On the civic level, however, the rejoicing of 404 was by no means a wholly misleading prelude to the history of the fourth century. The downfall of Athens (and the subsequent setbacks of Sparta) brought new hopes and opportunities to many Greek states, however briefly in some cases. Commercial development was no longer restricted to a few centers such as Athens, Corinth, and Syracuse, and Greece overall became considerably more wealthy. This wealth is ultimately manifested in both public and privately commissioned works, and the prettiness of much fourth-century art reflects burgherly complacency as well as 'refuge.'

The art of the first two decades of the fourth century is hardly revolutionary. Sculptors continued to work in the rich style, often infusing a new naturalism and intimacy, as we can judge best from a large output of Athenian relief sculpture: votives, document or record reliefs,[11] and funerary steles. During the course of the fourth century, these last become larger, carved in higher relief, and ostentatiousness was presumably the reason that their production was banned c. 317 by Demetrius of Phalerum. While it has been conjectured that some such monuments were carved slightly later, their manufacture effectively ends by 300, and this is also true of Attic votive reliefs. Robertson associates the beginning of this productivity with the completion of the Parthenon and the consequent unemployment of many sculptors;[12] since Athens was very active in building and adorning temples and shrines down to the end of the war, unemployment may have been a still greater factor c. 400.

The battle of Corinth, a defeat Sparta inflicted on Athens and its allies in 394, occasioned both public and private monuments to Athenian war dead. While only fragments of the former are preserved, the Dexileos stele (Plate 1, p. 14) has survived intact, a family memorial for a young cavalryman who is also mentioned in the inscription on the public memorial.[13] The stele over the cenotaph takes its motif, an unusual one for a grave stele, from the public relief: a heroic rider and fallen opponent. The weapon, one of several lost bronze attachments, crossed the diagonals formed by Dexileos' rearing horse and his spear's victim. The hard, schematic handling of the drapery has been much criticized but may have been as deliberately calculated as the emphatic crossed diagonals of the composition, to lend monumental solemnity to the rich style (the workmanship is excellent). The rider's head, however, has a fourth-century softness.

A truly transitional piece and datable almost to the year, the Dexileos stele comes from a period whose sculptural chronology has proved challenging. Claims that the reliefs of the Argive Heraeum and the Apollo temple at Bassae were completed after 400 are not widely accepted. A date well into the fourth century, however, has now been established for the work of Greek artists on Lycian monuments, once assigned to the end of the fifth.[14] The city reliefs from the Nereid monument at Xanthus, c. 380, and heroon at Trysa, c. 370 (see Plate 18) are especially notable as examples of Greek techniques applied to a venerable near eastern iconography; such an amalgamation (to borrow Childs' term) is surprisingly rare in the Hellenistic period. The Lycian reliefs, then, are not evidence for the appearance of Greek scene painting, landscape art, or book illustrations, as variously conjectured.

It is peculiarly frustrating that the painting of the late fifth and early fourth centuries is lost, since ancient literary sources claim that its achievements were notable. The great names are Apollodorus, Agatharchus, Zeuxis, and Parrhasius, the latter two the most likely to have worked appreciably after 400. While specific stories about their rivalry may be apocryphal, the testimonia overall indicate that their styles were in marked contrast. Parrhasius of Ephesus, remembered like Polygnotus a generation or two before as a master of characterization and atmosphere, was notably arrogant about his skills and accomplishments and influenced other artists even through his sketches. He excelled in representing volume through the use of outline; such specialized skill is displayed on the exceptionally fine white-ground *lekythoi* painted in Attica c. 400 and known as 'Group R.'[15] Zeuxis of Heraclea,[16] comparable to Parrhasius in skill, success, and pride, was said by Aristotle (*Poet.* 1450a24) to leave *ethos* or character

Plate 18 City relief from Heroon at Trysa, *c.* 370 BC. Kunsthistorisches Museum, Vienna. Photo courtesy of W. A. P. Childs.

out of his work.[17] His forte, also that of Apollodorus, was the use of light and shade. In this respect, he was more clearly in the mainstream of painting's evolution than Parrhasius, although the latter must have been more than a reactionary or formalist.[18] The two virtuosos are very fourth century in their individualism and in the divergence of their contemporaneous styles; the combined characteristics of their work exemplify much in fourth-century art – probably, given the high status of painting, because they influenced it profoundly. Their success can in large part be measured by Plato's condemnation of the illusionistic art of his time.[19]

While vase painting was inherently unsuited to either chiaroscuro or, in the manner of Agatharchus, perspective representation as first employed in stage scenery, both developments appear in early fourth-century vase painting, especially in South Italy. South Italian vase painting also reflects the theater in its liveliness, with a proclivity for caricature and comedy. A particularly vivid example from the 380s is the name-piece of the Dolon Painter (see Plate 19) depicting the ignominious end of the Trojan spy Dolon, an epic story used as *Iliad* 10 and retold in the tragedy *Rhesos*, perhaps contemporary with the painting. The eeriness of the rare night encounter, the terror of Dolon and the imminence of his death at the hands of Odysseus, who will promise him safety, and Diomedes, who will cut his throat, could not be more effectively portrayed.

A new medium closely related to vase painting and sometimes dependent on it is essentially a product of the fourth century: pebble floor mosaic, one example of which is probably to be dated before 398/7.[20] While pebble mosaics have a wide geographic distribution, Olynthus in the Thracian Chalcidice is especially rich in these (none post-dating the destruction of the city by Philip of Macedon in 348). Dionysiac and marine motifs, which both enjoyed remarkable popularity in Greek mosaic, are represented here. A marine mosaic in the Villa of Good Fortune can be dated close to 400 by stylistic and iconographic parallels; a seated Achilles receives new arms and armor from Thetis and the Nereids.[21] The Villa and other houses at Olynthus preserve traces of the sumptuous wall decoration in painted stucco which evolved into the 'First,' or 'Masonry Style,' of Pompeii. It was the excavations at Olynthus which first indicated to scholars the surprising comfort and luxury of fifth- and especially fourth-century domestic architecture. While the origins of Greek pictorial mosaics are mysterious, Masonry-style wall decoration can be traced back to Athens in the late fifth or early fourth century.[22]

Plate 19 Capture of Dolon, Dolon Painter, 380s BC. British Museum, London. Photo: British Museum.

Greek architecture changed profoundly after 400, and Dinsmoor stigmatized this turning point as 'the beginning of the decadence.'[23] His reference is especially to Doric temple architecture, and it might be asked whether such 'decadence' had not begun earlier, with the Periclean building program and even the Parthenon. Winter points out that, quantitatively, the Greeks built fewer temples, and fewer large temples, between 450 and 400 than between 480 and 450, despite the flurry of Athenian activity in the later fifth century (and Athenian inactivity before 450).[24] In terms of the Doric order, fifth-century Athenian temples were uncanonical and increasingly infiltrated by Ionic elements. The first significant building of the new century, and a notable one in any context, was the 'tholos' or round building constructed at Delphi around 390, whose function has been much debated. It has been called a treasury, a heroon, and a prytaneion; a recent discussion of the tholos type has plausibly associated many Greek round buildings, including the example at Delphi, with ritual dining, as well as offering much new information about the early development of the tholos.[25]

The one at Delphi had a very small sixth century predecessor; similarly, many fourth-century temples were replacements for archaic ones. Most, like the tholos, were modest in size. Most continued a late fifth-century trend of using slim proportions for the Doric columns of their exteriors, which increasingly featured less of the figural sculpture which had characterized the Doric order and more rich ornament in the Ionic manner. Interior decor was lavish; inside the Delphi tholos, all columns carried the Corinthian capital, introduced to Greek architecture towards the end of the fifth century and used sparingly,[26] and this interior colonnade, set close to the wall, was decorative rather than functional. The Delphi tholos combined many features of late fifth-century architecture which became characteristic of fourth-century temples. If these were more economical than the temples of the past, the reason may have been not so much a decline in religious fervor as a diversion of architectural expenditures towards development of the agora in an increasingly commercial and urbanized Greece.

'The sanctuary at Epidaurus was the most extensive religious building project of the fourth century.'[27] The great popularity of the healer Asclepius, the chief god at Epidaurus, is a phenomenon of the late fifth century which continues during the fourth. The Epidaurus complex eventually included a theater and a stadium. More directly connected with the cult were the Asclepius temple, built in the 370s, and the tholos, begun c. 360.[28] The latter again used Doric on the outside with Corinthian on the inside, and its decoration was extremely ornate. The temple, for which building records have survived, housed a gold and ivory cult statue which, like the architecture, was on a smaller scale than fifth-century forerunners. While there were no carved metopes, the temple carried full pedimental sculpture depicting the sack of Troy on the front and an amazonomachy on the rear. Some of the figures wear the clinging drapery of the rich style, its last major occurrence,[29] and even many of these display a new naturalism more fully evident in the denser drapery on some other fragments. The poses are complex, sometimes strained and contorted, conveying the intense emotion that is epitomized by the head identified as that of Priam about to be murdered by Neoptolemus.[30] The closest stylistic forerunners of Priam occur in the sculpture of the late fifth-century Argive Heraeum, and it has been suggested that Argives were the leaders in early fourth-century architectural design.[31] Both the Heraeum and the Epidaurus temple, however, betray Athenian influence as well, and the interplay between Athens and Epidaurus in creating art and architecture for the cult of Asclepius was evidently close and complex. Towards 380 appeared a major Asclepius type in sculpture, the Giustini, probably a Peloponnesian work but subsequently exercising enormous influence on the Athenian iconography of Asclepius.[32] Closer to 360, a follower of Polyclitus created the first influential sculptural image of Hygieia (Asclepius' daughter and cult associate), the Hope type.[33] Her head is completely in the style of the Polyclitan school; the stately beauty of her drapery has a marvelous rich-style antecedent in the armed Aphrodite found at Epidaurus (see Plate 20), whose quality has suggested a Greek original to some and whose contrasts of thin and heavy drapery have an almost geometric perfection.[34] The Hygieia, nevertheless, has sometimes been identified as the cult statue of the Athens Asclepieion, also attributed to the Athenian sculptor Cephisodotus.[35] We know this elder relative of Praxiteles (father? uncle?) primarily by his group of Eirene carrying the infant Ploutos: Peace fostering Wealth.[36] The appearance of this allegorical composition is so fully in reaction against the rich style that there have been attempts to date it to the fifth century;[37] most strikingly, the strong vertical fold falling from the knee of the free leg, a fifth-century stabilizing device makes (as Vierneisel-Schlörb puts it) an *echt Comeback*. Yet the intricate rendering of the minor folds is unknown to the fifth century, and there is decisive evidence that the original composition was set up in Athens to commemorate a general peace in the 370s, perhaps that of 371. While certainly *einansichtig* in Borbein's sense (that is, its spatial composition can be fully understood from a single vantage point),[38] the Eirene is less two-dimensional than usually stated, since several subsidiary vantage points offer a fuller appreciation of the spatial relationship between the adult and infant divinities.[39] Around this time, vase painting also shows a general trend away from the prettiness of the rich style towards increased sobriety and naturalism. It was a major painter, Euphranor, who most succinctly summed up the overall change: a Theseus by Parrhasius appeared to have been fed on roses; he himself had painted one fed on meat (Pliny *HN* 35.128).

The major holdout against the peace of 371 was Thebes. The surprising Theban victory over Sparta in that same year, at Leuctra, ended Spartan hegemony forever, and Thebes' invasions of the Peloponnesus in the 360s drastically altered the military and political situation in that region. Thebes' own hegemony was cut short by the death in combat of two brilliant leaders, first Pelopidas and then,

Plate 20 Armed Aphrodite from Epidaurus, copy of statue from the 380s
BC. National Museum, Athens, 262. Photo: Art Resource.

in the Theban victory at Mantinea in 362, Epaminondas. This battle was the subject of a highly praised painting by Euphranor,[40] while an equestrian statue of Pelopidas at Delphi, now lost, is the earliest recorded commission for the great Sicyonian artist who led sculpture into its Hellenistic stage: Lysippus. Meanwhile, victory monuments were also set up at Delphi by the Argives and the Arcadians, who had been hostile to Sparta.[41] These two sculptural groups followed the model of Lysander's monument and, despite their smaller size, challenged its significance by their close proximity. This was especially true of the Arcadian group, made by followers of Polyclitus, including one Argive who had also executed statues for the Lysander monument.

As a more practical form of defiance against Sparta, the Arcadians established a federal government, with the new city of Megalopolis as its capital. The architecture of Megalopolis was as ambitious as its name. The federal council-house, the Thersilion (named for its dedicant) was roofed, in accordance with the practice of Greek bouleuteria since the sixth century, yet its size was that of an assembly place; the Arcadian league had 10,000 representatives. Measuring 218 by 172 feet, it contained columnar supports arranged so as to obscure visibility as little as possible. Whatever the seating arrangements, they were soon supplemented by the largest theater ever built on the Greek mainland, whose capacity is estimated at 21,000 and which was constructed so as to form an annex to the Thersilion (see Plate 9, p. 58).[42] The obvious antecedents, not only for the theater but for the council-house, are fifth-century Athenian (as was the model for the federal constitution): the council-house in the agora, the many columned odeum built by Pericles on the acropolis, the Telesterion for the Mysteries at Eleusis.

The Athenians and Arcadians were allies in 371, but this situation changed within a few years; similarly, Arcadian hopes for federal unity were soon disappointed. A more lasting accomplishment of Theban arms was the independence of Messenia. Messenian refugees had shown themselves great fighters and ardent patriots as Athenian allies in the Peloponnesian War; Messenia's new freedom was now protected by fortification walls so sophisticated in design and so solidly constructed that they were once believed to be Hellenistic. Rather, partly on the basis of comparisons with Messenia, it now appears that several forts on the Attic–Boeotian border usually identified as Athenian and fifth-century should be reattributed to the Thebes of Epaminondas. As Aristotle (*Pol.* 7.10.8) prescribed, these fortifications were a defense psychologically, through their impressive appearance, as well as a practical barrier. That the fourth century was from its very start an age of imposing fortifications was not simply a reflection of troubled times. Fourth-century armies were more skilled than those of the past, because of both highly trained citizen soldiers such as the Thebans (from whom the youthful Philip of Macedon learned much) and the widespread use of mercenaries; siege engines and siege craft generally were more advanced.[43]

Persian intrigues and subsidies contributed to Greek unrest; a power in his own right was the Persian satrap Mausolus of Caria. His role in Greek affairs, however, was cut short by his death in 353, and he is instead remembered for his enormous marble tomb, which gave first the ancient, then the modern world a generic word (although it is uncertain when the 'Mausoleum' itself was first so designated).[44] Our most important testimonia for the Mausoleum are Vitruvius (De Arch. 7, preface 12–3) and Pliny (HN 36.30–1). The latter says it was built at the Carian capital Halicarnassus by Mausolus' sister-widow Artemisia, who left it unfinished on her own death in 351 – whereupon the artists finished it without pay. Probably it was begun by Mausolus and was under construction throughout the 350s. Pliny and Vitruvius record the architects as Pythius and Satyrus, the sculptors as Scopas, Leochares, Timotheus, and Bryaxis, adding that each of the latter worked on one side of the monument. There has been considerable skepticism about this division of labor and, partly as a consequence, about the famous sculptors named: Wace compared the Mausoleum's reported team-design to a hypothetical monument resulting from the quadripartite efforts of the modern sculptors Epstein, Moore, Gill, and Dick.[45] The parallel is misleading, since contemporary personal styles were less drastically different in antiquity. On the other hand, styles were more divergent in the fourth century than in the fifth; the sculptural remains show that stylistic diversity was tolerated on the Mausoleum as it had been in the sculpture of the Asclepius temple at Epidaurus.

The architects and sculptors were a decidedly Athenian–Ionian group: Pythius was from Priene (and, to judge from Vitr. 4.3.1, a chauvinistic Ionian and prominent critic of the Doric order),[46] Satyrus and Scopas were Parians, as was perhaps Timotheus, Leochares an Athenian, Bryaxis Carian by name and mainly Athenian by associations. The monument attributed to them, built for a Hellenized Asian ruler in an originally Greek, though cosmopolitan, city was more hybrid than might have been expected. Its thirty-six column peristyle stood on a high podium and was surmounted by a twenty-four stepped pyramid; these had precedents in local funerary architecture, although the pyramid is often thought to reflect Egyptian influence as well. The details of the Ionic columns followed Asian Greek practice, as did the dentils of the entablature. There were, however, three carved pictorial friezes; their placement has been much debated, but none was combined with dentils.[47] While the frieze had Near Eastern origins, its presence here is probably due to mainland Ionic practice, especially that of late fifth-century Athens.

Was the Mausoleum a monstrosity? British scholars inevitably compare the Albert Memorial (even favorably!),[48] but a better comparison might be the Victor Emmanuel Monument, whose pitilessly white Brescian marble clashes with the earth tones of its Roman surroundings; the Mausoleum was centrally and theatrically situated, and the sight of the chariot group at its apex may have been even more inescapable than the bronze wings on top of the Roman 'typewriter.' But aesthetic condemnation of so ruined a building must be tentative, especially if barbarian use of Greek elements is the ultimate target; we do not know what the Thersilion looked like, much less the Odeum of Pericles.

The many sculptural remains can still be appreciated, in some ways more than when they were *in situ*. The most arresting is the well-preserved colossal statue sometimes identified, not unreasonably, as Mausolus (see Plate 14, p. 117).[49] The head has a close resemblance to coin portraits of Mausolus; the features appear individualized, at the very least (like the hairstyle) non-Greek. The identification is perhaps supported by the colossal statue found in close proximity, often called Artemisia.[50] A woman in the same pose appears on a votive relief found at Tegea; she and a male figure flank an image of the Carian Zeus and are identified by inscriptions as Ada and Idrieus, the wedded siblings of Mausolus and Artemisia (the relief is most plausibly explained as an offering by a Carian artist who worked with Scopas and then accompanied him to Tegea, where Scopas designed a great temple now established as later than the Mausoleum).[51] Iconographically, then, 'Artemisia' is appropriate for a mid-fourth-century Carian ruler, rather than (for example) an ancestor (although it must be admitted that Idrieus on the relief bears no resemblance to 'Mausolus'). The colossal pair, along with most of the other free-standing sculpture from the Mausoleum, have been claimed as mid-Hellenistic additions, partly because of Mausolus' portrait-like face and the archaizing hairstyle of Artemisia (whose face is destroyed), partly because of the heavy 'baroque' drapery; most scholars have rejected this chronology, I think rightly.[52]

One of the few fragments of round sculpture which the revisionists had relegated to the fourth century is a vapid head with highly symmetrical hair and beard;[53] on the same scale (one and one-third life-size) but from an incomparably better workshop are a head of Apollo and a fragmentary bearded head.[54] It is unthinkable that any of these were by the same sculptor as the 'Mausolus'.

The friezes support the conclusion indicated by the statuary: different sculptors, some of them great artists, were involved. The motifs of two of the friezes were ones heavily used in fifth-century architectural sculpture, an amazonomachy and a centauromachy. The banality of this choice does not negate its irony: on the Parthenon both motifs were associated with the triumph of Greece over barbarian Asia. The third frieze depicted racing chariots appropriate to the funeral games staged for Mausolus, may have been placed in the interior, and was evidently quite repetitious; Ridgway aptly remarks that in Asia Minor, where the Greek frieze had its archaic beginnings, it now returns to its early decorative, non-narrative character.[55] The amazon frieze is the most extensively preserved, usually estimated at about one-quarter of its original length. The fragments vary not only in quality but in style; there may not be a single slab which has not at some time been attributed to each of Pliny's four sculptors. A beautiful fragment of the chariot frieze survives and has been attributed to Leochares himself.[56] Of the crudely executed centauromachy even less is preserved; it might be noted that two heads reflect what is usually thought to be the style of Scopas.[57] Robertson nicely summarizes ideas about Scopas:

> From the literary record it appears that one work of his at least, a maenad tearing a goat, made a strong impression of expressiveness and passion, qualities not on the whole sought in classical art, but found in certain sculptures which on other grounds can be associated with Skopas.[58]

The maenad is undoubtedly copied in the powerful Dresden statuette (see Plate 21).[59] The figure in frenzy twists her hips left, her shoulders right; her head is thrown back, her neck swells, her momentum makes her dishevelled hair stream down and her single scanty garment fly open. The maenad's pose, probably imitated on the amazon frieze of the Mausoleum, has its closest antecedents in

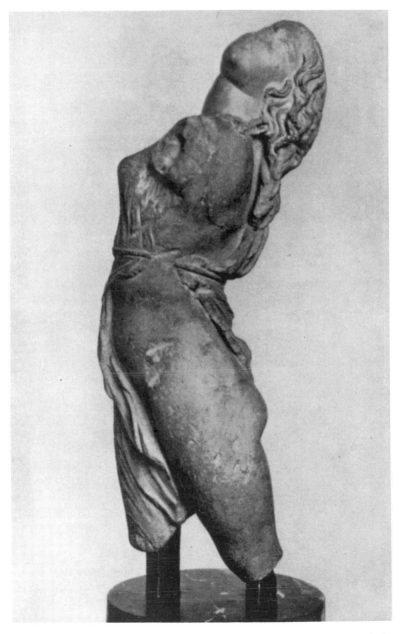

Plate 21 Statuette of maenad, copy of statue by Scopas 350s BC. Staatliche Skulpturensammlung (Albertinum), Dresden. Photo: Staatliche Skulpturensammlung (Albertinum) Dresden Museum.

the Epidaurus pedimental sculptures. There, intense emotion was also conveyed by at least one face, that of Priam. The face of the maenad is ruined, but there is unmistakable passion in the eyes, which are not only deep-set but overhung by muscle at the outer corners, and the mouth was lifted in the center as though breathing hard.

Similar heads are included among the battered fragments of pedimental sculpture from the Temple of Athena Alea at Tegea, which was designed by Scopas (Paus. 8.45.4–7) and built c. 345–35.[60] Arcadian local pride, tinged with anti-Spartan feeling, at least partially explains the temple's size and splendor, exceptional by fourth-century standards. The rich interior featured half-columns topped by the most robust Corinthian capitals ever carved, which supported an upper colonnade in the Ionic order. On the Doric exterior, the west pediment depicted the battle between Achilles and the Arcadian local hero Telephus; on the front was the hunt of the Calydonian boar. The sculptures are not explicitly attributed to Scopas, and their cursory execution overall marks them as workshop products, but plausibly carved to his design. The marble carvers show extensive knowledge of anatomy, along with awareness that their work would be positioned high above the viewer, where it would not be subject to close inspection; this calculation is characteristic of fourth-century architectural sculpture.

Another ambitious sculptural composition is credited not only to Scopas but (almost certainly wrongly) to his unassisted activity. Pliny (*HN* 25–6), after mentioning several of the artist's works, writes:

> But of the highest reputation, in the shrine of Gnaeus Domitius in the Circus Flaminius, are Poseidon himself and Thetis and Achilles, Nereids seated on dolphins and sea-monsters or sea-horses, also Tritons, the band of Phorkys, and many other sea creatures: all by his hand, a splendid work, even if it had occupied a whole lifetime.

These must have been pillaged from a Greek site, whether they were pedimental sculpture or a free-standing group. It has been suggested that the marine group was actually made by Scopas Minor, a late Hellenistic descendant of the fourth-century artist who worked in Rome, yet there is evidence that the motifs mentioned by Pliny appeared in fourth-century sculpture, in some cases with stylistic links to Scopas.[61] Marine groups and themes enjoyed popularity in a variety of media during the fourth century as well as the Hellenistic period, often used to illustrate Thetis and the Nereids bringing new arms and armor to Achilles (the mosaic from the Villa of Good Fortune is one example). Since Pliny does not mention the arms or Hephaestus (who made them) another myth may have been the subject, although unattested in Greek art: Achilles' final voyage to the Isles of the Blessed. Marine motifs eventually take on funerary significance, but the sculptures mentioned by Pliny are too ambitious even for a late fourth-century Athenian funerary monument.[62] Perhaps the finest of these is the Ilissus stele, made *c.* 340 and certainly by a first-rate artist.[63] The deceased, represented as a perfect young athlete, and a heavily draped elderly man confront each other across a space of a few inches which appears infinitely wide; at the young man's feet a little boy sits huddled and weeping. The pathos of death's separation is so effectively conveyed that Scopas has inevitably been suggested as the sculptor; the young man has some resemblance to the Meleager type preserved in many copies, and in turn often attributed to Scopas because of the style of the head and because Meleager was depicted in the East pediment at Tegea.[64] Scopas, however, cannot always have worked in the style of the Tegea sculptures, nor would all of his statues have expressed intense emotion; he made a statue of Hypnus (Sleep), and Pliny's passage calls his nude Aphrodite superior to the one by Praxiteles at Cnidus.

Conversely, pain and pathos were depicted by other fourth-century artists.[65] Pathos would have been appropriate to Silanion's portrait of Sappho; he also made a dying Jocasta in bronze, mixing the alloy with silver for the face, to show how her life was ebbing. Several fourth-century sculptors softened the usual austerity of Athena to represent her as approachable, even vulnerable. One example, a recently discovered bronze original at first attributed to Cephisodotus and more recently and plausibly to Euphranor, has not been without its modern critics:

> The sculptor has clearly modeled his statue on Pheidian Athena types, particularly the Parthenos, but in order to stress the goddess's engagement with and continuing benevolence toward her subjects he has abandoned their majestic, commanding posture. Instead, he opts for a relaxed contrapposto . . . and a gentle inclination of the head toward the observer. Such weakness in so masculine a deity is all but fatal . . . Athena was too tied in Athenian hearts to their years of greatness in the fifth century for her ever to be much of a success in the fourth.[66]

Euphranor was the only Greek artist to achieve fame as both painter and sculptor. Attempts to identify his sculpture are based on his cult statue of Apollo Patroos for the Athenian agora; this superb colossal work in marble has been rediscovered, unfortunately headless.[67]

Approachable, even intimate portrayals of the gods as the fourth century wished to see them were apparently the speciality of the Athenian sculptor Praxiteles, who inherited his trade and handed it down to his sons. Towards 340, he made two figures of Aphrodite: one draped, the other a revolutionary full nude for which his beautiful mistress Phryne is said to have posed. Offered their choice, the islanders of Cos favored the draped statue, and the nude went to Cnidus. Here, in close proximity to a Near Eastern religious tradition which gave enormous importance to female nudity, there may have been readier acceptance for what became the most famous and influential of all ancient statues (see Plate 22). However conventional the left hand's gesture of modesty has now become, there is an ambiguity about the pose reflected even in ancient anecdotes. Is the goddess proud of her perfection and tolerantly amused by the intruder – for the composition includes the spectator as perhaps did no earlier Greek statue? Or is Aphrodite more humanly startled by the intrusion, and so more closely related to previous Greek narrative tradition involving female nudity? Some copies, including the one illustrated, reveal a tension in both face and body which argue for the latter; in any case, the pose is not one at rest.[68] But Praxiteles' modern reputation for giving his figures a mood of languorous serenity involves other statues as well. The old debate over whether the Hermes holding the infant Dionysus – a marble group found at Olympia where Pausanias (5.17.3) saw it and attributed it to Praxiteles – is an original or a copy has increasingly given way to the argument that this is a Hellenistic work, although derived from Praxiteles' style.[69] There certainly exists a danger of over-simplifying the style of Praxiteles as well as that of Scopas, especially since it is so tempting to contrast the two. The very young and androgynous Apollo Sauroctonus, however, very probably goes back to a Praxitelean original, also the indolent youthful leaning satyr.[70] Overall, it still appears that Praxiteles, himself very prosperous, responded to a mood of well-being, even complacence, in Athens towards mid-century.

It was from such a mood that Demosthenes repeatedly sought to rouse the Athenians against the rapidly growing power of Macedon. His efforts led to the battle of Chaeronea in 338/7, where Philip

Plate 22 'Venus de Clerq,' statuette of Aphrodite, end of 2nd century AD. Artist unknown. Marble, height 0.972m. Copy of statue by Praxiteles for Knidos, *c.* 340 BC. Collection of the J. Paul Getty Museum, Malibu, 72.AA.93. Photo: J. Paul Getty Museum.

and Alexander won a decisive victory and assumed unprecedented supremacy over Greece. There was immediate impact on art as well as politics; two monuments set up within a few years of Chaeronea have particular significance in both respects.

The first of these was sculptural. Daochus, ruler of Pharsalus, had followed both a Thessalian and a family policy in collaborating with the Macedonians, and he commissioned nine statues in honor of his family at Delphi, where in the mid-330s he served as an official in the Panhellenic League established by Philip. The Daochus monument is our best-preserved free-standing sculptural group from Greece.[71] The row of statues stood within an architectural setting which restricted spectators to a single, rather distant view, as in the case of the nearby Lysander monument. It is possible that all nine statues survive: all but the first (on the east) are identified by inscriptions on the base. The uninscribed figure is now generally agreed to have been Apollo, perhaps the fragmentary seated figure recently discovered near the base; others assign this to the pediment of the Apollo temple.[72] Next, Acnonius, a late sixth-century Thessalian ruler wearing a tunic and short cloak, gestures as though introducing his descendants to the god. On his right stood his three sons, Agias, Telemachus, and Agelaus, who in the 480s won victories in all four Crown games; they were, respectively, pankratiast, wrestler, and boy runner, and their musculature is subtly differentiated according to event.[73] The nude athletes form a group within a group, probably linked by victory crowns placed in a rising line: Agias holding his lowered, Telemachus raising his to crown himself, Agelaus lifting his high (an unparalleled pose in Greek athletic sculpture) to form a pinnacle for the entire group. A complete contrast is Daochus I, heavily enveloped in a Macedonian cloak; he ruled peacefully in Thessaly for twenty-seven years in the late fifth century. His son Sisyphus I is again a contrast: a soldier, massively built and assertively posed, tunic clinging closely enough to outline his genitals. Of his son, Daochus II, the dedicant, only the feet are preserved at Delphi. I believe that this missing statue may be the torso found on Euboea and attributed to the workshop of the Daochus group;[74] while there are no joins, the pose is consistent with the position of the feet, the unusual irregular support behind these is continued by one at the bottom of the torso, and the drapery scheme is a suitable variant of the draped statues found at Delphi. The final figure is a nude youth leaning on a herm: Sisyphus II, the dedicant's son. The sculptors are unknown (Pausanias did not see this group, destroyed before his visit to Delphi), perhaps Thessalian. Without being first-rate artists, they skillfully varied and interrelated the line of figures; I am convinced by Fehr that they also characterized at least some of the figures by body language appropriate to their inscriptions. Agias plants his feet with a Heraclean effort appropriate to his epigram's paraphrase of the dying Heracles' boast in Sophocles' *Trachiniae* 1102: 'No one ever set up trophies over your hands.' Just as Daochus I's inscription stressed the justice and moderation of his long rule, his left arm is covered as a gesture of modesty used by Greek orators. Sisyphus I's statue has the swagger of his epigram, which praises his military prowess. Sisyphus II had no accomplishments to record; his youth precluded these, yet his promise (in the eyes of his father; nothing else is known of him) justified his presence here. His pose is easy and confident, even godlike; nude like the athletes, he already wears a victor's crown. Fehr argues persuasively that the statues and their inscriptions collectively embody the qualities of the good ruler as defined by Xenophon and Isocrates; with this monument, Daochus proclaimed his legitimacy as a Hellenic ruler, not merely a Macedonian vassal.

It is very possible, however, that the Daochus dedication was influenced by a Macedonian family monument set up a year or two earlier by Alexander, named for Philip and probably initiated by him. The Philippeion[75] was at Olympia, the greatest of Panhellenic sanctuaries, whose importance both kings fully recognized. The unknown architect designed a tholos, continuing the practice of using Corinthian capitals in the interior, but this time the exterior order was Ionic. The tholos contained portraits of Philip, Alexander, and other Macedonian royalty, made by Leochares in gold and ivory (Paus. 5.17.4): materials apparently reserved, until now, for statues of the gods, such as the nearby Zeus by Phidias. Miller's study of the architectural details has established the probability that the architect was Macedonian, following local practices also evident on the facades of slightly later Macedonian tombs. The circular plan may also be explained in terms of architectural tradition in Macedonia; there the tholos was associated with the cult of Heracles, whom Philip claimed as an ancestor.[76] The Philippeion may have immediately influenced another structure, the Athenian monument celebrating the victory won by the *choregos* Lysicrates in 334.[77] For the first time, Corinthian capitals were used for the exterior; as on the Philippeion, Asian dentils occur together with the carved frieze of mainland Ionic tradition.

Another Panhellenic sanctuary apparently owed its revival to Macedonian sponsorship. The Nemean games, removed to Argos in the fifth century, were restored to Nemea, which concurrently benefitted from an extensive building program. Its most important element was the stadium, which the athletes entered through a vaulted passageway; the dramatic effect created by the sudden emergence of the athletes into the area of competition has obvious parallels in modern athletic practice. Graffiti carved on the sides of the tunnel show that this also served as the locker room, and that the vault dates to the 330s or 320s: the earliest example in Greece.[78] An immediate Macedonian forerunner may have been the vaulted chamber II in the royal cemetery at Vergina. Some identify the tomb as that of Philip, assassinated in 336; others date it two decades later, as the tomb of Philip Arrhidaeus and his wife.[79] The vaulted entrance to the stadium at Olympia may therefore be of Macedonian rather than Roman origins.

The theater as a truly architectural form is a fourth-century development, although the one at Epidaurus, renowned in antiquity as the finest and the most beautiful (Paus. 2.27.5), is now dated to the end rather than the middle of the century.[80] Lycurgus' rebuilding of the Athenian Theater of Dionysus in stone probably belongs to the 330s; it is to this phase of the theater's history that scholars now assign the real beginnings of the scene building.[81] Tentatively dated to the fourth century is a theater at Vergina. Its proportions are anomalous: the permanent seating capacity was small, the orchestra far larger than any other known; while Greek theaters were often put to many uses besides theatrical performances, this example was designed expressly for ceremony. 'If this theater belongs to the middle of the fourth century,' observes Borza, 'we have the actual setting of Philip II's assassination.'[82]

The fourth century, especially its second half, was decisive for the development of the monumental stoa. While a few earlier stoas had attained considerable size, they were easily surpassed by the Echo Stoa and South Stoa at Olympia, the stoa in the Amphiaraion at Oropus, and especially the Stoa of Philip at Megalopolis. Macedonian subsidies for these have been suggested, but there is no certainty; according to Pausanias (8.30.6) Philip did not finance the one named for him. Despite their great length and consequent importance in defining public space, all these were limited in their impressiveness by the absence of a second storey.[83] This innovation probably first occurred on the Athenian acropolis c. 350, with the

East Stoa of the Asclepieion. At Corinth, early in the third century, the South Stoa combined the second storey with enormous length, pioneering the Hellenistic type.[84]

Probably datable just before 300, however, are two striking examples of religious architecture. The Temple of Apollo at Didyma, like most fourth-century temples, was built to the plan of an archaic predecessor, which in this case resulted in gigantic size.[85] The unusual interior, with its sunken open air court, was not inherited from the sixth-century plan. Access was through stairways covered by sloping barrel vaults; the Romans later tended to avoid this difficult construction in favor of stepped vaults. The sanctuary of Zeus at Megalopolis, on the other hand, is a remarkable anticipation of Roman design with its strict axiality and 'blueprint symmetry.'[86] Ardently pro-Macedonian, Megalopolis almost certainly possessed still another architectural distinction: the first of the few sanctuaries devoted to Alexander's cult.[87]

It was primarily through pictorial art that Alexander's fame and influence circulated.[88] He eventually gave Lysippus and Apelles the exclusive right to make his portrait in bronze and painting, respectively. Lysippus also made 'perhaps the most influential battle monument in all of ancient art,' a group of twenty-five equestrian statues commemorating the battle of Granicus; this stood at Dion, the sacred city of the Macedonians, until taken to Rome in 146.[89] At Delphi, a later group of bronzes depicting Alexander and his companions hunting a lion was a collaboration between Lysippus and Leochares,[90] whose careers were coeval. The groups are lost, except for the numerous works thought to reflect their appearance; a portrait of Alexander by the Athenian sculptor may survive.[91] The head, arguably an original, was found on the Athenian acropolis; Alexander's appearance is very youthful and, apart from the characteristic leonine hair, not individualized (its similarity to the head from the chariot frieze from the Mausoleum is the basis for the attribution to Leochares). Stewart compares a more animated Alexander also of Attic style, an original thought to come from Megara and now in the Getty Museum; he dates it to the 320s (see Plate 17, p. 190).[92] Fragments acquired with the Getty Alexander plausibly, although not certainly, belong with it as remnants of a marble group depicting a sacrifice. Lysippus was celebrated for his success in portraying Alexander as a ferociously energetic warrior, general, and ruler; little of this fire shows through in the copies identified with reasonable certainty. We are also poorly served by

271

copies of Lysippus' Apoxyomenus (athlete scraping himself with a strigil), a bronze made around 320 and by the beginning of the empire on public display in Rome, where it enjoyed enthusiastic acclaim (Pliny *HN* 34.61–5). The Vatican statue (see Plate 23)[93] can nevertheless be used as the starting point for consideration of Lysippus' style. Here we find many of the characteristics mentioned by Pliny and other ancient sources: slim proportions and small head, careful rendering of the hair and a naturalistic approach overall, and great attention to detail. Still more striking are the complexity and three-dimensionality of the pose. These aspects of his work are barely hinted at by the testimonia, but they clearly exercised enormous influence on early Hellenistic sculptors; many of whom were Lysippus' pupils, including several of his sons. Lysippus himself is said to have begun his extraordinarily long and prolific career as a foundryman, without a teacher in the conventional sense. Attempts to identify early works have been problematic. The Daochus dedication at Delphi is generally attributed to his assistants because we know that a statue of Agias by Lysippus once stood at Pharsalus; an inscription (now itself lost) on the base, very similar to the one at Delphi, adds the sculptor's name. Supposedly, at least some of the statues commissioned by Daochus copied bronzes made by Lysippus as early as mid-century. The skilled and eclectic marble-carvers who worked at Delphi, however, are unlikely pupils of the great specialist in bronze work. The dedication at Delphi, unlike the putative group at Pharsalus, has clear motivation for its time and place; it could then have inspired a belated victor statue of the great pancratiast Agias (and perhaps his brothers) in his home town. In that case, the Pharsalian Agias could be the original of the Vatican Apoxyomenus (several victor statues by Lysippus stood at Olympia, but these were seen by Pausanias long after his Apoxyomenus had been taken to Rome).

The finest of the several types of Socrates portraits probably shows us Lysippus' style in the 330s, but not before.[94] Another, and earlier, fourth-century Socrates portrait is perhaps by Silanion. It was he, more certainly, who made the definitive portrait of Plato.[95] The massive and somber head, while probably made soon after Plato's death in 347, is strongly individualized; at the same time, both the head and the seated, heavily cloaked figure established the basic philosopher-type of Hellenistic art. A more personal link between Lysippus and philosophy may be present in his statues of Heracles.[96] He made many statues of the hero (a Macedonian favorite and ancestor of Philip), in action

Plate 23 Apoxyomenus, copy of statue by Lysippus, 320s BC. Vatican Museum. Photo: Art Resource.

and more notably at rest; the latter motif had deep meaning for several Hellenistic philosophical schools. Lysippus' Farnese or 'Weary' Heracles, made around the same time as the Apoxyomenus, exists in numerous replicas, whose sub-types may be due to variants by copyists, by the artist himself, or both. The format is clear: massively muscled and convincingly fatigued, Heracles leans on his club; the three-dimensional spiralling pose eventually leads the eye around the back, where the right hand holds the golden apples of immortality. It was probably this Lysippan Heracles that stood in the agora of the sculptor's native Sicyon. Also in Sicyon was his bronze statue of Kairos, thoroughly Hellenistic in its complex allegorical depiction of 'opportunity,' 'the critical moment.' Long a standard topic in rhetoric, with obvious applicability to the careers of Alexander and his successors, Kairos may also have been central to Lysippus' artistic credo, as Stewart has ingeniously argued; there is reason to believe that the statue stood in front of Lysippus' house.[97]

An important early book on Lysippus summed him up as follows:

> intellectual vigor and technical expertness could not atone for the lack of creative genius and the highest perfection of taste . . . . Though our conclusion must be based on scanty evidence, it appears that Lysippus was a smaller man than either of his predecessors [Polyclitus and Scopas] . . . . We can not see in him a profoundly spiritual artist, who put his soul into every work. Skopas may have been such a man, but Lysippus worked too easily.[98]

The judgment combines the left-handed compliment inevitably aimed at the virtuoso with the criticism commonly made of Hellenistic culture as a whole. Suffice it to say that few artistic careers have approached that of Lysippus in accomplishment or importance.

In antiquity, the status of Apelles of Cos was even higher than that of Lysippus. Painting, the most admired of the arts, reached its greatest fame in the period from Philip through Alexander's successors, and Apelles' supremacy was unquestioned. Literary sources also indicate that he was a more amiable man than Parrhasius or Zeuxis, on easy and friendly terms with both Alexander and the rival painter Protogenes. This is hardly compensation for our loss of all direct knowledge of his work, as well as that of Protogenes. A more obscure contemporary, Philoxenus of Eretria, is perhaps the most tangible of all Greek painters, since his 'battle between Alexander and Darius' (Pliny *HN* 35.110; the only mention of this painter) is almost certainly copied with great accuracy in the late Hellenistic Alexander mosaic in Pompeii.[99] The battle here has been variously identified, most firmly and plausibly as Issus in 333, but as in Pliny the emphasis is on the encounter between the kings. Alexander charges from the left, profiled head relentless (the most powerful of all Alexander portraits), a dying Persian impaled on his *sarissa*; 'by his heroism this man has saved his king.'[100] Darius in his chariot stands high above the other combatants as he gestures in anguish towards the self-sacrifice. He is shown in three-quarter frontal view, his chariot and team skillfully foreshortened; the mosaic fully employs other painterly devices such as shading, cast shadows, and highlights. While the effect of massed figures is entirely convincing, there is no attempt to give the setting three-dimensional depth. The colors are restricted to the four of the classical palette: black and white, red and yellow. It is possible to forget that we are not looking at an early Hellenistic painting but a picture in the medium of tessellated mosaic developed in the third century.

The pebble mosaics of the late fourth century, especially those at Pella, bring us close to the new technique.[101] The stones are now very small, uniform, and closely set; most mosaics at Pella emphasize the outlines by lead strips (evidence of Classical mosaic's curious affinity with vase painting). The finest of the Pella pavements dispenses with the strips and beautifully balances the stylization appropriate to the medium and the current developments in painting (see Plate 24). Set within an elaborate floral border derived from the celebrated school of 'flower-painting,' two youthful hunters attack a downed stag. Shading, three-quarter poses, and overlapping are masterfully used against a neutral background. The artist would be unknown had he not (unlike other makers of pebble mosaics) signed his name: Gnosis. Comparable skill in representing human figures is displayed by the artists who painted on the tombs of Vergina and Leukadia.[102] It speaks well for the level of early Hellenistic painting that they were probably closer to journeymen than masters, and perhaps Macedonian; no Greek painter is recorded to have decorated Macedonian tombs. Two very recently discovered at Vergina are the most interesting. On the wall of Tomb I (tentatively identified as Philip's by Borza)[103] the abduction of Persephone by Hades in his chariot is depicted with virtuoso rapid brushwork that contributes to the painting's remarkable liveliness.[104]

Much less well-preserved is a hunting scene on the facade of Tomb II. The forest setting has exceptional emphasis compared with the

Plate 24 Stag hunt mosaic by Gnosis, at Pella, late fourth century BC. Pebble mosaic pavement. Photo: Archaeological Museum, Pella. Courtesy of Dr I. M. Akamaris

relatively small men and animals. There is admittedly nothing here to support crediting the invention of landscape painting (such as the Odyssey frescoes) to Greek rather than Italian artists.[105] The Macedonian tombs, however, have already provided many surprises for students of both Greek and Roman painting. At Leukadia, large painted figures are framed by architectural elements as in the Pompeian Second Style; a vaulted chamber from the third century anticipates by more than a century the earliest known example of Second-style painting in Italy.

During the course of the fourth century, 'it is extremely important to remember that mainland Greece is ceasing to be the determinant of what is Greek.'[106] Future excavation in Macedonia may be expected to contribute substantially to our knowledge of fourth-century art.

NOTES

1 On the differences between dedications at Olympia and those at Delphi see F. Felten, 'Weihungen in Olympia und Delphi,' *Ath Mitt* 97 (1982), 79–97.

2 On the reconstruction I follow D. Arnold, *Die Polykletnachfolge*, Berlin, Mann, 1969, pp. 97–109 and A. H. Borbein, 'Die griechische Statue des 4. Jahrhunderts v. Chr.,' *JdI* 88 (1973), 77–9. For a survey of free-standing groups see H. L. Schanz, *Greek Sculptural Groups*, New York and London, Garland, 1980, pp. 62–6 on Lysander's monument.

3 See B. R. Brown, *Anticlassicism in Greek Sculpture of the Fourth Century BC*, New York, New York University Press, 1973, p. 47. Her book is a useful and stimulating discussion of the fourth century and the reflections of political and economic change in fourth-century art. Cf. M. Robertson and J. J. Pollitt, 'What is "Hellenistic" about Hellenistic Art?,' in P. Green, ed., *Hellenistic History and Culture*, Berkeley, University of California Press, 1993, pp. 67–103.

4 G. Flaubert, *Oeuvres Completes de Gustave Flaubert. Correspondance*, second ser., Paris, L. Conard, 1926, p. 298 (letter to Louis Bouilhet, February 10, 1851).

5 J. J. Pollitt, *Art and Experience in Classical Greece*, Cambridge, Cambridge University Press, 1972, pp. 115–25.

6 E.g., R. M. Cook, *Greek Art*, New York, Farrar Straus Giroux, 1973, p. 9. R. Carpenter, review of Pollitt, *Art and Experience, AJA* 77 (1973), 349. Cf. M. Robertson, *The Art of Vase Painting in Classical Athens*, Cambridge, Cambridge University Press, 1992, p. 235.

7 The term High Classic has sometimes been used – but also, confusingly, applied to mid-fifth-century art.

8 The phrase is from E. R. Dodds, *Plato. Gorgias*, Oxford, Clarendon Press, 1959, p. 8.

9 See R. Lattimore, *Poetry of Greek Tragedy*, New York, Harper & Row, 1958, pp. 110, 117–20.

10 M. Robertson, *History of Greek Art*, Cambridge, Cambridge University Press, 1975, p. 373.
11 These, which have the advantage of being dated, have received very full treatment in M. Meyer, *Die griechischen Urkundreliefs*, Berlin, Mann, 1989.
12 Robertson, *History*, pp. 363–4.
13 See Robertson, *History*, pp. 368–9, A. Stewart, *Greek Sculpture. An Exploration*, New Haven, Yale University Press, 1990, pp. 22–3, 172–3; more fully, S. Ensoli, *L'Heroon di Dexileos nel Ceramico di Atene*, Rome, Memorie della R. Accademia Nazionale dei Lincei, 1987, ser. 8, 29, fasc. 2.
14 See especially W. A. P. Childs, *The City Reliefs of Lycia*, Princeton, Princeton University Press, 1978. The chronology and conclusions presented below are his; I am greatly indebted to Professor Childs for supplying the photograph.
15 See A. Rumpf, 'Parrhasios,' *AJA* 55 (1951), 1–12.
16 Probably Heraclea on the Black Sea not in Italy, according to W. Ameling, 'Der Herkunft des Malers Zeuxis,' *EA* 9 (1987), 76.
17 See J. J. Pollitt, *The Ancient View of Greek Art*, New Haven, Yale University Press, 1974, pp. 194–9.
18 On Zeuxis and Parrhasius see V. J. Bruno, *Form and Color in Greek Painting*, New York, Norton, 1977, pp. 31–4.
19 Cf. Bruno, ibid., pp. 34–5, E. C. Keuls, *Plato and Greek Painting*, Leiden, Brill, 1978, W. A. P. Childs, 'Platon, les images et l'art grec du IVe siècle avant J.C.,' *Rev. Arch.* 1994/1, pp. 33–56.
20 See Robertson, *History*, pp. 486–8.
21 See S. Lattimore, *The Marine Thiasos in Greek Sculpture*, Los Angeles, Institute of Archaeology, University of California, 1976, p. 29.
22 Bruno, 'Antecedents of the Pompeian First Style,' *AJA* 73 (1977), pp. 316–17.
23 W. B. Dinsmoor, *The Architecture of Ancient Greece*, New York, Biblo and Tannen, 1950, p. 216.
24 F. E. Winter, 'Tradition and Innovation in Doric Design IV: The Fourth Century,' *AJA* 86 (1982), 388–99.
25 F. Cooper and S. Morris, 'Dining in Round Buildings,' in O. Murray, ed., *Sympotica*, Oxford, Clarendon Press, 1990. For the Delphi *tholos* see H. Berve, G. Gruben, M. Hirmer, *Greek Temples, Theaters, and Shrines*, New York, Abrams, 1963, pp. 341–2, and G. Roux, 'La tholos d'Athena Pronoia dans son sanctuaire de Delphes,' *CRAI* 1988, pp. 290–309.
26 For the suggestion that the Corinthian capital was a 'particularly sacred form' (which I find unlikely) see J. J. Pollitt, *Art in the Hellenistic Age*, Cambridge, Cambridge University Press, 1986, pp. 247–9.
27 Brown, *Anticlassicism*, pp. 8–15, with a good summary of the important features.
28 For the temple see Winter, 'Tradition,' pp. 395–8: for the *tholos*, Berve, *Greek Temples* pp. 360–1.
29 The dancing girls on the Acanthus Column at Delphi are a possible late fourth-century example; for the monument and its date see B. S. Ridgway, *Hellenistic Sculpture* I, Madison, University of Wisconsin Press, 1990, pp. 22–6.

30 For the pedimental sculptures see Robertson, *History*, pp. 397–402, Stewart *Greek Sculpture*, pp. 170–1 (for the Priam head, fig. 459).
31 See Winter, 'Tradition,' pp. 397–8, 400.
32 On the Asclepius Giustini see now M. Meyer, 'Erfindung und Wirkung. Zum Asklepios Giustini,' *Ath Mitt* 103 (1988), 119–59, whose chronological arguments are convincing; previously suggested dates had ranged from the late fifth century to the mid-fourth.
33 R. Kabus-Jahn, 'Studien zu Frauenfiguren des 4. Jahrhunderts v. Chr.,' PhD Diss., Freiburg, 1963, pp. 85–7, G. B. Waywell, *The Lever and Hope Sculptures*, Berlin, Mann, 1986 pp. 68–9.
34 See Kabus-Jahn, ibid., pp. 81–5, Robertson, *History*, pp. 402–3.
35 See Robertson, *History*, 395, Stewart, *Greek Sculpture*, p. 83. For a rebuttal to the theory that the Asclepius Giustini and Hope Hygieia were the Athenian cult statues see especially G. Heiderich, 'Asklepios,' PhD Diss., Freiburg, 1966, pp. 26–8, cf. B. Vierneisel-Schlörb, *Glyptothek Münich: Katalog der Skulpturen. 2. Klassischen Skulpturen des 5. und 4. Jahr. v. Chr.*, Munich, Beck, 1979, pp. 216–24.
36 On Eirene and Ploutos see especially E. La Rocca, 'Eirene e Ploutos,' *JDI* 89 (1974), 112–36, and Vierneisel-Schlörb, pp. 255–73, more briefly Robertson, *History*, pp. 383–6.
37 R. Carpenter, *Greek Sculpture*, Chicago, The University of Chicago Press, 1960 p. 159, while dating the Eirene to 376, called it 'not only a frigid allegory but a severe and unseductive study of the impenetrably draped feminine form.'
38 Borbein, 'Statue,' p. 139; on the Eirene, pp. 115–19.
39 Groups uniting a larger and a smaller figure were a fourth-century speciality, see especially E. Künzl, 'Fruhhellenistische Gruppen,' PhD Diss., Cologne, 1968, pp. 8–41; on the Eirene, pp. 9–12.
40 The painting was in the Athenian agora; Mantinea was a defeat for the allies Athens and Sparta, but Epaminondas' death nullified the Theban victory, and Euphranor concentrated on a related engagement in which the Athenian cavalry distinguished itself. See Robertson, *History*, pp. 433–5.
41 See Schanz, *Greek Sculptural Groups*, pp. 55–60.
42 Sadly, it has now been disproved that the scene building of the theater, which stood between it and the portico of the Thersilion, was on wheels so that it could be rolled out of the way; see C. Buckler, 'The Myth of the Movable *Skenai*,' *AJA* 90 (1986), 431–6.
43 While Greek fortifications were long somewhat neglected by scholarship, two excellent recent studies are F. E. Winter, *Greek Fortifications*, London, Routledge & Kegan Paul, 1971, and A. W. Lawrence, *Greek Aims in Fortification*, Oxford, Clarendon Press, 1979; for Messene see respectively pp. 113–14, 164–5 and pp. 382–5. The fourth century fortifications of Attica have received additional attention in J. Ober, *Fortress Attica*, Leiden, Brill, 1985. For the reattribution of the border forts, see F. A. Cooper, 'Epaminondas and Greek Fortifications,' *AJA* 90 (1986), 195 and J. M. Camp, 'Notes on the Towers and Borders of Classical Boeotia,' *AJA* 95 (1991), 193–202.

44 See S. Hornblower, *Mausolus*, Oxford, Clarendon Press, 1982, pp. 232–3, and, for a comprehensive discussion of the Mausoleum, pp. 223–74. A useful brief account is C. Scarre, 'A Tomb to Wonder At,' *Archaeology* 46 (1993), 32–9.

45 A. J. B. Wace, 'Design and Execution,' *ASAA* 22–6 (1944–5), 109–12. Those who believe that famous artists were falsely credited by local tradition note that Vitruvius hesitates between Timotheus and Praxiteles (whose participation in fact is not as impossible as usually claimed).

46 See Pollitt, *Ancient View*, pp. 243–4 and J. C. Carter, *The Sculpture of the Sanctuary of Athena Polias at Priene*, London, Thames and Hudson, 1983, pp. 26–33.

47 This probably occurred first on the mainland, where it is attested in the 330s. See D. S. Robertson, *Greek and Roman Architecture*, Cambridge, Cambridge University Press, 1945, p. 145 and below.

48 See Hornblower, *Mausolus*, p. 257, n. 229.

49 There are many skeptics; recently, see Ridgway, *Hellenistic Sculpture*, pp. 109–10. For the statue see especially Robertson, *History*, pp. 457–8 and G. B. Waywell, *The Free Standing Sculptures of the Mausoleum at Halicarnassus*, London, British Museum, 1978, no. 26.

50 Cf. Robertson, *History*, pp. 457–8, Waywell, *Mausoleum*, no. 27, Stewart, *Greek Sculpture*, p. 181, fig. 535.

51 For the Tegea relief see Hornblower, *Mausolus*, pp. 240–1.

52 On the controversy see Robertson, *History*, pp. 449, 458, and Hornblower, *Mausolus*, p. 272, n. 405, with references. The question is not as closed as they assume, cf. C. M. Havelock, *Hellenistic Art*, New York, Norton, 1981, pp. 35–6 (a persistent revisionist).

53 Stewart, *Greek Sculpture*, fig. 526.

54 Robertson, *History*, pls 144b, 144c.

55 B. S. Ridgway, 'Notes on the Development of the Greek Frieze,' *Hesperia* 35 (1966), 202.

56 See Hornblower, *Mausolus*, pp. 235, 269, n. 375, and below.

57 For the frieze, see Hornblower, ibid., p. 268; for the heads, E. Buschor, *Maussollos und Alexander*, Munich, Beck, 1950, figs. 47–8, 53–4.

58 Robertson, *History*, p. 452. For Scopas in general see A. Stewart, *Skopas of Paros*, Park Ridge, Noyes, 1977.

59 See Stewart, ibid., pp. 91–2.

60 See especially N. J. Norman, 'The Temple of Athena Alea at Tegea,' *AJA* 88 (1984), 169–84, also Winter, 'Tradition,' pp. 389–94. For the sculptures see Stewart, *Skopas*, pp. 5–84; for the style of the heads, pp. 73–6.

61 Cf. Lattimore, *Thiasos, passim*, Stewart, *Skopas* pp. 99–101.

62 For an elaborate example recently discovered in the Piraeus see Ridgway, *Hellenistic Sculpture*, pp. 31–3.

63 See Robertson, *History*, p. 382, Stewart, *Greek Sculpture*, pp. 92–4, figs. 517–19.

64 See Ridgway, *Hellenistic Sculpture*, 87–9.

65 See Pollitt, *Art and Experience*, p. 147.

66 Stewart, *Greek Sculpture*, p. 179. Cf. Robertson, *History*, p. 386, pl. 126b, and, for another emotional Athena, 402, pl. 129c.

67 See S. Adam, *The Technique of Greek Sculpture*, London, Thames and Hudson, 1966, pp. 94–7, O. Palagia, *Euphranor*, Leiden, Brill, 1980, pp. 14–25.
68 See Stewart, *Greek Sculpture*, pp. 177–8, Ridgway, *Hellenistic Sculpture*, p. 14.
69 See Stewart, ibid., pp. 177, 198, Ridgway, ibid., pp. 91, 105, n. 34.
70 For these see Robertson, *History*, pp. 388–90, Stewart, *Greek Sculpture*, pp. 178–9.
71 Cf. Adam, *Technique*, pp. 97–102, T. Dohrn, 'Die Marmor–Standbilder des Daochos–Weihgeschenks in Delphi,' *Antike Plastik* 8 (1968), 33–54, Borbein, 'Statue,' pp. 79–84, B. Fehr, *Bewegungsweisen und Verhaltnisideale*, Bad Bramstadt, Moreland, 1979, pp. 59–66, Ridgway, *Hellenistic Sculpture*, pp. 46–9.
72 See Ridgway, ibid., 19–20.
73 See N. J. Serwint, 'Greek Athletic Sculpture from the Fifth and Fourth Centuries BC', PhD Diss., Princeton University, 1987, pp. 384–91. I am grateful to Professor Serwint for sending me a copy of her dissertation.
74 See Dohrn, 'Daochos Weihgeschenks,' p. 46, pl. 37; he does not make this identification and believes that the statue of Daochus II was nude.
75 See S. G. Miller, 'The Philippeion and Hellenistic Macedonian Architecture,' *Ath Mitt* 88 (1973), 189–218, also Robertson, *Architecture*, p. 145, Dinsmoor, *Architecture*, pp. 236–8.
76 See T. H. Price, 'An Enigma in Pella: The Tholos and Herakles Phylakos,' *AJA* 77 (1973), 66–71.
77 See Robertson, *Architecture*, pp. 144–5, Dinsmoor, *Architecture*, pp. 237–8.
78 For the vaulted tunnel see M. Goethals, 'The Stadium,' in S. G. Miller, ed., *Nemea. A Guide to the Site and Museum*, Berkeley, University of California Press, 1990, pp. 184–91; for early vaulted construction in Greece, also T. D. Boyd, 'The Arch and the Vault in Greek Architecture,' *AJA* 82 (1978), 83–100.
79 See Borza, pp. 256–66 on the controversy; he favors the latter identification. While Vergina is generally thought to be ancient Aegae, the early Macedonian capital, this has now been contested by P. B. Faklaris, 'Aegae: Determining the Site of the First Capital of the Macedonians,' *AJA* 98 (1994), 609–16.
80 See Pollitt, *Art and Experience*, pp. 170–1.
81 See R. E. Wycherley, *How the Greeks Built Cities*, Princeton, Princeton University Press, 1978, p. 211.
82 See Borza, p. 256 (and above, n. 79).
83 See F. E. Winter, 'Ancient Corinth and the History of Greek Architecture and Town Planning,' *Phoenix* 17 (1963), 275–92.
84 The South Stoa was long dated to the 330s; see J. J. Coulton, *The Architectural Development of the Greek Stoa*, Oxford, Clarendon Press, 1976, pp. 50–1.
85 See Pollitt, *Hellenistic Age*, pp. 236–8.
86 See J. Russell, 'The Origin and Development of Republican Forums,' *Phoenix* 22 (1968), 322–4.

87 See E. Fredricksmeyer, 'Three Notes on Alexander's Deification,' *AJAH* 4 (1979), 1–9.
88 See A. Stewart, *Faces of Power*, Berkeley, University of California Press, 1993; more briefly, Pollitt, *Hellenistic Age*, pp. 19–46.
89 See Stewart, ibid., pp. 123–30; the quotation is from Pollitt, *Hellenistic Age*, p. 41.
90 See Stewart, ibid., pp. 270–3.
91 See Stewart, ibid., pp. 106–13.
92 Stewart, ibid., pp. 116–21, 209–14.
93 See especially K. Moser von Filseck, *Der Apoxyomenos des Lysipp*, Bonn, Rudolf Habelt, 1988, also Stewart, *Greek Sculpture*, p. 187.
94 Cf. Pollitt, *Hellenistic Age*, pp. 52–3, Ridgway, *Hellenistic Sculpture*, pp. 79–80, Stewart, *Greek Sculpture*, p. 188.
95 Cf. Robertson, *History*, p. 509, Pollitt, ibid., p. 64, Stewart, ibid., pp. 179–80.
96 See Pollitt, ibid., pp. 49–52.
97 A. Stewart, 'Lysippan Studies. 1. The Only Creator of Beauty,' *AJA* 82 (1978), 163–72; cf. Pollitt, ibid., pp. 53–4.
98 F. P. Johnson, *Lysippos*, Durham, Duke University Press, 1927, pp. 262–3.
99 Cf. Robertson, *History*, pp. 497–503 (skeptical about the connection with Philoxenus), Pollitt, *Hellenistic Age*, pp. 45–6, Stewart, *Faces*, pp. 130–50.
100 Stewart, ibid., p. 144.
101 See Robertson, *History*, pp. 486–9, Pollitt, *Hellenistic Age*, pp. 210–5.
102 See Robertson,, ibid., pp. 565–73, Pollitt, ibid., pp. 188–93.
103 Borza, p. 266.
104 See Pollitt, *Hellenistic Age*, p. 191.
105 For a recent review of this question see Pollitt, ibid., pp. 185–209.
106 W. Childs, review of Waywell, *Mausoleum*, in *AJA* 84 (1980), 387.

SELECT CRITICAL
BIBLIOGRAPHY

(Works cited in the notes are mostly omitted here. Readers should consult there too for relevant literature.)

INTRODUCTION

Some additional works deserve mention. W. R. Connor, 'Historical Writing in the Fourth Century BC and the Hellenistic Period,' in *The Cambridge History of Classical Literature*, eds P. E. Easterling and E. J. Kenney, Cambridge, Cambridge University Press, 1985, pp. 458–71, provides a useful survey of historical literature. A popular form of historical writing, particularly in Athens, was local history; for a recent discussion of this genre see P. Harding, *Androtion and the Atthis*, Oxford, Clarendon Press, 1994. An interesting work, one outside the Attic literary tradition (reflecting as well the temper of the times) is Aineias the Tactician, *How to Survive Under Siege*, trans. D. Whitehead, Oxford, Clarendon Press, 1990. Plutarch's *Lives*, so important to the study of the fourth century, are readily available in the Penguin edition, Plutarch, *The Age of Alexander*, trans. by I. Scott-Kilvert, with an introduction by G. T. Griffith, Harmondsworth, Penguin, 1973 (or the Loeb edition [Greek text with translation], by B. Perrin, Cambridge, Harvard University Press, 1914–26). Diodorus of Sicily, whose work covers the fourth century, is available also in the Loeb edition of C. H. Oldfather and C. B. Welles, 12 vols, Cambridge, Harvard University Press, 1933–67; a useful discussion is K. Sacks, *Diodorus Siculus and the First Century*, Princeton, Princeton University Press, 1990.

ATHENS

As in many ways, Athens dominates the body of surviving ancient literature. The many writings of Xenophon, *Memorabilia* (*Memoirs of Socrates*), *Anabasis* (or *March Up Country*), and *Hellenica*, refer to affairs in Athens as elsewhere in the Greek world; these are all available in Penguin and Loeb editions. A good sampling of Attic oratory may be found in A. N. W. Saunders, ed. and trans., *Greek Political Oratory*, Harmondsworth, Penguin, 1970. Many other sources, including the many inscriptions, are available in a number of collections (see above references, pp. 7, 9).

Two studies that complement works on Athenian democracy cited above are R. Osborne, *Demos: The Discovery of Classical Attika*, Cambridge, Cambridge University Press, 1985, and R. K. Sinclair, *Democracy and Participation in Athens*, Cambridge, Cambridge University Press, 1988. Prominent fourth-century Athenians, Aeschines, Demosthenes, and Phocion, have been examined in depth recently (see above references, pp. 38–9) and important but less well known figures are treated by G. Cawkwell, 'Eubulus,' *JHS* 83 (1963), 47–67 and R. Sealey, 'Callistratus of Aphidna and His Contemporaries,' *Historia* 5 (1956), 178–203. For Athenian social and economic issues, J. K. Davies, *Athenian Propertied Families, 600–300 BC*, Oxford, Clarendon Press, 1971, is fundamental, and P. Millett, *Lending and Borrowing in Ancient Athens*, Cambridge, Cambridge University Press, 1991, provides a stimulating discussion of business and economics as well as contemporary sources.

SPARTA

No single book treats all aspects of Sparta in the fourth century, though several works examine some aspect of the subject. Recommended among general works is P. Cartledge, *Sparta and Laconia: A Regional History, c. 1300 to 362 BC*, London, Routledge & Kegan Paul, 1979, which gives a brief treatment of Sparta between the end of the Peloponnesian War and the Battle of Mantinea. A recent examination of post-Peloponnesian War Sparta is C. J. Tuplin, *The Failings of Empire: A Reading of Xenophon's Hellenica, 2.3.11–7.5.27*, Historia Einzelschriften, 76, Stuttgart, Franz Steiner, 1993. Sparta's king Agesilaus has received much attention recently: P. Cartledge, *Agesilaos and the Crisis of Sparta*, Baltimore, Johns Hopkins University Press, 1989, is a more detailed study of Sparta from 404 to 362, with focus on social and economic questions, than a study of Agesilaus. C. D. Hamilton, *Agesilaus and the Failure of Spartan Hegemony*, Ithaca, Cornell University Press, 1991, attempts to view the period from the standpoint of political and diplomatic history with some emphasis on the personality and character of Agesilaus. E. David, *Sparta Between Empire and Revolution, 404–243 BC*, New York, Arno, 1981, focuses on social, economic, and political developments, again from the end of the Peloponnesian War through the reforms of the early third century. Its early chapters are relevant and useful. A similar study of Sparta's ally and rival Corinth may be found in J. B. Salmon, *Wealthy Corinth. A History of the City to 338 BC*, Oxford, Clarendon Press, 1984, pp. 342–412.

THEBES AND CENTRAL GREECE

The authoritative account for Thebes and central Greece in the fourth century is J. Buckler, *The Theban Hegemony, 371–362 BC*, Cambridge, Harvard University Press, 1980. Boeotian history from the Peloponnesian War to the beginning of the Theban supremacy is usefully surveyed in R. Buck's *Boiotia and the Boiotian League, 432–371 BC* (Edmonton, University of Alberta Press, 1994). Aspects of Theban–Athenian relations in a period of transition are treated in M. Munn, *Defense of Attica: The Dema Wall and the Boiotian War of 378–375 BC*, Berkeley, University of California Press, 1993. For Thessaly, H. D. Westlake, *Thessaly in the Fourth Century BC*, London, Methuen, 1935, remains valuable. J. A. O. Larsen, *Greek Federal States*, Oxford, Clarendon Press, 1968, provides an invaluable study of the federal constitutions of Boeotia and Thessaly and smaller federal states of central Greece. The affairs of Delphi and its Amphictyony are usefully surveyed by H. W. Parke and D. E. W. Wormell, *The Delphic Oracle*, vol. 1, *The History*, Oxford, Blackwell, 1956.

THE EASTERN GREEK WORLD

There is no single work devoted to the fourth-century Eastern Greek world. G. E. Bean, *Aegean Turkey*, London, John Murray, 1979, and A. H. M. Jones, *The Cities of the Eastern Roman Provinces*, rev. M. Avi-Jonah *et al.*, Oxford, Clarendon Press, 1971, provide brief sketches of the topography, history, and remains of individual cities through the Roman period. Some cities have provided subjects of recent monographs: S. M. Sherwin-White, *Ancient Cos: A Historical Study From the Dorian Settlement to the Imperial Period*, *Hypomnemata* 51, Göttingen, Vandenhoeck & Ruprecht, 1978; G. A. Shipley, *A History of Samos*, Oxford, Clarendon Press, 1987.

Several collections of translated sources attest fourth-century Eastern Greek matters: these include M. M. Austin and C. B. Welles, both cited in the notes. Among ancient sources, Diodorus, books 14–20 cover the whole of the period, while Arrian, *The Anabasis of Alexander*, trans. A. de Selincourt, with introduction by J. R. Hamilton, Harmondsworth, Penguin, 1960, treats the 330s and 320s to Alexander's death.

There are numerous modern works that touch upon Eastern Greek affairs and their dealings with both Greeks and non-Greeks alike. J. M. Cook, *The Persian Empire*, New York, Schocken, 1982, provides a good introduction to the institutions, practices, and personages of the empire which included much of the Eastern Greek world during the fourth century. The beginnings of Macedonian involvement in the eastern Greek world are discussed in J. R. Ellis, *Philip II and Macedonian Imperialism*, London, Thames & Hudson, 1976. The best recent treatment of Alexander's career and policies, which includes a section on Alexander and the Greeks of Asia, is A. B. Bosworth, *Conquest and Empire: The Reign of Alexander the Great*, Cambridge, Cambridge University Press, 1990. After Alexander's death, Antigonus the One-Eyed dominates the Eastern Greek world, and R. A. Billows, *Antigonos the One-Eyed and the Creation of the Hellenistic State*, Berkeley, University of California Press, 1990, exhaustively examines his career and policies.

THE GREEKS IN SICILY AND SOUTHERN ITALY

The relevant books of Diodorus (13–21) are available in the Loeb edition (cited above); for Plutarch's Lives of Dion and Timoleon, use either the Loeb translations or the Penguin edition, Plutarch, *The Age of Alexander*. For close investigation of part of the source tradition, see L. J. Sanders, *Dionysius I of Syracuse and Greek Tyranny*, London, Croom Helm, 1987, a book narrower in scope than its title would suggest, and not for beginners (see the balanced assessment by R. G. Lewis, *CR* 103 [1989], 285–6).

The only recent monograph on Dionysius, that of B. Caven, *Dionysius I: Warlord of Sicily*, New Haven, Yale University Press, 1990, needs to be read with caution. In particular, the attempt to assess Dionysius more favorably than the prevailing tradition, while deserving serious consideration, does not always convince (see the review of R. J. A. Talbert, *AJP* 113 [1992], 455–7). Sharper, though briefer, discussions of fourth-century Sicily (the latter two ending with Timoleon) may be found in M. I. Finley, *Ancient Sicily*, London, Chatto & Windus, 1979, chs 5–8; J. K. Davies, *Democracy and Classical Greece*, London, Fontana, 1978, chs. 10 and 12. In addition, note S. Berger, *Revolution and Society in Greek Sicily and Southern Italy*, Historia Einzelschriften 71, Stuttgart, Franz Steiner, 1992. R. J. A. Talbert, *Timoleon and the Revival of Greek Sicily*, Cambridge, Cambridge University Press, 1974, does not claim to be a full study of its central figure. A valuable conspectus of the Italiotes is to be found in K. Lomas, *Rome and the Western Greeks, 350 BC–AD 200: Conquest and Acculturation in Southern Italy*, London, Routledge, 1993.

MACEDONIA AND THE NORTH

The sources for the rise of Macedon are scattered in various authorities, but a good place to start would be Diodorus, book 16. A distinctly Athenian view of Philip and the Macedonians appears in the rhetoric of Demosthenes, especially his *Olynthiacs* and *Philippics*, several of which may be found in *Greek Political Oratory* referred to above. Another important source is Theopompus of Chios, recently studied by M. A. Flower, *Theopompos of Chios*, Oxford, Clarendon Press, 1994.

For background on the Macedonian state and kingdom, see N. G. L. Hammond, *The Macedonian State: The Origins, Institutions and History*, Oxford, Clarendon Press, 1989, and R. M. Errington, *A History of Macedonia*, Berkeley, University of California Press, 1990. A cultural counterpart to these is R. Ginouvès, *et al.*, *Macedonia From Philip II to the Roman Conquest*, Princeton, Princeton University Press, 1994, which provides a picturesque account of ancient Macedonian society and the material remains of its culture. Philip II dominates, naturally, both Macedonia and the period and this is reflected in the many biographies and studies of him that have appeared over the last twenty-five years. These include works by G. L. Cawkwell, *Philip of Macedon*, London, Faber & Faber, 1978 and J. R. Ellis (referred to above) and most recently that of N. G. L. Hammond, *Philip II of Macedon*, Baltimore, Johns Hopkins University Press, 1994.

RESISTANCE TO ALEXANDER

The single most important ancient source for the life and exploits of Alexander is Arrian, who lived in the second century AD, but who compiled his work from (mostly) reliable contemporaries including Ptolemy and Aristobulus. His *Anabasis of Alexander* (cited above) is available in both Penguin and Loeb editions (for the latter see the edition of P. A. Brunt, *Arrian*, 2 vols, Cambridge, Harvard University Press, 1976–83). Another important source for Alexander is Q. Curtius Rufus, a first-century Roman, who wrote of Alexander's exploits in dramatic fashion and represents a more popular, sometimes less reliable, tradition (cited above, p. 220, n. 28, with Atkinson's commentaries).

There are many works available that examine Alexander and his conquests. Accessible works include P. Green, *Alexander of Macedon, 356–323 BC*, rev. edn, Berkeley, University of California Press, 1991, and U. Wilcken, *Alexander the Great*, ed. E. N. Borza, New York, Norton, 1967 (though somewhat dated); the picturesque *The Search for Alexander* by R. L. Fox, Boston, Little, Brown & Co., 1980, provides many illustrations and vigorous interpretation.

THE SUCCESSORS OF ALEXANDER

Primary sources for the era of Alexander's successors are fragmentary and difficult to find. Plutarch's life of *Demetrius* (available in the Penguin edition, *Age of Alexander* cited above) offers much useful information, as does the *Eumenes* (available in the Loeb edition); Diodorus books 18–20, most readily available in the Loeb edition, provides a good narrative. Other sources, including inscriptions, may be found in M. M. Austin, *The Hellenistic World from Alexander to the Roman Conquest* (cited above, p. 136, n. 14).

The most recent relevant narratives are in *CAH*² (1984), vol. 7, 1: ch. 1, F. W. Walbank, 'The Sources for the Period,' and ch. 2, E. Will, 'The Successors of Alexander.' On the politics and culture see P. Green, *Alexander to Actium: the Historical Evolution of the Hellenistic Age*, Berkeley, 1990, chs. 1–8. Some scholarship is more specialized to the period: H. Bengtson, *Die Diadochen. Die Nachfolger Alexanders des Grossen 322–281 v. Chr.*, Munich, Beck, 1987, P. Cloché, *La dislocation d'un Empire: les premiers successeurs d'Alexandre le Grand (322–281/280 avant J.C.)*, Paris, Payot, 1959, detail the struggles of Alexander's successors. W. Heckel, *The*

Marshals of Alexander's Empire, London, Routledge, 1993, provides an excellent summary of the main characters, updating H. Berve, *Das Alexanderreich auf prosopographischer Grundlage*, 2 vols, Munich, Beck, 1926. Recently, a number of biographical studies of some of the main characters have appeared: these include R. A. Billows (p. 286 above); J. D. Grainger, *Seleukos Nikator: Constructing a Hellenistic Kingdom*, London, Routledge, 1990; H. S. Lund, *Lysimachus: A Study in Early Hellenistic Kingship*, London, Routledge, 1992. Macedonian imperialism, especially in regard to this era, is a long-studied theme, but of particular interest is R. A. Billows, *Kings and Colonists: Aspects of Macedonian Imperialism*, Leiden, Brill, 1995, esp. chs. 3–7.

ART AND ARCHITECTURE

M. Robertson, *History of Greek Art*, Cambridge, Cambridge University Press, 1975, provides a comprehensive and exceptionally sensitive overview of fourth-century pictorial art, with particular attention to painting; equally valuable and stimulating are the works of J. J. Pollitt cited in the notes above. For further discussion of wall painting, see V. Bruno, *Form and Color in Greek Painting*, New York, Norton, 1977. For sculpture, A. Stewart, *Greek Sculpture. An Exploration*, New Haven, Yale University Press, 1990, is fundamental; major developments in the fourth century are addressed by A. Borbein, 'Die griechische Statue des 4. Jahrhunderts v. Chr.,' *Jahrbuch des k. archaologischen Instituts* 88 (1972), 43–212 and B. S. Ridgway, *Hellenistic Sculpture* I, Madison, University of Wisconsin Press, 1990. An important specialized study is R. R. R. Smith, *Hellenistic Royal Portraits*, Oxford, Clarendon Press, 1988.

A new survey volume on Greek architecture has long been needed, and one by R. Rhodes is forthcoming. Meanwhile, highly recommended are F. E. Winter's essay on temples, 'Tradition and Innovation in Doric Design IV: The Fourth Century,' *AJA* 86 (1982), 387–400, and R. E. Wycherly, *How the Greeks Built Cities*, London, Macmillan, 1962, which emphasizes planning. A thorough study of an architectural type especially important in the fourth century is J. J. Coulton, *The Architectural Development of the Greek Stoa*, Oxford, Clarendon Press, 1976. Still useful, although somewhat out of date, is M. Bieber, *History of the Greek and Roman Theater*, Princeton, Princeton University Press, 1961.

INDEX